Mothers and Ch

Mothers and Children

Feminist Analyses and Personal Narratives

Susan E. Chase
and Mary F. Rogers

Rutgers University Press
New Brunswick, New Jersey, and London

Library of Congress Cataloging-in-Publication Data
Chase, Susan E., 1954–
Mothers and children : feminist analyses and personal narratives / Susan E. Chase and Mary F. Rogers.
p. cm.
Includes bibliographical references and index.
ISBN 0-8135-2875-5 (cloth : alk. paper) — ISBN 0-8135-2876-3 (pbk. : akl. paper)
1. Motherhood. 2. Mother and child. 3. Feminism. I. Rogers, Mary F. (Mary Frances), 1944– II. Title.

HQ759.C48 2001
306.874'3—dc21

00-039032

British Cataloging-in-Publication data for this book is available from the British Library

Manufactured in the United States of America

For my mother, my sister, and my daughter

SEC

In memory of Bertha Fuehlen Maire
and Florence Yount Rogers

MFR

Contents

Acknowledgments

My first thanks go to Mary Rogers for coming up with the idea of working on this book together. My admiration and respect for her ideas, her writing, her personal and professional generosity, and her love of life have been deepened by our collaboration.

I am grateful to my friends, some of whom are also colleagues, for our ongoing discussions about the trials, joys, and politics of motherhood. Joli Jensen, Nelly Vanzetti, Ann Blakely, Jessi Rowe, Colleen Bell, and Vibs Petersen have been particularly important to me during my work on this book. These discussions helped me to remember why I was spending so much time and energy on this project.

Members of my family have also engaged me in countless conversations about the day to day realities of parents' and children's lives, forthright conversations about our fears, doubts, and satisfactions as we watch our children grow. For these conversations and for their continuous support and encouragement, I thank my parents, my siblings, and their partners: Elizabeth and George Chase, Stephen and Carolyn Chase, Carl and Cincia Chase, Cynthia and Steve Keating. My mother, Elizabeth, read and commented on each of my chapters. I always draw strength from her interest in my work.

I will never forget the great insight and enthusiasm with which the students in my Motherhood and Feminism class approached the many topics covered in this book. I learned a lot from our sometimes heated debates as well as from the many personal stories they shared in and out of the classroom. They provided feedback on every article we read, which was very useful as Mary and I drafted the initial ideas for this book.

The University of Tulsa Faculty Research Grant Program provided funds that allowed me to hire others to help with the incredible amount of work that goes into researching and writing a book. I received careful, efficient assistance from Jill Hayes, Sara Booher, and Sharon Haltom. Allison Cosslett deserves special thanks for helping with the permissions process and the preparation of the final manuscript.

I would not have been able to research and write this book without the help of women whose work is woefully underacknowledged and underpaid in our society: child care workers and preschool teachers. Because I trusted the caregiving and teaching skills of many women over the last several years, I was able to turn my attention to this book and my teaching without worrying about my daughter during the day. I especially appreciate Renee Smith, Annamarie Farone, and Karen Christensen.

When I told my daughter, then three years old, that I was writing a book about mothers and children, she asked, "What about daddies?" Her question speaks volumes about her father, my partner, John Anderson. I am deeply grateful to John for his loving co-parenting and his willingness to take more than his share of responsibility for Marie when deadlines for this book loomed large. He also offered helpful feedback on all of my chapters. Finally, I thank Marie for bringing motherhood into my life and helping me to see the world once again through a child's eyes.

SEC

This project has enriched my consciousness of caregiving, community, and homemaking. Above all, I thank Susan Chase for all this enrichment. A model colleague, an indefatigable friend, and a consummate scholar, Susan has inspired me a great deal over our many months of working and learning together.

I also thank other women whose caregiving sustains me day in and day out, whose presence in my life makes for wonder, passion, and surprises as well as togetherness. Christy Garrett knows my profound indebtedness to her, and I happily proclaim it anew. Martha Rogers is probably less aware of how much her sisterly friendship strengthens me, and I now remind her of that happy circumstance. Gloria Mattingly also energizes me, and I thank her for consistently reminding me, "Take time, Mary."

I also thank the following mothers whose loving labors offer singular examples of life well lived: Lola Buonanno, Dorothy Juhlin, Michelle Murphy McCann, Catherine McVey, Lois Natanson, Arline Riordan, and Gen Rogers. Thank you all for showing me the way and for brightening the world at the same time.

MFR

Introduction

The novelist Jane Smiley suggests that "motherhood is the most public of personal conditions."[1] In that swift observation she points to an irony bound up with motherhood. On the one hand, it is an unutterably personal array of experiences. Its joys and challenges, its pains and rewards, come to women as they care for their unique, irreplaceable children. On the other hand, motherhood has decidedly public dimensions. It preoccupies policymakers and advice givers, health care professionals and religious functionaries, child care workers and educators. It is also public in a more mundane sense. Many Americans feel entitled to judge mothers whom they see with their children in the mall, on the bus, in the neighborhood, or on the TV news, even when they know little or nothing about those mothers' or children's lives.

Why is the very personal mother-child relationship such a public concern? Why do so many people care about motherhood and what mothers do? In large measure the answer is obvious. Mothers are typically the primary caretakers of children; to the extent that a society's members care about their future, they care about motherhood and how mothers raise their children. But widespread agreement about mothers' importance to their children's development does not translate into consensus about maternal practices and priorities. Who should (and should not) be a mother? What makes a woman a good (or a bad) mother? Who, besides mothers, should be responsible for the next generation: fathers, extended families, paid caregivers, the society at large? What kinds of responsibility and authority should those others have? What kinds of support and resources do mothers need? Which mothers deserve that support and those resources? Finally, who gets to decide? Whom should we consider experts on these matters? Questions such as these get debated regularly in schools, courts, welfare offices, the halls of Congress, and living rooms across the country. When motherhood takes center stage, heated debate often ensues.

Public interest in motherhood is complicated by motherhood's personal dimension. Every adult was once a helpless infant, dependent on someone else for survival and nurturance. It doesn't take a psychoanalyst to figure out that a person's attitude toward motherhood in some way reflects his or her childhood and family experiences. If nothing else, the personal dimension of motherhood lends an intensely emotional character to the public debates. In the words of philosopher Sara Ruddick, "A hot emotional atmosphere surrounds the 'mother' whenever she appears on a feminist, academic, or political stage. Allegedly adult and public discussions become suffused with passions of childhood: love, hate, blissful and wretched dependency; grievances no mother can assuage, longings no mother can satisfy."[2] Clearly, it is difficult to approach the topic of motherhood dispassionately.

In the midst of passionate public discussions of motherhood, what often gets lost is the realities of mothers' lives, indeed, the incredibly diverse realities of mothers' needs, struggles, joys, and hopes and dreams for their children. In *Mothers and Children*, we bring those diverse realities to light. We show how mothers' lives and their relationships with their children are shaped by the public dimensions of motherhood, and by social, cultural, economic, and political factors far beyond mothers' control. One of our aims is to help readers grasp the diverse, complex realities of mothers' and children's lives. Another is to help readers understand and participate more thoughtfully in the raging public debates about motherhood.

A Feminist Sociological Perspective

We approach the huge, profound terrain of motherhood and mothering as feminist sociologists. This means that we focus on certain kinds of questions: How are ideas about motherhood shaped by social and historical conditions? How do ideas about motherhood change over time and vary across social contexts? Who has the power to make their definitions of motherhood and good mothering stick? How is that power exercised through specific social institutions and cultural ideologies? What are mothers' own perspectives on motherhood and mothering? How are the perspectives of diverse groups of mothers similar or different? How do mothers respond to the dominant definitions of motherhood? Do they accommodate or resist those definitions, or find themselves doing both?[3]

As feminist sociologists, we make certain assumptions as we explore these questions. The first is that women's lives are every bit as valuable as men's are. While it may seem difficult to find anyone who seriously disagrees with that assumption, many people act as if women's lives count less than men's do. Our society's lack of respect for nurturing and caregiving, work typically done by women at home and in the labor force, speaks to this problem. Similarly, most people may not openly advocate that men get higher-paying jobs or more attention or better service than women do, but many people continue to take those patterns for granted and find nothing fundamentally intolerable about them. As feminists, we find any favoritism or privilege or inequality based on gender unacceptable. Thus, we have a lot of problems with the typical arrangements between women and men in families, workplaces, and other institutional arenas.

Second, we assume that women's dreams, aspirations, fears, and goals are diverse and will become more so as further opportunities open up to them. While we esteem mothers and value child rearing and other forms of nurturance, we do not assume that these are women's only or even primary forms of work and caring. We believe that our society's institutions should strongly support parenting, especially by women, so that parents have opportunities to spend adequate time both with their children and in pursuit of other commitments and interests. We further believe that children benefit from caring, respectful attention from many adults and that diverse forms of noncustodial nurturance of children should be recognized, encouraged, and supported.

Third, we assume that women generally face resistance, if not resentment, when they give their self-development considerable priority. Widely expected to live in service of others, both at home and in the workplace, most women cannot expect reliable support when they attend to their own needs in obvious, habitual ways. Often facing resistance and lacking support for their self-nurturance, many women are angry, though they may not express their anger publicly. We assume, then, that many mothers are frustrated, not by their mothering or their children, but by the lack of support they receive and the price they are expected to pay for their maternal commitments.

Finally, we assume that the very diverse circumstances of mothers' lives shape their particular experiences, needs, and desires. A mother's age, race, ethnicity, social class, sexual orientation, and abilities or disabilities make a big difference to the challenges she faces as she goes about her everyday life, the kinds of resources and support she is able to draw on for mothering, and the social expectations concerning her motherhood. For example, a forty-year-old, partnered Chicana lesbian professional giving birth to a premature baby has needs and experiences that differ dramatically from those of a poor, white, unpartnered teen mother trying to finish her education while raising her child alone. We assume, then, that no one policy or theory can address every mother's situation.

Our feminist sociological perspective provides a powerful standpoint for exploring the diverse realities of mothers' lives and relationships with their children. It helps us to investigate incisively how those realities take shape from the social, cultural, political, and historical dimensions of motherhood.

Feminist Analyses and Personal Narratives

Mothers and Children consists of ten analytical chapters, which we have written singly and jointly, and which draw heavily on feminist theory and research on mothers, mothering, and motherhood. This literature includes not only sociology but also anthropology, psychology, history, and philosophy. One idea that pops up frequently in reviews of this literature is that mothers' voices are too often missing from it.[4] Thus, we decided to include one or more personal narratives following each of our chapters, narratives written mostly by mothers (or others who care for children) about their mothering, their relationships with children, or the joys and difficulties of mothering under specific conditions. We chose personal narratives that illustrate the lived realities of the topics covered in each chapter.[5] Because lived experience is complex, many of the narratives speak to issues raised in other chapters as well. As the subtitle of *Mothers and Children* implies, then, our book includes both feminist analyses of a wide range of topics concerning motherhood and mothering and mothers' own perspectives on those topics. Yet we don't mean to create a dichotomy between the feminist analyses and the personal narratives. We wrote our chapters in the first person, and we often include our own or others' personal stories as we analyze each topic. Similarly, many authors of the personal narratives integrate feminist analyses into their reflections.

Mothers and Children is organized around three main themes that we culled from the vast and growing feminist social science literature on motherhood. In part 1, "Social Constructions of Motherhood," we explore an idea central to contemporary feminist writing about mothers. The idea that motherhood is socially constructed means that it has no fixed universal shape. Its shape varies with the contours of culture and the dictates of history. What motherhood can be and what it is expected to be shift as we cross cultural and historical boundaries. Even within the contemporary United States, different groups of people develop different meanings of motherhood—for example, about whether motherhood can properly include employment outside the home. In part 1 we argue that the dominant social constructions of motherhood—including those of some lawmakers, child professionals, and scholars—have been and continue to be detrimental to mothers and their children. We also argue that feminist critiques of those social constructions help us to bring mothers' and children's needs to the forefront.

Part 1 opens with Susan Chase's chapter on "Motherhood and Feminism." This chapter anchors our book by debunking the myth that feminists do not care about mothers and children and replacing it with a portrait of the complex relationship between contemporary feminism and motherhood. Chapter 1 illustrates that complex relationship by examining three central issues: diversity in feminist approaches to motherhood, feminist debates about maternal bodies, and tensions in the feminist embrace of motherhood. These three issues broadly parallel the three major themes, the three parts, of our book.

Their diverse stances notwithstanding, feminists commonly criticize certain social constructions of motherhood. Chief among these are the hackneyed labels of "good" mother and "bad" mother. Susan addresses these social constructions in chapter 2. These labels are so pervasive and taken for granted in American culture that mothers themselves are often harshly self-critical. Feminists take issue not with mothers' desire to do a good job but with how social institutions and ideologies construct "bad" mothers without genuine regard for children's or mothers' well-being. This chapter focuses on mothers who are especially vilified in the United States: lesbian mothers; poor, single, teen mothers; and drug-dependent pregnant women.

In chapter 3, "The Institution and Experience of Motherhood," Susan focuses on the historical roots of the contemporary labeling of good and bad mothers. Thus, this chapter traces the development of the institution of motherhood in Western societies over the last few centuries. (The idea that motherhood is an institution means that in any particular time and place, laws, traditions, and ideologies, as well as social, economic, and political structures shape mothers' identities and practices.) This chapter shows how the institution of motherhood has constrained virtually all mothers. At the same time, it has revered white, middle- or upper-class, heterosexual, married, and able-bodied mothers, at the expense of all others. In addition to criticizing the institution of motherhood, this chapter explores women's diverse experiences of motherhood, experiences that are shaped by—but not wholly determined by—the institution.

Chapter 4, "Fatherlessness, Men, and Mothering," is the last of the chapters organized around the theme of socially constructed motherhood. Here Mary Rogers examines the recent deluge of popular and academic literature lamenting "father absence" in American society. That literature carries powerful messages about what mothers' priorities should be and how necessary fathers are to good mothering. At the same time it sends messages about the supposed inferiority of stepfamilies and other forms of child nurture that depart from the nuclear family made up of a married heterosexual couple sharing a household with one or more of their own biological children. This chapter debunks these messages while showing that feminist critiques of the "father absence" literature do not discount fathers' caregiving. The personal narratives accompanying this chapter illustrate men's loving involvement with children.

The second major theme in *Mothers and Children* revolves around motherhood and embodiment. While feminists emphasize that motherhood is socially constructed—that it is an institution created by society rather than a biological destiny for women—they do take seriously the biological fact that only women give birth. Thus, part 2, "Maternal Bodies," focuses on the various ways that Western societies and women themselves have attended to the physical aspects of becoming a mother and mothering. Here we argue that mothers' bodies have long been and still are a site of cultural and political struggle. Indeed, the regulation of women's sexuality and reproductive processes is central to the institution of motherhood.

In chapter 5, "Mothers, Sexuality, and Eros," we take up a topic that usually evokes keen ambivalence and discomfort. It is also a topic where mothers' voices are least likely to be heard: the connections between women's sexuality and their motherhood. Because modern cultures commonly treat motherhood and sexuality as incompatible, good mothers are presumed to be asexual (or incidentally sexual) persons. We join those feminists who seek to reclaim and redefine the erotic, making room for mothers' sexuality as well as maternal eroticism. This chapter also explores breastfeeding as a concrete practice through which mothers' pleasures have often been denied. In an effort to bring to light the deep love and passion many mothers feel for their children, we explore the idea of the mother-child relationship as a romance with all the playfulness, intense emotion, and diffuse eroticism that implies.

Chapter 6 looks at the dramatic embodiment of motherhood during pregnancy and childbirth. These experiences are at once physical, social, emotional, cognitive, cultural, and spiritual. In the United States, as elsewhere, they are also typically medical experiences. In "Pregnancy and Childbirth," Susan presents the centuries-long struggle for control over maternal bodies, with the medical profession the qualified winner over midwifery and holistic approaches. How different women experience pregnancy and childbirth also gets attention here, especially how women accept or resist the medical model of birth. This chapter ends with feminist ideas about living within, thinking from, and trusting maternal bodies, ideas intended to illuminate and ultimately to help change the social and ideological conditions under which most women currently give birth.

Chapter 7, "Family Making and Reproductive Technologies," looks at embodiment from a related but obverse angle. Here Mary focuses on the experiences and emotions of people who very much want a child but are unable to conceive one, and she discusses the reproductive technologies that sometimes enable them to have a child. This chapter also considers how women's bodies most often get invaded and manipulated in the process of trying to overcome infertility. At the same time many of the innovations in reproductive technologies ultimately aim at ending the need for pregnancy. An overarching goal, then, is to curtail the embodiment of pregnancy and childbirth by moving not only fertilization but also gestation to the laboratory. This chapter relies on phenomenological as well as feminist perspectives to grapple with these and other reproductive issues.

The theme that organizes part 3 is "Mothering in Everyday Life." Since mothering is usually a round-the-clock, day-by-day undertaking, it can pervade a woman's daily round of activities. Even when she is not with her children or specifically tending to their needs, a mother often has her child(ren) in mind. Often, too, her consciousness is given over to planning, scheduling, and all the other invisible efforts whereby children's meals get made, soccer practice gets put on the weekly schedule, and school visits get arranged. Or her consciousness may be weighed down with worries about what she will feed her child when the cupboard is bare with eight more days before the next disability check arrives. Or. . . . A mother's work may indeed never be done. A lot of that work is invisible not only because it is home-based but also because it is consciousness-based. Mothering is, then, as thoroughly a matter of everyday consciousness as it is a matter of everyday hugging, meal preparing, listening, wiping clean, and tucking in. The three chapters that make up part 3 argue—sometimes explicitly, sometimes implicitly—that we must understand these and other realities of mothers' everyday lives if we are to imagine what social and political changes are needed to promote mothers' and children's welfare.

In chapter 8, "Mothers and Children Over the Life Course," we focus on relationships between mothers and children and how those relationships change over time. Because the joys and frustrations of mothering depend heavily on the circumstances of particular mothers' and children's lives, we narrow our focus to just a few specific situations: mothers and adolescent daughters struggling with the issue of teen sexuality; mothers dealing with the trauma (for both mothers and daughters) of father-daughter incest; and feminist mothers facing the daily challenges and satisfactions of raising daughters and sons. One important idea unifies these various situations: mothers, children, and the professionals involved in their lives need to accept that good mothers are not perfect human beings. A woman can be a good mother and still have flaws, needs, desires, and a life of her own.

The next chapter explores various forms of "othermothering" in American society. Broadly speaking, othermothering embraces all those forms of child nurturance done by girls and women other than the primary mother of a child. As Mary shows in chapter 9, much othermothering is done by grandmothers, aunts, godmothers, family friends, stepmothers, foster mothers, and paid caregivers. This chapter illuminates the realities of mothering as a collaborative undertaking. It aims to raise our awareness of just how many people it really does take to raise a child. If, as the West African proverb puts it, it takes a whole village, then virtual villages of women are busy at the task. Social recognition of their collective work is minimal, however, in countries like the United States.

In chapter 10, Mary brings part 3 to a close with a focus on "Mothering as Political Action." A burgeoning literature has built up around the notion that motherhood often leads women into grassroots politics, local activism, and social-change efforts from the neighborhood level to the global level. This chapter begins with a look at maternal activism during the Progressive Era and then turns briefly to two instances of post–World War II activism: getting state-funded child care in California and the founding of La Leche League. The remainder of the chapter focuses on activist motherhood in the contemporary world, particularly welfare-rights and toxic-waste activism. In closing, Mary assesses maternalism as a political-action paradigm that is often (but not necessarily) feminist in its tone and substance, if not in name.

Mothers, Children, and Feminism

Although the three themes, the three parts of our book, are distinct, we hope you will come away with a sense of their connectedness. For example, how motherhood is socially constructed in any particular time and place impinges on women's experiences of their maternal bodies and shapes the expectations surrounding their everyday mothering. Conversely, only when we pay close attention to mothers' everyday experiences are we informed enough to contribute to discussions about how motherhood should be socially constructed. Again, we believe that understanding the realities of mothers' lives—an understanding grounded in mothers' own perspectives—should be pivotal to public debates about motherhood.

As is probably clear by now, feminism not only infuses our approach to motherhood and mothering but also constitutes a central topic throughout our book. The relationship between contemporary feminism and motherhood gets addressed in chapter 1 and the relationship between feminism and maternal activism gets addressed in chapter 10. We consider feminist perspectives on specific motherhood topics in the rest of the chapters.

Some readers may find the feminist perspectives we present gloomy or even painful. We acknowledge that feminist critique can feel painful because it requires that we look squarely at the negative consequences of dominant social constructions of motherhood. While many, if not most, mothers derive great pleasure and joy from their children, they also experience ambivalence, pain, and sometimes trauma in the course of their mothering. Many mothers face poverty, violence, and mental or physical exhaustion. Feminist sociological critique rejects the cultural tendency to understand these experiences as individual problems and explores instead how they are rooted in our society's general disregard for mothers' and children's needs.

A feminist sociological perspective also allows us to address a most vexing question: Why is social change so slow? Why, if social institutions and cultural ideologies change over time, have they been persistently detrimental to mothers and children? Sometimes particular groups of people have the power to define reality and to influence policy, laws, and public attitudes, and thus to control mothers' and children's lives. For example, in chapter 2 we find that some lawmakers have this kind of power; in chapter 4, certain scholars;

and in chapter 6, medical professionals. But many times the social processes at issue are broader and more diffuse. Social, economic, cultural, and political factors often coalesce in ways that make the current status quo seem inevitable. These broader social processes are at work, for instance, in the construction of motherhood as asexual (chapter 5) and the construction of othermothering as unusual and problematic (chapter 9).

Feminist critique may be painful, but it is ultimately empowering. We do not have a gloomy outlook on the future of motherhood. Feminist critique has certainly helped to improve mothers' lives, especially over the last several decades. The insight that motherhood is socially constructed has freed women to construct motherhood differently. In general, American women now have more freedom than ever before to consider motherhood an option rather than a destiny, and more opportunities to combine motherhood with other commitments. In addition, feminists have exposed both the unjust and unrealistic cultural expectation of perfect mothering and its flip side: pervasive mother-blame for all our society's ills. They have shaken the tenacious belief that good mothering is the prerogative only of white, middle-class, heterosexual, married, able-bodied women. They have challenged the taboo on mothers' sexuality, created more options for birthing women, and insisted that women's interests be placed at the center of debates about reproductive technologies. They have long argued that mothering requires a lot of support, and that children should be treated as a societal not an individual responsibility. They have demonstrated that feminist mothering helps both daughters and sons to grow into strong, nurturing adults. In short, feminist ideas and activism have made an enormous difference in contemporary American society, whether the general public is aware of that or not. Overall, feminist sociological critique is empowering because it opens our eyes to social and historical processes that shape our everyday lives. We need to understand these processes if we are to imagine and work for social change.

Ahead of us, then, lies a rich, challenging, and crucial domain of experiences and ideas to consider with great care. As you turn the many pages of this book, it might help to keep in mind that we all come to the topic of mothers and children with a good deal of experience, whether as mothers or other caretakers of children, or as children of mothers. We have all been mothered in one way or another and that makes this topic emotionally weighty. The politically charged character of public debates about motherhood also raises the stakes for all of us. As you read the feminist analyses and personal narratives ahead, we hope you will find yourself thinking in new ways about relationships in your life, about mothers and children in the world around you, about the centrality of caretaking and nurturing to the well-being of communities, and about the many public dimensions of motherhood.

PART

1

Social Constructions of Motherhood

CHAPTER 1

Motherhood and Feminism

What do you think of when you hear the words *mother* and *motherhood*? What about *feminist* and *feminism*? And what comes to mind when you imagine these two sets of terms together—*motherhood and feminism*? These are the questions my undergraduate students and I discussed on the first day of a seminar I taught on "Motherhood and Feminism."[1] Reflecting on mothers and motherhood, the students focused on relationships between mothers and children, characterizing them in both positive and negative terms: intense bond; huge responsibility; unconditional love; lifelong commitment; smothering; abandonment. They also described the work of mothering: providing; educating; guiding; disciplining; protecting; sacrificing; comforting; supporting; organizing; cleaning; attending to the details of children's lives.

Their ideas about feminists and feminism included some derogatory portrayals: antimale; male bashing; anger at the world. Perhaps because my seminar was an elective rather than a required course, most responses leaned in positive directions. They articulated feminist goals: empowerment; liberation; building bridges and opening doors; recognizing that women are not treated equally in this society and working for change; recognizing the value of each person, especially of women; standing up for oneself as a woman; understanding the links between personal and political beliefs and actions. And they described the qualities of feminists: a militant, vigilant woman; a strong, forceful, persuasive, proud leader; a woman who is comfortable with herself no matter the context; an independent, self-assured woman who believes she is capable of doing anything she sets her mind and heart to do.

Most interesting was how students linked—or didn't link—motherhood and feminism. Here the responses were sparser. Several stated that the terms contradict each other, pointing to a conflict between the urge to sacrifice and nurture on the one hand and the strength and independence of feminism on the other. One simply wrote "blank," indicating that nothing came to mind. For other students, however, the combination evoked specific images: a supermom juggling work, children, and self; a gender-neutral child; the power that being a mother gives a woman; the struggle to equalize duties within the

This chapter was written by Susan E. Chase.

household; the desire to nurture someone without giving up individual dreams and goals.

The trouble some students had connecting motherhood and feminism reflects a widespread myth in American culture that feminism and motherhood have nothing to do with each other. Even today, the myth persists that feminists do not care about or are hostile to mothers and children. The connections other students drew between motherhood and feminism reflect a realistic, if partial, image of feminism's compatibility with motherhood. Indeed, since the 1960s feminists have devoted much attention to analyzing motherhood and its effects on mothers, addressing the problems mothers face in their everyday lives, and advocating feminist parenting as beneficial for both daughters and sons.

This chapter is about both the myth and the reality. In a sense our entire book puts the myth to rest; it demonstrates how feminist theory and research promote a sound understanding and appreciation of motherhood, and how feminist activism promotes mothers' and children's well-being. But in this chapter I focus directly on the relationship between feminism and motherhood. First, I present some of the diversity in feminist approaches to motherhood, diversity reflecting feminists' varying social and historical circumstances. Second, I look at feminist debates about the social consequences of the fact that only women give birth. Third, I explore how feminists have embraced motherhood, showing that, contrary to myth, the preponderance of feminist approaches to motherhood have been positive. While this chapter belongs to part 1 because it focuses on feminist constructions of motherhood, these three sections raise issues that broadly parallel parts 1, 2, and 3 of the book, respectively.

Finally, at various points in the chapter and in the concluding section as well, I address how the myth of feminism as antimother and antichild arose and why it persists. Throughout, my overarching aim is to replace that myth with a portrait of the complex, multifaceted, ever-shifting relationship between feminism and motherhood.[2]

Diversity in Feminist Approaches to Motherhood

How have feminists of different historical periods thought about motherhood? How are feminists' perspectives on motherhood shaped by their differing social locations?

First-Wave Feminism

Known at the time as the "woman movement," first-wave feminism arose in the 1840s in the context of abolitionism. As (mostly) northern, white, middle-class women participated in the fight against slavery, they began to think about their own subjection as women. Their male peers in the abolition movement often prohibited them from speaking in public and participating equally in their organizations. And in the society at large, women could not vote, attend university, or pursue a profession. If they married, they lost all rights to their wages and property.[3]

These early feminists did not challenge the idea that women were responsible for family life. Rather, they concentrated on "the political, economic and psychological effects of women's enforced dependence on men."[4] In a historical context where all women were denied the rights of citizenship, it made sense—at least from the point of view of the relatively privileged women who led the movement—that issues of motherhood would take a back seat. Indeed, there is only one mention of motherhood in the 1848 Seneca Falls "Declaration of Sentiments and Resolutions," widely viewed as the first feminist document in the United States. The signers of this declaration protested the fact that in the case of divorce, fathers, simply because they were men, were given guardianship of the children by law.[5] Yet, as Sojourner Truth pointed out in her famous 1851 speech "Ain't I a Woman?" motherhood was a major site of oppression for women under slavery.[6] Slave owners controlled black women's motherhood through rape and the forced separation of mothers and children when one or the other was sold.[7]

In the nineteenth century, the meaning of motherhood for white middle-class feminists and nonfeminists included not only the bearing and rearing of children but also the nurturance of husbands, extended families, friendship networks, and cultural institutions.[8] During the late nineteenth and early twentieth centuries, women activists—often called maternalists—used these nurturing responsibilities to justify their incursion into a wide array of political activities. For example, they fought for "mothers' pensions" for poor and working-class mothers, a topic Mary Rogers returns to in chapter 10.[9]

Early Second-Wave Feminism

Second-wave feminism developed under a different set of historical conditions; consequently, it produced a different set of ideas about motherhood. Called the women's liberation movement in its early years, second-wave feminism arose in the 1960s in the wake of the civil rights, New Left, antiwar, and counterculture movements.[10] Women of different races and class backgrounds began to protest their second-class treatment within these movements as well as in the society at large. In this wave of feminism, motherhood was, and continues to be, high on the agenda.[11]

M. Rivka Polatnick's study of two 1960s feminist groups merits extended attention because she looks closely at their approaches to motherhood, demonstrating that each group's perspective is grounded in its particular social location. One group consisted of poor and working-class African American women from two communities in the New York City area, Mount Vernon and New Rochelle. Pat Robinson, a radical social worker employed by Planned Parenthood, helped bring these two networks together. The Mount Vernon (MV) women, many of whom were already mothers, became politically active in the early and mid-1960s when they protested poor housing conditions and organized a welfare rights group. They also created a Saturday freedom school for children to counteract the alienating education poor African American children received in the public schools. The New Rochelle (NR) women were younger and mostly childless when they became politically active around the time of Martin Luther King Jr.'s assassination in 1968. Like the MV women, their activism was child oriented. They tutored young children and organized recreation programs and a freedom school. The NR women were beneficiaries of the civil rights movement as well as slightly more advantaged class backgrounds. As such, they had (limited) opportunities to attend local colleges and they were motivated to postpone having children for awhile. Most had children later.[12]

The other group—the New York Radical Women (NYRW)—consisted primarily of young, white, middle-class women with college degrees. Most of the core members were single, heterosexual, and childless. As one of the many groups under the rubric of radical feminism, their activism involved raising consciousness about the inequities in conventional sex roles, and challenging those inequities politically, theoretically, as well as in their personal lives.[13] Although most of the core members of NYRW never became mothers, some of them expressed regret about their childlessness when Polatnick interviewed them in the 1980s and 1990s. Polatnick herself belonged to the NYRW for several months; unlike most of the members, she eventually had a child in her late thirties, a decision influenced by her research on these two feminist groups.[14]

The Mount Vernon/New Rochelle group viewed motherhood positively and saw it as a source of power for women. The New York Radical Women viewed motherhood as oppressive; becoming a mother meant sacrificing new possibilities (680). Despite this stark contrast, Polatnick points to commonalties in the two groups' perspectives. Both believed that women's self-determination depended on women's ability to control their reproduction. For the MV/NR women, this took the form of defending their right to the birth control pill For the NYRW, it meant advocating the legalization of abortion (694–695). (The birth control pill was not widely available until the mid-1960s and abortion was illegal until 1973.)

Furthermore, both groups believed that too much responsibility for mothering oppressed women. The MV/NR group felt the burden lay in having too many children, while the NYRW saw having any children at all as oppressive. Both groups argued for shared child rearing, but they imputed different meanings to the concept. The MV/NR women lived in communities where child rearing was shared within women's networks, with men playing relatively minor roles. For the NYRW, shared child rearing meant equal parenting with fathers and the need for publicly funded child care centers. Finally, the MV/NR women associated child rearing with social activism; caring for one's own children coexisted with caring for the needs of the community's children. By contrast, the NYRW perceived motherhood as getting in the way of social activism (695–697).

The ideas of the MV/NR women need to be understood in relation to African American and African traditions: othermothering (see chapter 9); associating motherhood with power; and sharing economic resources among kin (697). Their ideas also need to be understood in the context of black radicalism in the mid-1960s. As historian Lauri Umansky observes, many black activists were frustrated with the limits of the integrationist philosophy of the civil rights movement. They were enraged by unwanted sterilizations of women of color, the disproportionate deaths of black men in Vietnam, violence against blacks on American streets, and persistent attacks on the black family (culminating in the notorious 1965 Moynihan Report, which vilified a culture of poverty in black communities for which black "matriarchs" were held responsible). In this milieu, many African Americans moved toward black nationalism, which argued that African Americans have political, economic, and cultural interests distinct from those of white Americans or the United States as a nation.[15]

Given the threat of genocide, black nationalists encouraged black women to have children. Some claimed that the birth control pill was a tool of white society's genocidal efforts in African American communities.[16] But when the MV women received a statement to that effect from a group of black male activists, they responded angrily. "Poor Black sisters decide for themselves whether to have a baby or not to have a baby." They argued that the pill gave them "freedom to fight genocide of Black women and children. . . . Having too many babies stops us from supporting our children, teaching them the truth . . . and fighting Black men who still want to use and exploit us."[17]

The ideas of the NYRW also arose from their particular social location. As activists in the New Left and counterculture movements, they had already been exposed to radical critiques of the traditional nuclear family.[18] These women had grown up with the 1950s ideology that a woman should find her identity and satisfaction in marriage and motherhood. Yet having been educated alongside their male peers, they had unprecedented opportunities for self-development and achievement. At this point in American history, white middle-class women began to enter in much greater numbers the prestigious, traditionally male professions such as law, medicine, and higher education. Not only were they more privileged in these ways than the MV/NR women, they were also more likely to live far from their families of origin, and much less likely to be involved with children in their daily lives.[19]

As Polatnick points out, both the MV/NR women and the NYRW made an important contribution to women's liberation. At the same time, each group's contribution contained a risk.

> The MV/NR group's genuine high regard for motherhood was an important message to a society that celebrated mothers at the superficial level but devalued them at deeper levels. Their community-based child rearing challenged the mainstream notion that the mother should handle all the parenting. By connecting mothering with community activism, the group countered the dominant image of the mother immersed in domesticity. Their child-centered values bade defiance to the societal obsession with self-interest and materialism. (701)

However, by "putting children first" these feminists may have risked putting themselves last (701).[20] For their part, the NYRW's contribution lay in their bold challenge to the sacredness of motherhood and their validation of other options for women. On the down side, their approach seemed to support the society's devaluation of mothering.[21]

In narrative A, writer Alix Kates Shulman recounts her experiences in becoming a feminist. She was in her mid-thirties and a mother when she joined the NYRW and other groups. Although her age and motherhood made her an atypical NYRW member, her story shows how a mother can find feminism empowering and how a feminist can find motherhood empowering. Feminism gave her license to cultivate her independent interests, and it gave her tools to advocate social change for the benefit of children, such as eliminating sexism in children's books.

One source of the myth of feminists as antimother and antichild is a distortion of the early history of second-wave feminism. On the one hand, that myth mistakes some white, middle-class women's feminism for feminism in general; it ignores the diversity of viewpoints among those feminists as well as the ideas of other feminists such as the MV/NW women. On the other hand, it misinterprets those white, middle-class women who rejected motherhood. Their critique of the cultural assumption that marriage and motherhood alone should satisfy women does not mean that they rejected mothers and children (see chapter 3). Furthermore, we need to keep in mind that privileged women in the 1960s and 1970s encountered more difficulties than privileged women do today in seeking to combine motherhood with rewarding professional employment. Among other obstacles, maternity leaves were rare and day care was not widely available. In fact, whether they were mothers or not, early second-wave feminists fought for high quality, affordable day care. One of their infrequently noted accomplishments was the creation of communally run child care centers, which aimed to provide, among other things, a nonsexist curriculum.[22] In any case, early second-wave feminists—the two groups Polatnick studied, along with many other groups—created a distinction between "woman" and "mother" that has benefited women, feminist or not, ever since.

The feminist constructions of motherhood that I have presented so far are just the tip of the iceberg. In the rest of this chapter as well as in various chapters and personal narratives throughout our book, we shall find that motherhood holds different meanings for different feminists. Of course, feminists are not the only ones who develop ideas about motherhood. The rest of the chapters in part I address social constructions of motherhood that feminists have criticized, the constructions of lawmakers, politicians, medical experts, welfare professionals, and scholars who have something other than the well-being of mothers and children in mind.

Feminist Debates about Maternal Bodies

Does the fact that only women get pregnant and give birth oppress or empower women? Should pregnant women be treated differently from or similarly to men in the workplace? Feminists have wrangled over these questions and, equally important, moved beyond the dichotomies they presuppose.

Oppression and Empowerment

Concerning women's bodies, some early second-wave feminists espoused ideas that could easily be interpreted as antimother. Shulamith Firestone is the best known of these. In *The Dialectic of Sex*, published in 1970, she argued that women's bodies are the source of women's oppression. Before the development of reliable birth control, in her view, women were completely subject to the biological processes of childbirth, breastfeeding, and the care of infants, which led to their dependence on men for survival. Because she viewed the female body as a prison, Firestone argued that women would achieve freedom only when technology released them from pregnancy and childbirth altogether.[23]

Those who claim that feminism is antimother frequently point to Firestone as proof. Yet her work has received far more attention than warranted by the historical record. Ann Snitow aptly describes Firestone's book, along with a few others, as "demon texts" for which feminism has been apologizing ever since.[24] Many of Firestone's peers—other early second wave feminists—criticized her *biological determinism*, the idea that specific characteristics of our bodies determine our place in society. They also criticized her faith in scientific technology. Following the lead of the New Left and counterculture movements, which espoused a holistic approach to nature and human bodies, most feminists at the time were suspicious of technology.[25] This suspiciousness continues to this day in many feminist circles, as we shall see when we get to pregnancy and childbirth in chapter 6 and reproductive technologies in chapter 7. Indeed, while Firestone launched her critique of biological sex differences, a much more positive, and much less acknowledged, feminist discourse about maternal bodies was emerging. The women's health movement portrayed pregnancy and childbirth as empowering aspects of women's lives.[26] And on a theoretical level, many feminists over the years have argued that maternal bodies are a source, or at least a potential source, of women's empowerment.[27]

Mary O'Brien, a philosopher and midwife, is among those theorists. She contends that "reproductive consciousness" differs for men and women. "Man is related to his child only by thought, by knowledge in general, rather than by experience in particular—whereas motherhood is a unity of consciousness and knowing on the one hand, and action (reproductive labor) on the other."[28] Men's awareness of their separation from the process of reproduction could produce great respect for women's reproductive capacities, as was the case in many ancient societies.[29] O'Brien speculates, however, that the origins of patriarchy lay in men's reproductive consciousness. She defines *patriarchy* as "the power to transcend natural realities with historical, man-made realities." By "natural realities" she means the difference between women and men's relations to reproduction. By "historical realities" she means the institutions and ideologies men created in response to their lesser part in reproduction. In short, men sought to dominate women and to assert their rights to children in order to compensate for their alienation from reproductive processes and powers.[30]

As O'Brien acknowledges, the historical accuracy of this argument is difficult to prove or disprove. It has also been the source of much debate. Feminist historian Gerda Lerner, for example, takes issue with O'Brien's single-cause explanation of patriarchy.[31] Nonetheless, many feminists note that Western culture's devaluation of women's bodies and childbirth figure centrally in patriarchy. After analyzing several major Western texts—from Homer and Plato to Marx and Tolstoy—Robbie Pfeufer Kahn concludes that many of these texts elevate "the instructive properties of death," but few address the meanings that birth offers.[32] The flip side of this devaluation of birth is found in Western science's appropriation of female procreativity. According to Evelyn Fox Keller, for example, scientists used the metaphor of pregnancy and birth as they produced and tested the atomic and hydrogen bombs. The A-bomb was "Oppenheimer's baby"; the H-bomb was "Teller's baby." Far more than a code to conceal the scientists' activities, this metaphor was adopted by the U.S. government and eventually by the public. Keller points out the irony of physicists usurping birth metaphors in the production of instruments of death.[33]

In any case, the vast majority of feminists have opposed Firestone's idea that biological sex differences inevitably produce social inequality between men and women. To the extent that maternal bodies are a site of women's oppression, it is not because that oppression is "natural" but because patriarchal (and racist and classist) societies have devalued, controlled, or appropriated women's reproductive capacities.

Difference and Sameness

Women's increasing participation in the labor force during the second half of the twentieth century led to other feminist debates about maternal bodies. What kinds of policies and laws would best support women's efforts to achieve equality in the workplace? What does equality for pregnant women mean in this context?

A little background: In the early twentieth century, feminist reformers lobbied for protective legislation for women workers who, like men, typically labored under unregulated, harsh conditions. Protective legislation limited the number of hours women could work, sometimes prohibited them from night work, and excluded them from jobs considered physically or morally dangerous. For example, women were restricted from metal grinding, underground mining, operating elevators, carrying mail, reading meters, and bartending. Racism infused these laws: domestic and agricultural work, the occupations in which most African American, Chicana, and Asian American women were likely to work, were typically exempt.[34]

By the 1960s and 1970s the social and political landscape had changed. While women of color had been in the labor force at greater rates than white women, the labor force participation rates of all groups of women—including mothers—increased rapidly. Furthermore, antidiscrimination legislation had been enacted, partly through the efforts of liberal feminists, who were particularly focused on legal reform concerning women's paid employment. The Equal Pay Act of 1963 required equal pay for equal work, prohibiting at least on paper the widespread practice of employers paying women less than men for identical work. Title VII of the Civil Rights Act of 1964 prohibited employers from discriminating on the basis of race, sex, national origin or religion, challenging the common practices of advertising and hiring on the basis of such characteristics.[35]

Within the social and political context of the 1960s and 1970s, then, the costs to women of protective legislation clearly outweighed the benefits. In fact, protective legislation left a legacy that harmed women employees well into the 1970s. Employers could both fire pregnant women and refuse to hire them. Regardless of a woman's desire or ability to work, employers could put pregnant workers on mandatory maternity leave with neither benefits nor job security. The upshot was that women often lost seniority, promotions, and retirement benefits they would have otherwise earned.[36]

In the 1970s, the Supreme Court twice upheld the denial of employment benefits to pregnant women. At the same time, however, feminists were key actors in pushing for a new approach to pregnancy, an approach assuming that most women are long-term participants in the labor force and that, broadly speaking, women and men are more similar to than different from each other (69). Congress ratified this new approach when it passed the Pregnancy Discrimination Act (PDA) in 1978. In order to comply with the PDA, employers are required to treat pregnant workers on the basis of their ability to work. As long as a pregnant woman is able to work, an employer cannot fire her or force her to take a leave of absence. If she is not able to work, an employer must treat her like other workers who are unable to work for a period of time. For example, if an employer allows temporarily disabled employees to return to their old jobs, pregnant workers must also have that option (72). Although the PDA was a clear victory in the sense of supporting pregnant women's right to work, the actual treatment a pregnant woman received depended on her employer's particular policies. Moreover, the PDA soon came into conflict with state legislation designed to help pregnant women by providing benefits that were not given to other workers (73).

At this point, feminist lawyers and legal scholars found themselves on both sides of the ensuing legal battles. While feminists on each side supported pregnant women's right to a disability leave mandated by the state, and agreed that employers should comply with both state laws and the federal PDA, their reasoning and remedies differed. The debate among feminist legal scholars turned on whether to emphasize women's difference or women's sameness, divergent approaches that sociologist Lise Vogel describes as "special treatment" and "equal treatment" (77). Each side viewed equality for women in the workplace as the goal but disagreed about the best method for achieving it. On one side, feminists portrayed pregnancy as a unique condition requiring "special attention if equal employment opportunity standards are to be met, and if women are not to be disadvantaged as workers" (86). On the other side, feminists "depicted pregnancy as a unique condition that is nonetheless comparable to other conditions affecting workers—conditions that invariably involve special needs which society ought to accommodate. Disability due to pregnancy should not . . . be privileged over temporary inability to work caused by other conditions" (87).

Notice that when feminists seek to promote equality for women within systems controlled by elite men (in this case, the legal system and the labor force), it is difficult to avoid the idea that those men—and male bodies—are the standard. It is difficult to move beyond assuming either that women need to accommodate themselves to that standard or that women need special help because they deviate from it.

In 1987, the Supreme Court (in *California Federal Savings and Loan Associa-*

tion v. Guerra) upheld the California state law that gave specific benefits to pregnant women, ruling that the PDA was "a floor beneath which pregnancy disability benefits may not drop—not a ceiling above which they may not rise" (88). While feminists on both sides viewed this as a victory for pregnant women, it still left open the question of whether women's difference from or similarity to men should be emphasized and codified in federal law concerning employment.

To a certain extent, that question was answered by the Family and Medical Leave Act (FMLA), signed into law by President Clinton in 1993. Feminist policy analysts designed the FMLA in the wake of the debate over pregnancy disability leave statutes (155–156). This law requires employers with fifty or more employees to give men and women up to twelve weeks of unpaid leave per year upon the birth or adoption of a child, the serious health condition of an immediate family member who needs care, or a serious health condition that renders the employee unable to work.[37] According to Vogel, this legislation "addresses the special needs of pregnancy and motherhood within a gender-neutral legal framework that encompasses a spectrum of workers' special needs." Although the FMLA is clearly stingy when compared to the social benefits accorded workers in most European countries, it is the most protection American employees, including employed mothers, have ever had. Vogel argues that the gender-neutral framework of the FMLA is the most advantageous for women employees, especially given the history of how different treatment (such as protective legislation) has disadvantaged women. The gender-neutral framework, she claims, makes room for—while not singling out—the uniqueness of pregnancy and other maternal conditions. She contends that this policy transcends the sameness/difference dichotomy by including both.[38]

Pregnancy and childbirth have compelled the attention of feminists in part because of discrimination against pregnant women in the labor force. Recently, however, Robbie Pfeufer Kahn has called on feminists to redress their inattention to breastfeeding.[39] While most women can continue employment through much if not all of their pregnancies, and childbirth itself is short, breastfeeding—especially extended nursing not supplemented with formula—seems to impinge to a much greater extent on women's attempts to achieve equality at home and in the workplace. For example, most employed women do not have enough privacy and flexibility in their jobs to allow them to pump breast milk a few times a day at work.

Kahn suggests that feminists have neglected the topic of breastfeeding because it embodies a serious dilemma. On the one hand, feminists want to respect the needs, powers, and pleasures of maternal bodies, which have conventionally been devalued. On the other hand, feminist attempts to do so can be misinterpreted as biological determinism and used to justify restrictions on women's labor force participation (33). Rather than becoming mired in this dilemma, however, Kahn begins with a strong commitment to breastfeeding as a practice that benefits both mothers and children (and thus benefits society as a whole). She treats the mother-child dyad rather than the autonomous individual (usually assumed to be male) as the primary unit in society. Putting maternal bodies rather than male bodies at the center of her analysis, she argues that changes could be made to facilitate long-term breastfeeding, such as the reorganization of work spaces and schedules (386).

While Vogel claims that equality is best achieved through a gender-neutral framework that allows for the uniqueness of maternal bodies, Kahn supports a difference framework that demands changes so that equality for women is possible.[40] Thus, in her own way, Kahn, like Vogel, attempts to transcend the difference/sameness dichotomy. In an important sense, of course, we are talking about apples and oranges. Vogel addresses the legal system's treatment of pregnant women in the labor force, while Kahn focuses in a broader sense on the organization of and assumptions embedded in work and family institutions.

Part 2 of this book will take up the topic of maternal bodies again. While differences among feminists will also surface in those chapters, most contemporary feminists protest the cultural separation of motherhood and sexuality, and the medical profession's wresting of control from women in pregnancy and childbirth. Reproductive technologies are more contentious among feminists because the question of where women's interests lie is less straightforward.

Tensions in the Feminist Embrace of Motherhood

By the mid-1970s, most white, middle-class feminists (including many who had earlier rejected motherhood) embraced a positive evaluation of motherhood that has continued to the present.[41] For example, in 1978, activist and writer Robin Morgan proclaimed, "It is refreshing at last to be able to come out of my mother-closet and yell to the world that I love my dear wonderful delicious child—and am not one damned whit less the radical feminist for that."[42] Yet the feminist embrace of motherhood has been riddled with tensions: how to value and respect mothers without idealizing them, erasing differences among them, or celebrating them at the expense of non-mothers.

Idealizing Mothers and Erasing Differences among Them

Beginning in the early to mid-1970s, cultural feminists developed theory that stressed differences between men and women.[43] Some cultural feminists elevated all women's potential for motherhood to an essential, unifying principle. Jane Alpert, for example, argued that whether women are mothers or not they possess procreative potential, which leads to the development of empathy, intuitiveness, and other "feminine" traits.[44] In this view, women are basically alike and their biological capacity for motherhood should be the basis of feminist consciousness. Thus, some cultural feminists succumbed to the biological determinism Kahn works to avoid in her discussion of breastfeeding.

Umansky interprets this development within cultural feminism as an attempt to resolve tensions that had arisen between groups of women, particularly over issues of sexuality. Lesbians often felt marginalized within feminist groups that focused on heterosexual women's issues, while heterosexual women often felt defensive in light of some lesbians' claim that heterosexuality is inherently oppressive to women. Tensions between white and black heterosexual women arose when sexual relationships between black men and white women became more common during the civil rights movement. African American women repeatedly voiced their concern and sometimes outrage about this sexual pattern, but for the most part white feminists remained silent.[45]

According to Umansky, cultural feminism failed to overcome these tensions because it disguised rather than addressed them. For example, it created an image of the maternal figure as a sensuous but asexual being (124). This set women up to choose either sexuality or motherhood, a problem we address in chapter 5. Cultural feminists also tended to ignore the realities of mothers' lives, which reveal the immense class, race, and sexual differences among them (111). African American women were particularly disturbed by this erasure of difference (120). Indeed, many African American women felt the need to organize on their own because neither white women's nor black men's groups addressed their needs and issues. In 1973 they founded the National Black Feminist Organization (108).

Analyzing Motherhood, Mothers, and Mothering

Many feminists rejected this totalizing approach to motherhood and continued their struggles in the realm of practical politics, for example, by fighting for reproductive rights and day care (118). In addition, by the late 1970s and early 1980s, many feminist scholars were attending to motherhood in a wide range of ways that suggested a positive evaluation without idealizing it. Assuming that what mothers do is important, academic feminists from an array of disciplines examined the daily experience of mothering from both mothers' and daughters' perspectives, and they analyzed the feelings, values, and rituals of motherhood. Their work made mothering visible and "furthered the centrality of motherhood to feminist theory" (132).

Let's take a brief look at one influential text from this period—philosopher Sara Ruddick's 1980 article, "Maternal Thinking"—in order to flesh out one feminist version of what it means to value and respect mothers. Grounding her ideas in philosophical traditions that assume "*all* thought arises out of social practice," Ruddick begins by suggesting that maternal practice is governed by three interests: preserving the life of the child; nourishing the child's physical, emotional, and intellectual growth; and shaping the child's growth in ways that are acceptable to the mother's social group. As mothers engage in these everyday practices, the argument goes, they have the potential to develop specific intellectual capacities, to assume certain metaphysical attitudes and to affirm particular values.[46] By focusing on mothers' *practices*, Ruddick treats what mothers do as important and rejects cultural feminism's tendency toward biological determinism.

A mother's commitment to preserving life in the face of life's fragility can produce an attitude Ruddick calls "holding." This attitude is governed by "the priority of keeping over acquiring, of conserving the fragile, of maintaining whatever is at hand and necessary to the child's life." By elevating keeping over acquiring, maternal thought rejects "the instrumentalism of technocratic capitalism." Preserving life also encourages humility, "a metaphysical attitude one takes toward a world beyond one's control." Humility "accepts not only the facts of damage and death, but also the . . . increasingly separate existences of the lives it seeks to preserve." While humility can degenerate into melancholy, Ruddick suggests that cheerfulness—which she carefully distinguishes from a cheery denial of problems—is another aspect of maternal thinking. "In a daily way, cheerfulness is a matter-of-fact willingness to continue, to give birth and to accept having given birth, to welcome life despite its conditions. When things fall apart, maternal cheerfulness becomes evident courage" (350–351).

For its part, the practice of fostering a child's growth encourages thinking in which "[i]nnovation takes precedence over permanence, disclosure and responsiveness over clarity and certainty." This openness to change differentiates maternal thought from scientific thinking, which typically relies on the results of repeatable experiments. Because children are constantly growing and changing, maternal thinking requires continual learning (352–353).

When Ruddick turns to the maternal practice of shaping the child's growth in ways that are accepted within the mother's community, she warns that this practice can be harmful to children. "This may mean training her daughters for powerlessness, her sons for war, and both for crippling work in dehumanizing factories, businesses, and professions. It may mean training both daughters and sons for defensive or arrogant power over others in sexual, economic, or political life" (355). The solution to this problem, Ruddick claims, is the feminist transformation of maternal thought. If a mother develops a feminist consciousness, she will resist teaching her child to conform to social values that injure self and others (356–357). Although liberating, this is no easy project, as we discuss when we get to feminist mothering in chapter 8.

Ruddick contends that maternal thought can be valuable far beyond the confines of the domestic realm because it rejects capitalism's instrumental treatment of people. Maternal thought, informed by feminism, can lead to a public commitment to the preservation and growth of all children (359, 361). Ruddick developed her ideas further along these lines in her 1989 book *Maternal Thinking: Toward a Politics of Peace.*[47] The strengths and limits of maternalism in the environmental and peace movements are one topic of chapter 10.

Ruddick's contribution lies in her respectful treatment of mothers' everyday practices and thought, and her theorizing of their public value. Nonetheless, some feminists have interpreted her theory as universalizing the experiences of white, middle-class mothers and thus marginalizing other mothers' practices and thought.[48] In her effort to "shift the center" away from such mothers, Patricia Hill Collins describes the mother-work of poor and working-class women of color as revolving around physical survival, the struggle for power within oppressive institutions, and the maintenance of racial or ethnic identities under pressures to assimilate.[49] On a different level, Ellen Ross points to the limits of Ruddick's "measured cadences." Referring to the death of her six-year-old child, Ross laments that Ruddick's ideas "could not encompass the intensity of my own grief or joy in motherhood."[50]

Poet, writer, and musician Joy Harjo speaks implicitly to these criticisms in narrative B. As a young, single, Native American mother, she worked at low-wage jobs, tried to get an education, and attempted to heal the wounds of her own childhood. Although she certainly wanted to preserve her children's lives and foster their growth, her struggles sound more like the mother-work of physical survival, fighting for power within oppressive institutions, and maintaining racial identities in a racist society. When Harjo recounts the story of her teenage daughter running away from home, leaving no clue of her whereabouts, we hear resonances of Ross's intense grief. Harjo takes us inside a world where few social advantages can be taken for granted; all the while, though, her love for her children rings out loud and clear.

Celebrating Mothers at the Expense of Nonmothers

Let's return to the general topic of this section: the shift early on within second-wave feminism to a positive evaluation of motherhood. What brought about this change? Umansky contends that it was influenced in part by black feminists' earlier embrace of motherhood. In addition, many observers suggest that as educated, white, middle-class feminists heard their biological clocks ticking, they began to rethink their earlier choice to forego motherhood. Most early second-wave feminists did eventually have children. In fact, this pattern of delayed childbearing characterized privileged American women generally. Birth rates dropped in the American population as a whole during the early to mid-1970s, but especially among the educated, white middle class. The availability of birth control and abortion and expanding opportunities for higher education for women explain this drop. Moreover, by the mid-1970s, a large number of feminists were entering academia, and they brought their interest in motherhood to their professional research. They founded new academic journals, and traditional academic publishers began to publish feminist scholarship.[51]

But Umansky also points to a much broader influence: "[The] profamily rhetoric of the political and intellectual community at large." Although it is usually considered the brainchild of conservative politicians, she argues that the focus on "traditional family values" infused rhetoric across the political spectrum. While many feminists strongly rejected this rhetoric, some were influenced by it (137–138). Ann Snitow offers a similar view. "[I]n the rising national babble of pronatalism in the 1980s, listening to the mothers was a project subtly susceptible to co-optation."[52]

Snitow is particularly concerned that the feminist embrace of motherhood erases the experiences of women who do not have children, whether voluntarily or not. She argues that second-wave feminism set out to demystify the experiences of both mothers and nonmothers but has been less successful at imagining how a full and deeply meaningful life is possible for women without children (33). She suggests that the backlash against feminism in the 1980s as well as the snail's pace of social change encouraged pronatalism among feminists.[53] While divorce rates and women's paid employment have increased, women still do not have adequate day care, enough support from male partners, and workplaces attentive to employees' family responsibilities. "Our discouragement is, in my view, the subtext of most of what we have written about motherhood in the past decade. I think women are heartbroken. Never has the baby been so delicious. We are—in this period of reaction—elaborating, extending, reinstitutionalizing this relation for ourselves."[54]

In recent years, feminists have begun to attend more closely to the experiences of women who do not have children.[55] Gayle Letherby argues that just as feminists have articulated motherhood's complexity and mothers' ambivalence, they need to do the same for nonmotherhood and women who are childless.[56] Carolyn Morell begins this process by noting that our language betrays the cultural devaluation of women who do not have children. "Childless" and "nonmother" imply an absence or a void, suggesting that the standard is a woman with children. The term "child-free" is also problematic, according to Morell, because "[i]t suggests that women who do not have children of their own want to be rid of children, as in those who promote a 'union-free' or 'smoke-free' environment." The implication that women who do not have children are hostile to them is neither accurate nor helpful.[57] Many nonmothers, for example, have strong relationships with nieces, nephews, godchildren, or other children who are part of their work or personal lives (see chapter 9).

In sum, when feminists embrace motherhood, they take on a set of challenging tasks. They must study the diversity and complexity of mothers' lives, resisting the temptation to assume that any one group of mothers represents all others and exploring the historical, social, and political circumstances that shape different mothers' lives and choices. They need to examine the wide range of feelings—joy, sorrow, ecstasy, rage, and ambivalence—that mothers have about mothering and their relationships with their children. They must respect the hard work and thought entailed in nurturing and providing for children, including the social justice activism that mothers and nonmothers sometimes engage in on behalf of their own and others' children. Last but not least, they need to understand the situations of women who do not have children, whether voluntarily, involuntarily, or ambivalently.

These feminist challenges have shaped Mary Rogers's and my work throughout this book, both in writing our chapters and in choosing the personal narratives. Yet there is a particularly strong connection between this discussion and part 3, "Mothering in Everyday Life." The chapters there look squarely at (some of) the joys and traumas that arise in mothers' relationships with their children, the contributions of other mothers (including nonmothers) to the care of children, and mothers' political activism.

Feminism and Motherhood: Myths and Realities

There is no doubt that since the beginning of the second wave of the women's movement, motherhood has been high on the feminist agenda. Yet the relationship between feminism and motherhood is complex. At different times, in different contexts, and from differing social locations, feminists have treated motherhood as an oppressive *and* an empowering experience; a source of alienation from *and* connection to their bodies; a form of work that is enervating *and* rewarding; a relationship that constrains women's autonomy *and* invites their personal growth; a cause for distance from *and* a bridge to other women; a motivator of conservative *and* progressive political action. Given the diversity of women's experiences of motherhood, given our culture's simultaneous idealization and vilification of mothers, and given our psychological bonds (for better or worse) to those who mothered each of us as individuals, it should be no surprise that feminist approaches to motherhood have been so multifaceted.[58]

Nonetheless, the simplistic myth of feminists as antimother and antichild persists. I have traced the roots of that myth to misinterpretations of some white feminists' critique of motherhood as oppressive; to ignorance about African American feminists' approaches to motherhood; to exaggerated attention to the ideas of Shulamith Firestone (among others); and to a focus on some early second-wave feminists' ideas to the exclusion of all that feminists have done since then.

But this myth has other sources as well. Feminist ideas have been demonized by media pundits and politicians and sometimes by people whose ideas gain currency *because* they are criticizing feminism. Among the most successful in getting their voices heard are women who claim sympathy to feminism and yet blame it for women's sorry state. In the mid-1980s, Sylvia Ann Hewlett became one such public figure. In *A Lesser Life: The Myth of Women's Liberation in America,* she stated that "many contemporary feminists have reviled both mothers and babies," and she accused feminists of doing nothing to help them.[59]

As Michele M. Moody-Adams explains, this feminist bashing exploits many women's insecurities; it persuades them that embracing feminism would mean giving up "their 'essential' womanhood, along with all the institutions, practices, and prerogatives attached to it." Moody-Adams contends, to the contrary, that feminist ideas, such as a woman's right to autonomy and self-determination, can enhance a woman's commitment to her family.[60] For example, a mother who takes paid employment to provide for her family needs to be committed to her own autonomy in order to get and persist in that employment. And a mother who wants to teach her daughters self-respect and to teach her sons respect for women needs to model those attitudes in her own actions. In any case, Mary Rogers takes up a more contemporary and subtler version of feminist bashing in chapter 4, where she looks at current attention to fatherlessness as a public issue. Hewlett pops up again in that context.

Finally, a related source of the pernicious myth about feminism is the general ignorance and considerable misinformation in our society about women's movements. When I hear students express negative opinions about feminism, I ask them where their ideas come from. How do they know that feminists are male-bashers, mother-haters, or allergic to children? Usually this question catches them off guard, and they are hard pressed to answer it. They may say they've heard such things on TV or radio, perhaps from Rush Limbaugh, or from their parents, teachers, or other influential adults in their lives. But they don't know the source of these adults' opinions. Sometimes a student will say s/he knows someone, often a teacher, who calls herself a feminist and who seems angry. When I ask what that person is angry about and whether her anger is justified, the answers are usually vague.

My point here is not to rail against students but to suggest that it is easy in our society to develop strong negative opinions about feminism. Despite the presence of women's studies in academe, the contributions of feminist activism and scholarship are more often than not absent from our educational curricula from kindergarten through higher education. To the extent that feminist contributions have been integrated into the curriculum or have influenced educational practices and policies, they are not usually recognized as such. Rather than hear students accept uncritically what others say about feminism, I'd like them to ask their own versions of Dale Spender's question, "Why Didn't I Know?" In the late 1960s Spender and her peers wondered whether women before them had ever protested women's lot in life. Much to their surprise, they found a vibrant history of feminist creativity, scholarship, and activism, which they had never learned about in school. Spender concluded that she didn't know this history because "[t]hese women and their ideas constitute a political threat and they are censored."[61] I find that when students and others make similar efforts to understand feminism's history and contributions, great things begin to happen.

For instance, on the last day of my "Motherhood and Feminism" seminar, we took turns talking about what we had learned from the wide range of readings we had covered as well as from our lively and sometimes heated conversations over the course of the semester. Two themes arose from this discussion. Some students learned most about feminism's focus on different groups of mothers, whose specific desires, needs, and frustrations need to be examined in their own right, in light of the many social factors shaping those experiences. Some students, however, learned that feminists care about children and that a commitment to children must include concern for mothers, who continue to shoulder most of the responsibility for children in our society. We traced the sources of these two themes and talked about how they need not be perceived as contradictory. This, I thought, was a great beginning.

NARRATIVE A

A Mother's Story

Alix Kates Shulman

• • •

I was born on August 17, 1932, in Cleveland. My father was a lawyer, my mother a housewife who'd been forced by the then-current laws to quit her teaching job when she married. I had a conventional white middle-class suburban childhood, except that my father and I had wonderful ongoing intellectual rapport. He was a family man; he set up a card table in the living room to write his briefs, and I learned to write by watching him. He encouraged me, gave me books we could discuss. My mother was also a reader, and my father used to say, "Your mother is really the

From The Conversation Begins: Mothers and Daughters Talk about Living Feminism, *edited by Christina Looper Baker and Christina Baker Kline. Copyright © 1996 by Christina Looper Baker and Christina Baker Kline. Used by permission of Bantam Books, a division of Random House, Inc.*

smart one." But since my parents followed traditional gender roles, it didn't seem to matter that she was smart and in college. (At six, I watched her walk down the aisle in cap and gown to receive her BA.) She became a project designer for the WPA—a job she loved but gave up when World War II started, because otherwise, with two breadwinners in the family, my father would have been drafted. After the war she bought into the back-to-the-kitchen propaganda and became an unpaid community organizer, sometimes contemptuously referred to as a "clubwoman." Because I loved them both, in my teens I felt divided by my parents' values: the social strivings of my mother versus the self-contained independence of my father.

• • •

In 1953, at twenty, I went off to Columbia as a graduate student. I wanted to be a philosopher, but women were not philosophers then. Seeing all three women in my department treated like freaks, I soon married a fellow graduate student, dropped out of school, and became an editor to support us. My marriage was empty and lasted only five years. Then in 1959, feeling the press of time, I married the father of my children, who looked to me like a family man. That marriage lasted twenty-five years. At first it was exciting, romantic, close. But after we had children, it became embattled.

With the birth of my children (a boy and a girl, the fifties' ideal family) my whole life changed. Now it belonged to others. In my first marriage I had earned money and maintained my independence and spunk; in my second marriage I gave up freedom for family. Having chosen to become a mother, I gave it my all; soon being a good mother became my new purpose in life, which I pursued with pleasure and verve. Still, some part of me mourned my lost independence, and some instinct kept me from withdrawing from the world entirely. Terrified of not being able to support myself if my husband ran out on us (and from the moment I had children it was clear the honeymoon was over), I tried always to have some freelance job to do at home—for emergency money and to keep a toe in the world, especially after my husband began having affairs. No matter how vulnerable and humiliated I felt over the loss of my independent self, at least I still lived in Greenwich Village; I hadn't given up utterly and moved to the suburbs, where I would have been totally dependent.

I loved raising my children in the city, where I could participate in the civil rights and antiwar movements (albeit as a woman) and take my children to play in Washington Square Park. I delighted in watching them grow and acquire language. I taught them to read and draw, sew and cook, do new math. I took them often to the library and read them books. The first books I wrote were for them, for children—that's how I became a writer.

One day in 1967 a friend who had heard young feminists talking on the radio called me excitedly and said, "These women sound like us! We have to go to a meeting." Suddenly the world opened up and everything felt possible again. Soon I joined Redstockings, WITCH, New York Radical Feminists. I couldn't get enough.

I never felt any conflict between the movement and motherhood. Feminism healed my conflicts. Once I joined the movement I never again felt I had to sacrifice anything or choose between being a mom and having my own independent life. To me, all the sacrifice and compromise preceded feminism, and feminism reversed them. In fact, it was as a mother that I most deeply engaged with feminism. I spoke up for mothers, defended mothers. To the young women in my group I was that rarity, a genuine mother-housewife, who could speak of motherhood not from theory but from experience.

Not that being a mother in the women's movement was easy; motherhood was always one of the great explosive divides. Women without children often felt stereotyped by society as incomplete women, failures; those with children felt confined and marginalized. Each side thought the other privileged. Single women without children said, "You have the respect of society"; mothers said, "You have freedom." There wasn't much mutual understanding. But in my own life, motherhood and feminism were integrated from the start. One of the first projects I organized, Feminists on Children's Media, the pioneer group investigating sexism in children's literature, I embraced as both mother and feminist. (In 1969 the American Library Association offered us a big slot at their convention, and we met every month for a year in my apartment, preparing a talk, a slide show, and a bibliography, "Little Miss Muffet Fights Back." Few librarians had heard the word *sexism* before we presented our program.)

By then I was writing—short stories and children's books. But I always felt I had to fit writing into the interstices between domestic and maternal duties. I would drop the children at nursery school, run home, take the phone off the hook, and write for three hours until I had to pick them up, which was the end of my writing day. I wrote *Memoirs of an Ex-Prom Queen* that way—the most efficient writing I ever did.

I thought I was lucky to have work I loved that I could do at home, because it enabled me to be a full-time, hands-on mother. I considered that a great gift to both me and my children, ensuring them both my maternal presence and the model of my passionate engagement. But it turns out what they saw was something else: a disciplined, invulnerable person, with standards hard for them to live up to, who was always working.

I took over the study for my office—a beautiful little room overlooking Washington Square Park. I worked there every day. My husband was in some ways supportive, but in other ways he subverted my work. Even after I began publishing, he acted as if I had no right to that room (he had two offices!) or to my own time. No longer the submissive, compliant wife we had both expected me to be when we married and had children, I fought back, even though my ideal had been the gentle family I'd been raised in. My husband was a fierce fighter, and in fighting him I became fierce myself—something I now regret. When he was away (which was much of the time), the children and I were harmonious and close, but when he was home there was contention. Back then I thought the children could only benefit from those principles I struggled so hard for. But what they experienced was conflict between their parents, not my principles. Our constant conflict was hard on them, as was our divorce, years later.

In 1969 I wrote "A Marriage Agreement," published in the underground feminist journal *Up From Under.* By proposing that men and women play equal roles in taking care of their children and their households, it was a defiant manifesto proclaiming the status quo no longer acceptable. As the subject of a 1972 six-page spread in *Life* magazine, it caused a furor. When *Redbook* reprinted it, thousands of women wrote in. Some asked, "How did you get your husband to agree?" The answer is, either he agrees or the marriage is over; but I never said so outright, and I began to feel there was something inauthentic about my not making clear how much struggle was involved.

Despite our best efforts, our agreement didn't work very well. My husband tried to pass as a feminist, but in fact he was very angry. It was as if he had been deprived of his birthright—a helpmate who would have dinner on the table and the children ready for bed when he came home. I think my husband was humiliated by feminism. He was no longer the king, the center. I wanted him to take responsibility; he wanted to escape. Once he left for a year and then returned "for the children's sake," but the marriage was essentially over. By then we lived separate lives, separate sex lives, everything.

• • •

In some ways, the true erotic center of my life was the women's movement. That was where my passions lay—I was energized, stimulated, excited by our meetings, conversations, my women's group. The new ideas were erotically charged for me. With feminism I became self-confident, and I dumped my self-hatred and the feeling that I was this yucky, creepy female. Suddenly, being female was honorable; it was great. Dropping my body shame, I was finally able to have orgasms and to ask for what I wanted physically. I felt respected as I hadn't before. So feminism and sexuality and sexiness and erotic energy and power were all connected for me.

A movement so charged and challenging for me, I thought, must have a similar effect (through osmosis?) on my children. I assumed that my daughter, a female, would be as invested as I in feminism's success, that my son would be the "new man" for the "new woman." I never realized that my children could feel displaced by or jealous of my work. It didn't occur to me that they might experience the movement as a barrier between them and their mother.

I may have been fuzzy about love when it came to men, but I knew what it meant when it came to children. My children were the center of my world, the transforming experience of my life. All my novels are about the centrality of the mother-child relationship.

Polly was four when I became a feminist. I felt saved by feminism and believed Polly was saved along with me. My in-laws treated my son and daughter quite differently: They wanted my son to shine and Polly to be a sweet, passive girly-girl in pink dresses. I felt my feminism rescued her from that fate. From the beginning I took Polly seriously. I think feminism enabled me to nurture her best qualities: her startling perceptiveness, her wit, her depth, her wide-ranging talents. We were very close. Despite our differences, from the temperamental to the metabolic, we always had a conversation that was real and deep and never stopped, and I loved her as I loved myself.

As a child, Polly had a certain feminist consciousness. In junior high she founded a math club to train younger students for the math team and a literary magazine to be run collectively, without an editor—a feminist ideal. In elementary school she befriended a pariah and made people change their behavior toward her. Thinking back, I'm struck by how brave, independent-minded, and principled she's always been, though she's not an activist in the conventional sense. What you breathe as air isn't what challenges you, and she grew up breathing the air of feminism. The problems of her generation are different from those of mine, and in some ways I can't comprehend them. The world she inhabits is a hard world because, although more is permitted women now, so much more is expected of them. Which means increased pressure and anxiety. The idea that I could save her along with me was a utopian delusion—the idea, which some of us held for a brief moment, that by making feminist changes we'd somehow make things easy for our children. The big problems—sexism, racism, violence, poverty—are probably as great as before, though different.

NARRATIVE B

A Mother's Story

Joy Harjo

My daughter, Rainy Dawn, was born in Albuquerque, New Mexico, on a hot July afternoon, when everyone was wishing for rain. Rain is important in the Southwest, and her birth meant regeneration for our family. Rainy had come to me in a dream, a dream in which we laughed and talked, and I agreed to make a place for her. Before that dream I did not plan to have another child. I already had a son, Phil, and knew the struggle to raise children with grace was difficult, especially without the resources of close family or money.

When I was growing up, girls were expected to become nurses, teachers, or brides. Even at a young age I was horrified that most of my peers saw marriage as their life goal. I wanted to be an artist and had no intention of becoming a wife or mother. To be married and have children signaled the end of a creative life for most women. It did for my mother. She used to write songs on an old Underwood typewriter in the kitchen after she'd cooked and cleaned the house. That was during the few years before she went to work more than forty hours a week as a cook and/or waitress.

• • •

My parents married during the post–World War II boom, the great arc of the American dream, and they tried to assimilate. My dad worked in manufacturing. His mother died when he was young; his father beat him, then sent him to the Ponca City Military Institute. My father was a sensitive man who had built a shell around himself. Seeing through his shell, I felt close to him. My mother, a homemaker, had grown up in poverty. As a mixed-blood [Cherokee, Irish], she lacked self-esteem and felt powerless. Her in-laws, a prominent [Muscogee] Indian family with money, looked down on her, she said, because she came from nothing. I was frustrated by her inability to act on her own and our behalf. Now I realize that she did the best she could.

I was born in 1951 in Tulsa, Oklahoma, the first of my mother's family to be born in a hospital. During the birth my mother and I almost died, and I was kept alive on a breathing machine. Three siblings followed, each two years apart. Our house began to topple when my father became a violent alcoholic and beat my mother and us children. He brought other women into our home. I encouraged my mother to leave him because of his growing violence and disrespect. I was my mother's confidante and felt responsible for taking care of her, but I also felt that I was betraying my father.

• • •

When I was fifteen a chance occurrence altered the current of my life. I was preparing to go away to Indian school, excited about the prospect of being with other Indian students and out of my turbulent home. As we were leaving the Bureau of Indian Affairs, my schooling arranged, my mother added, "And she's a very good artist." The BIA representative then told us about an experimental school in Santa Fe that stressed the arts. I was accepted.

The Institute of American Indian Arts in the late sixties brought together Indian students from all over the country to create art—music, poetry, painting, sculpture, and drama. We used both traditional techniques and more modern European-inspired methods, often a combination of both. I became involved in creating an exciting show, "Deep Roots, Tall Cedar," which blended traditional tribal motifs with contemporary drama. . . . Being part of such a creative endeavor was an awakening for me. It stirred my pride. It was about being proud of my people and my history instead of ashamed.

At sixteen I became pregnant by a fellow Cherokee artist. I began working at a pizza parlor in Tulsa when my son was seven weeks old, and I married his father on my eighteenth birthday. I didn't love him, but I wanted my son to be legitimate, a major concern in those years. During the marriage I worked at several jobs, from cleaning hospital rooms in Tulsa to pumping gas in a miniskirt at the Shell Gas Mart after moving back to Santa Fe. Half my paycheck went to child care. My husband was supposedly looking for a job, yet he never seemed to find one. Besides my son, I was also raising my husband's young daughter, Ratonia. I hired a baby-sitter to look after the children. Apparently she looked after my husband, too. After three difficult years I left. I only regret not taking Ratonia with me.

On the University of New Mexico campus I joined the Kiva Club, the Indian student club, which provided a warm environment of support. We became a major force for change for tribal communities. I worked on a project to put Indian history into textbooks and returned to my first love, painting. Through the Indian movement I became aware of the larger struggle, which was also my personal struggle. The civil rights movement encouraged us to proclaim beauty in our difference. As we began to understand that oppression had become our eyes, ears, and tongues, we rose up together with pride and a greater love for ourselves.

I have called myself a feminist and practice feminism, but I prefer Alice Walker's term *womanist*. In the early days of the women's movement I felt excluded. I was an Indian woman and a mother, and feminism did not particularly address my concerns. Today I call myself a worker for human rights, but women's rights are a central and crucial part of my work. Each of us is born of woman, and women are the central transmitters of culture; yet women still are not valued in the dominant culture.

My first year at the University of New Mexico I met an Acoma poet—the first Indian poet I ever met. I was excited to discover that poetry can be constructed of things that make up everyday life. Through his influence I rediscovered my love of words and language. I began to write poetry seriously for the first time. We were together for only a short time, however, before I realized that he had a serious drinking problem. It was a dreary time, dealing with the erratic behavior of a binge alcoholic as I raised my son (and then daughter) and attended the university. Now I have to wonder what I was thinking then. I wouldn't put up with such behavior from anyone now. My only explanation is that because I was raised in a home with an alcoholic father, I was still acting out of instinct.

Rainy was born in 1973. Like her brother, she came into the world under difficult circumstances. The consequences have reverberated through the years, sometimes quite painfully. Such experiences either become useful knowledge or destroy you. Whether a woman wants to or not, she often acts out her mother's struggle in some manner. Caught up in mere survival, I lacked the perspective needed to work it out at the time, and I left Rainy's father, when she was still an infant.

Often the worst pain women endure is over our children. At fourteen my son was desperately searching for a father. We lived in a Chicano neighborhood in Santa Fe, and he began to model himself after gang members. To be initiated he had to commit a theft. He did and was caught. Other families watched behind the safety of their windows as my son was handcuffed and taken away in a police car.

Rainy was quieter, seemingly more complacent than her brother. A beautiful and intuitive child, she carried within herself a deep wisdom as well as the pain from all the shuffling between apartments and houses in our moves related to school, jobs, and relationships. But she also missed the steady presence of a father. Her rebellion near the age of fourteen was unexpected and therefore deeply disturbing. I think when children are raised by one parent, that parent becomes the focus of all rebellion, rage, and anger. Without the safety net of an extended family, we all fell for a while.

• • •

When Rainy was sixteen there were more rumblings of trouble. She became obsessed with a Navajo boy who had carved her initials on his hand. He resembled her father at that age and had already been kicked out of school once for misbehavior. I sensed they were doing drugs and drinking, so I showed up at the school unannounced to bring her home—something I should have done sooner. But before I finished signing her out, before I'd even seen her, she left on the back of a motorcycle with her boyfriend. For two months I didn't know her whereabouts, though she was rumored to be on the streets of Gallup, a border town notorious for its cruelty toward Indians. These were the worst months of my life.

When Rainy returned with her boyfriend, she was pregnant. My granddaughter Krista was born in July 1990. Rainy had some difficult times with this boyfriend, who was dangerous and violent. Once, just before Christmas, I had to rescue her and the baby from the street in the middle of the night. It was a dangerous area; the baby had no shoes, and they were wrapped in a blanket.

Fortunately, circumstances have improved for all of us. Rainy is now a full-time student at the University of New Mexico, studying creative writing. She gave her first poetry reading recently and has the makings of a fine poet. The man she is with respects her. My granddaughter Krista is quite a storyteller and is constantly making art. My son works on the railroad in Wisconsin. His daughter, Haleigh, is also a vivacious storyteller. We miss them, being so far away.

Rainy and I have a symbiotic tie. Her life in many ways has followed the pattern of my own. This connection has been a blessing, although it has complicated our relationship. Rainy had to struggle to make her own place in the world, just as I had to struggle to make mine. When my children were young, we were surrounded by conflict. I didn't want to deal with it, so I closed myself off emotionally. I hadn't come to terms with my own terrors, and anything resembling anger evoked fears. I was so often absorbed in my own problems, I didn't know how to reach out to make our relationship work.

I regret not being more present for my children. I missed them terribly during the years I had to work so hard, attend school, and make sure they were taken care of in basic ways. I cooked for them—we didn't eat junk food—and made most of our bread. They had new clothes for school and whatever I could buy with my often-meager scholarships, grants, and jobs. I was the only person steadily there for them, and I deeply loved them. But what they really needed was more of my attention, a sense of family. It took many sacrifices to become a writer in a culture that does not value artists or women. I think Rainy understands that.

I want Rainy to feel her own center of power, born of her sense of compassion, her great love for the children of this land, and her creativity. She's beginning to, the way I knew she would. These lines from "Rainy Dawn," published in *In Mad Love and War,* express my love for her: "And when you were born I held you wet and unfolding, like a butterfly newly born from the chrysalis of my body. And breathed with you as you breathed your first breath. Then was your promise to take it on like the rest of us, this immense journey, for love, of rain."

Life is precious and it goes on. I see it in the gifts of my children and their children. Knowing this restores me, restores all of us.

CHAPTER 2

"Good" Mothers and "Bad" Mothers

We all know the ideal of the good mother. Above all, she is selfless. Her children come before herself and any other need or person or commitment, no matter what. She loves her children unconditionally yet she is careful not to smother them with her love and her own needs. She follows the advice of doctors and other experts and she educates herself about child development. She is ever present in her children's lives when they are young, and when they get older she is home every day to greet them as they return from school. If she works outside the home, she arranges her job around her children so she can be there for them as much as possible, certainly whenever they are sick or unhappy. The good mother's success is reflected in her children's behavior—they are well mannered and respectful of others; at the same time they have a strong sense of independence and self-esteem. They grow up to be productive citizens.

All mothers, even the most privileged, feel the pressure of this glorified image of the good mother. I certainly feel it. For example, when my daughter (then one year old) started to sit in a corner by herself at day care, crying or sucking her thumb, all eyes turned to me. The caregivers, the center director, and the social worker I consulted began to ask questions about what was going on at home. Was I under a lot of stress? Were John and I getting along? Was I working too hard? I liked these professionals and felt they cared about my daughter and me. But while their questions were gentle, I was suddenly on the defensive. The quality of my mothering was at stake.

From the moment a woman announces she is pregnant or adopting a child, she is bombarded with advice from doctors, family, friends, and strangers—much of it unsolicited and most of it contradictory—about how to be a good mother. Every action is morally freighted: taking or refusing painkilling drugs during childbirth; bottle-feeding or breastfeeding; deciding whether the child should sleep alone or in its parents' (or parent's) bed; allowing or prohibiting junk food and TV; working outside the home or staying home. Even the most mundane actions carry moral weight. Some of my students in the "Motherhood and Feminism" seminar talked about sneaking in half an hour of exer-

This chapter was written by Susan E. Chase.

cise after finishing their courses and studying for the day, before picking up their kids at day care. They didn't want their children or the caregivers to know they had the audacity to spend time taking care of themselves. I have experienced this too.

Although the good mother ideal is depicted in terms of what she does, it embodies certain unspoken assumptions about who she is. It is rarely said out loud that the good mother is a white, able-bodied, middle, upper-middle, or upper class, married heterosexual, but that is what the ideal conveys.[1] If mothers who fit those characteristics feel the pressure of the good mother ideal, how much more pressure do those mothers feel who are not so privileged?

This chapter is about the social construction of "bad" mothers, and by extension, "good" mothers. It is about the social processes through which many mothers are deemed bad even when they don't deserve that label. Of course, some mothers are bad. Some mothers neglect, abuse, and even kill their children. But they will not be my focus here. Rather, I will consider mothers who are deemed bad on the basis of their social characteristics or unfounded assumptions about the damage they cause their children.

During the twentieth century, American culture targeted three types of "bad" mothers: those not in nuclear (heterosexual, married) families; those who can't (or who are perceived as refusing to) protect their children; and those whose children seem to go wrong.[2] Today many mothers are deemed bad in one or more of these ways. In this chapter, however, I focus on three groups of women who are especially stigmatized in contemporary American society: lesbian mothers; poor, single, teen mothers; and drug-dependent pregnant women. As we shall see, these women are unjustly vilified for who they are as well as for what they do. Lesbian mothers and poor, single, teen mothers do not live in nuclear families. Drug-dependent pregnant women are charged with failing to protect their fetuses. And all three are presumed to have children who go wrong, who become homosexuals, delinquents, criminals, welfare dependents, and burdens to the rest of society. But despite significant differences among these women, a similar process of social construction vilifies them all.

Lesbian Mothers

Lesbian mothers raise children in a variety of family situations.[3] Some rear children on their own or with the help of an extended family; some co-parent with a lesbian partner; and some share parenting with male friends, husbands, or ex-husbands. Estimates of the number of lesbian mothers in the United States range from two to four million.[4] Nonetheless, in American society, lesbian motherhood has been considered an oxymoron. How can a woman who eschews heterosexual intimacy be a mother? When anthropologist

Ellen Lewin began research on lesbian mothers in the late 1970s, her colleagues doubted that she would find enough subjects for her study.[5]

Although specific data are not available, it is likely that most children of lesbian mothers today were conceived in the context of heterosexual marriage.[6] Nonetheless, beginning in the mid-1970s, lesbians became increasingly interested in becoming mothers on their own or with women partners. Lesbian feminists began to develop a positive discourse of chosen motherhood, a discourse that continues to gather momentum today.[7] A lesbian baby boom, as it is often called, developed in the context of rising numbers of single mothers in the population at large, the women's movement's embrace of positive discourse about motherhood, the rise of the gay liberation movement, and the greater availability and popularity of assisted conception.[8]

Because "lesbian mother" is generally assumed to be a contradiction in terms, some lesbians find that motherhood makes their sexual orientation invisible to others. A woman with a child is presumed to be heterosexual.[9] Much more problematic is the assumption that lesbians must be bad mothers or shouldn't be mothers at all. Lesbians are deemed bad mothers in part because, like gay men, they are associated in the popular imagination with sexual activity. As such, they cannot, presumably, be competent mothers. "The pursuit of sexual gratification, according to this reasoning, is antithetical to the kind of altruism expected of mothers."[10] The image of mothers as asexual dates back to the Victorian cult of true womanhood (see chapter 3). Although this ideological separation of motherhood and sexuality has been used most egregiously to the detriment of lesbian mothers, it is harmful to all mothers.

Lesbians who had children while married often fear that they will lose their children after the marriage ends. For the past century, women have almost always been awarded custody, based on the assumption that children and mothers belong together. In this light, the pattern of denying custody to lesbians underscores the depth of our society's presumption that they are bad mothers. In some cases, lesbians (and gay men) have lost custody and had their visitation rights restricted solely on the basis of their sexual orientation. This is called the "per se" approach, "which presumes that the homosexuality of a parent, by itself, is sufficient to bar an award of custody or visitation." This approach disregards the gay or lesbian parent's child-rearing skills or relation to the child.[11]

Even mothers who would be considered exemplary if they were heterosexual have been denied custody for no other reason than their sexual orientation. For example, in 1975, Mary Jo Risher, a thirty-nine-year-old white woman, lost custody of her nine-year-old son. Risher was a nurse with a college degree, a former Baptist Sunday school teacher, and a PTA president. She and her partner, also a solid member of the community, had been living together for three years in a stable, committed relationship. Although several psychologists reported that Mary Jo's son had an "exceptionally loving stable family life," custody was awarded to Risher's ex-husband, who was remarried to a "full-time" wife.[12]

Even in those cases where lesbians have been granted custody, it is usually under "highly compromised conditions, often with the stipulation that they not live with their partners or not allow their children to have contact with them."[13] Such restrictions have also applied when women have been denied custody but granted visitation rights. Paradoxically, these restrictions create obstacles in lesbian mothers' efforts to be good mothers. For example, these restrictions encourage lesbian mothers to conceal their partners from their children. If the children find out, they may feel confused and deceived. Furthermore, under these restrictions, lesbian mothers can not demonstrate to their children the everyday normalcy of lesbian relationships.[14]

Although some lesbian mothers and their children have been punished unduly by the per se test, the majority of jurisdictions in the United States have used the "nexus" test. This test focuses on "only those factors that can be shown to have an identifiable connection with the welfare of the child. Moral beliefs, stereotypes, and social biases that cannot be shown to have a substantial connection to the best interest of the child are not considered by the court." This standard, however, has been used to deny lesbians and gay men custody on the grounds that children would suffer peer and community harassment and that their normal heterosexual development would be impaired. Some courts have gone so far as to presume that lesbians and gay men are likely to abuse children sexually.[15]

Let's address these charges by consulting social science research. In reviewing recent studies, psychologist Charlotte Patterson finds no empirical evidence for the fear that children are at risk for sexual abuse when they are in the custody of gay or lesbian parents. Child sexual abuse is committed primarily by adult men, and gay men are no more likely than heterosexual men to abuse children.[16]

What about the sexual identity development of children? Drawing on two decades of research comparing the children of divorced, custodial lesbian mothers and divorced, custodial heterosexual mothers, Patterson concludes that children of the former are no more or less likely than children of the latter to grow up to be unhappy about their gender, to be outside the typical range of behavior and preferences for their gender, or to be gay or lesbian. Nor are there differences among the children in terms of psychiatric and behavior problems, personality, self-concept, moral judgment, or intelligence. Likewise, a recent study of lesbian couples whose children were born through donor insemination or adoption after mothers acknowledged lesbian identities found that "according to the standardized assessment techniques . . . both mothers' and children's adjustment fell clearly within the normative range."[17]

These findings should reassure legislators and judges that there is no reason to fear lesbian mothers' influence on children. Nonetheless, I want to point out that the research itself treats heterosexuals as the norm and presupposes heterosexist assumptions: growing up to be gay or lesbian is abnormal, and only the conventional range of masculine and feminine behaviors is normal.

Perhaps the most difficult charge to address is that peer and community harassment will harm children of lesbian mothers. Personal accounts certainly indicate that children encounter homophobia from peers and teachers, among others. Yet there is no evidence that children's development is impaired by such encounters.[18] Significantly, a New Jersey Superior Court of Appeals argued in 1979 against the presumption of harm:

> If defendant [a lesbian mother] retains custody, it may be that because the community is intolerant of her differences these girls [her daughters] may sometimes have to bear themselves with greater than ordinary fortitude. But this does not necessarily portend that their moral welfare or safety will be jeopardized. It is just as reasonable to expect that they will emerge better equipped to search out their own standards of right and wrong, better able to perceive that the majority is not always correct in its moral judgments, and better able to understand the importance of conforming their beliefs to the requirements of reason and tested knowledge, not the constraints of currently popular sentiment or prejudice.[19]

While some lesbian mothers defend themselves in custody or adoption cases on the grounds that they and their families are as normal and healthy as heterosexual families, some turn this defensive argument on its head by claiming that children benefit from growing up with a lesbian mother or mothers. Children in lesbian families—like children in many other kinds of families—learn firsthand that our society is structured by inequalities. This lesson can be a source of strength.[20]

Lesbians who want to adopt or care for foster children rightly fear that their applications will be rejected because of their sexual orientation. In the mid-1980s, for example, Massachusetts created a policy that favored "traditional" families and that required all applicants for foster children to state their sexual orientation. Many social service professionals protested the policy because they feared that foster children would suffer from the emphasis on family structure rather than caring relationships. The policy remained in effect until 1990.[21] Not surprisingly, some women decide to conceal their sexual orientation and/or their partners in order to increase their chances of adoption. The effort involved in such concealment can produce great stress in a relationship.[22]

New Hampshire and Florida are the only two states that specifically ban lesbian and gay adoption and foster parenting, yet many other states prevent them in practice. In December 1997, New Jersey became the first state to make explicit in its adoption policy "that gay and unmarried couples would be measured by the same standards as married couples." The upshot is that gay and unmarried couples in New Jersey are now able to adopt a child jointly in a single proceeding, rather than having to go through the adoption process twice. In recent years, joint adoptions by gay and lesbian parents have been taking place quietly in a number of states. New Jersey's law is important because it explicitly prohibits different treatment on the basis of sexual orientation.[23]

Lesbians who seek to adopt children or who wish to use donor insemination to conceive a child challenge not only the norm of the heterosexual family but also the norm of the biological family. Despite growing numbers of families built on non-genetic ties—such as adoptive and stepfamilies created by divorce and remarriage—the ideal continues to revolve around biological connection. Whether heterosexual or lesbian, unmarried women were denied access to donor insemination prior to the 1980s; their access continues to be restricted today. When married women are artificially inseminated by donor sperm with the consent of their husbands and under the supervision of a physician, the husband becomes the legal father and the donor has no right to fatherhood. For unmarried women, however, "there is no man to stand in as a 'pretend' biological father."[24] Nonetheless, lesbians continue to choose motherhood via donor insemination (an easy, nonmedical procedure) either through sperm banks (where donors are anonymous) or male friends who donate sperm on terms that range from no further involvement to co-parenting.

Despite strong evidence that good parenting is unrelated to sexual orientation, punitive laws, policies, and cultural assumptions continue to construct lesbians as bad mothers. Even the ten states that have laws prohibiting discrimination on the basis of sexual orientation in employment, housing, credit, or public accommodations, do not necessarily prohibit discrimination in areas concerning parenting.[25] Given this state of affairs, lesbian mothers' everyday practices often have a political edge. Journalist Phyllis Burke writes, "When my lesbian partner had a child through assisted conception, I could no longer pass for straight. I was propelled into a world where every act, no matter how everyday, became political, whether I wanted it to be or not. Everything, from taking our child to the doctor for a checkup to enrolling him in nursery school, brought with it a kind of visibility I had always avoided."[26] Thus, lesbian mothers may discover that speaking forthrightly about their families with doctors, teachers, and others is essential to resisting the heterosexism they and their children typically face.

Poor, Unmarried, Teen Mothers

On the day we discussed teen motherhood in my "Motherhood and Feminism" seminar, a young white woman declared, "Teen pregnancy is always a bad thing," expressing a cultural assumption about too-young parenthood. A twenty-three-year-old African American retorted, "I got pregnant the first time I had sex at fourteen and I gave birth at fifteen. I now have three children and I'm married to the father of all three. I break all the stereotypes and I wonder how many more teen moms there are like me." Indeed, two other women in the class, now in their early twenties, both white and married, had been teen mothers. One has three children; the other has one. At the end of the semester I had the pleasure of watching all three young women graduate. All have plans for graduate school and professional careers.

Despite stereotypes, some teen mothers are married. In 1998, 22 percent of babies born to teens had married mothers.[27] In addition, some pregnant teens get married soon after they give birth.[28] The three former teen mothers in my class are part of an invisible group of young mothers; they are not the ones that politicians and pundits carry on about, even though, ironically, they may have been at the time of their first pregnancies. Their current marital status, social class (struggling but not poor), and educational achievement protect them from public scorn.[29]

It is poor, single teen mothers who are castigated in the popular imagination as bad mothers, as women who should not be allowed to be mothers at all. Politicians, the media, and the public blame these mothers for a host of social ills: poverty, crime, violence, drugs, family breakdown, and the disintegration of social values.[30] Yet there is a profound disjunction between the rhetoric and the facts about teen mothers. We need to know the facts and we need to know why the rhetoric—the blame heaped on poor teen mothers—is out of sync with the facts.

In the United States, teen pregnancy became a public issue in the early 1970s and has continued to be so. This time period, however, has seen a decline in birthrates among teenagers in this country.[31] In the 1950s and 1960s the level of teenage births was much higher than it was in the 1970s and than it is today. The high point for teen births was 1957, when there were 96 births per 1,000 women ages fifteen to nineteen. Furthermore, from 1991 to 1998, teen birth rates nationwide declined substantially with the sharpest declines among black teenagers. The overall rate in 1996 was 54.7 per 1,000 women.[32] While the stereotype of the teen mother is a black woman, 57 percent of all babies born to unmarried teenage mothers were born to whites in 1990.[33] Given the more rapidly declining birth rates of black teens in the 1990s, the percentage of teen mothers who are white would be even higher today.

The fact of declining birthrates among teens, however, has done nothing to alleviate public preoccupation with teen mothers as a major social problem. It is assumed that their "bad" decisions about sex and childbearing cause them and their children to live in poverty. Consequently, they live off welfare, soaking up the hard-earned tax dollars of "normal" Americans. An often-cited statistic is that half of all families on welfare at any given time began with a teen mother. Yet this statistic disguises the fact that teen mothers made up less than 10 percent of Aid to Families with Dependent Children (AFDC) recipients at any particular point in time. Furthermore, sociologist Kristin Luker points out that 80 percent of teen mothers were already poor by the time they became pregnant. "Many of these young mothers would be poor (and would have children who grew up to be poor) no matter how old they were when they gave birth."[34] Thus, it is incorrect to assume—as so many politicians do—that "teenage pregnancy causes and perpetuates poverty in the United States."[35]

But doesn't welfare just encourage teen mothers to sit around eating Big Macs, waiting for their checks to come in? Doesn't it motivate them to have more children earlier? Contrary to myth, the average size of a family receiving AFDC in 1993 was 2.9 persons, typically a mother and two children. AFDC benefits in all fifty states were well below the poverty line, ranging from Mississippi, where benefits were 13 percent of the poverty line ($120 per month), to Alaska, where benefits were 79 percent of the poverty line ($923 per month).[36] Payments to foster parents can be four times greater per child than AFDC payments to mothers, clearly indicating that social support is available for some kinds of parenting but not for others.[37]

Teenagers, like other women, generally receive welfare for short periods of time. Nearly 75 percent of AFDC recipients collected benefits for less than three years. Furthermore, researchers have found either no relationship or a very weak relationship between welfare policies and unwed teenage motherhood. For example, states that give relatively large payments do not have higher rates of single teen motherhood than states that are stingier. Likewise, on the international level, the United States has one of the highest rates of married or unmarried teen motherhood but offers less assistance to single mothers than any other industrialized country.[38]

The stinginess of the welfare system in this country—the below-poverty-level support—goes back to assumptions embedded in the initial creation of the federal system in the 1930s. While unemployment compensation and old-age insurance were both conceived as entitlements earned by and replacing a male wage and as subject to neither means nor moral tests, support to poor mothers was deemed an unearned benefit subject to both tests.[39] Unlike most European countries, where support for parenting is perceived as a communal responsibility and as promoting the welfare of the entire society, the United States has a tradition of treating children as a private, individual responsibility.

Contrary to the image of teen mothers as irresponsible welfare cheats, social science research demonstrates that most poor young mothers work hard to keep their families intact and healthy under extremely difficult conditions. The lack of decent affordable housing, health insurance, and child care makes daily life stressful for poor young mothers, even when other family members are supportive. Furthermore, the inevitable childhood illnesses, and even bad weather (which may halt public transportation), "threaten the precarious worlds of these young families."[40] Recall that Joy Harjo (the author of narrative B) struggled with these problems and more as a teen mother.

Given the hardships, wouldn't poor, single teen mothers be better off if they just waited a few years before having children? Not necessarily. Luker argues that delaying childbearing would have little effect on their lives because "the same social conditions that encourage [poor] teenagers to have babies also work to prevent them from ever being 'ready' to be parents in the way that a white, middle-class public might prefer."[41] Moreover, the assumption that teen motherhood is inherently developmentally unhealthy obscures the wide range of individual experiences and levels of maturity among teen mothers.[42]

Poverty is foremost among the social conditions that encourage early childbearing among poor teens and that make waiting no solution at all. Recall Luker's observation that 80 percent of teen mothers were poor before getting pregnant. Many poor teens who lack good educational and occupational opportunities look to motherhood as the most rewarding form of employment they can get. On top of poverty, shifts in gender roles, high divorce rates, and a shrinking market of well-paying jobs for men with a high school education encourage single childbearing among teens (as well as older women).[43]

More than in previous decades, women today, of all races and classes, are expected to contribute financially to the support of their families. But while a woman is less likely to expect to depend on a man economically, she is also not likely to expect a male partner to share equally the burdens of child rearing and homemaking. In addition, marriages have a fifty-fifty chance of ending in divorce; divorced mothers have a fifty-fifty chance of receiving all of their court-ordered child support payments; and divorced fathers who have remarried visit their children less often than unwed fathers (136).

Furthermore, well-paying blue-collar jobs—and male wages—are declining. Many sociologists argue that because men are confronting increasingly restricted economic opportunities—the loss of unionized jobs; the split of the labor market into high-skill, well-paid jobs and low-skill, poorly paid jobs; the proliferation of service jobs—they are less likely to perceive themselves or to be perceived by others as marriageable. These trends have affected African Americans more than whites, but it is likely that as these trends continue, they will affect poor whites as much as poor blacks, leading to an increase in single-parent families among whites (166–167).[44]

These social and economic factors make marriage less attractive to and less possible for teens who get pregnant today than for teens who got pregnant in the 1950s. But why are teens getting pregnant in the first place? Premarital sex has become increasingly common over the last century in part because people are getting married later and in part because of our society's transformation from rural, kinship-based communities to a modern, industrial complex. That transition "tends to disconnect sex from marriage." In fact, throughout the "developed world," teens are engaging in premarital sex. Although some observers suggest that the greater availability of contraception beginning in the late 1960s encouraged teen sex, this explanation (and its implied solution—make contraception unavailable) is simplistic. For example, when federal funding of family planning services dropped sharply in the 1980s, teens' sexual activity continued to increase.[45]

Over the last few decades, the general pattern among teens has been toward increased contraceptive use. Nonetheless, some teens use contraception more effectively than others do. Higher socioeconomic status and educational aspirations are related to more consistent contraceptive use. Older teens are more consistent users than younger ones in part because they get better at it over time (143–144). Another important factor is the stage of a relationship. Even though being a "nice girl" no longer means never having had sex, it may mean not having had too much. A teen can show that she is a "nice girl" by being unprepared for sex, by not preparing to use contraception (147). However, as a relationship develops and is defined as serious and as a teen connects her sexual desire to "true love," she may become ready to get and use contraception (149). The upshot is that some teens get pregnant the first time they have sex because they are not using contraception or because they are using it inadequately. Some get pregnant during transitions in relationships, and others get pregnant because they are using no contraception at all (145).

What about abortion? Among teens, abortion rates are related to class, and to a lesser extent, race. While less than 50 percent of poor young women abort accidental pregnancies, 75 percent of affluent young women do so. Half of black and Hispanic teens and 60 percent of white teens terminate their pregnancies. The more opportunities for educational and occupational success a young woman expects to have, the more likely she is to get an abortion (154).[46]

In sum, the evidence clearly shows that young women who have grown up poor and who have few educational and occupational opportunities are more likely to become teen mothers than are their more affluent peers. Early motherhood may inhibit or postpone educational and occupational success for middle-class teens, but for poor teens, educational and occupational success are usually far out of reach whether or not they delay childbearing. Why wait? Not waiting may even be advantageous given that they can make moral claims on kin for help when they are young in a way that they would not be able to when older. Furthermore, given that fertility and health decrease with age, especially among poor women, early childbearing makes sense.[47] Just like everyone else, poor teens act in ways that are logical within the particular circumstances of their lives.

If social science research debunks the myth that poor, single teen mothers cause their poverty and that of their children, why is the myth so resilient? Rickie Solinger contends that the facts don't obliterate the myth because something else is going on. Politicians, policy makers, and pundits use the rhetoric of reproductive choice—a watered-down version of reproductive rights—to discredit mothers who are perceived as making bad choices. Paradoxically, second-wave feminism contributed to this rhetoric by challenging the ideology that motherhood is women's natural, biological lot.

> Those women—poor, young, and especially poor, young, and of color—who appeared to behave reproductively as if biology were (still) destiny and had "too many" children were targeted as retrogressive by population controllers, by politicians interested in stimulating hostility to welfare recipients, and by others: Not only were these females irresponsibly backward, because they were non-users or ineffective users of birth control; they were also violating the first principle of modern womanhood—rational exercise of choice. The attacks marginalized poor women in general as aberrant; they also deepened the alienation between middle-class white women and those with fewer resources. The former were in the process of *defining* their reproductive *right* to choose, as the latter were, often, *being defined* as resisting their alleged *duty* to choose.[48]

The rhetoric of choice—that individuals freely choose among good and bad options—invites us to evaluate the decisions people make. This rhetoric has so permeated our culture that it is difficult even for well-intentioned, middle-class people not to think of poor, single teen mothers as having made bad choices. But we need to recognize this rhetoric as what it is: a powerful discourse that scapegoats poor teens by turning our attention away from deep structural problems in our society, especially persistent poverty. Poor teens are likely to continue to have higher rates of early childbearing than their more privileged peers as long as they lack good, realistic educational and occupational opportunities. In the meantime, as scapegoats, they are punished by increasingly stingy and restrictive social support systems.

The Personal Responsibility and Work Opportunity Act of 1996 (PRA) ended the federal guarantee of assistance to poor families (meager though it had been since its inception in the 1930s). Dismantling AFDC, the federal government now gives block grants to the states, which amount to much less money than went into AFDC. The PRA enacts new restrictive measures, such as a lifetime limit of five years for assistance; the requirement that recipients find work within two years; and the denial of assistance to single mothers less than eighteen years old who have not completed high school, are not in school, and/or do not live with a parent or guardian.[49] This "end to welfare as we know it" has been implemented without the creation of a sufficient number of jobs paying a living wage, or adequate provision of affordable, quality day care. It certainly has been implemented without concern for the well-being of poor, single mothers and their children.[50]

Jillynn Stevens, the author of narrative C, recounts her own experience of poverty and welfare as a way of challenging stereotypes about young, single mothers who need the support of the state to survive. Once she recognized her own abilities and strengths (a major struggle for many women), she became determined to get an education and to pursue a profession. AFDC benefits enabled her to do so. Sadly, poor mothers today can not depend on welfare in order to get an education because of changes brought about by welfare reform and the PRA.[51]

Drug-Dependent Pregnant Women

Perhaps the most despised "bad" mothers of recent years are pregnant women addicted to crack cocaine. Like lesbian and poor, single teen mothers, they are accused of hurting their children and are disciplined by punitive policies and laws. Unlike lesbian and poor, single teen mothers, however, crack-dependent pregnant women have been prosecuted and imprisoned for harming their fetuses and children. Charges include "distributing drugs to a minor, child abuse and neglect, reckless endangerment, manslaughter, and assault with a deadly weapon."[52]

Given the seriousness of these charges, why would feminists want to extricate drug-addicted pregnant women from the bad-mother label? Some crack-addicted pregnant women may indeed be negligent or worse, and some may be incapable of caring for their newborns. Of course their infants should be removed from them under those circumstances. However, my aim in addressing the social construction of drug-dependent pregnant women as bad mothers is to show how that social construction diverts attention from the realities of the situation, how it singles out poor women of color for punishment, and how it absolves the society at large for the broader social problems affecting their lives.

Crack-addicted pregnant women came to public attention shortly after crack cocaine became widely available in the United States in the early 1980s. Health professionals noticed an increasing number of babies born prematurely with serious health problems. In response, the major news media produced a deluge of stories about "crack babies" and their mothers. Lawmakers and prosecutors also sprang into action. In 1990, legislators in thirty-four states wrangled over bills concerning prenatal substance abuse, debating whether it should be treated as a crime or a public health issue.[53] Although no state has specifically criminalized prenatal drug exposure (it does constitute civil child neglect in a small number of states), criminal charges have been filed under other state laws, such as drug possession and delivery, child abuse, and homicide. The American Civil Liberties Union estimates that more than 160 women had been prosecuted in 26 states by 1992.[54]

As Laura E. Gomez points out, it didn't take long for the American public to catch on. In 1989, an ABC poll revealed that 82 percent of Americans agreed with the statement that "a pregnant woman who uses crack-cocaine and addicts her unborn child should be put in jail for child abuse" (26). Because prenatal drug exposure was easily linked, at least in the public imagination, to drug abuse, child abuse, and bad mothering, it quickly evoked outrage and virtually invited prosecution. Here was a story with an easy-to-blame perpetrator and a completely innocent victim (100).

What are the realities embedded in this story about criminal mothers and damaged babies? Let's start with the number of "crack babies." In 1989, Dr. Ira Chasnoff, founder of the National Association for Perinatal Addiction Research and Education, published the results of a study based on the urine samples of women who had recently given birth in thirty-six public urban hospitals. Extrapolating from his finding that 11 percent of newborns had been exposed prenatally to alcohol or illicit drugs, he reported that "375,000 American babies annually were prenatally exposed to 'some amount of alcohol or illicit drug.' " The next day, newspapers across the country distorted the findings with headlines about an "epidemic" of "375,000 *crack* babies" and the like. In their reporting, many newspapers ignored the study's inclusion of alcohol and other drugs besides crack, and they amplified the study's finding of "exposure" to "harm" and "addiction" (22; emphasis in original).

Like the media, medical researchers themselves bear some responsibility for the public's misunderstandings about prenatal drug exposure. On the crucial question of the harm crack cocaine causes newborns, researchers first raised alarm and then urged caution about their earlier findings. Like initial research on any medical topic, earlier studies (in this case, from 1985 to 1990) were relatively unrigorous and their findings speculative (22–25). Dr. Chasnoff and his colleagues found that "prenatal cocaine exposure was associated with premature birth, lower birth weight, and smaller size. . . . Cocaine-exposed babies also exhibited higher rates of physical, mental, and emotional irregularities; in severe cases, they manifested withdrawal symptoms, including irritability and inability to be calmed by caretakers" (23).

Research published after 1990 was more likely to be longitudinal, testing the impact of drugs on children's development over two or three years. At this point researchers took into account the great difficulty of testing the effects of just one drug; crack users might also use other drugs, alcohol, and tobacco (23–25). Acknowledging such factors, the Chasnoff team presented its findings on three-year-olds: " 'Contrary to information in the popular media, not all substance-exposed children suffer the same poor prognosis. In fact, generalizations about the fate of drug-exposed children must await additional research into the outcome of the broader population of drug-exposed children, examining the roles of maternal and environmental factors' " (25).

As researchers have looked at such factors, they have found that regular prenatal care and good nutrition lessen the harmful effects of prenatal crack exposure, even if a woman continues to use drugs during pregnancy. Often, however, proper health care and diet are not accessible to crack-dependent women, many of whom are poor, homeless, sick, and physically abused.[55] Legal scholar Dorothy Roberts points out that news stories often represent the pregnant drug user as a prostitute, trading sex for crack and violating every possible quality of a good mother.[56] Belying this revolting image, however, researchers find that most pregnant women who use or are addicted to drugs know that their actions may injure the fetus and many try to stop using drugs.[57]

Although it is common for medical researchers to change their conclusions over time (think of the ever-changing recommendations we hear concerning nutrition and diet), some medical researchers began to question their own profession on the issue of prenatal drug exposure. " 'How did it happen that an epidemic of such proportions was declared so quickly? What were the forces within science and our society that propelled the early reports of cocaine effects to such prominence?' " A similar reevaluation occurred within the media. Newsmakers challenged their own stories about the extent and severity of prenatal drug exposure. But these new reports did not capture the public's attention because they lacked the sensational, gripping character of the earlier ones.[58] This soul-searching suggests that something was going on besides the desire to save the lives of innocent babies.

When we look at the testing, reporting, and prosecution of pregnant drug users, we find that race and class play an important role. Because of their greater surveillance by governmental institutions—public hospitals, welfare agencies, probation offices—poor black women who use drugs are more likely to be suspected of drug use, tested, reported, and prosecuted than middle-class white women. Public hospitals, which serve poor minority communities, do almost all of the testing for prenatal drug use, which they then report to child welfare or law enforcement authorities.[59]

By contrast, middle-class women are usually treated by private physicians who are unlikely to test their patients for drug use and even less likely to report them to authorities. Even if doctors suspect drug use, they tend to treat it as a disease rather than a crime. When doctors serve patients of their own class and race, they are likely to empathize with them, to live in the same communities, and to depend on them for referrals. It's hard to imagine a private physician handing an affluent white woman a letter warning her that the office is cooperating with law enforcement officers and that she might be arrested if she tests positive for drugs. But such has been the treatment of poor women of color at the Medical University of South Carolina, a state hospital in Charleston.[60]

One study of pregnant women in Pinellas County, Florida, examined the results of tests on women who received prenatal care in public health clinics and in private obstetrical offices. Although the study found similar rates of substance abuse in black (14.1 percent) and white women (15.4 percent), "Black women were *ten times* more likely than whites to be reported to government authorities. Both public health facilities and private doctors were more inclined to turn in Black women than white women for using drugs while pregnant." Evidence that black women have been prosecuted disproportionately can be seen in the states that have taken the most punitive approach. By 1990, ten out of eleven criminal cases in Florida were against black women. In South Carolina, seventeen of the eighteen women charged with criminal neglect of a child or distribution of drugs to a minor, were black.[61]

Racism and classism clearly contribute to the disproportionate testing and prosecution of poor women of color. Yet, given widespread outrage about crack babies, the number of prosecutions nationwide has been surprisingly low.[62] The most common punishment for pregnant women or new mothers who test positive for drug use is not criminal prosecution but the permanent or temporary removal of children. Poor black mothers by the thousands have lost custody of their infants on the basis of a single drug test. A dozen states have statutes requiring that positive newborn drug tests be reported to child welfare authorities; in addition, many hospitals in all fifty states use child abuse notification laws to report positive tests. Positive drug results in some states lead automatically to neglect and custody proceedings. In New York City, for example, crack exposure is the most common reason for the placement of newborns in foster care. While these practices may seem motivated by concern for the infants involved, they are highly problematic. A positive drug test shows only that the mother used drugs shortly before giving birth. Such tests do not reveal the severity of the mother's drug use, they do not confirm harm to the baby, and they do not tell us about a woman's ability to mother.[63]

Could it be that crack-dependent mothers deserve to lose their infants because they have refused to get help for themselves through drug treatment programs? In Charleston, South Carolina, law enforcement officials collaborated with the state hospital, the Medical University of South Carolina, which serves poor people of color, to offer drug rehabilitation for first-time offenders. Failure to comply would lead to prosecution. However, many women testing positive for drug use were doomed to fail because they were handed a letter with an appointment date they could not control, and they were offered no assistance with child care or transportation to the treatment center. Indeed, nationwide, pregnant addicts are either barred from treatment centers or find that the centers are not organized to meet their needs. Lack of child care may be the greatest barrier to treatment. Typically, residential treatment programs do not admit children, and outpatient clinics do not generally provide childcare. Finally, when women fear that they will lose their children or that they will be threatened with criminal sanctions, they are unlikely to seek treatment or to discuss their drug problems with health care providers. They may even avoid prenatal care altogether.[64] In this sense, the punitive treatment of crack-dependent pregnant women exacerbates rather than alleviates the problem.

How are we to understand what is really going on in this construction of drug-dependent pregnant women as bad mothers? Many observers, including feminist scholars, point to the convergence of two social trends, both of which escalated in the mid-1980s when crack cocaine was first viewed as a social problem. First, the "war on drugs" increased federal spending on drug interdiction from $200 million in the early 1970s to $13 billion in 1992. Instead of drug abuse prevention and treatment, the majority of these funds went to law enforcement. As a result, during the 1980s, arrests for all drug offenses more than doubled, and arrests for drug possession increased by more than 800 percent.[65]

Second, the rhetoric of fetal rights gained cultural force. Philosopher Susan Bordo criticizes this rhetoric by showing how it depends on an invidious distinction in our legal tradition, a distinction that unfairly burdens pregnant women. American legal tradition assumes that people are "embodied subjects"—persons whose bodily integrity must be respected to the point that they cannot be coerced to undergo minor surgery even to save the life of a close family member. Yet, the law has treated pregnant women, especially poor women of color, as "de-subjectified bodies." This disrespect for the personal and bodily integrity of pregnant women is seen in practices such as involuntary sterilization and involuntary cesarean sections, as well as the prosecution of pregnant drug users.[66]

The powerful rhetoric of fetal rights holds dangers for all pregnant women. Smoking cigarettes, working at jobs declared hazardous to fetal health, and even drinking an occasional glass of wine can make a pregnant woman a "bad" mother. Several of my students who wait on tables in restaurants declared that they would refuse to serve a glass of wine to a pregnant woman. But poor women of color are singled out for excessive punishment as "bad" mothers. As we have seen, they suffer disproportionate testing, reporting, removal of children, and prosecution for use of crack cocaine.

Roberts contends that it is not a concern for black infants that has whipped the state and the public into outrage about crack babies. Rather she argues that the singling out of crack-dependent, pregnant black women is the latest manifestation in a long history of the state's control of black women's reproduction. From the days of slavery to the present, black women's motherhood has been manipulated in the interest of the dominant white society, which has produced the images of "Jezebel" (the immoral black mother), the "Mammy" (the negligent black mother), the "Matriarch" (the black unwed mother), and the "Welfare Queen" (the devious black mother). Indeed, that society has produced no positive images of black motherhood. Roberts concludes that black women have been punished for having babies throughout the history of our nation, except when their children have been perceived as useful to the society at large, as slaves or as low-wage workers.[67]

Roberts also points to the history of state neglect of black infants. "When a nation has always closed its eyes to the circumstances of pregnant Black women, its current expression of interest in the health of unborn Black children must be viewed with distrust." The state's indifference to the well-being of black children is revealed in the high black infant mortality rate. In 1996, the mortality rate for black infants was 14.7 per 1000 and 6.1 for white infants. Poverty and inadequate health care are the major causes of black infants' high mortality rates. Although crack contributes to low birth weight (a leading cause of infant death), crack "is a small and recent addition to an old story." A genuine concern for the well-being of black infants would require a national commitment to alleviating the poverty and inadequate health care that disproportionately affect black communities.[68]

Common Threads in the Social Construction of "Bad" Mothers

Despite very real differences among the groups of mothers I have discussed, several threads weave their stories together. All three groups are subject to disciplinary policies and laws: lesbians are threatened with the denial of custody and limits on visitation rights; poor, single teen mothers are punished by an increasingly stingy and restrictive social support system; and drug-dependent women face prosecution and the removal of their children to foster care. All three groups are subject to unfounded cultural assumptions: lesbian mothers create a harmful environment for their children; poor teen mothers cause their children's poverty; crack-dependent pregnant women love drugs more than they love their babies. I have drawn on social science research to disentangle the realities from the cultural assumptions that support punishment.

But that disentanglement is not sufficient. In each case, deeper ideologies are so powerful that debunking the specific myths of harm caused by these "bad" mothers may leave the ideologies intact: lesbianism is unnatural; a poor teen's "choice" of motherhood is obviously a bad choice; poor black women's reproduction should be controlled because they don't deserve to be mothers in the first place; poor children, especially poor children of color, are worthless. These ideologies themselves need to be analyzed; I have barely begun here to locate their social and historical origins.

Another common thread is the rhetoric of concern for children that gets used to revile "bad" mothers. If our society were truly committed to children, it would support rather than demonize the diversity of family forms we now see among us. Lawmakers and policy makers would prioritize alleviating the poverty of nearly one-fourth of our nation's children. They would view as a national shame the fact that 40 million Americans lack health insurance, and they would create a national health care system like those in nearly every other industrial nation.[69]

It is not only women who are harmed by their social construction as bad mothers; so too are their children. Children are harmed when they are taken from lesbian mothers who love and nurture them. Children are injured when their teen mothers suffer the inordinate stress of surviving on inadequate social support programs and equally inadequate minimum-wage jobs. Children are harmed when they are pried from drug-dependent mothers who want very badly to kick their habit but who are effectively denied the help they need to do so. Their children will likely languish in foster care rather than being given support in their mothers' homes.[70] Children are harmed when their mothers must divert energy from them to fight unjust treatment, whether in court, the welfare office, or the public hospital.

Mother-blame is pervasive in our society. Jane Taylor McDonnell, in Narrative D, reminds us that even white, well-educated, middle-class mothers are blamed for their children's problems, in her case, her son's autism. While she has many more resources and social advantages to draw on than poor, single teen mothers or drug-addicted pregnant women do, she, like them, confronts a similar process of social construction. In each case, specific ideologies and institutions are mobilized to chastise mothers for their "deviance." McDonnell's rich descriptions of her anguish, frustration, anger, and self-doubt give us insight into the range of emotions that every "bad" mother is likely to feel.

Whenever we hear the charge of bad mothering, we need to pause to consider what is going on. What are the social and historical conditions shaping these mothers' lives? What are the ideologies and cultural assumptions shaping public perceptions of them? And most important of all, what is at stake, and for whom, in their social construction as bad mothers? More often than not, "bad" mothers function as scapegoats, as diversions from the horrendous social problems of our time: persistent poverty, and pervasive racism, sexism, and heterosexism.[71] Understanding the social construction of bad mothers should be an essential part of the education of lawmakers, policy makers, prosecutors, doctors, educators, child welfare professionals—everyone who has the power to affect the lives of mothers and their children.

NARRATIVE C

Investing in the Future

by Jillynn Stevens

My car was gone. I stood in the parking lot of the student family housing at the University of Utah and stared in disbelief. Immediately I assumed that it had been stolen. I ran back into my apartment and, with my two young children watching, called the University Police to report my missing Caprice Classic. "Your car has been repossessed," the dispatcher informed me. Repossessed. How could this happen?

I called the bank as soon as it opened, insisting there must be some mistake. "There have been no payments made on your car for three months." It was incomprehensible. Slowly, the awareness of what must have happened emerged. Fourteen months ago, in October 1980, my ex-husband had been ordered to pay $300 in child support. We agreed he would make the $200 car payment and send me the balance. I had received my monthly check without fail and had no indication that he hadn't been making the car payment as promised. The startling reality that my already fragile existence could be so shaken by his whims left me feeling raw and naked; vulnerable in my dependence, at the same time I was fighting so hard for independence. The day ended with the return of my car—but I was forever changed. I promised myself that no one would have that much power over my life again.

When I was growing up in a rural southern Utah town, no one had ever mentioned college as an option. It was assumed that, as a female, I would marry and raise my children in a conservative Mormon home. Married at seventeen, I followed the prescribed role, but found myself growing increasingly despondent and dissatisfied. In 1979, I sought counseling from a local therapist. He listened and helped me understand that my sense of emptiness stemmed from the fact that I had no developed opinions, no sense of self; in short, no identity. I had been following a script written by my ancestors (both women and men), my patriarchal church leaders, the media, and local and national politicians. But it was not my story. During therapy, my counselor taught me the beginnings of identifying and listening to my own voice. He gave me a battery of psychological tests and convinced me that I could be successful in college.

I began my college education in 1980 as a single mother. In the face of disapproval and clearly breaking from tradition, I separated from my husband of over six years and moved some 300 miles to Salt Lake City with my children. Erin was four and Brenan one. I enrolled in classes at the University of Utah, worked part-time as

From The Women's Review of Books *14, no. 5 (February 1997): 15–16. Reprinted by permission of the author.*

a waitress, and moved into student family housing. That first quarter was wrenching. I was painfully shy and felt sharply conspicuous, having yet to convince myself that I could actually compete with traditional students (I was all of 24). When I received my first grades in college and found that I got an A in biology, I was convinced that an error had been made.

• • •

I come from a working-class family . . . in which higher education was primarily viewed with suspicion as indulgent, eccentric and unnecessary in an environment valuing plain, old-fashioned hard work and the traditional family ethic. Further, the leaders of the Mormon church are considered prophets, that is, they literally relay the word of God to the world. They continue to instruct women to stay at home and care for their children. Work outside the home is emphatically discouraged; when absolutely necessary, it should be limited to providing essentials only. Women who work are often in conflict about deviating from their prescribed role as mother and helpmeet to their husbands. Those who go to college give primacy to finding a husband, ideally a returned church missionary.

I am the only woman on my mother's side of the family to have obtained an undergraduate degree, and the second on my father's side. Only two of my thirty-four cousins and four siblings have completed a four-year college education. That I am currently working on my doctoral dissertation (the first one ever, in my family) is no small feat!

The day my car was repossessed I was in my sophomore year. By that time, I was deeply committed to my education and refused to allow anything to get in the way. I made the decision to apply for Aid to Families with Dependent Children [AFDC] in order to provide myself with a consistent income. Nothing could have prepared me for the humiliation and dehumanizing experience of applying for financial assistance at the local welfare office.

After filling out the appropriate forms, I met with a case worker. Ironically, my car became a sticking point. "Your car is worth too much for you to qualify for assistance." Without appearing to be confrontational or disrespectful (for this would surely result in immediate denial of help), I explained that I owed more on my car than it was worth. Then the issue of student financial aid surfaced. I was receiving a Pell Grant, a state grant and a small merit scholarship; I had borrowed money from the National Direct Student Loan program; and I was approved for financial help from the Division of Rehabilitation for the costs of tuition and books. Today, this might be called "packaging" income. I had learned to be creative in accessing resources. Even if I was approved for AFDC, it would barely cover my rent. Food Stamps would help with the cost of groceries. My tuition and books would be paid for by Rehab, and student aid covered my car payments, insurance, clothing, non-food items (not covered by Food Stamps), gasoline, utilities and other necessities.

It quickly became apparent that the more I disclosed to the case worker, the more doubts about my eligibility arose. I learned the cardinal rule: offer only the barest information necessary. By this I don't mean being dishonest, just meager with information. I walked out of the office with a list of official documents I had to produce in order to be considered for assistance.

After a great deal of scrutiny I obtained AFDC. For three years I went to the grocery store late at night to avoid people looking at me askance as I paid for food for my family with Food Stamps. I endured the endless questions about my education and income at the welfare office and I learned not to look the case workers in the eye or appear too intelligent. I dressed down when going to the welfare office to get my monthly payments reinstated when some error in their record-keeping meant that my checks stopped coming. In short, I became dependent on a system that not infrequently failed to send my Food Stamps or welfare check because a worker forgot to check some box on a form. Paradoxically, I felt belittled and insignificant each time I met with a case worker to review my progress toward self-sufficiency.

All told I received around \$10,800 in monthly checks and approximately \$5,000 in Food Stamps during the time I was on AFDC. The state also paid for childcare while I was in classes. In a society that stresses reciprocity and the work ethic, what did I give back? Once I graduated (cum laude) with two undergraduate degrees, I began working full-time for approximately \$17,000 per year. At the same time, I started graduate school in the field of Social Work. In 1990, I graduated Phi Kappa Phi with a Master of Social Work degree and began working at a rural community mental health agency as an out-patient therapist for \$30,000 per year. Eighteen months later I was promoted to a program director position and earned \$42,000. I also had a small private practice and carried a crisis pager for an additional \$5,000 annually.

In 1994 I moved back to Salt Lake City when I was accepted into the PhD program at the University of Utah Graduate School of Social Work. I worked full-time for the first year and then part-time during the second year. After completing all my required course work, I became reemployed on a full-time basis at \$45,000 per year. I also teach as an adjunct faculty member for the Graduate School, provide consultation services, and work a few crisis shifts, earning an additional \$15,000 annually.

Since 1988 I have paid approximately \$58,000 in federal and state income taxes. In addition, I have made regular payments, including interest, on my student loans. During that time I purchased two homes, became a partner on a duplex (income property), bought three cars, a few pieces of furniture and a healthy wardrobe (hey, I deserve it!). I am currently helping my twenty-year-old daughter pay for her own college education.

My three years on AFDC cost the state and federal government around \$15,800 in monthly checks and Food Stamps. I figure we can call it even on the childcare and Medicaid (which I rarely used), in the face of my proficiency as a consumer. To date, the government has realized, at minimum, a \$42,000 profit from investing in me while I pursued my education—a 266 percent return rate. And at forty, I still have a good twenty to twenty-five years of employment to go. If I maintain my current income over twenty years, I will pay a minimum of $200,000 in additional federal and state income taxes. The bottom line is that society stands to earn a net gain of at least 1533 percent on its investment in my education.

Of course, promoting financial independence is not the only justification for providing the safety net of welfare. Viewing welfare as a waste of taxpayer dollars undermines the fact that it is an investment in families: single parents, infants, toddlers, grade-school kids and teenagers.

Over the sixteen years I have been pursuing higher education I have known many women who temporarily put their dignity—but never their integrity—aside to ask for help in permanently escaping the burdens of poverty. Those women embraced the responsibility of parenting and providing for their families with the courage needed to forestall the impact of stereotyping and scapegoating that goes along with being on welfare. In a patriarchal society, those with power have identified poor women and their children as the cause of most of society's ills. In the construction of this reality the dominant have, again, devalued the role of mothering and termed deviant those mothers unwilling to negotiate the dual roles of parenting and working at a dead-end job.

The dissertation research I am now doing analyzes the impact of education, both economically and personally, on welfare recipients' ability to realize self-sufficiency. Frankly, in my experience, education stands out as being the best intervention available, hands down, for those recipients who want to pursue it. Certainly, the potential improvement in the earning capacity of women is greatest when a woman can truly compete for skilled employment, even in a "free" market economy that continues to pay women less for the same work their male counterparts perform.

Women and their families can not and will not become self-sufficient by accepting jobs that pay at or slightly above the minimum wage with few or no benefits. President Clinton has stressed the importance of education for all Americans. Apparently "all Americans" excludes poor women and their children. The Personal Responsibility and Work Opportunity Reconciliation Act of 1996 (H.R. 3734) emphasizes getting women to accept work, any work, and imposes time-limits for them to do so, without addressing the human impact that working full-time, and still falling below the federal poverty line, has on a family. It is a very lucky welfare recipient whose case worker encourages her to obtain her GED (General Equivalency Diploma) before going to work; one who advocates the pursuit of higher education is all but unheard of.

Not every woman on welfare will want to go to college. More often than not that is because, like myself at first, they never think it is an option and believe they are not smart enough to be successful in school. But for those women who brave their case workers, the red tape of applying for financial aid, the intimidating process of petitioning to and being accepted into college, finding housing and transportation, registering for classes and showing up, and ultimately discovering their personal contribution to society . . . fragment . . . by . . . fragment, I say to state and federal policy-makers, GET OUT OF THE WAY. Help welfare recipients attain economic independence: pay the monthly check, cover the costs of childcare, give Food Stamps, provide medical insurance. Why? Because the story you never hear is that, used effectively as a tool to combat poverty, welfare works.

NARRATIVE D

On Being the "Bad" Mother of an Autistic Child

Jane Taylor McDonnell

I remember I was standing with a young teacher on the playground of a London nursery school, watching my son Paul, then three. He had already been given every medical and psychological test known at the time but was not yet diagnosed as autistic.

"He doesn't look anyone in the eye, does he?" the teacher remarked.

"No, well . . . ," I began. "But he does with me . . . most of the time." Why did I bristle at this comment? Partly it was because I thought it was so unfair. His father and I had always known Paul to be an affectionate, alert, intelligent child; his was a happy temperament, we had always thought, an "easy" child, but not too easy. He was healthy, well grown, loved us and his wonderful college babysitters, was passionately interested in his books and demanded to be read to for hours each day. Furthermore, he had always been appropriate in the expression of his feelings (sadness, joy, frustration, fear).

But now in London these things were beginning to seem less important than the fact that he was having so much trouble speaking and was obviously getting more and more frustrated as a result. Slowly, a deepening anxiety was crowding out our earlier feelings of pride and joy in this wonderfully "original" child. I was almost desperate to get some kind of diagnosis for Paul and some help for his delays in learning, and I was especially vulnerable now to any implied criticism.

I thought of all this, as we watched Paul together, this teacher and I. And then she asked: "How many hours do you spend in the library every day?"

From "Bad" Mothers: The Politics of Blame in Twentieth-Century America, *edited by Molly Ladd-Taylor and Lauri Umansky, New York University Press, 1998. Reprinted by permission of the press, editors, and author.*

I was startled—then stunned and angry. When Paul was enrolled in the school at the beginning of the fall, I had offered some information about all of us. We were an academic family, living for a year in London. I taught women's studies and my husband taught English at the same college. I was writing a book (trying to), and spent three or four hours in the London Library every day reading Victorian novels written by women: Harriet Martineau, Margaret Oliphant, Lady Blessington.

This teacher's questions had now gone beyond friendly interest; they seemed intrusive and unwarranted. They also seemed to be of a piece with other questions and comments made by the headmistress. Everyone in the school appeared to be preoccupied with the fact that I was leaving my child in a nursery school as I went off to a library to research a book, and with the fact that the child's father or a babysitter sometimes dropped him off at the school or picked him up after his three hours there. Did they think that because I was an English teacher, I was putting undue pressure on my child to speak, or that because I spent several hours a day in the library, I was neglecting my child?

Could I have been imagining all this? Imagining also the pursed lip, the head turned aside, the glance away from me to Paul, then uneasily back to me again? But I knew they never asked these same questions of Paul's father.

It was true, on the other hand, that Paul had several odd behaviors at this time. He was fascinated with a couple of little balls colored blue and green, part of a construction set, which he recognized as similar to two large marbles he had lost a few months before. His high-pitched delight at rediscovering "boo bah, bee bah" (blue ball, green ball) did seem to be out of all proportion to any possible importance they might have to any normal child.

Paul's other nursery school fascination was with the toilets. As soon as he arrived in school each day, he ran off to the bathrooms and started flushing each of the little toilets. He then hung his head almost down into the bowl as he listened to the sounds of the rushing water, perhaps checking for minute differences in pitch and motion. This, needless to say, was considered extremely odd behavior by all the teachers at the school.

His quirks made me anxious and confused. I wanted to defend him, to let these teachers know how wonderful he really was. At the same time I couldn't deny his developmental delays or pretend that he was learning in the same way other children did. I had a whole set of contradictory feelings about myself as well. I wanted to be reassured that I was doing a great job, but at the same time I wanted my doubts and fears for him to be acknowledged. I wanted it both ways.

But more than anything else, of course, I wanted to be recognized as a *good mother.* And as a good mother, I wanted to be acknowledged as smart and well informed about children, as well as self-aware, kind, generous, energetic, resourceful, relaxed, and funny! I wanted desperately to believe that all my years in graduate school and in the classroom teaching had prepared me to be a better mother, not a crippled one. I did not want to think that the sensitivity and awareness developed through literature was in any way different from that used directly with people. In my great plans for myself it was all supposed to be of one piece: raising children, writing books, and teaching students. I wanted my life to be full of all these riches, and I had always been deeply resentful of any attempts to make women choose between children and work.

So now, in this London nursery school, I felt that my deepest self was being attacked. I thought of the time when the headmistress suggested I talk to the mother of a little boy who was deaf. "She's such a *sensible* Mum," she had pointed out to me. "She has really devoted herself to that child." This mother had spent the first three months at the nursery school with her child. She came every morning with him and stayed the whole time, I was told, "until he was completely used to the school."

I resisted the headmistress and the other teachers in the school, but still the niggling doubts were there, the tiny pinpricks of poisonous anxiety. And in the meantime, Paul was getting worse, much worse, in his school behavior, becoming more and more wild. I tried sitting with him in the circle of the children on the floor as they sang songs or played clapping games. He twisted sharply away from them now, something he had not done before. If another child approached, he simply ran away. More and more he was locked into his obsessions: flushing toilets, arranging little colored balls, flicking light switches, searching for a screwdriver to take things apart.

Six months before this, we had gone to Paul's pediatrician in Minneapolis and asked that he be tested because of his speech delay. The doctor had been alarmed. Here was a beautiful, healthy child who *seemed* so normal in every way—except for a puzzling lack of speech and a certain withdrawal from human contact.

The doctor suggested that I read *Dibs in Search of Self,*[1] the story of a bright but speechless child who had been rejected by his surgeon mother, and who had withdrawn into his own little world until a loving teacher rescued him. I had already read the book and was stunned by the doctor's suggestion that there was a message for me in those pages. The book had suggested that mothers (otherwise well-meaning, intelligent, kind women) had the power to deprive their children of a sense of self, to destroy them at their very core, to kill their "souls," as people a generation or two ago might have put it. It attributed an awesome power to the mother, and it was a power to harm, but not to heal. It seemed that professional help was called for in restoring children to a healthy sense of self.

My reading of *Dibs* had led me to other books about disturbed children, and I had discovered that the worst mother in twentieth-century psychological literature is quite possibly the mother of the autistic or schizophrenic child. These two conditions, now widely accepted as neurological (autism) or biochemical (schizophrenia) in origin, were once conflated, and both were thought to be psychogenic, caused by bad mothers. Possibly the most extreme case made against such mothers, but also one of the most widely read and highly influential, was Bruno Bettelheim's *The*

Empty Fortress: Infantile Autism and the Birth of the Self,[2] where the author argued that autism was caused by the cruelly rejecting mother. This mother, in fact, was similar—in her complete disregard for the welfare and even the humanity of her child—to the SS guards of concentration camps. Here is a passage from the beginning of the book:

> In the German concentration camps I witnessed with utter disbelief the nonreacting of certain prisoners to this most cruel experience. I did not know and would not have believed that I would observe similar behavior in the most benign of therapeutic environments [Bettelheim's Orthogenic School in Chicago], because of what children had experienced in the past [at home with their mothers].(57)

Bettelheim, who had himself suffered imprisonment in Dachau and Buchenwald, goes on to draw a sustained analogy between the behaviors of the kind of prisoner who became mentally ill under those conditions and the well-known behaviors of the autistic child (63–85). He notes that the prisoners often expressed a sense of rage at any change in their immediate environment, just as autistic children rigidly insist on sameness. Mutism in the prisoner and in the autistic child are both traced to pervasive feelings of helplessness and hopelessness, in the child's case to the mother's withdrawal of the breast. The prisoner's "nearly continuous daydreaming was a close parallel to the self-stimulation of autistic children. . . . The purpose, in each case, was to blot out recognition of an immediate threatening reality" (67). Both often show a strange insensitivity to pain. Both carry their bodies in a similar way and often have a shuffling gait. They might both be emotionally depleted to the point of "catatonia," "melancholic depression," complete "loss of memory," or "disregard of reality" (64).

Gaze avoidance is similar in both the autistic child and the prisoner. Bettelheim argues that "the averted gaze of autistic children, their looking vaguely in the distance without seeming to see, and their concentration on things close at hand when there is nothing to see but their own twiddling fingers . . . is essentially the same phenomenon as the prisoner's averted gaze. . . . Both behaviors result from the conviction that it is not safe to let others see one observing" (67).

Finally, even the mental skills which autistic children often show are discredited, labeled as essentially disturbed behavior. "If another parallel were needed, the often remarked-upon autistic repetition of 'empty' rote learning, lists of names or dates, and the like seems to include some of the same reasons why prisoners favored similar activities: to prove to themselves that they had not lost their minds . . . even though they could not use (them) to better their fate" (67–68).

Bettelheim concludes this introductory passage to *The Empty Fortress* by disavowing any further analogy between the SS guards and mothers of autistic children, but he does so in a very surprising way:

> Here I wish to stress again the essential difference between the plight of these prisoners and the conditions that lead to autism and schizophrenia in children: namely that the children never had a chance to develop much of a personality. Thus, to develop childhood schizophrenia it is enough that the infant be convinced that his life is run by insensitive, irrational powers that have absolute control of his life and death. (68)

In other words, the only real difference between the SS guard and the mother of the autistic child is that the mother gets to the child much earlier in life. She is in the unique position of being able to damage him (I say "him" because autism is much more common in boys than in girls) before he has even had a chance to develop a personality. Some prisoners, as Bettelheim well knew, were able to resist the destructive forces on their personalities and to carry on later in life, after liberation, with a traumatized, but essentially intact, mind and spirit. The autistic child never will have such a chance.

One of the most interesting things about Bettelheim's argument is that the autistic child's behavior is taken as proof of etiology; in other words, the fact that autistic children show some of the same behaviors as traumatized concentration camp prisoners suggests that they have been hurt by comparable circumstances in their own lives. And these circumstances, according to his argument, have to have been created by their parents, specifically by their mothers.

Now, three decades after Bettelheim's book was published, this analogy between autistic children and the inmates of concentration camps, between SS guards and the mothers of autistic children, seems preposterous. But we must remember also that Bettelheim's is only the most extreme statement of a view still widely held. Many other writers were convinced that autism was psychogenic,[3] and introductory textbooks used in college psychology classes still sometimes repeat this view. Leo Kanner, who first used the term autistic to describe these children, also claimed that they were treated to "coldness, obsessiveness, and a mechanical type of attention" by their mothers. He argues that the children's "withdrawal seems to be an act of turning away from such a situation."[4] These women he called "refrigerator mothers," a term that stuck and came to be repeated for many years after he first used it.

But perhaps more important than these egregious examples of mother-blaming in the professional literature is the "trickle-down" effect of such views on both the general populace and, even more, on public school teachers, social workers, family doctors and pediatricians, school psychologists, and the like—the people who are most likely to have contact with autistic children and their parents. It seemed pretty obvious to me that Paul's teachers in London, as well as his doctor in the United States, had been trained to view this kind of disability as psychogenic in nature, and specifically as caused by some flaw in the mother.

Such notions have been very resistant to change, in spite of the fact that autism is now widely understood as a neurologically based developmental disorder that affects not just the rate at which skills are learned but also the way in which they are learned. Overwhelming evidence now exists for sensory dysfunction in autism, and it is interesting to see how an alternative explanation to Bettelheim's is now emerging for each of the behaviors he interpreted as caused by trauma similar to that experienced in the concentration camps.[5] Now we know that autistic children have disturbances in one or all of the senses: sight (accounting for the famous gaze avoidance, the use of peripheral vision, and such strange fixations as the "twiddling" fingers Bettelheim mentions); hearing (hypersensitivity, especially to loud or abrasive noises, which accounts for much of their withdrawal); taste and smell (possibly explaining the eating oddities and the "anorexia" that Bettelheim believed to be a self-imposed starvation to escape a threatening world); touch (the "tactile defensiveness" which a baby may show when picked up and cuddled by a parent and which many psychologists cited as the child's learned response to a mother's ambivalence); and proprioception or the sense of the body in space (toe walking or shuffling gait).

Difficulty in coordinating shifts of attention (for example from a person's voice to his or her face and eyes) and in integrating information from several senses at once are now recognized as neurologically based, rather than a defense against a rejecting mother. This probably accounts for the autistic person's problems with complex and rapid social interactions, as well as for his narrowly focused learning—the rote learning that Bettelheim named as neurotic. Finally, and maybe most importantly, a problem with regulation of the nervous system and the enormous stress which autistic people typically feel causes their withdrawal, tantrums, or self-stimulation, all ways of reacting to or blocking out an overload of sense impressions.

Why were professionals so ready to blame mothers for a childhood disorder such as autism? I think there are several reasons, and I have elsewhere offered possible answers to this question.[6] For one thing, because these children often "look" so normal and frequently have very good health, many experts on autism have resisted looking for an organic or medical explanation. And of course there has been a general tendency of twentieth-century environmentalists, as well as Freudians, to trace aberrant behavior in children back to parents.

There is another possible reason for this readiness to blame mothers for a child's autism, however, and that is the frustration that many well-intentioned professionals feel when confronted by these children, who so often seem not to get better even with heroic efforts at treatment. Eric Schopler, himself one of the leading professionals in the field of autism, has written persuasively of the temptation to scapegoat parents.[7] Among the reasons given are the professionals' own "confusion and lack of knowledge" about the causes and optimum treatment of autism, their fear and anxiety, and the projection onto the child of their own guilt at not being able adequately to treat him:

> The clinician confronted with an autistic child has the additional burden of coping with the child's difficult interpersonal behavior. The child may be negativistic and irritable. . . . This interpersonal avoidance and disorganization is often communicated to the clinician. He feels . . . insignificant to the child. The resulting sense of helplessness in the adult is not easily expressed against the child, and considerable pressure develops to explain the child's impossible behavior in terms of his parents. (238)

Schopler also suggests that "feelings of inferiority may lead to scapegoating . . . and when the progress in treatment is uneven, the clinician's role as an authoritative expert is seriously threatened" (238–239). "Conformity" may be another reason for blaming parents. "When the predominant orientation of a clinic is the psychoanalytic framework, then the emphasis on parental pathology for explaining children's difficulties is a shared belief among the staff " (239). And finally, when there are so many possible causes of the child's behavior to consider (perceptual and sensory dysfunction, dietary and metabolic problems, neurological involvement, genetic flaws, as well as the possibility of traumatic experiences), simplification is a real temptation, since it "provides for economy and energy in directing aggression" (239).

In addition, Schopler identifies ways in which parents can play into the hands of scapegoating professionals. I would suggest that what he says about "parents" applies particularly to mothers. Mothers are already "embarrassed by their child's peculiarities," and as targets of blame they have "little possibility for retaliation because the scapegoater is stronger . . . in terms of prestige." The mother is already so used to being attacked that her resulting demoralization makes it harder for her to fight back. And finally, "the victim is accessible." "In their desperate search for help," and after exhausting all other possible avenues of help, parents may seek out a diagnosis from the very professionals who are likely to offer psychogenic explanations of their child's disorder (240).

So what does all of this add up to? If the subtle hints dropped in the London nursery school constituted the only time I encountered blame as a mother, or if the frustration of an otherwise kindly pediatrician who suggested I read a book about a cured child was the only time someone suggested my child was withdrawing because I had rejected him—then probably not much. But this kind of blame, which was usually indirect and often appeared as much in what was not said as in what was said, happened over and over as Paul was growing up. It's true I was especially sensitive, all the more so because I was relatively well informed, relatively well-read in the literature. But one more event, which happened when Paul was in middle school, deserves mention. It shows again how widespread this belief in the psychogenesis of autism was, and it happened not so many years ago.

Paul was not happy in his neighborhood middle school, and a couple of concerned teachers, as well as a friend who was an activist on behalf of children, suggested that we visit schools in Minneapolis, some forty miles away from our home. One of these schools looked particularly promising. It had been set up to address the problems of children with various learning disabilities. It boasted very small classes, dedicated teachers, and a lot of attention paid to the individual learning styles of children. The teachers obviously worked very hard and seemed to have been very successful in building self-esteem among these children, who quickly learned to take a lot of responsibility for their own education.

For all these reasons, this school seemed perfect for Paul. Even though he had the diagnosis of autism, his learning difficulties as well as his remarkable strengths (as shown on test scores and in other ways) seemed to qualify him as an obvious fit for their program. After touring the school and becoming more and more convinced it was the right place for Paul, we sat down for the interview with the principal. I felt very hopeful that at last Paul could get a really superior education and one suited to his particular learning style.

The principal, however, listened to us for about forty-five seconds. As soon as he heard that Paul was diagnosed with "high functioning autism," he stopped us.

"I can't take him," he said.

We were stunned and wanted to know why not.

"He's autistic," he continued. "And I am one of those people who really does believe that autism is caused in the home. It's psychological in origin. That means we simply can't do anything for him here."

And with that, he closed the interview.

Notes

1. Virginia Axline, *Dibs in Search of Self* (New York: Ballantine, 1964).

2. Bruno Bettelheim, *The Empty Fortress: Infantile Autism and the Birth of the Self* (New York: Free Press, 1967).

3. See review by J. N. Hintgen and C. Q. Bryson, "Recent Developments in the Study of Early Childhood Psychoses: Infantile Autism, Childhood Schizophrenia, and Related Disorders" *Schizophrenia Bulletin* 5 (1972): 8–4.

4. Leo Kanner, "Problems of Nosology and Psychodynamics in Early Infantile Autism," *American Journal of Orthopsychiatry* 19 (1949): 416–26.

5. See, for example, Christopher Gillberg and Mary Coleman, *The Biology of Autistic Syndromes,* 2d ed. (New York: Cambridge University Press, 1992).

6. Jane Taylor McDonnell, *News from the Border: A Mother's Memoir of Her Autistic Son* (New York: Houghton Mifflin, 1993); and Jane Taylor McDonnell, "Mothering the Autistic Child," in *Narrating Mothers: Theorizing Maternal Subjectivities,* ed. Brenda Daly and Maureen Reddy (Nashville: University of Tennessee Press, 1991).

7. Eric Schopler, "Parents of Psychotic Children as Scapegoats," in *Classic Readings in Autism,* ed. Anne M. Donnellan (New York: Teacher's College Press, 1985), 236–41.

CHAPTER 3

The Institution and Experience of Motherhood

Where do the highly charged images of "bad" mothers discussed in chapter 2 come from? Why is the glorified image of the "good" mother, a white, upper- or middle-class, heterosexual woman, married to the father of her children? Why is it so hard, even for women who fit these characteristics, to live up to the ideal of good mothering? This chapter addresses these questions by focusing on the idea of motherhood as an institution. After exploring this idea, I examine how the institution of motherhood developed in Western societies over the last few centuries, creating ever-changing standards for mothering and burdening mothers differently, depending on their social location. I then turn to feminist social science research that shows how women's experiences are shaped by the institution of motherhood. Finally, I address a question that kept tugging at my students in the "Motherhood and Feminism" seminar: what are the consequences for children of feminists' critiques of the institution of motherhood?

The Idea of Motherhood as an Institution

In chapter 1, we saw that many feminists in the late 1960s and early 1970s rejected the cultural assumptions that motherhood is women's primary identity and that mothers alone are responsible for their children. In 1974, sociologist Jessie Bernard, in her significant but undervalued book, *The Future of Motherhood*, elaborated this critique and developed the concept of motherhood as an institution. "Motherhood is more than the biological process of reproduction," Bernard writes. "As an institution it consists of customs, traditions, conventions, beliefs, attitudes, mores, rules, laws, precepts, and the host of other rational and non-rational norms which deal with the care and rearing of children."[1]

To think of motherhood as an institution, then, is to focus on a society's specific mechanisms for shaping what mothers do and how they feel about what they do, as well as others' treatment and expectations of mothers. In other words, as an institution, motherhood is a human invention rather than

This chapter was written by Susan E. Chase.

a natural phenomenon. This idea allows us to consider how motherhood changes over time and varies across societies. Bernard argues that "[m]otherhood as we know it today is a surprisingly new institution. It is also a unique one, the product of an affluent society." Throughout most of history and in most societies, women have been central to the economic survival of their families and communities and have not spent their time exclusively in the care of children (7). Indeed, an anthropological review of 186 contemporary societies reveals that, after infancy, mothers have primary responsibility for children in only 20 percent of the societies.[2]

Bernard criticizes the modern Western institution of motherhood, especially its requirement that mothers suppress their own needs and desires, as oppressive to women. Moreover, she argues that it is not good for children. It is difficult for mothers to give children the tender, loving care they need when they shoulder the entire burden of child care twenty-four hours a day, when they are isolated from others who could help, and when child care is supposed to be their sole activity. Referring to early second-wave feminists, Bernard comments, "[Women] are daring to say that although they love children, they hate motherhood."[3]

Adrienne Rich also criticizes the institution of motherhood in her classic text, *Of Woman Born: Motherhood as Experience and Institution*, published in 1976. She decries motherhood as a patriarchal institution, by which she means that men, as politicians, scientists, doctors, religious leaders, fathers, and husbands, have exerted legal, technical, and ideological control over all aspects of reproduction as well as the social meanings attached to motherhood and nonmotherhood. Rich is particularly concerned about women's lack of control over their own bodies. She argues that women's relationships to children will be released from the bonds of the patriarchal institution of motherhood only when women control whether, when, how, and under what conditions they will have children. Like Bernard, she distinguishes women's potentially empowering experiences of motherhood from the oppressive institution.[4]

The institution of motherhood is integral, Rich claims, to the functioning of society as a whole. "Institutional motherhood revives and renews all other institutions" (45). In other words, by subordinating herself to husband, doctors, religious and political leaders, and by suppressing her own needs in order to serve those of her children, the "good" mother supports the dictates of traditional religions and the medical profession, and supplies the nation with well-socialized, productive citizens. Indeed, the institution of motherhood is so pivotal to the survival of other social institutions that it is difficult to think of it as an institution at all. Other institutions are usually embodied in a building such as the Vatican (Catholicism), the Pentagon (the military), or the Capitol (government). But "[w]hen we think of the institution of motherhood, no symbolic architecture comes to mind, no visible embodiment of authority, power, or of potential or actual violence. Motherhood calls to mind the home, and we like to believe that the home is a private place" (275).

Rich smashes that illusion of privacy by reminding us that mothers' lives are conditioned by social, economic, and political factors beyond the home. Such factors include the gap between men's and women's wages, which encourages women to depend on marriage for economic support; the devaluation of women's work in the home and the assumption that it contributes nothing to economic production; the treatment of unmarried women's children as illegitimate; the long struggle to criminalize marital rape (not until 1993 did all fifty states have such laws[5]); the lack of low-cost, high-quality child care; the skimpiness of social benefits for low-income mothers; the marketing of dangerous contraceptive devices; and "the token nature of fatherhood, which gives a man rights and privileges over children toward whom he assumes minimal responsibility." These factors influence mothers' relationships with their children whether they are aware of it or not.[6]

Bernard's and Rich's conceptions of motherhood as an institution were, and still are, revolutionary. Yet both were thinking primarily about white, middle-class women. Many feminist scholars, particularly women of color, have criticized that narrow view, and they have examined the consequences of the institution for other groups of women. They have demonstrated how it constrains mothers differently depending on their race and class, and they have explored how various groups of mothers construct different ideas about motherhood.[7] This diversity becomes clear when we examine the history of the modern institution of motherhood.

The Development of the Modern Institution of Motherhood

Before the eighteenth century, Europeans did not have a concept of instinctive maternal love. Upper-class European mothers did not think they should love all of their children equally, they did not necessarily mourn when their children died, and they were not expected to care for their children themselves. In France, aristocratic and bourgeois women (and, in the eighteenth century, urban women of the poorer classes) frequently sent their children away to wet nurses. Wet-nursing allowed well-off women to engage in the social and intellectual activities they valued. They considered breastfeeding immodest and disgusting, and doctors supported them in choosing social obligations over caring for their children.[8]

A society's ideas about mothers' responsibilities (or lack thereof) are closely tied to its ideas about children. During the Middle Ages, Europeans thought of very small children as animal-like and as having a natural tendency to evil. If children survived to the age of six or seven, they were considered old enough to participate in adult activities such as work, worship, play, and street life. They were expected to contribute to the family's survival, wealth, and status, and to help protect the family and community.[9] For centuries, parents, as well as the society at large, valued children only to the extent that they were useful. In the American colonies in the late 1700s, for example, "[t]he nations' leaders, delighting in the contributions of little children to economic independence, struggled to secure national protection for infant industries but did not find it necessary to protect the 'little fingers' that worked them."[10] Although mothers and fathers took delight in their children and may have felt great affection for them, parents were neither expected nor encouraged to express such feelings, as they are today.[11]

In the seventeenth and eighteenth centuries, Europeans' ideas about childhood and motherhood began to change. In the middle classes especially, the idea slowly developed that children were innocent (rather than evil and animal-like), that childhood was a special period of human life, and that motherhood was a crucial social role. Breastfeeding one's own children—and only one's own children—became more common, while swaddling (tightly wrapping infants to make them easier to carry and control) became less common. The new value attached to children was evidenced in the special clothing, toys, books, schools, and even caskets built solely for children. The increasing popularity of family portraits, as well as portraits of children alone, also indicates this change.[12]

In the United States, the modern institution of motherhood developed in the context of the Industrial Revolution, the American Revolution, and Protestant evangelicalism. The Industrial Revolution transformed the domestic, agricultural economy in which women played a major productive role. In the new industrial society, the factory or office, rather than the home or family unit, organized production. This split between the domestic realm and the productive, economic realm led to the doctrine of separate spheres for women (domestic) and men (economic) among the white middle and upper classes. The separation was not only physical but also ideological. The economic sphere was thought of as masculine and competitive, and as requiring rugged individualism, while the home was supposed to offer feminine warmth and shelter, an antidote to the cruel outside world.[13]

The American Revolution, for its part, fostered the development of what historians call Republican Motherhood, which connected good mothering to the task of nation building. Although women were denied the rights of citizens, they were expected to provide their sons with the moral education befitting citizens who would serve the nation well. At the same time, the Calvinist belief in original sin eroded as the idea of children's innocence and potential for development took hold. For the first time in Western societies, mothers became responsible for their children's moral behavior and well-being.[14]

Together, these historical forces produced the Victorian cult of true womanhood, which flourished throughout the nineteenth century and had an ambiguous impact on white, middle-class women. On the one hand, it increased their status. Rather than being affiliated, as they had been before, with sexuality, cunning, and immorality, women were now thought of as pure, pious, domestic, and submissive. Perceived as morally superior to men, "true women" had dignity, and their authority at home increased; previously fathers had held authority over child rearing. Moreover, women now had strong justification for their education. They needed to learn the use of reason in order to do a good job raising the future leaders of the country. On the other hand, the cult of true womanhood set very restrictive standards for mothers' behavior. Any expression of her own needs or interests—any deviation from self-sacrifice—brought familial and community censure upon a woman.[15]

Public acknowledgment of the increasing importance of mothers in children's lives is revealed in changes in custody law during the nineteenth century. Until mid-century, fathers were almost always given custody rights to minor legitimate children. (Recall that this was the one injustice concerning motherhood that was included by first-wave feminists who signed the 1848 "Declaration of Sentiments and Resolutions" discussed in chapter 1.) Thereafter, as courts began to focus on the welfare of the child, they increasingly assigned custody of young children to mothers, under the assumption that children needed their mothers' love. At the same time, women were more carefully scrutinized for their capacities as good mothers. In legal terms, power over children was transferred from fathers to the courts.[16]

Race, Class, and the Nineteenth-Century Institution of Motherhood

The "true woman" and "good mother" of the nineteenth century reflected conditions and ideologies within the dominant white upper- and middle-class society. Most women of color and white working-class women faced conditions that precluded the separation of economic and domestic spheres.[17] Indeed, slave mothers were denied their rights to motherhood altogether because slaveholders decided which female slaves would be used as "breeders" and which would have their children taken away and sold. "Owners, in other words, got to decide which enslaved women were mothers, and which ones were not."[18]

Sociologist Evelyn Nakano Glenn points out that even after slavery was abolished, African American women in the South, Mexican American women in the Southwest, and Asian American women in California and Hawaii were excluded from the cult of domesticity. Because the dominant white society sought to take advantage of the low-cost labor of women of color as domestic servants, agricultural workers, and low-level workers in institutional settings, there was little concern for their family lives or economic well being. "[P]eople of color were treated as individual units of labor, rather than as members of family units." Their value as cheap labor was more important than their value as mothers. Unlike white middle-class women, they were neither expected nor allowed to be full-time mothers. Rather, they moved back and forth between domestic and economic realms on a regular basis. Under these circumstances, providing economically for the family became a normal part of mothering, and responsibility for children was often distributed among family members and other women in the community. Thus, caring for children was not seen exclusively as women's work. While the dominant society treasured the idea of the private household, working-class communities of color developed a broader sense of domestic cooperation.[19]

During the early years of the nineteenth century, the experiences of white, urban working-class populations (both native born and immigrant) shared some similarities with those of working-class people of color later in the century. Far from following the doctrine of separate spheres, men, women, and children all contributed to the family economy, often working at low-wage temporary jobs. Families, including women raising children on their own, survived by assisting each other on a daily basis with child care, domestic labor, and economic subsistence. "Women in this context were surely not 'angels of the hearth' free to dedicate themselves to conscientious child rearing, home decorating, and philanthropy."[20] As a result, they were easily and often labeled "bad" mothers.[21]

This class- and race-based categorizing of mothers persisted as "scientific motherhood" took hold in the late nineteenth century. At this point, the dominant society viewed childhood as a phenomenon to be studied by the growing phalanx of experts such as doctors and psychologists. Mothers were now expected not only to love their children but also to educate themselves about child development, an activity requiring the freedom from labor force participation available mostly to white middle-class women.[22] Previously, children had been viewed as innocent; now the experts considered them full of dangerous impulses—not the impulses of a demon as had been believed two centuries earlier, but rather the "natural" drives of the young human, such as masturbating, sucking its thumb, and dominating its parents. Mothers needed to curb these impulses through rigid scheduling and behavior modification.[23]

Scientific motherhood flourished at the same time that evolutionary theory established a supposedly scientifically based hierarchy of races that placed Caucasians at the top and assumed that only women of that race could be good mothers. "Women of 'superior' heredity could ensure not only the well-being of their families but also the future of the nation (since they raised the next generation of citizens) and the progress of their race!" While evolutionary theory increased the stakes for good mothering, it also enhanced the authority and prestige of white middle-class mothers at the expense of all others.

The "scientifically" established inferiority of African Americans, Native Americans, and southern European immigrants further justified their exclusion from the ideology that children need their mothers' care and educated guidance. This virulent racism and classism strengthened the dominant society's expectation that mothers of color should serve its interests through low-wage work, without concern for their children, who were also often compelled to labor.[24] These are the historical roots of the contemporary scapegoating of poor black mothers. The assumptions that poor black children are worthless unless they serve the interests of the dominant society, and that poor black women have no right to control their reproduction, are deeply embedded in American history.

Reform Movements and the State in the Late Nineteenth and Early Twentieth Centuries

Beginning in the late 1800s, white, middle-class moral reform movements arose, targeting the children of poor white and immigrant families. Their goal was to "save" the children by assimilating their families to the norms and practices of middle-class society. These reform movements facilitated the rise of the helping professions, including those concerned with child welfare, adding to the growing public attention to families. At the same time, the power of the state was increasing in the form of child labor laws, stricter enforcement of compulsory schooling laws, and the establishment of the juvenile court system. In 1912, the federal government established the U.S. Children's Bureau to monitor the working conditions of children. Soon thereafter, the Children's Bureau published *Prenatal Care* and *Infant Care*, which quickly became government best-sellers. In addition, the kindergarten movement emerged, the Playground Association of America began to promote playgrounds as an alternative to the dangers of street life, and the federal government established Mother's Day.[25] As before, however, these developments led to drastically different outcomes for women of different social classes. "The well-to-do became childsavers and the protectors of the family; and poor mothers became eligible for salvation or for damnation."[26]

The white, middle-class, child-saving movements made some headway in assimilating poor and immigrant families to middle-class norms in part because they had the force of the state behind them. The family economy of the working class was certainly disrupted by compulsory education and child labor laws. Prohibited from paid labor, children were no longer major contributors to their family's survival, although they often continued to earn money by doing less remunerative work such as housework and running errands. Compelled to attend school, older children could no longer spend much time caring for younger siblings.[27] Consequently, working-class women's labor patterns began to change. At the beginning of the twentieth century, mothers who worked outside the home did so while their children were very young. When their children were old enough to work for pay and thus contribute to the family income, mothers left the labor force. By the middle of the twentieth century, mothers typically remained home while their children were young, seeking paid employment when all of their children were in school.[28]

These changes coincided with powerful efforts on the part of working-class men and capitalists to solidify the family-wage, a wage supposedly adequate for a male breadwinner to support his family. During the early twentieth century, the federal government also passed protective labor laws, which restricted the number of hours women could work and excluded them from certain jobs altogether. Protective legislation may have improved the lot of some working women, but most feminist historians now view such laws as harmful in the long run.[29] The upshot of all of these developments was that the cult of domesticity began to infiltrate at least some white working-class communities.[30]

While some poor and working-class families were now more likely to get needed assistance, for example, through public health programs, they were also more vulnerable than ever to scrutiny and more subject to a narrow range of acceptable behavior. "In attempting to 'save' children—and make them 'American'—social workers frequently engaged in disputes over childrearing with immigrant and working-class mothers." For example, reformers insisted that "[a] good American mother . . . did not swaddle her infant or give her a pacifier. She did not feed her baby garlic or sausage or tortillas. . . . When her children were sick, she turned to a doctor. A good mother would not place a talisman around her child's neck to ward off the evil eye."[31]

Furthermore, the white middle-class reformers generally ignored poor and working-class children of color. These children, however, captured the attention of middle-class reformers in their own communities. Black women reformers, like their white counterparts, believed that a man's family wage was important, but unlike white women reformers, they assumed that employed women were here to stay and that there was no point in discouraging women from working outside the home or making children suffer for it. Because government programs and white organizations excluded people of color, black welfare reformers built private institutions to take care of their own people: schools, child care centers, old people's homes, and health clinics. Black women showed their greater acceptance of employed mothers by giving high priority to day nurseries. Historian Linda Gordon suggests that if these reformers had been able to implement their vision, "the working mothers of the past few decades would have been much better supplied with child care and other measures to lighten the double day."[32]

The Institution of Motherhood in the Twentieth Century

Child-rearing experts played a pivotal role in shaping the institution of motherhood during the twentieth century. As the physical health of children improved and infant mortality rates declined, doctors and psychologists turned their attention to the mental and emotional development of children, and hence to the behavior of those deemed responsible for it—mothers.[33]

During the 1930s, when the permissive era of child rearing began, child rearing became explicitly child centered. This was a departure from child rearing organized around the good of the family and the nation, which had reigned throughout the previous century and a half. The paramount aim in the earlier period was to train the child to adopt adult sensibilities and demeanor and ultimately to produce proper adults. "By contrast, the most striking feature of permissive-era advice is the idea that the natural development of the child and the fulfillment of children's desires are ends in themselves and should be the fundamental basis of child-rearing practices."[34]

During the early decades of this child-centered era, which continues today, mothers faced a set of paradoxical demands. On the one hand, they were told that their unconditional love was absolutely essential to their children's healthy psychological development. Any unconscious hostilities they harbored would seriously harm their children. On the other hand, mothers were warned that their love could easily slip into dangerous overindulgence and overprotection. Thus, mothers needed the careful guidance of experts to negotiate this treacherous psychological terrain.[35]

These paradoxical admonitions coincided with an increasingly privatized ideal of motherhood. Whereas mothers of all races and classes in the nineteenth and early twentieth century relied on networks of women kin, neighbors, and friends to learn about mothering, the childrearing experts of the 1920s and 1930s—particularly pediatricians—encouraged white middle-class mothers to rely on doctors' expertise alone. Middle-class women's dependence on domestic servants also decreased at this time. Pediatricians "renounced servants and nurse-maids, and proclaimed motherhood as a mother's exclusive duty. . . . [T]he contrast between the mother and the servant provided pediatricians with an opportunity to offer white middle-class women a superior status vis-a-vis the servant." Although the well-being of the child was supposedly at stake in this privatized image of motherhood, the growing power of the experts was also at stake. Pediatricians encouraged this definition of motherhood at least in part because of their occupational dilemmas, particularly their concern about gaining authority in middle-class households. They feared competition from women's networks, which mothers had previously turned to for support and advice.[36]

Changes in women's educational, political, and occupational prospects also influenced the institution of motherhood during the twentieth century. In 1920, women reached a zenith of 47.3 percent of all students enrolled in institutions of higher education, a proportion that declined in subsequent years and was not surpassed until 1980.[37] Also in 1920, the first wave of feminism finally won the vote for women. Along with the new stresses and responsibilities surrounding motherhood, these achievements, and their implication that women were independent citizens equal to men, may have contributed to an increase in the proportion of women who remained childless. More than 25 percent of women born between 1900 and 1909 were permanently childless, a much larger proportion than among women in earlier and later decades. About one-third of African American women born between 1900 and 1919 did not have children.[38] In response to women's changing roles, doctors, psychologists, social scientists, and social reformers started to use the rhetoric of women's rights and fulfillment. However, they limited women's fulfillment to the heterosexual, middle-class marriage.[39]

Despite the experts' efforts to encourage middle-class women to seek fulfillment within the companionate marriage and the privatized version of motherhood, they could not contain the trend of women's increasing employment outside the home. In 1890, 18.2 percent of women fourteen years or older were in the labor force; by 1995, 58.9 percent were employed.[40] The war industries during the early 1940s created new opportunities for paid work for women but these closed after the war. Nonetheless, women's work for pay has continued to increase unabated since then.[41]Today women of all races are employed in approximately equal proportions.[42]

As white middle-class women entered the labor force in ever-greater numbers, child-rearing experts offered drastic warnings about this supposed problem. Perhaps most significant at mid-century was British psychiatrist John Bowlby, who proposed that a mother's absence was devastating for a child's emotional development. He based his ideas on studies of war orphans and institutionalized children. Others followed up Bowlby's research and came to the conclusion that good mothers stayed out of the labor force.[43] Thus emerged a "bad" mother who was usually white and middle class: the cold, selfish, ambitious career woman.

Of course, the dominant society did not treat the employment of working-class women of color as a problem for children's well-being. Rather, as before, it expected these mothers to work outside the home. The state institutionalized this expectation through "employable-mother" rules, which declared that when work was available mothers were ineligible for Aid to Families with Dependent Children (AFDC). These rules were applied specifically to African American women, whom employers wanted as seasonal field laborers and whom middle-class women wanted as domestic workers.[44]

During the latter half of the twentieth century, mother bashing of all groups continued to intensify. Women of color who conformed to the dominant society's expectation of them—that they work outside the home for low wages—did not escape the label of bad mothering. Beginning in the 1960s, black single women supporting families were denigrated as "matriarchs." They were accused of depriving black men of their manhood by usurping their place as household heads. Consequently, according to this racist stereotype, they caused a host of social ills. Even white middle-class women found themselves in a no-win situation in the postwar years: they were expected to be self-sacrificing, stay-at-home mothers, but in doing so they were accused of causing all of their children's as well as society's problems. Mothers were considered too protective, too dominating, too affectionate, or too distant, and the result was a nation populated by children who became delinquents, criminals and alcoholics.[45]

In recent years, middle-class mothers who work outside the home have achieved begrudging acceptance from the society at large, as long as their children remain their top priority. But the married, middle-class, stay-at-home mother remains a resilient icon of good mothering. During the 1992 presidential campaign, Hillary Clinton was portrayed as an ambitious career woman who controls her husband, and Barbara Bush was pictured as a devoted mother and housewife. When Hillary Clinton attempted to prove her womanhood by publicizing her recipe for oatmeal chocolate chip cookies, Barbara Bush presented her own richer, less fiber-conscious version. The media had a field day.[46]

Even though women's labor-force-participation rates are at their highest ever, with no sign of abatement, the ideology of "intensive mothering," as sociologist Sharon Hays calls it, is at its most extreme. This ideology is expressed in contemporary child rearing manuals, which many mothers read. Outsold only by the Bible in the entire history of publishing, Dr. Spock's *Baby and Child Care* has sold 40 million copies in six editions. Penelope Leach's *Your Baby and Child* has sold 1.5 million copies, and T. Berry Brazelton's *Toddlers and Parents* and *Infants and Mothers* together have sold 715,000 copies. These best-selling books "assume that child care is primarily the responsibility of the individual mother," and they recommend methods that are "child-centered, expert-guided, emotionally absorbing, labor-intensive, and financially expensive."[47] A tall order for mothers who are increasingly employed outside the home.

Finally, laws and policies concerning reproduction shaped the institution of motherhood throughout the twentieth century. Not until 1965 did the Supreme Court remove the last restrictions on married couples' use of contraception, citing the right to privacy. It took a few more years for that right to be extended to everyone.[48] In 1973, the Supreme Court legalized abortion. In 1977, however, the Hyde Amendment prohibited the use of Medicaid funds for abortions, severely limiting poor women's access to abortion. Revealing its priorities for poor women, the government continued (and continues) Medicaid funding for sterilizations.[49]

While unwanted childbearing was the lot of countless women for much of the twentieth century, unwanted sterilization was the lot of others. In the early decades of the twentieth century, the most horrifying antimother laws allowed the involuntary sterilization of people considered "feebleminded." Sterilization programs reached their height during the 1930s, but they continued for several more decades. By the 1960s at least sixty thousand people had been legally sterilized without their consent. Before the Depression, sterilization programs aimed to prevent the birth of children with genetic defects. During the Depression their goal shifted to preventing the parenthood of those considered unable to care for their children, children who would thus become a drain on public resources. At this point as well, women were more likely than men to be sterilized involuntarily.[50] Well into the 1970s poor women were sterilized without their consent and/or under threat of having welfare benefits withdrawn. These practices and laws disproportionately violated the rights of people of color. In 1978, the Department of Health, Education, and Welfare finally published rules restricting sterilizations performed under government programs such as Medicaid and AFDC. Involuntary sterilizations may have abated at that point, but they were not stopped altogether.[51] Adrienne Rich recalls her own experience in the 1970s, when she sought sterilization after her third child: "[W]hile the medical establishment was reluctant to sterilize women like myself, the same professionals and the federal government were exerting pressure and coercion to sterilize large numbers of American Indian, Black, Chicana, poor white, and Puerto Rican women."[52]

Women's Experiences of Motherhood

The history of the modern institution of motherhood shows that married, white middle-class mothers have been venerated at the expense of all others. At the same time, the institution has created unrealistic expectations even for mothers who most closely fit the ideal. But understanding motherhood as an institution is different from understanding how women experience mothering. How do women of various social groups feel about their children, the work of mothering, partners who share (or don't share) child-rearing responsibilities, and other aspects of their lives, such as paid employment? While talking to friends and intimates about these issues may be common practice, mothers have begun to go public with their experiences, as evidenced by the recent outpouring of mothers' personal narratives.[53] Indeed, most of the narratives in our book touch on women's experiences of motherhood in one way or another.

Accompanying this chapter, Sylvia Pashkin's story (narrative E) offers a clear picture of how a woman can feel so constrained by expectations embedded in the institution of motherhood that she must leave her children in order to regain a sense of self and psychological well-being.[54] Pashkin challenges us to think about ideologies embedded in that institution: children need their mothers no matter what; a mother must be the primary parent; and a woman automatically becomes a bad mother when she puts her own needs first. Jeannine O. Howitz (narrative F) also rebels against the institution of motherhood by refusing to give into the assumptions that mothering is an instinctive activity rather than work, that only mothers who are employed in the labor force are "working mothers," and that only mothers who work at home are "full-time mothers." In addition, Howitz shares her sense of the rewards and stresses of both mother-work and paid employment.

While the institution of motherhood constrains women in many ways, women do not always experience mothering as oppressive. In her study of predominantly white working-class and middle-class mothers, sociologist Martha McMahon found that they felt deeply connected to their children, that they embraced motherhood as integral to their identity, and that they experienced mothering as a profound process of self-transformation. Acknowledging the taboo against expressing or even feeling negative emotions concerning one's children, McMahon notes that "*None* of the middle-class mothers and 11% of the working-class mothers said they would *not* have children again" if they had the chance to do things over. Those few who said they would not have children again were mothering alone under difficult circumstances. Yet even they "were not ambivalent in their feelings of commitment toward the children they now had."[55]

McMahon observed significant class differences in how the women described the moral transformation they underwent upon becoming mothers. The middle-class women focused primarily on personal growth and development, as well as a "changed relationship with the universe, the rest of humanity or some generalized other" (147). For example, they spoke about motherhood as helping them to see the strengths and weaknesses in their own characters and as encouraging them to become less self-centered without being self-sacrificial (152, 155). By contrast, working-class mothers described their self-transformation as a matter of learning to accept the lack of choices in their lives and the need for self-abnegation. "Motherhood meant 'settling down' " (164–165).

While McMahon respects the high value women place on motherhood, she interprets their experiences in light of motherhood's institutionalized form. Once women actually become mothers, their everyday activities lead to self-transformations that encourage them to embrace that institution's ideologies. McMahon points to the irony "that women can come to reproduce the romanticized image of mother, which in turn functions to produce much of the ambivalence and pressure women feel about motherhood" (275).

The institution of motherhood is most oppressive when women do not fit that romanticized image whether by virtue of their marital status, race, class, or sexuality, as we saw earlier in this chapter as well as in chapter 2. But that institution also weighs heavily when women of any social group can not bring their emotions into line with its dictates. In her study of white middle-class women suffering from postpartum depression, sociologist Verta Taylor eschews psychological explanations in order to understand women's emotions—guilt, anxiety, depression, and anger—in a wider social context. She quotes as typical the words of one woman who suffered a yearlong depression after the birth of her first child:

> I had in mind this cooing, laughing baby, someone I could love and have that special kind of close relationship with that you can't have unless you're a mother . . . so I was a bit let down when in the hospital I was handed this sleeping infant who didn't seem to care whether I was there or not. It just wasn't what I expected. Here was this baby I was supposed to love, and I just didn't feel a thing. I literally went numb. I can't tell you how guilty I felt.[56]

Because the institution of motherhood promotes the idea of natural, instinctive mother-love, a woman may be deeply disturbed if she does not feel immediate love for her child.

Many of Taylor's interviewees felt anger and resentment toward husbands or partners who did not share child care and household responsibilities. They also felt hostility toward physicians who failed to acknowledge their suffering or who encouraged them to accept maternal self-sacrifice as integral to good mothering. Some women directed anger at their children, the most stigmatized emotion. The medical discourse on postpartum illness assumes that women's anger derives from individual abnormality. Rejecting that discourse, Taylor points to injustices embedded in the institution of motherhood as the source of women's anger (52–54).

Mothers' ambivalence—and the difficulty women have acknowledging and expressing it—is a major theme in feminist studies of mothers' experiences.[57] Psychologist Shari Thurer tells the story of a client who had spent two terrifying years caring for her very ill child. The mother had to monitor her child's breathing every night, perform complex nursing procedures, and fight medical bureaucracies to insure that her child got the best care. After her daughter recovered, the mother developed severe agoraphobia.

> This bravest of young women was now afraid to leave her home. Her panic turned out to be self-punishment for ambivalent feelings, now breaking through, about her little girl and the traumatic course of events. While her child was acutely ill, my patient had functioned on automatic

> pilot; but now that her youngster was out of danger, she found herself dreaming of murdering her. It was all so irrational: her little girl was the most precious thing in the world to her. . . . What this mother came to recognize was that her resentment toward her child was understandable in light of the hell she had been through when caring for her and that despite her suppressed rage, she had functioned wonderfully. Coming to accept her own ambivalence helped her shed the crippling agoraphobia.[58]

Thurer traces this mother's difficulty in accepting her ambivalence to the "myth of motherhood that defies common sense" (xxiii). Mothers are held responsible for everything that happens concerning their children, but many mothers do not have the support they need to do the difficult work of "intensive mothering" expected of them.

Interestingly, Sharon Hays found that the predominantly white, mostly married, upper-middle, middle-, and working-class women she interviewed wholeheartedly embraced the ideology of intensive mothering, whether or not they worked outside the home. Nonetheless, both stay-at-home and employed mothers expressed ambivalence about their situations, each acknowledging the pressures embodied in the stereotype of the cranky, bored, frumpy housewife on the one hand, and the stereotype of the harried career woman on the other. Notably, not only stay-at-home mothers but also employed mothers defended their situations using the ideology of intensive mothering. Employed mothers argued that their employment is good for children because it provides financial resources (such as saving for college), it exposes children to caregivers who further their development, and it increases the quality of the time mothers actually spend with their children. Employed mothers also argued that their own happiness is pivotal to good mothering, making a small dent in the ideal of motherhood as utter selflessness.[59]

Sociologist Denise A. Segura argues that the ambivalence many women experience when juggling paid employment and mother-work is shaped by culture and social conditions. Interviewing women of Mexican descent, both native-born Chicanas and resident immigrant Mexicanas, Segura found significant differences between the two groups. Having grown up in a social context where economic and household work were integrated, the Mexicanas treated employment as part of motherhood. The Chicanas, however, had been raised in a culture "that celebrates the expressive functions of the family and obscures its productive economic functions." Not surprisingly, then, they were more likely than Mexicanas to believe that mothers should stay home with their children. Even those Chicanas in the labor force were more likely than the Mexicanas to feel ambivalent about their employment.[60]

While many mothers struggle to live up to the ideal of intensive mothering, some face conditions that ensure their failure to do so. Alison Griffith and

Dorothy Smith show how single working-class mothers are particularly disadvantaged in relation to that ideal. For example, school administrators and teachers expect that parents, usually mothers, will spend time and money facilitating their children's education. But these expectations take for granted middle-class knowledge, time, and resources. Even at the kindergarten and elementary school levels, mothers are supposed to prepare their children by teaching them to use scissors, paint, and glue, helping them to learn colors, and socializing them to follow directions. Hence, single working-class mothers, who often have neither the time nor the resources to meet the schools' expectations, are deemed unhelpful, bad mothers.[61] Even as a professional and partnered mother, I find it difficult to keep up with my daughter's preschool's requests for materials and participation: "Have your child bring or wear Winnie-the-Pooh items today"; "Come to the Mother's Day Tea on Friday morning"; "We need parent volunteers to watch the children during the Teacher's Appreciation Luncheon," and so forth. How much more difficult it is for single, working-class mothers.

Yet that challenge does not begin to capture the experiences of mothers who struggle to resist the racism their children encounter in schools, or who fight to keep their children in school at all.[62] Sharon R. Liff listened to homeless mothers living in temporary New York City shelters as they worried about the negative impact homelessness has on their children's education. One mother stated, for example, "Annie's in fourth. She belongs in sixth. Elizabeth's in third. She belongs in fifth. And it all has to do with moving around so much. I know they're not that smart but they're not stupid at all."[63]

As this small sampling of feminist research on mothers' experiences demonstrates, women mother under very diverse conditions, from many different social locations, and with a wide range of emotions. It is also clear that the institution of motherhood shapes, but never fully determines, their experiences.

What About the Children?

Some students in my seminar worried that contemporary feminism's critique of the institution of motherhood leaves children in the lurch. Children need unconditional love, they argued, a thoroughly modern idea that I also embrace. If the institution of motherhood needs to be destroyed because of the various harms it causes mothers, then how will children get the unconditional love they need?

Over the last three decades, a common thread has woven together feminist answers to this question: children get the unconditional love they need when mothers are supported in the difficult work of mothering. Mothers who are partnered need an ongoing commitment from their mates to some form of co-parenting.[64] Mothers who work outside the home need the support of "coordinated care" from child care workers.[65] They need employers to implement family-friendly policies, and they need the support of the state in the form of laws protecting their right to take time off to care for children (or other family members) without threat to their jobs. The Family and Medical Leave Act of 1993 is a small step in this direction. Employed mothers also need employers to retire the image of the ideal employee as one without family responsibilities. Sadly, that image is still alive and well in the United States, as demonstrated in an exchange during June 1998 on the SWS (Sociologists for Women in Society) e-mail network. Participants seriously discussed whether women applying for academic jobs should reveal that they have children. Finally, all mothers need cultural recognition that mothering is work pivotal to the well-being of the society as a whole.

Many Americans may agree that mothers deserve and children would benefit from these familial, community, institutional, and cultural supports. Yet many people are likely to imagine the mothers discussed in the previous paragraph as either married and amply supported by a husband, or stably employed at a job with decent wages and good medical insurance. Many people blanch at the idea that our society should provide subsistence (never mind comfortable) levels of support for mothers who have made the wrong "choices": mothers who are single, poor, and without the qualifications for professional, middle-class, or stable working-class jobs. At the basis of this resistance is not only the individualistic ideology that a person's station in life is of her own making, but also the less acknowledged ideology (discussed in chapter 2) that poor children and their mothers are unworthy of any support.

Let's pause to absorb the implications of this idea. When we hear cries of concern about "our nation's children," whether from politicians, pundits, scholars, or the neighbor next door, we need to ask which children they have in mind. The history reviewed in this chapter should convince us that it is not a concern for poor children that has led the dominant society to blame their mothers for "bad" mothering. Indeed, it is the classist and racist devaluing of poor children and their mothers that has shaped the conditions of their lives and precluded their achievement of "good" mothering.

Mothers who are poor and parenting on their own (whether out of preference or not) have less access than other mothers to the material, institutional, and cultural supports every mother needs. For example, poor single mothers often can not afford high-quality day care and find themselves in the impossible position of having to choose between leaving their children in unsatisfactory conditions or quitting their jobs. These mothers need the social provisions of the state. But "welfare" is woefully inadequate to their need, it is heavily stigmatized, and it is temporary. Many critics worry that the Personal Responsibility and Work Opportunity Act of 1996 will increase the poverty of women and children because job training, child care, and transportation programs are inadequate and because the available jobs are low-wage, low-skill, and often temporary and inflexible. Current welfare "reform" exacerbates the contradictions poor mothers have always faced.

Gwendolyn Mink reminds us that current welfare reform is grounded in the devaluation of mothers' work of caring for children.[66] Such devaluing is clearly evident in the stereotype of the middle-class mother and homemaker who plays tennis or golf or lounges next to the pool all day long. It is also obvious in the notoriously low wages paid to child care workers, the vast majority of whom are women. In the 1970s, the U.S. Department of Labor assigned higher skill ratings to dog pound attendants and zookeepers—two male-dominated jobs—than to nursery school teachers and day care workers.[67]

But mother-work is especially devalued when mothers and children are poor. Mink points out that current welfare law coerces poor single mothers by law—and *only those mothers*—to work outside the home. Unlike women with more economic resources, poor, single mothers have no right to choose whether or not to work outside the home. They have no right to choose to care for their own children in their homes. Furthermore, Mink chides those white middle-class feminists who assume that women's equality and autonomy are always gained through wage work. As we have seen, for poor and working-class women, white or of color, employment has been in part a mark of subordination. Their low wages have kept them poor and they have been limited to work that serves the dominant society's needs. "Thus the rights to have and care for their own children—to work inside the home—have been touchstone goals of their struggles for equality." Paradoxically, current welfare law assumes that any work outside the home is more valuable than caring for one's own children, even work caring for other people's children.[68]

Feminist critiques of the institution of motherhood are motivated by a deep commitment to children's well-being, and they are grounded in the belief that most mothers love their children and desire to do what is best for them. Adrienne Rich's hopeful words from 1976 emphasize the power of mothers' enduring relationships with their children, despite society's devaluation of their caretaking work:

> [W]hat can give us enormous hope . . . is all that we have managed to salvage, of ourselves, for our children, even within the destructiveness of the institution: the tenderness, the passion, the trust in our instincts, the evocation of a courage we did not know we owned, the detailed apprehension of another human existence, the full realization of the cost and precariousness of life. The mother's battle for her child—with sickness, with poverty, with war . . . —needs to become a common human battle, waged in love and in the passion for survival. But for this to happen, the institution of motherhood must be destroyed.[69]

Rich reminds us that destroying the institution of motherhood as it has developed in Western societies does not mean abolishing relationships between mothers and children. The institution of motherhood is part of the structure of our society and is tied up with other institutions: government, economy, education, medicine, religion. If we are committed to the well-being of all mothers and all children, and to strong relationships between all mothers and their children, we will need to re-create the institution of motherhood, as well as the host of institutions upholding it.

NARRATIVE E

She's Leaving Home

Sylvia Pashkin

"You should be cast to the outer regions of hell for what you have done" was what one acquaintance said when I left my husband, my son aged eleven and my daughter of six to pursue an independent life.

This was just the most virulent of the comments I had to face; others have denounced me as callous, selfish and unnatural. Each time the spears are launched, and they still occasionally are, they bring home to me how much of a threat I am, how much of a taboo I have broken.

By the late seventies, I had a dream house, designed by my architect husband, two happy, high-spirited children and all the trappings of an affluent and undemanding lifestyle. To all but the most perceptive eye, I had it all—but in the middle of all this, I was experiencing a growing and frightening sense of personal emptiness. Like other women, I had internalized all the available notions of what it is to be a "good wife" and a "perfect mother." Yet the domestic, private world I lived in made me feel powerless and invisible. True I taught part-time, English as a foreign language, but this was very far from what I believed myself capable of achieving.

My husband was a paternalistic, powerful man, far more capable than me in a worldly sense. When we first married seventeen years before, I admit I revelled in my lack of personality and the protection he afforded me. But I was beginning to grow up and much of my dissatisfaction was echoed by the women's movement which made me question, still more, the point of the roles I played.

I was dissuaded from looking for full-time work by my husband, and since I had very little self-confidence, I allowed myself to be persuaded that my first duty was to

From New Statesman and Society *3, 95 (April 6, 1990): 13–14.*

my home and children. For a while longer, I remained a Ming vase—passive, precious, fragile but also isolated and immured.

Then, I suddenly decided to lose weight. If I could control nothing else I could control my body, I told myself. I lost a great deal of weight very quickly, and there followed a period of enormous personal elation. In a renegade frame of mind, and with no other means of self-expression at my disposal, I embarked on a series of bizarre affairs in my effort to escape the family. The last of these affairs was very destructive. My mental state was unstable—the slimming drugs I had taken were amphetamines and, quite suddenly, I plummeted from euphoria to total despair. I became catatonically depressed.

I could not speak and I could not move. I crawled around the house on my hands and knees. My husband gave me every kind of support but he was helpless in the face of this devastating condition. I sought help in therapy but it was useless. I needed a quicker cure than their long-term ministrations might bring. Nor did the lavish doses of psychotropic drugs like Largactil, offered by one eminent psychiatrist, help either—they dulled me into insensibility. Even in that state I realized that no one recognized my condition as a valid response to an intolerable situation. They all wanted to thrust me back into the family, to return me to "normal".

I am still not sure how, but I slowly recovered. I clawed my way up the steep sides of a black well, into which I hope never to return. As I got better, I knew that to survive I had to leave, to reconstitute myself in another place and alone. At home I was asked to give so much—to be everything to the children and nothing to myself. I wanted to be a mother on my own terms—and wanted things motherhood couldn't give me. The children cancelled the possibility that I might be something to and for myself. I knew if I stayed, nothing would change and I would die—I would be killed with kindness.

And what of my children? There is a photo of them, taken just before I left; for me it marks an empty and desolate moment. They are standing in the garden, laughing; and I can't help feeling that their laughter since that time has always been tinged by sadness and loss. But I could not have looked after them—they had a loving father who offered them stability and security, emotionally and materially. They had their home and school and friends—all the continuity they needed and I was so detached at that point, so empty of all feeling with simply the will to re-create myself. At that time, I did not want them with me.

So in 1982, I left. Walking from the bedroom carrying a small suitcase to the front door was the longest journey I shall ever make. My husband thought that given the requisite time and space, I would return, whole again; but like many other people, I knew when I closed the door of my home, I would never go back. I would not allow myself.

When I first left I stayed with my mother. She was generous but very frightened for me, and she thought what I had done was horrendous. Then I found my own flat and lived in considerable penury compared to what I had known. Many friends turned away, shocked and threatened by my action. Some husbands considered me subversive, a Pied Piper who might turn up one day on their doorstep, trill enticingly and seduce their wives away.

One close woman friend, particularly harsh with me at the time, has recently done what I did and left her children. It's possible, I now think, that those initial cruel reactions from women were their way of denying they were capable of the same thing.

I, however, had problems beyond those imposed upon me by my friends. I had to find the energy to put myself back together again—to create a life that was mine and to become someone I could be proud of. I enrolled as a full-time MA student at London University and got a further degree in Media Studies and became a freelance media writer, editor and researcher. I co-founded a radical poetry group, organised three major poetry festivals and coedited two anthologies.

I have kept on good terms with my husband though we got divorced. We kept matters amicable between us so that the children would suffer as little as possible from my departure. I saw the children whenever I wanted but I was a "Sunday mother" with all the problems usually experienced by men, except that no one invited the children and myself to join them for Sunday lunch. Maybe it was for the best—at least the children didn't have to share me with others. Nevertheless, seeing them under those conditions was sometimes bleak and often fraught—another Chinese meal, another museum, the zoo again.

And there has been grief and pain and anger. However much I have tried to explain my reasons for leaving—and they make sense to me—the children have not been able to come to terms with my leaving. If I say I love and have always loved them—they wonder, how I could leave them. In the early days when I went to see them, they were all grieving for something—which was me—but I could not give myself back.

In the years I have been away, I have often felt very isolated and realised how little the matter of women leaving their children has been discussed, let alone accepted. In 1988 I published a detailed account of my experience to see what the response would be. I was deluged with letters from women in a similar position as well as from children whose mothers had left.

The women's letters reflected many of my own feelings—sadness, a sense of bereavement, anger at the double standard, low self-esteem and outrage at people's prejudice and the stigma attached to being a woman apart from your children.

More than one letter read "I stopped telling people that I had children that did not actually live with me because the reaction I got was a bad one." The high level of self-justification in the letters encouraged me to want to write about this decision which is so harshly judged and condemned. The women all loved and missed their children and, although not with them full-time, were concerned and still felt themselves to be mothers though not in the accepted sense.

These letters and my own situation made me see that there is a dangerous social myth abroad that leads people to believe in an innate maternal instinct, and any woman who strays from the total fulfillment of this destiny is considered aberrant—women who wish to remain child-free, who have their children adopted, who have abortions or act as surrogates or suffer from post-natal depression as well as the women who live apart from their children. Why should the love of a mother not be akin to other forms of human love—fragile, imperfect and uncertain—it too can change.

Now that I am stronger and can look after myself, I love my children differently from when they were young—it is a richer love and I think they understand that. My son is away in the Far East, prior to going to university. A letter arrived last week and among the ecstatic descriptions of the Thai islands, he wrote, "I lost a lot when you and Dad divorced. A part of my soul has had to re-build itself and this has not been an easy journey—one that you yourself have travelled but simply by another route . . . you are my mother. I realised it is not simply for this I love you—it is for the love I receive from you and not your role in my life".

We are faced with choices—I made one not usually considered open to women, but eight years on and holding this letter in my hand, the conscious intelligence of my son's remarks give me heart. I think I made the right decision: my ex-husband, my children and myself have survived, and, while I acknowledge that my leaving has hurt them in many ways, I believe that if I had stayed, a worse and more damaging scenario might well have ensued.

NARRATIVE F

Reflections of a Feminist Mom

Jeannine O. Howitz

I am seven months pregnant, slithering along my kitchen floor. The ruler I clutch is for retrieving small objects lost in the dust jungle beneath my refrigerator. After several swipes I come up with a pile of dirt and a petrified saltine, so I get serious and press my cheek against the floor, positioning my left eye just inches from the target zone. I spot it—the letter "G," a red plastic refrigerator magnet. "Here it is!" I cry, hoisting myself up to offer this hard-won prize to Sophie, my momentarily maniacal toddler. Her face collapses into a sob as she shrieks, "NOT THAT ONE!"

Sophie is twenty-two months old, and in the final stages of potty training, which I remember as I feel a gush of warm and wet on my outstretched leg. Wet clothes

From On The Issues, The Progressive Women's Quarterly *2 (fall 1993):15–16. Reprinted by permission of* On the Issues.

bring more tears (hers, not mine), and I quickly strip off her clothes, then pull off my own with one hand while I slice and peel an apple with the other. I might have barely enough time while she eats to run upstairs, grab dry clothes, and toss the dirty ones into the basket before I'm urgently missed.

That was how I came to be standing in the middle of my kitchen with the magnificence of my naked abdomen hanging low and wide on a clammy June afternoon. The sweat of my exertion had just begun trickling between my breasts when the phone rang. It was an old friend with whom I'd been out of touch for a while. I panted hello, eyeing Sophie as she climbed up and out of her booster chair to totter precariously on the table top. "What are you doing home?" my friend wanted to know. "Don't you work at all anymore?"

Don't you work at all anymore? Again and again since entering the life phase which positioned my work in the home, I have encountered the judgments, however unconscious, of those whose definition of work excludes most of what I do. The same system that discounts my labor scoffs at its rewards, which, like my productivity, are impossible to measure by conventional standards. By limiting our view to one which allows only for paid employment, usually only that located outside the home, to be included in the understood meaning of the word "work," we support the process through which all that we do and all that we are as women is ultimately devalued and despised.

Like most labels applied to women's roles, "working mother" is extremely inaccurate and defeating, because it foolishly implies that there is another type of mother: the non-working variety. Being a mother is work. On the other hand, it is equally absurd to call mothers who are not employed outside the home "full-time mothers," as this unfairly suggests that employed mothers are only mothers part-time. Ridiculous as they are, these labels go largely unchallenged, even by many feminists. They are a sinister trap, imprisoning women in feelings of inadequacy about whatever roles we have chosen or been required to perform.

The same process that forces a woman to say "I don't work" when she performs 12 to 16 hours of unpaid labor every single day at home ultimately transforms most female-dominated professions into mere chores that women and men alike come to consider less desirable and important than other types of work. Once stamped with the kiss of death "women's work," we can forget entitlement to the same respect and fair wages a man would get for equivalent labor.

Before motherhood, I sold advertising at a newspaper, with hopes of working my way into editorial. However, my sales performance exceeded standards, and I was quickly promoted to a well-paying position in management which required me to build a classified department from the ground up. I forged ahead until my daughter was born, when, after reexamining our options, my husband and I decided one of us should stay home with her. Although he was happily working in his chosen field, John's income as a schoolteacher was half that of mine, which rendered him the financially logical choice for at-home parenthood. But it was I who jumped at the chance, albeit scary, to shift the gears of my career and of my life.

When my maternity leave was up, I told the publishers that I wouldn't be returning to the office. Surprisingly, they offered me the chance to bring my daughter to work with me. I was thrilled; those long days at home with an infant weren't exactly what I had imagined. I discovered that although I didn't always enjoy my job, I did enjoy the recognition it provided me—something I found was not a part of the package for home-working moms. While my sister spoke with unveiled envy about all the reading and writing I would now be accomplishing, in reality I was lucky if I brushed my teeth. So I took the deal.

Seven weeks old on her first day at work, Sophie fascinated the staff as only a newborn can. A two-minute trip to the copier often turned into a half-hour social ordeal as one person after the next stopped to exclaim over her. She was a great diversion for a young and predominantly single staff. I had no idea, as a new mother, how fortunate I was to have an extroverted baby. It was my own introverted nature that suffered from the constant sensory bombardment. I was uncomfortably aware of my special status, and fighting a losing battle to hide how much time it actually took to care for Sophie on the job.

In a culture where women feel guilty to call in sick to work when a child is sick, it was tremendously difficult to be in an office setting, drawing a full salary, and to say, "Sophie's crying now—this phone call, this meeting, this project, whatever it is, will have to wait." In a society that expects workers to give 150 percent dedication to the job, and considers motherhood a terrible detriment to productivity, it was incredibly stressful and even painful at times to experience such a personal conflict in a very public setting when the two worlds collided.

For six months, I toted a baby, a briefcase, and a diaper bag back and forth from home to my office, which at first housed the crib and swing, after which came the walker, the play gym, and the toy box—not to mention the breast pump equipment and mini-diaper pail. I could hardly see my desk, let alone get to it. Not that it mattered, because by that time I wasn't doing any work that required a desk. It had gotten crazy, and I knew it. The circles under my eyes and my continued weight loss told me it was time for a change.

I explored every alternative I could think of, from researching and visiting daycares to negotiating with my employers for a part-time or home-based position, or a combination of the two. However, my key position on the management team required a full-time presence in the office.

Offering my resignation was an extremely difficult decision, particularly in light of my gratitude for the progressive opportunity to have my daughter on-site. My employers and I finally agreed to view my departure as the beginning of an indefinite unpaid leave that left the door open for my possible return at some unpredictable future date.

A two-month notice allowed me to finish up the last big sales project of the quarter, while my daughter was cared for by a neighbor. I got an unforgettable taste of the superwoman syndrome, rising at 5 a.m. and dashing out the door by 6 to drop Sophie off and commute an hour to the office for a grueling nine-hour day. This was followed by a long drive in Minnesota winter rush-hour traffic to pick my daughter up and go home, and was topped off with a couple of frantic hours that my husband and I spent getting everyone fed and Sophie bathed and to bed so that we could start all over again after what felt like a quick catnap. Relief overcame me as my last day at the office arrived, and I packed my diaper bags for good.

Our plans had always included my return to full-time paid employment upon our children's entry to school, which meant that, for the benefit of our financial solvency, we should have another baby quickly if at all. We chose "quickly," and shortly after our daughter's first birthday I was pregnant again.

I started stringing for our local newspaper, rushing out to city council and school board meetings as soon as my husband dragged himself through the door at seven o'clock. I got paid a measly 25 dollars a story, but since the meetings were at night and I could write the stories at home, I didn't have to pay for childcare. Moreover, it was the first time I saw my writing published; it signaled a turning point for me as I finally made the leap from advertising to editorial.

Since then, I've stuck to what I'm passionate about as I navigate the uncertain waters of these transitional years. I've redefined my priorities, and am using this time to lay the groundwork for a career that is going to work for me long after my children are grown. Like the many women who grow home businesses while growing young ones, I've discovered meaning in my personal work that was previously absent.

These days, since I do perform paid work from home, I could have an easy answer to "Don't you work at all anymore?" I could say that I am a freelance writer working at home. It's true, and since I know, based upon my own research, that it gains me a great deal more respect in the eyes of the asker than saying that I'm home with the kids, I'm tempted to offer it up. But I won't because every time I do, I'm perpetuating a system that defines work only in terms of what men have traditionally been paid to do, and discounts most of what women have traditionally done for centuries.

I have to make perfectly clear when I say that I work at home, I'm talking about the childcare and the home maintenance activities which utilize my talents as a manager, nurturer, healer, wise woman, acrobat . . . and retriever of small objects lost in the dust jungle beneath my refrigerator. Otherwise, people automatically dismiss these activities and conjure up a false image of an orderly day spent at the computer doing paid work. This strain toward clarity requires a lot more effort than calling myself a full-time mom, or proclaiming that I'm taking time off to be with my kids (motherhood is not a vacation), or, worst of all, concurring that no, "I really don't work at all anymore." It demands concentration and patience, but it can be done.

We must find new words, or new combinations of and meanings for old words that more accurately reflect our reality. When we don't—when we resign ourselves to the old words that apportion us less worth than we deserve because it's less awkward and just plain easier—we are validating a description of ourselves that we know to be false. This danger is like that of looking into a fun house mirror, without challenging the falsehood of the contorted stranger staring back at you. Eventually, you're going to believe what you see is you, and that twisted version of yourself becomes the only truth you know.

CHAPTER 4

Fatherlessness, Men, and Mothering

During the 1990s father absence began getting lots of attention. Sylvia Ann Hewlett and Cornel West's *The War against Parents* exemplifies the latest wave of concern about father absence. Their book's subtitle—*What We Can Do for America's Beleaguered Moms and Dads*—points to how parenting often gets distorted as a public issue. When "parenting" moves onto a public agenda, "moms" and "dads" get lumped together in ways that mask their practical differences.[1] When Hewlett and West talk about how little time *parents* spend with their children, for example, they erase the greater practical challenges mothers usually face and the heavier guilt and social censure they are likely to experience on that count. Significantly, too, one way of overemphasizing fathers' involvement with their children is to talk about parents as if their gender were irrelevant or at least secondary.

Hewlett and West go much further, though. Woven into their discussion of beleaguered parents in general is unusual concern for fathers in particular. Their book's index includes only four lines of page references for "mothers" but fourteen for "fathers." These authors offer no chapter on mothers but two on fathers—"The Disabling of Dads" and "Escape Routes: Promise Keepers and the Nation of Islam." Given that most mothers have primary responsibility for daily child care, that most single-parent households are headed by women, and that mothers face increasing demands beyond the home, what does Hewlett and West's disproportionate concern with fathers mean?

Among other things, it means that they join a social movement building up around the premise that father absence is socially catastrophic. Their book is but one of many recent publications calling for the restoration of mom-dad family units while arguing that single-parent households cost children as well as society a great deal. Even though the evidence to date is inconclusive, pro-father publications keep proliferating. The antifeminist, antimother messages often found in them, whether intended or not, reinforce what many people already believe and what many policy makers seem hell-bent on doing anyway.

This chapter was written by Mary F. Rogers.

The Alleged War against Parents

For several decades North American feminists have been struggling to make motherhood less costly by making discrimination against pregnant women and mothers illegal and by raising public awareness about employed mothers' second shift of unpaid labor following their shift of wage labor.[2] Now some nonfeminist scholars and activists are trying to make fatherhood less costly for men. Here, though, cost has to do not with undue strain on physical and emotional energies but with undue diminution of paternal control alongside alleged financial hardship among noncustodial divorced fathers. To get a feel for this ideological terrain, let us look at some ideas Hewlett and West showcase in their book. These ideas are common to "family restorationists" or "New Familists."[3]

The first idea is that today's American fathers are hard pressed to be effective parents. In their second chapter Hewlett and West introduce a section entitled "Fathers under Siege." This brief foray, which anticipates two later chapters on fathers, centers on the thirty years of changing divorce statutes and social welfare policies that "make it extremely difficult for a large proportion of American men—somewhere between a third and a half—either to live with or to stay in effective touch with their children."[4] Hewlett and West offer no evidence about how many of these men want to reside with or stay in relatively close touch with their daughters and sons. Instead, they postulate a social conspiracy among government, business, and popular culture.

The second idea is that irresponsible fatherhood is thus understandable, though not excusable. Hewlett and West, for example, construct a shoddy defense of so-called deadbeat dads, those court-ordered to contribute to their children's financial support who chronically fail to do so. They lament the "demonization of deadbeat dads" (40), which allegedly began with a 1989 report indicating that more than one-fourth of nonresidential fathers were neither a part of their children's lives nor providing them any financial support. Hewlett and West concede that that pattern is "shocking" and "shameful." Yet they argue that "almost 40 percent of the 'absent fathers' described in this report had neither custody nor visitation rights and therefore no ability to connect with their children."

"Almost 40 percent" leaves a hefty percentage of these nonpaying fathers "connected" with their children. Further, even without custody or visitation rights a determined parent can "connect" with a daughter or son using the U.S. Postal Service, the regional Baby Bells, or e-mail. Hewlett and West ignore the issue of why some fathers have no visitation rights. One supposes that the most common reasons are that they did not fight for them or were denied them due to past inappropriate behavior. Anyway, fathers' relationships with their children have no bearing on their responsibility to contribute to their children's support. Hewlett and West imply otherwise. They not only deem it "odd" to call fathers " 'absent' when they have no right to be present" but also cite a study showing that noncustodial mothers provide financial support for their children at an even lower rate than fathers. Conveniently set aside is any acknowledgment of mothers' lower average incomes and the more tragic circumstances that typically separate them from their children, for example, addiction or neglect.[5] Hewlett and West conclude, "It is probably unrealistic to think we can keep in place all the obligations of traditional parenthood without its main reward: loving contact with a child. Yet, rather than create policies that help noncustodial parents connect with their children, all we seem capable of doing is cracking down some more on deadbeat dads" (40).

The third restorationist idea is that disconnected fathers—those not living with their children by virtue of never having married the mothers or having divorced them—cost their children and society a great deal. Drawing selectively on social scientists such as Sara McLanahan and Gary Sandefur and family restorationists such as David Blankenhorn and David Popenoe, Hewlett and West (162–165) emphasize the academic, psychological, financial, and behavioral problems it promotes. Moreover, they insist that "the missing ingredient in the single-parent family is not simply a second adult who can provide supervision and involvement but the *biological father*" (165, emphasis added).[6] The single-parent household at issue, then, is the single-mother one, even though about 15 percent of single-parent household involve fathers.

A fourth restorationist idea that Hewlett and West advance is that we should "probably not" even "be surprised by the connection between father absence and child abuse" (166). This idea is usually only implied in the New Familism with the notion that mothers and children are best protected (as well as supported) when husbands and fathers live with them. More common in the restorationist literature, though not typical, is the notion that a "child welfare bureaucracy" now engages in "parent bashing" and the "victimization of *parents*" (113, emphasis added). Given that most child abuse charges are leveled against men, the bashing and victimization at hand much more concern fathers than mothers.

Hewlett and West cite several extreme examples, one involving a man allegedly charged with child abuse for tickling his nine-year-old stepdaughter's stomach. Richard Wexler's *Wounded Innocents: The Real Victims of the War Against Child Abuse*, the source of this example, indicates that the stepdaughter initially described behaviors that were likely abusive; the charge of child abuse was ultimately dropped when the child recanted some of her allegations. Thus, Hewlett and West not only use an extreme example but also mispresent it by omitting the initial allegations. Also from Wexler's book, they cite instances where "[p]arents were labeled child abusers for not letting a child watch television after 7:30 p.m. or for giving a child money to go to McDonald's for breakfast too often" (114). Wexler himself never documents these instances. Likewise, Hewlett and West cite no source when they conclude that "only a third [of child abuse charges] are ever substantiated, and of these only a fifth involve elements of serious endangerment" (115). Here, in effect, Hewlett and West assign greater weight to parents' rights and dignity than to child protection. All the while, fathers' rights and dignity are most at issue, albeit implicitly, as seems also to be the case with Wexler.

A fifth notion linking Hewlett and West with other family restorationists is that fatherlessness derives in part from feminism. Hewlett and West soft-pedal this notion, but it does crop up several times in their book. They first mention that "radical feminists tend to see motherhood as a plot to derail equal rights and lure women back to subservient, submissive roles within the family" (95). Hewlett and West neither document nor illustrate that point, let alone concede that radical feminists' influence has been limited at best. Later the scope of their charges widens:

> Over the past three decades, important segments of public opinion have become convinced that fathers don't matter—a point of view encouraged by modern feminism, which for all its enormous value has indulged in some excesses. Most damaging has been a set of attitudes that center on the expendability of men. Ideas that women don't need men, women can do whatever they want without men, men are responsible for all the evil in the world, children need only a loving mother, and men only teach children how to be patriarchal and militaristic have become standard fare on the cutting edge of the women's movement. (161)

Similarly, in connection with the Promise Keepers, Hewlett and West claim that "[f]eminists and their allies on the left are offended by the idea of any group's encouraging men to reassert leadership within the family" (198). They downplay such concerns by insisting that what the Promise Keepers mean "is a matter of some dispute."

Before long, Hewlett and West mention Betty Friedan's *Feminine Mystique* (1963), which they take as symptomatic of a "strand of feminist thought" emphasizing "women's family roles as inherently oppressive." Hewlett and West generalize that some modern feminists want to separate not only from men but also from children in order to lead "autonomous existences" (200). Their treatment of feminism is more straightforward than most in the restorationist literature. The more typical formulations make no mention or only passing mention of feminism. Rather they stress that since the 1960s (when second-wave feminism emerged), Americans (read American women) have become more individualistic and self-centered.

A sixth idea advanced by Hewlett and West that also shows up elsewhere is that absent fathers are often, perhaps typically, fathers in pain. Hewlett and West emphasize that many absent fathers yearn to spend more time with their children or even live with them. Many say they "never wanted their marriages to end." Hewlett and West wonder, "Given the anguish wrapped up in separation from children, . . . why so many divorced fathers eventually choose to sever all ties with their kids." According to them, the main reason is that "[v]isiting their children only serves to remind these men of their painful loss, and they respond to this feeling by withdrawing completely" (169). These authors focus on the "male yearning" for "connectedness" (183) without noting the relationship between remarriage and the cessation of contact with children from earlier relationships. Besides emphasizing the pain of absent fathers, Hewlett and West stress the "tidal wave of critical thinking and punitive action" fathers have faced. They conclude, "If the past few decades have been a systematic war against parents, the battles against fathers have been particularly ugly and fierce" (173).

Hewlett and West see these battles as having a history. They trace their history, at least among African Americans, back to the nineteenth century. Slavery, they argue, affected mothers and fathers differently:

> Even under slavery, females were able to fulfill their most elemental gender-specific role: they could be mothers and nurse their babies. Males, however, were completely stripped of their identity as men. One of their basic roles—to provide —was assumed by the white master. Their other basic function—to protect—was something they were utterly powerless to do against the white man's overwhelming force. (181–182)

Here Hewlett and West ignore the violations of motherhood that "breeder slaves" faced, the ambivalence (at best) of nursing white babies at the expense of their own black or mulatto babies, and the grim uncertainties of family life wrought by the auction block. Also ignored are the daring acts of male slaves intent on providing and protecting even at the cost of their own lives. One can only suppose that those acts of resistance increased during the Jim Crow era.[7]

In addition to these six ideas, Hewlett and West's rhetorical gestures link them with other New Familists. The most characteristic of these are brief caveats to assure readers that the authors support liberal social values, above all, women's rights. For instance, Hewlett and West concede that "a child can certainly be well raised by a single mother—or father—who is devoted to that child's well-being" (165). Similarly—and parenthetically—they insist that they are aligned "firmly with progressive folk who have fought recent attempts to diminish or destroy homosexual rights or the legal right to an abortion" (197). Also parenthetically, they "unequivocally reject any form of racism or anti-Semitism" (205).

Such brief caveats scarcely counteract Hewlett and West's largely uncritical stance toward the Promise Keepers and the Nation of Islam. About the former they claim that "if we are interested in enhancing this nation's store of parenting energies, there is much to work with in the Promise Keepers movement" (200). About the latter they conclude, "It seems safe to assume that many of the more elaborate and fantastical of Elijah's beliefs were intended to be symbolic and allegorical rather than factual in nature" (204). But Hewlett and West know that the shortcomings of both groups[8] are more profound than their facile generalizations let on:

> If the leaders of Promise Keepers were to affirm homosexual and women's rights and stay out of the abortion wars and if the leaders of the Nation of Islam were to repudiate anti-Semitism and patriarchy, it would be a giant step forward. Then it might be possible for progressive folk to pay attention to what is really going on in these movements and to respond constructively. For if we continue to look at Promise Keepers and the Nation of Islam and see only patriarchy reestablished or gay-bashing celebrated, we lose out on a rare opportunity to take the agony of crippled men and turn it into something good: a new commitment to husbandhood and fatherhood. (211)

This quote not only reiterates Hewlett and West's explicit theme of painful fatherhood but also points to an implicit theme, namely, compromised husbandhood. Another formulation pointing to these twin themes is Hewlett and West's reference to "the all-out war our society has waged against *husbands* and fathers" (189, emphasis added). That reference alludes to what underlies a great deal of the New Familism. Husbands' rights are at issue, even while fathers' rights—often discussed in parental terms—command the lion's share of explicit attention.

Before further linking Hewlett and West's work to the New Familism, let us look briefly at how they would establish a cease-fire in the war against parents. Like many family restorationists, they want divorce made less accessible, particularly among parents. In the latter case they recommend a "three-year waiting period, during which time [the parents] would be obliged to seek marriage counseling" (242). Hewlett and West's recommendations are more daring, though, than those of most family restorationists. They advise that federal law require a ten-day paid leave for new fathers (243). Even bolder is their recommendation that state laws should guarantee "generous visitation rights" and require that they be used: "If a noncustodial parent . . . has not seen his child in, say, three months, that parent should be fined or otherwise put on notice that such conduct is unacceptable" (244). Downright radical and equally problematic is Hewlett and West's insistence that parents should be able to vote for each of their children under eighteen years old, which "would almost double the potential size of the parent vote" (241). These proposals amount to a reduction of married parents' freedom, even to leave abusive or miserable marriages, alongside electoral discrimination against nonparents (who probably vote in favor of children's welfare as often as parents do).

The New Familism: A Circle of Family Restorationists

In the forty-three footnotes of their sixth chapter, "The Disabling of Dads," Hewlett and West cite David Blankenhorn's work six times, David Popenoe's twice, and Jean Bethke Elshtain's once. Also cited is a 1996 fact sheet from the National Fatherhood Initiative (NFI). Blankenhorn, Popenoe, Elshtain, and those leading the NFI belong to a small circle of New Familists who, with a few other social scientists and policy advocates, are coordinating a movement to put divorce, fathers' rights, and child abuse on the public agenda. Significantly, Hewlett and West coauthored a 1998 article entitled "A Parenting Movement," and Blankenhorn has coedited an anthology entitled *The Fatherhood Movement*.[9]

Another key organization in the restorationist movement is the Institute for American Values (IAV), which Blankenhorn directs. As Judith Stacey indicates, the IAV was once codirected by Blankenhorn and Barbara Dafoe Whitehead, who wrote the 1993 *Atlantic Monthly* article applauding Dan Quayle's diatribe against fictional unwed mother Murphy Brown.[10] Stacey notes that the research arm of the IAV is the Council on Families in America and that Blankenhorn directs the NFI. Currently, Elshtain chairs the Council on Families as well as the IAV's board of directors.[11] The inner circle of New Familists also includes Hewlett. In *When the Bough Breaks: The Cost of Neglecting Our Children* (1991), she says her "largest intellectual debt" is to Blankenhorn, Elshtain, and Popenoe (among others).[12] Hewlett's intellectual affiliation with these family restorationists puts her in problematic company from both feminist and social-scientific points of view. That affiliation also partly accounts for the tone and content of Hewlett and West's book.

This section of the chapter focuses on three authors whose works illuminate the New Familism. First comes Popenoe's *Disturbing the Nest: Family Change and Decline in Modern Societies* (1988). After also looking at another of Popenoe's books, I move to Whitehead's *The Divorce Culture* (1997). I then turn to Dana Mack's *The Assault on Parenthood: How Our Culture Undermines the Family* (1997) before returning to Hewlett's work.

Popenoe is a sociology professor and academic administrator at Rutgers University. *Disturbing the Nest* focuses on Swedish society.[13] It deploys a rhetoric of family decline centered on the family's loss of functions and its diminishing importance. "In Sweden," says Popenoe, "the institution of the family has declined further than in any other society" (xii). *Disturbing the Nest* documents that "decline" and comments on its ramifications.

For Popenoe, family decline means such things as that nearly half of Swedish babies are born to nonmarried women and that nearly one-fifth of Swedish households with children are headed by single parents (xiv, 174). For Popenoe, such "decline" has a number of causes. First, "self-fulfillment" and "egalitarianism" have superseded familism (9). Second, changing gender roles promote familial instability by weakening marriage (224, 225). Popenoe observes that "gender-role equalization has progressed further in Sweden than it has in most other countries. It may be precisely this reality that has strained the Swedish marital relationship" (229). Third, Popenoe claims that radical feminists mostly applauded family decline as a "positive human achievement" and that women's rights have reached an apparent apex in contemporary Sweden (31, 176). These developments, he repeatedly implies, promote family decline. Swedish mothers don't stay at home "as much as they used to"; Swedish husbands are "losing some power and authority over family decisions"; "power within the home is becoming more symmetrical"; parents "have been turning away from the care and support of children" (199, 301, 309).

Popenoe says little about the ill effects of Swedish family "decline." His discussion is limited to looking at a few mild-mannered statistics on the problems of Swedish young people that are probably related to family changes (316–321). Nearly as remarkable as Popenoe's failure to say much about the negative effects of so-called family decline in Sweden is his protofeminist explanation of that decline:

> [W]omen with newfound economic security no longer need to be bossed around by a husband on whom they were once financially dependent. Women in bad marriages no longer need to stick it out because of economic necessity. A woman can tell a man who wants to marry her that she does not need a breadwinner . . . what she wants is a friend, an intimate companion, and someone who will equally share with her the domestic work load of a family. (222)

In societies like Sweden and the United States Popenoe thus sees a "postnuclear-family trend" associated with women's advancement, which is part and parcel of a larger cultural trend toward individualism (230, 295, 328). (Like Popenoe, Hewlett and West [95–96, 134] also lament the growth of individualism since the mid-1960s.) Popenoe implies that that trend ties in with a "new version of rights discourse" that has been gaining force "over the past 30 years" (x).

Eight years after the publication of *Disturbing the Nest*, Popenoe's *Life With-*

out Father appeared. Its subtitle suggests its biases: *Compelling New Evidence That Fatherhood and Marriage Are Indispensable for the Good of Children and Society*.[14] Its acknowledgments also point to Popenoe's slant on the family. There he mentions meetings of the Council on Families in America, described as an "interdisciplinary group of family experts and scholars *from across the political spectrum*" (8, emphasis added). Popenoe, who does not mention the formal connection between the Council and the IAV, thanks more than a dozen Council members, including Hewlett as well as Elshtain, Whitehead, and Blankenhorn.[15] He also cites two members of the NFI which, to repeat, Blankenhorn directs. Finally, Popenoe cites Amitai Etzioni as "particularly influential." Later, we will look at the overlap between the New Familists and the Communitarian movement launched by Etzioni.

Life Without Father considers the "dramatic decline of marriage" in American society brought about by a high divorce rate as well as a high incidence of "unwed motherhood." These developments have led to a "new fatherlessness" (2). Popenoe focuses on fatherlessness in the belief that fathering ("more cultural") necessarily differs from mothering ("more natural") and is essential for children and society (135). He links fatherlessness with "crime and delinqency; premature sexuality and out-of-wedlock teen births; deteriorating educational achievement; depression, substance abuse, and alienation among teenagers" as well as growing poverty among women and children (3). Using a sociobiological perspective and drawing from polemical as well as sociological works, Popenoe claims adequate fathering usually comes only from biological fathers. He also argues that involved fathering anchors men in society and stabilizes their behavior.

Popenoe believes American fathers have long "been losing authority within the family and psychologically withdrawing from a direct role in childrearing" (6). His main concern again lies with the "past three decades" of "continuing social decline," which includes a "divorce culture" (13, 28–29) rooted in individualism and self-absorption. Popenoe laments a "growing culture of nonmarriage" based on the notion that "fathers are unnecessary, superfluous, obsolete" (35). He concludes that American society has gotten too individualistic (48). Popenoe favors the 1950s, when the modern nuclear family enjoyed a "final moment of flowering" (135).

Although Popenoe has little explicit to say about feminism here, he does emphasize that "A contrary perspective on recent family-related cultural trends . . . sees the father-mother nuclear family as inherently authoritarian, our cultural past as pervasively negative, and 'alternative family forms' as representing social improvement" (193). Since he goes on to mention patriarchy and domestic imprisonment, one can be confident Popenoe is talking about a feminist perspective. Soon he reiterates his opposition to this perspective: "Fathers are not merely would-be mothers. The two sexes are different to the core, and each is necessary . . . for the optimal development of a human being" (197).

Put differently, "Parental androgyny is not what children need." Nor, says Popenoe, does androgyny "seem to provide a good basis for a lasting marriage" (212). Rather, "women as a general rule should be the primary caretakers of infants at least during the first year to eighteen months of life." Moreover,

> out-of-home child care normally should be limited to not more than ten to twenty hours per week for at least the first year of life; a number of studies have found negative effects on child development when out-of-home child care exceeds this amount. After age three there is little evidence that high-quality day care has negative effects . . . and the amount of time spent in day care and preschool activities can increase. (214)

Popenoe also recommends a "two-tier" divorce system where couples with children would face a "longer waiting period" plus "mandatory marriage counseling or marital education" (222–223).

Whitehead's work resonates with Popenoe's. *The Divorce Culture* does not include "feminism" in its index but does have entries for "individualism," "father(hood)," and "single-mother(hood)." Whitehead acknowledges her "colleague and friend David Popenoe" as well as Norval Glenn, a sociologist whom Popenoe also acknowledges. Scott Coltrane aligns Whitehead's work with the "similar message . . . championed by [her] colleagues at the Institute for American Values and its Council on Families." He mentions Blankenhorn, Popenoe, and Elshtain as contributors to "a public campaign to revive the supposedly failing institution of marriage." Additionally, Coltrane cites Glenn's study of college textbooks on families that decried their "anti-marriage" stance. Coltrane reports that the IAV, which published Glenn's study, "printed 10,000 copies . . . , distributing them to publishers, college instructors, and the popular press."[16]

Whitehead, whose advanced degrees are in social history, observes that after the 1950s, Americans shifted "away from an ethic of obligation to others and toward an obligation to self."[17] More pointedly, she claims "the new divorce era began . . . when women were gaining new freedoms and opportunities in the world of work and public life" (45). Whitehead devotes a lot of attention to single mothers, treating their motherhood partly as an "expressive pursuit" (62–65). She argues that from the mid-1960s—the past thirty years again!—"liberal opinion increasingly devoted itself to championing the rights and interests of single mothers and to condemning those who raised concerns about the impact of divorce on children as illiberal" (80). Logically enough, Whitehead emphasizes the advantages of an "intact two-parent family" for children. The "long-term damage experienced by a *majority*" of children of divorced couples includes "disruption in their relationship with their fathers" (103).

While advancing arguments akin to Popenoe's, Whitehead takes potshots at new reproductive technologies as well as feminist notions of equality. She likens artificial insemination, for instance, to the sexual exploitation of women's bodies: "The instrumental use of men's bodies to gratify women's desires for solo motherhood raises the same concerns that women have rightfully raised about men's exploitative use of women's bodies to satisfy their desires" (146). Also problematic is Whitehead's insistence that "marriage as a 50–50 deal . . . is likely to be both tense and unstable." She says "marital commitment" rests on "the giving over of oneself to another" (193).

Appearing the same year as Whitehead's book was Mack's *Assault on Parenthood*. Mack's title resonates with Hewlett and West's, while her acknowledgments resonate with those of Popenoe and Whitehead. She is "grateful for the support of [her] colleagues at the Institute for American Values as well as the network of scholars affiliated with the Council on Families in America." She names Blankenhorn, Elshtain, Glenn, Popenoe, Whitehead, and Hewlett. For the most part, Mack's book revolves around her problematic contention that most "social scientists, political commentators, and journalists admit that both out-of-wedlock childbearing and divorce put kids at risk and that the crisis of youth has a lot more to do with family structure than we previously thought."[18] Like Hewlett and West, Mack wonders whether child protection has gone too far in American society. Her second chapter, "Child Welfare, Family Destruction," claims that "overreporting of child maltreatment has become the greatest single problem of the child welfare system" (59). Like Hewlett and West, Mack cites the case of the man accused of child abuse "for tickling his nine-year-old stepdaughter on the tummy."

Mack also dwells on child care outside the home, arguing that "Nowhere . . . are the cross-purposes of parents and professionals so evident as in the recent government push to expand day care and early preschool programs for the poor, at a time when middle-class parents are reassessing the supposed social and educational benefits of group care for young children" (179). Mack says the evidence about "even the highest-quality group care experiences in early childhood—whether in a daycare or preschool environment—is very discouraging" (181). In that same chapter, "The Workfare/Day Care Trap," Mack cites Blankenhorn to support her assertion about the "worst pathologies of inner-city youth" deriving from the "conspicuous absence of healthy male role models in their homes and neighborhoods." Before long, she lambastes feminists such as the "ideologue Betty Friedan" who "hold[s] up the model of the working mother as the epitome of women's liberation" (194). Mack concludes that characterizing feminists as "spoiled is painfully accurate" (196).

Contrasting with their supposed self-centeredness is the New Familism, the focus of Mack's ninth chapter.

The New Familism centers on parents' rights and family privacy. For Mack this "familism" rests on "a culture of no-compromise, a culture whose primary message could be depicted by a 'Keep Out!' sign" (306). From her point of view this countercultural familism pits itself against a culture where

> a powerful contingent of political and professional advocacy organizations, ranging from the American Civil Liberties Union and People for the American Way to Planned Parenthood, . . . the National Organization for Women, and the League of Women Voters, is determined to convince the public that parents don't need rights and would only abuse them. (286)

Like other New Familists reacting against this "family-hostile culture," Mack sees divorce among its "chief evils" (300).

Hewlett's *When the Bough Breaks* adopts the same stance toward divorce, which she sees as a cause of fathers' lesser involvement with their children over the past thirty years (95–6). Another source of children's familial losses during this period is feminism:

> In progressive circles, discomfort with the family enterprise became particularly pronounced in the 1960s with the emergence of the women's liberation movement. Modern feminism began as a critique of the family. . . . For Friedan and other leaders of the movement, liberation meant moving out of the domestic sphere. (185)

Hewlett concludes that under these circumstances "there is often no one at home to look after the children or worry about the moral tone of society" (280). She thus makes daughters' and sons' presumed losses something that mothers perpetrate. As in her work with West, however, she insists that "the plight of our children is not solely or even mainly a woman's issue" (95).

Having come full circle back to Hewlett's work, we might gain further insights into the New Familism by looking briefly at some of Etzioni's thinking. Long a prominent sociologist, Etzioni is perhaps best known now for launching the "Communitarian movement, . . . an environmental movement dedicated to the betterment of our moral, social, and political environment."[19] The movement launched its own journal, *The Responsive Community*, in 1991. There is considerable overlap between this movement and the New Familism.[20] Although some key players in each movement are the same, such as Elshtain, my focus is their thematic overlap. To illustrate it, I look at Etzioni's chapter on "The Communitarian Family" in *The Spirit of Community: The Reinvention of American Society*.

Like Hewlett, Etzioni explicitly refuses to make the "parenting deficit" women's responsibility or a women's issue. Early in the chapter he insists that "the issue is the dearth of parental involvement of both varieties: mothers and fathers" (55). At the chapter's end Etzioni reiterates that "both parents share the responsibility to attend to their children. The community should not stigmatize but appreciate those who do" (88).

Yet some of Etzioni's observations undermine these stances. He emphasizes, for instance, that "it is the parents who flew the coop," not the children. Significantly, he immediately adds that "Those who did not leave altogether increased their investment of time, energy, involvement, and commitment outside the home" (56). Etzioni is pointing his finger at mothers, since in industrial societies fathers had long since flown the coop as breadwinners. He also observes that films like *Kramer vs. Kramer* helped to legitimize women's equal right to "find themselves, to discover their identities, and to follow their careers the way men do" (63). Etzioni goes on, "Some blame this development on the women's rights movement, others on the elevation of materialism and greed to new historical heights. These and other factors may well have combined to devalue children" (63). Before long, Etzioni's gender-inclusive usages again point to women rather than women and men alike, just as his earlier use of "parents" implied "mothers." He writes, "Parents in a Communitarian family . . . are entitled not just to equal pay for equal work, equal credit and housing opportunities, and the right to choose a last name, they also must bear equal responsibilities—above all, for their children" (63).

Similar to such rhetorical sleights of hand are Etzioni's hints at what counts as a "real" family. He notes that most "preschool children (about 78 percent) live in *functioning families* of one kind or another." Etzioni goes on to cite the percentage of families with children where "the father works outside the house and the mother is at home," where "both parents work full-time," and where "the married mother works part-time." He immediately says, "The two-parent family is less common than it used to be, but it is far from dying out" (73). For Etzioni, then, "functioning families" means not all two-parent families, which include both cohabiting heterosexual and homosexual couples parenting together, but specifically dad-mom families. "Functioning families" also excludes single-parent households headed by women or men, homosexual or heterosexual. Moreover, dad-mom families are at their best when at least one parent "stays home." Etzioni advocates child allowances over income tax exemptions for children because the latter favors dual-employed parents "over those households in which one of the parents (or both, in part) stay home to attend to the children." Etzioni concludes, "A public policy that relies on child allowances is one that is truly pro-family" (84).

Like many family restorationists, Etzioni bemoans the ill effects of child care outside the home. For children under two years old, such care is best avoided at all costs. Even those two to four years old, Etzioni believes, may not "cope well with a nine-to-five separation from a parent" (59). Thus, he advises parents to consider doing their paid work in the home, sharing jobs, working different shifts, or one parent working full-time and the other working part-time outside the home (70).[21] He also advises Americans to discourage divorce by shifting their values away from consumerism and careerism toward familism, responsibility, and community.

Unlike many New Familists, Etzioni does briefly admit that his viewpoint is partly a matter of interpretation. Discussing divorce's effects on children, he says, "There may be alternative explanations for some of these findings, and they are far from universally accepted. For example, Jessie Bernard, a distinguished sociologist and feminist, reviewed several early studies of stepchildren; she found a more varied and complex picture than the studies cited above" (77). On that note let us turn to a more varied and complex picture than the one the New Familists sketch.

Fatherlessness, Motherlessness, and the Postnuclear Family

Alternative pictures of today's American families are widely available, especially from social scientists specializing in the study of the family. In fact, some of them have formed an organization that offers correctives to the restorationists' picture of family life in American society. Named the Council on Contemporary Families, this organization's board of directors includes Judith Stacey and other prominent social scientists, such as Stephanie Coontz, Barbara Risman, and Arlene Skolnick.[22] These and other social scientists largely agree on some key ideas that challenge restorationist thinking.

First, fatherlessness cannot in and of itself have the consequences sometimes attributed to it. Statistical correlation in no way implies cause and effect. That father absence is associated with lower academic achievement, for instance, does not mean that the former leads to the latter. Both factors could be effects of some other factor such as chronic, intense conflict between mother and father. Besides, if fatherlessness had the causal impact the New Familists assign it, its effects should show up virtually everywhere that fatherlessness widely occurs. In actuality, however, Sweden "has almost the same percentage of woman-headed single families as the United States but only a fraction of the teenage pregnancy rate, delinquency rate, and other problems."[23] As we saw, Popenoe's own study implies as much. Moreover, crosscultural comparisons show that "[t]he local setting is a particularly important and relevant part of single mothers' lives. . . . Single mothers' neighbourhood support networks represent local structures of interaction, giving them access to resources or being resources in themselves. "[24] American single mothers commonly lack adequate social support.[25] Also, the support African American children get from family members besides their parents may explain why they "show fewer deficits than their white counterparts" from single-parent households.[26] As Alisa Burns and Cath Scott put it, "Children can get by with one parent but not so successfully with only one adult supporter."[27]

Second, changes in family structure often parallel other changes in social structure, especially the economy. Both the industrialization of Western Europe and North America and economic development around the globe today show how economic change promotes nuclear units where one or more adults leave the home daily for the job market. The latter market, interplaying with welfare policies and other social factors, dramatically affects rates of impoverishment and single-mother households. In American society, for example, "there are neither enough good jobs nor enough good husbands to provide every American woman with enough money to support a family."[28]

Third, like the effects of economies, those of divorce vary with social, cultural, and legal contexts. Overall, divorce "typically has complex costs and benefits for individual children."[29] In any event "Loving, harmonious families are unlikely to break up."[30] Furthermore, a lot of the ill effects associated with divorce may derive from "aspects of family functioning that were present before the divorce."[31] Thus, comparing children of divorced parents with children of nondivorced parents means, on average, comparing children who have lived in stressful, conflict-ridden households with those who live in less stressful, less conflict-ridden households. Without controlling for the character of daily interactions and family culture as well as social context, studies comparing children from "broken" and "intact" families cannot single out the effects of divorce per se.

Fourth, even studies without that shortcoming cannot show which statistically significant associations are humanly significant. Michael R. Stevenson and Kathryn N. Black generalize that "offspring of divorced and never-divorced parents differ in a variety of ways, but . . . most of these average differences are not large. In fact, in some content areas, although statistically significant, the differences are trivial."[32] Sara McLanahan, the author with Gary Sandefur of an influential study widely cited by New Familists, makes the same point differently: "If all children lived in two-parent families, teen motherhood and idleness would be less common, but the bulk of these problems [the family restorationists typically cite] would remain."[33]

About divorce restrictions, McLanahan observes that making it harder to divorce makes "marriage less attractive relative to cohabitation." Like some of the other recommendations that family restorationists advance, those about waiting periods for divorce take no account of gender differences. When a husband resists a divorce, waiting periods can put a wife and their child(ren) at risk of extreme stress, if not physical intimidation and violence. Family restorationists also fail to take gender into account at other junctures. When they insist, for instance, that they mean for both fathers and mothers to be seriously involved in raising their children, they conveniently set aside the deeply gendered (and gendering) world of marriage and family. The New Familists write as if wives and husbands can negotiate a practical equality as parents that even feminist parents find difficult to achieve together.

Although the New Familists seem sociologically naive, little naivete would seem to be at work here. Instead, their works illustrate how "often the rhetoric of 'strengthening families' conceals efforts to reimpose traditional forms of patriarchal control over women" and children.[34] Overall, these authors augment a countermovement against feminists as well as against lesbians and gay men.[35] To that extent, the New Familism resonates with or even augments the fathers' rights movement, a part of the men's rights movement that emerged in American society in the 1980s.

The fathers' rights movement seeks to "increase men's legal control over their children outside marriage while effective day-to-day care of children remains where it always has been—with mothers."[36] Whether they participate in the fathers' rights movement or not, many divorced, noncustodial fathers seem bent on increasing their prerogatives without much increasing their responsibilities. Terry Arendell's study of seventy-five divorced fathers in New York State showed, for instance, that more than three-quarters felt victimized by their divorce, and most felt that the child support demanded of them was excessive. Yet their average payments were only $283 per month, or less than $75 a week. Arendell found that "[e]ven men paying less than $100 a month argued that their support payments exceeded children's needs" and that many dismissed maternal custody as a "logical outcome" of mothers' primary caregiving.[37] At least one study has shown that such sentiments are common in fathers' rights groups. By and large, such fathers want to restore their "predivorce role." Because they take for granted mothers' child rearing, they tend to "discount or ignore" it while sizing up their postdivorce situations.[38]

Largely accepting a gendered division of household labor or setting gender entirely aside, at a minimum the New Familists typically offer rhetorical support for such stances. All the while, they also provide rhetorical support for such groups as the Promise Keepers, which involves "an antifeminist reassertion of essentialist views of male and female differences" and support for the "traditional two-parent family."[39] One feminist observer concludes that a "fantasy of benevolent domination" informs the Promise Keepers' perspective.[40]

To say the very least, family restorationists oversimplify the research literature on single-parent households and divorce. They also oversimplify—if only by omission—the gender dynamics whereby mothers end up doing the lion's share of child nurturing in two-parent households. They oversimplify their recommendations, too. Nowhere in the New Familist works at hand, for instance, are there recommendations about how to raise boys to be more nurturing, how to get fathers more positively involved with their children on a daily basis, or how to help mothers be comfortable with greater sharing of child-nurture responsibilities.

Yet a rich literature does address those very challenges. Kathleen Gerson has shown that involved fatherhood is likelier when the mother is strongly oriented to work (paid or not) outside the home, when a father's paid work leaves him time for additional modes of personal expression, and when men have gratifying interactions with children. Others have shown that "generative fathering" and "fatherwork" can deepen men's involvements with their children and that fathers' feminism promotes their greater involvement.[41] The studies are many, but family restorationists pay them little or no attention. What seems most at issue among the New Familists is the dramatic shift away from the nuclear family toward diverse family configurations. That shift, which entails a diminution of husbands' and fathers' historical rights and prerogatives, drives New Familists' concern with child protective services, custody laws, visitation rights, and "child support" at the expense of attention to children's well-being and rights. In the end the New Familism is more about family structure than children's welfare.

Irwin Garfinkel, Jennifer L. Hochschild, and Sara S. McLanahan imply as much when they describe a 1994 conference attended by academicians as well as representatives of various agencies, institutes, and foundations. The conference focused on policy issues concerning children. In its aftermath these three scholars concluded that "[s]ome of the dissension was ideological. Proposals that came closest to the sensitive issues of gender roles and racial interactions . . . produced the hottest debate and the least consensus. Disparate values about parental authority and children's rights also underlay intense discussions of school-based health clinics and child abuse."[42]

These scholars' perceptions extend to the New Familist literature. As Stacey and others have observed, what passes for discourse about children's well-being is often more about restoring the neotraditional nuclear family where fathers' roles, rights, and responsibilities are more clear-cut and less demanding.[43] During the "good old days" implied in this literature dads knew that their preferences held sway, that their work lay mostly beyond the home, and that they had a lot of latitude about how involved they would be with their daughters and sons. Significantly, Wini Breines, Margaret Cerullo, and Stacey saw all of this coming more than twenty years ago. They said then what needs reiterating now, namely, that "Soaring divorce rates . . . are evidence not of biological dictates nor of the end of ego strength but of the crisis in personal life generated by an oppressive, inegalitarian social order."[44] Fatherlessness as such thus merits no high priority on public agendas. In any case, those intent on making it a public issue need to emphasize that "we can reject the idea that fathers are superfluous without simultaneously reinvigorating old-time fatherhood and skewering those trying to build more egalitarian forms of parenting.[45]

In narrative G, Scott Coltrane illustrates such balance and inclusiveness. His is a narrative that, while first-person, builds up more around his professional judgments than his paternal experiences. Narrative H also departs somewhat from the other narratives we have read thus far. In it, R. W. Connell briefly touches upon how he nurtures his young child as he writes into the night. His narrative is noteworthy because of how matter-of-factly it speaks to the satisfactions of paternal nurturance and involvement. Finally, Steven Harvey, in narrative I, speaks in greater detail about those same paternal satisfactions. All three readings illustrate that Popenoe and other family restorationists notwithstanding, fathers can indeed "mother."

NARRATIVE G

Parenting in Transition

Scott Coltrane

While shopping for groceries a short time ago, I ran into Terry, a bright and vibrant attorney friend I hadn't seen in several years. As we stood in front of the produce bins, Terry used car keys to entertain a fidgety two year old and described the difficulties of balancing family and career: "I'll bet you can't imagine me as the domestic type, but things have changed since we had Megan. Now all I want to do is stay home and take care of her, and everyone at the office is questioning my commitment to the firm."

Listening to a monologue on the joys of baby care, I marveled at how this fast-track attorney had softened and slowed since we'd last seen each other. I found myself musing about some primal parenting instinct that had caused a profound re-ordering of priorities. As the conversation went on, I learned that Terry's new domestic commitments carried a steep price. According to colleagues, Terry was no longer considered "serious" about work and had been subtly relegated to a slower and less prestigious career track. The dilemmas Terry was facing are now commonplace for working mothers, but what makes this story unique is that Terry is a father.

When women sacrifice careers to have children, we consider it normal or even natural. So deep is our belief that mothers ought to value family over paid work, that we hardly give it a second thought when new mothers quit their jobs or cut back their hours of employment. When women approaching thirty still consider

From Family Man: Fatherhood, Housework, and Gender Equity *by Scott Coltrane.*

their careers to be more important than having babies, they tend to be chastised and labeled selfish. When employed mothers (which is most mothers these days) leave their young children in someone else's care during the work day, neighbors and in-laws still shrug their shoulders and wonder if there isn't something wrong with her. If mothers put their kids in child care to do something for themselves—like take a walk, go to a movie, or socialize with a friend—they are especially vulnerable to attack. As sociologists and psychologists have noted, our culture holds unrealistically high expectations that mothers will sacrifice their own needs for their children.

Compared to the complete self-sacrifice expected of mothers, being a father in our culture carries far fewer burdens. Whereas nineteenth-century fathers in Europe and North America were expected to be family patriarchs and stern moral teachers, twentieth-century fathers have been relatively uninvolved in the daily routines of family life. In common English language usage, to father a child means to provide the seed, to donate the biological raw material, to impregnate. Of course, people also expect fathers to be providers, which in the modern context means earning the money to pay the bills. But compare this to our unspoken and taken-for-granted expectations of mothers. To speak of *mothering* implies ongoing care and nurturing of children. *Fathering*, on the other hand, has typically implied an initial sex act and the financial obligation to pay.

Looking at the meaning of common parenting terms alerts us to the fact that mothering and fathering are gender-laden activities. What it means to be a woman or a man in our culture has been tied up with, and in a sense created by, what it is that mothers and fathers do within and for families. A woman who spoon feeds an infant, unceremoniously wipes a toddler's runny nose, or tenderly comforts a crying child is seen as exhibiting "motherly" love. In contrast, "fatherly" love is suggested by very different activities: perhaps playing catch on the front lawn; a suppertime lecture about the importance of hard work; or a tense evening chat with a teenage daughter's prospective date. We assume that mothers and fathers are very different, that they do different things with their children, and that these differences are fixed and natural. These assumptions mask the fact that ideas about parenting, and the actual practices of parenting, are constantly changing.

What parents do with and for children, like all forms of human activity, responds to the shifting demands of life within specific social and economic contexts. As the world around us evolves, so do our parenting practices. The simple fact of change is more "natural" than any supposed underlying genetic or spiritual reasons for mothers or fathers to act differently. Despite all the political and religious rhetoric about a mythical past when "family values" were secure, parenting and family life have always been subject to change and are going to continue changing as we move forward into the future. Instead of wringing our hands and trying to recapture some idyllic bygone era, we ought to pay more attention to why the changes are occurring and begin exploring how we can better adapt to them as we struggle to meet the needs of all family members. . . . The family changes we are facing will be neither easy not uniformly positive, but they do carry the potential of richer lives for men, more choices for women, and more gender equality in future generations.

• • •

At least in the ideal, modern fathering is no longer just procreation and bill paying. For contemporary fathers like Terry, becoming a father means reordering priorities and making a commitment to physically and emotionally care for children. The things Terry talked about in the supermarket—providing routine care for his baby daughter, feeling emotionally connected to her, and wanting to spend more time with her—are the sorts of things we have expected from women when they become parents. In fact, Terry created a stir at his office only because he was the "wrong" gender: he was a father acting like a mother.

According to recent media imagery, Terry is no longer an oddity. Single fathers and male nannies populate TV situation comedies as never before, and muscular men cuddling cute babies are used to sell everything from life insurance to fast food. While there are reasons to be skeptical about some of these idyllic portrayals, the line between fathering and mothering is beginning to blur. Even large scale government surveys are reporting substantial increases in the numbers of fathers who take care of children while mothers work.[1] It is becoming fashionable for fathers to act more like mothers; to shed their privileged outsider status and assume an active role in the routine care of their children. In short, it seems that American fathers are increasingly likely to be nurturing family men rather than the distant providers and protectors they once were.

• • •

Men's involvement in families, or lack of it, is a relatively new topic of concern for researchers and is part of a renewed interest in women's lives led by feminist scholars. My interest in these issues coincided with my own children's births over a decade ago. Unsatisfied with a peripheral role in their upbringing, I changed jobs several times, and eventually returned to graduate school to study sociology. While at the University of California, I studied with Nancy Chodorow, who recently had written *The Reproduction of Mothering*, an influential book on why women mother (and coincidentally, why men do not). Her complex neo-Freudian theory placed much emphasis on the establishment of gender identity within families where mothers do all the child care. She described an unconscious process wherein male children compensate for a deep and painful sense of betrayal by the mother through their rejection of things feminine, including the feminine parts of their own psyches.

Superficially, my own case seemed to contradict Chodorow's theory, insofar as I was raised by a nurturing stay-at-home mother and a distant breadwinner father. If the capacity and motivation for nurturing children is dependent on early childhood experience, then why was I, having been raised almost exclusively by my mother, so interested in being a nurturing caregiver to my own kids? With further study, I learned that Chodorow was suggesting that the capacity for nurturing exists in both boys and girls as a result of early experiences with a parent—usually the mother. It's just that men tend to suppress and devalue the soft and vulnerable parts of their psyches in an unconscious effort to maintain a firm sense of masculinity. But that sense of oppositional masculinity seemed so fragile and insecure to me that it appeared to be an oppressive trap. From my own experiences of personal growth as a child care worker in college, I wondered if caring for children might not provide other men with opportunities for fuller emotional lives. Could men reclaim a more complete sense of manhood that was not based on rejecting the softer or more "feminine" sides of themselves? That question led me on a search for the reasons why men might be drawn to caring for their children and into the realm of the sociology and social psychology of gender and families.

I was impressed by Chodorow's idea that gender socialization and the formation of masculine and feminine selves, with accompanying patterns of gender inequality in the larger society, were perpetuated through the organization of parenting. I became interested in the social forces that promoted men's assumption of family work and began to study the potential outcomes of involved fathering. I soon discovered that scholars had paid scant attention to fathers before the 1970s. Most psychologists and sociologists had assumed that fathers were peripheral to family functioning, even if their presence was usually deemed desirable. More recently, researchers have begun to help us understand how fathers directly and indirectly influence children and other family members, and how men's family involvements intersect with other aspects of their lives.[2] The few studies that have been conducted with men who are highly involved with their children suggest that fathers can "mother" in the sense that they can interact with and care for infants much like women do. What's more, the children of fathers who share responsibility for the everyday details of their upbringing tend to exhibit enhanced intellectual, cognitive, social, and emotional skills.[3] But a puzzle remains. Despite the potential payoffs of fathers taking a more active role in the family, large-scale surveys still show that most men avoid doing routine child care or housework. What's going on? Why is family work obligatory for women and mothers, yet still optional for men?

Regrettably, most of the popular books on men's changing family roles don't move us very far in answering these questions. We also have a few books by psychologists and social workers who present personal accounts from nurturing fathers struggling to become single parents or attempting to share parenting with their wives.[4] Although these advocates of the "new father" give us a glimpse into the inner lives of nurturing men and provide some useful advice to men who want to care for children, their analyses typically leave women out altogether. By focusing only on the men, and by ignoring most of the larger social, political, and economic contexts and consequences of their actions, these authors fail to give us a complete picture of men's family roles.[5]

Notes

1. See, for example, Martin O'Connell, *Where's Papa?, Father's Role in Child Care* (Washington, D.C.: Population Reference Bureau, 1993); Barbara Vobejda and D'Vera Cohn, "Dad's Help Seen Reducing Need for Day Care," *Los Angeles Times*, May 21,1994.

2. For reviews of research on fathers by psychologists, see Ross Parke, *Fathers* (Cambridge: Harvard University Press, 1981); Michael Lamb, *The Role of Father in Child Development* (New York: Wiley, 1981); and Henry B. Biller, *Fathers and Families: Paternal Factors in Child Development* (Westport, Conn.: Auburn House, 1993). For recent sociological studies of fathers, see Kathleen Gerson, *No Man's Land: Men's Changing Commitments to Family and Work* (New York: Basic Books, 1993); Shirley M. H. Hanson and Frederick W. Bozett, eds., *Dimensions of Fatherhood* (Beverly Hills, Calif.: Sage, 1985); Jane C. Hood, ed., *Men, Work, and Family* (Newbury Park, Calif.: Sage, 1993); Robert A. Lewis and Robert E. Salt, eds., *Men in Families* (Beverly Hills, Calif.: Sage, 1986); William Marsiglio, ed., *Fatherhood: Contemporary Theory, Research, and Social Policy* (Newbury Park, Calif.: 1995). For an excellent history of U.S. fatherhood, see Robert L. Griswold, *Fatherhood in America* (New York: Basic Books, 1993).

3. Kyle Pruett, *The Nurturing Father* (New York: Warner, 1987); Norma Radin, "Caregiving Fathers in Intact Families," *Merrill-Palmer Quarterly* 27 (1981): 489–514; Norma Radin, "The Influence of Fathers upon Sons and Daughters and Implications for School Social Work," *Social Work in Education* 8 (1986): 77–91; Barbara Risman, "Can Men Mother?" in B. Risman and P. Schwartz, eds., *Gender in Intimate Relationships* (Belmont, Calif.: Wadsworth, 1989); E. Williams, N. Radin, and T. Allegro, "Children of Highly Involved Fathers: An 11 Year Follow-up" (University of Michigan, Ann Arbor, 1991), cited in *Babies and Briefcases,* Hearings before the Select Committee on Children, Youth, and Families, House of Representatives, One Hundred Second Congress, First Session, June 11, 1991 (Washington, D.C.: U.S. Government Printing Office), 78–85.

4. Pruett, *The Nuturing Father*; Geoffrey Greif, *The Daddy Track and the Single Father* (Lexington, Mass.: Lexington Books, 1985). For an account of middle-age sons longing for contact with their fathers, see Samuel Osherson, *Finding our Fathers: The Unfinished Business of Manhood* (New York: Free Press, 1986).

5. For a more nuanced and critical look at shared parenting from a practicing feminist therapist, see Diane Ehrensaft, *Parenting Together* (New York: Free Press, 1987). On the subject of men's reactionary responses to women's modest gains, see Scott Coltrane and Neal Hickman, "The Rhetoric of Rights and Needs: Moral Discourse in the Reform of Child Custody and Child Support Laws," *Social Problems* 39 (1992): 40–61; and Susan Faludi, *Backlash: The Undeclared War Against American Women* (New York: Crown, 1991).

NARRATIVE H

The Materiality of Theory

R. W. Connell

I am sitting in a small room at the back of a brick house in south London, looking at a row of brick houses across a row of backyards, some with dogs that do not observe curfew. We are living with a close friend who has been fighting for women's interests in British trade unions, a long and grinding struggle. For globe-trotting intellectuals, London is the place to be in 1984: a woman prime minister is in power; the miners are on strike. It is the year of George Orwell, the year our daughter is born, the year of writing [my book] *Gender and Power*.

Literally writing, with a pen. I have a sensuous relationship with the text flowing slowly onto the page, not just a cerebral one; a relationship compounded of body, clothes, chair, ink, paper spread on the table, stillness of the room, light falling from the window, scurries in the backyards. These physical matters seem to be part of the way ideas solidify and sharpen, the way prose gets shaped.

The baby is involved with this text-making, sharing a lot of it asleep in a carry cot on the floor behind me. She gradually swims up to the top end and gets stuck with her head in a corner, at which point her grunts and gurgles change tone, I get up and lift her back to the bottom, and she starts the journey again. Sometimes the grunts turn to grousing, a familiar aroma steals across the room, and it is time for a paragraph break.

I mostly do the midnight feed, which gives Pam the chance of a solid sleep and me an excuse to be up late. I like writing at midnight. With the house still, and no lights on but the desk lamp (bad for the eyes!), I seem to be in the middle of a vast, dark space stretching out in all directions to the stars and nebulae. The only things sounding in it are the words I write and the grunted comments of the next generation.

From Feminist Sociology: Life Histories of a Movement, *edited by Barbara Laslett and Barrie Thorne. New Brunswick, N.J.: Rutgers University Press, 1997, 158–159.*

NARRATIVE I

A Geometry of Lilies

Steven Harvey

Flowers can bloom from the mathematical mind. Matt, the mathematician in the family, wrings petals from paper by practicing origami, the ancient, Oriental art of paper folding. Given enough paper and time, he can create a garden of intricate shapes. It is the complexity of origami that drives him—a hundred folds for a single design is not uncommon—but what he does has its own grace, a thumb-twisted elegance. The result is a wondrous mix of clarity and clutter, a paper knot in the form of a rose, perhaps, or a daisy, a creation that seems light and whimsical, the intricacy relegated to accordion folds hidden away.

With practice Matt learned most of what he needed to know and eventually mastered the subtleties of the art. In minutes now he can turn a sheet of colored paper into a flower, a donkey, or a star. No flat page in the house is safe. A quick inspection of one shelf turns up a dog, a swan, a camel, a grasshopper, a pig, and a panda. Pterodactyls, wings clipped snugly to the next shelf up, hover menacingly above the scene. I love to watch him amid such clutter create designs, his fingers producing abundantly within the constraints of his own devising. Love and discipline meet in these shapes, a boundless, creative energy in the mix. I see in them a rough draft for the geometry of lilies and catch a glimpse of the folds in our lives as well.

"There's something to keep you busy for the next twenty-one years," my brother-in-law said folding back the baby's blanket when Matt was born. Barbara—the new mother—and I looked at each other, dumbstruck, but after a night in which both of us had walked the crying baby we knew he was right. Something had changed. Until that time our lives had seemed one long Sunday afternoon, the only imposition on romantic bliss an enormous lab-collie that scratched the door on rainy nights. Now a baby!

It was not the work that worried me. An eager volunteer, I charged into dribbled breakfasts of strained peas, limped through afternoons hauling a tot on my hip, and dragged my feet all night over a square of carpet in the nursery, flopping in bed at dawn, a weary veteran, tired but okay. I could deal with drudgery, but the lost spontaneity ate at my soul. In my memory I see Barbara taping a calendar to the refrigerator the day we brought Matt home. I bet the hospital supplied it. From now on we live according to a schedule—that was the message sent with our folded bundle.

From A Geometry of Lilies *by Steven Harvey. Columbia: University of South Carolina Press, 1993, 129–131 and 41–42. Reprinted by permission of the press.*

We're not talking about a big loss here. Barbara and I were not flower children, but we did at times just take off, telling no one. I remember before Matt was born, going to the pancake house at midnight on a whim and eating a big breakfast. Barbara was in her ninth month, then, and I should have realized when she waddled with me to the checkout that changes were on the way. I didn't. "No dust upon the furniture of love": it could have been our motto. Two weeks later when the source of Barbara's waddle slept in my lap, we ate pancakes at home and turned in by ten.

We devised escape plans, of course, like everyone, hiring baby sitters and imposing on grandparents in order to slip away and taste the old freedom, but such wanderlust required planning, jottings on the calendar, groveling phone calls, and haggling over money. Moments away became precious, not to be squandered on the casual or frivolous; they were big events with maps, and grandma waving goodbye from the porch, and suitcases thrown in the back of the station wagon. Such occasions required haute cuisine. Sadly, I haven't had a midnight breakfast at the pancake house since.

And what does the poetry between the lines of our calendar say now?

Monday:	Alice (gym) 3:30 Elementary (Alice) 6:30 Soccer 5:30 Band Boosters
Tuesday:	Soccer 4:30 S & A 5:30 Nessa
Wednesday:	PICTURE DAY! Dr. Revell 10:30 Alice Marcia's 7:30 Body Shop!
Thursday:	(Sam) Elementary 7:00 Hum Workshop Lynne's 6:00
Friday:	Elementary 11: 00 Body Shop! 3:45 (Sam)
Saturday:	Franklin's brunch Matt Magazine Sale Key Club Party! Body Shop!

Dinner Dale
Soccer Game 4:00

Sunday: To Tennessee!

Ah, Sunday. Ah Tennessee! Leave soccer and PTA and gym behind. That's the wish.

• • •

My daughter Nessa sashays through the house in a long white robe that nightly falls from my wife's shoulders. To keep the hem from dragging the floor, Nessa stands tall and hitches the terry cloth up under her belt. The sleeves fall over her hands, but she takes up the slack by holding her arms out wide and high like a ballerina. Affecting a prissy look, she tours the downstairs, a celebrity throwing kisses to her one adoring fan, me. Eventually she returns to the clutter of her room with all the elegance of Columbia amid scattered toys of the New World.

Clothes, I'm reminded, make the child.

Our children regularly ransack a brightly painted army locker stuffed with dress-up outfits. The remnants of many Halloweens burst over the edges when they undo the latch. Orange plumes rise from the heap and tumble to the floor. Feathers, flounces, and furbelows float through clammy fingers; beads, bells, and boas leap to greedy hands. Swords and armor, brocaded dresses and flimsy chiffon things, Dracula's cape and Robin Hood's vest—these and various unidentifiable sequined suits magically appear to children who open the Pandora's box and try it all on. Fancy hats are saved for last, the straw bonnet, witch's cone, or plastic centurion helmet lending panache to any motley outfit.

In our house, dress up is the rule. It is not uncommon to sit down to Saturday breakfast with a bare-chested, pint-sized barbarian wearing a wide-brimmed pointed hat, a bandana, three necklaces, a sequined belt, and a plastic sword shoved down his pantleg. "Pass the sugar, *please*," you say in such company.

The costumes come, of course, with characters. Afternoons Nessa rounds up her gauzy and besequined little brother and sister for a game of Michelle and Lavinia. The kids are Baby Alice and Baby Sam who brave a terrifying world along with a gang of abandoned, imaginary waifs, Michelle, Lavinia, and Baby Perry, to name a few. Nessa is the school teacher, the mother, or the ever-vigilant elder sister saving her troupe from villains and the ravages of nature. Some days our bed—the site of many adventures—is a ship at sea carrying these charmed souls away from dangerous and exotic lands to safety in England or France. Other days it's a prairie schooner rumbling through hostile territory, tomahawks whizzing overhead. All the while Nessa, the ubiquitous nanny, scares the wits out of her tiny charges with wild-eyed screams about squid! and winds! and flaming arrows!

In Nessa's mind anything can happen. "'Tend like we're in the middle of the ocean and sharks are everywhere," she says in her make-believe singsong. Invented skies darken the Karistan sea as some fresh calamity strikes from the gloom. Fins rise out of the carpet. A snout appears. All is not well for our trembling band. Suddenly a slimy, disembodied hand—conjured up by words—flops over the gunwale! Alice screams, Sam runs into the bathroom crying, and all hell breaks loose until I, walking blithely across water, bring the ship crashing into calmer seas by telling them to hold down down the racket.

At night, when the children go to bed, I come across the plastic and lace of who they were strewn everywhere, evidence that we shed many outfits on the way to becoming ourselves. One trip through the downstairs and my arms are full.

• • •

PART

2

Maternal Bodies

CHAPTER 5

Mothers, Sexuality, and Eros

Throughout American culture mothers are widely supposed to be neither sexy nor sexual. Mothers can be attractive, to be sure, but the expectation is that their maternal commitments preclude being sexy, too. When the topic of motherhood and sexuality was discussed in Susan's seminar on Motherhood and Feminism, several students announced unequivocally that they could not think of their mothers as sexual persons. One told a story about herself as a five-year-old walking into her parents' bedroom while they were making love. She yelled at her mother—not her father—"You're a sinner!" Amidst laughter, the students recognized that they were denying their mothers, indeed all mothers, full subjectivity. But that intellectual insight did not dislodge their deeper attachment to the motherhood/sexuality divide. Over the past several decades, cultural images of chaste mothers have lost ground, but mothers' sexuality is still widely treated as mild-mannered and properly domesticated.

The divergence between maternity and sexuality points to the modern Western mind/body split, which in turn separates spirituality from sensuality and cognition from emotion. Like other cultural binaries, these presuppose either/or thinking; one cannot be both spiritual and sensual, just as one cannot be both maternal and sexual. Maternal desexualization also derives from a cultural pattern whereby women's passions and erotic energies are stifled or even denied in the interest (it seems) of attuning them more to men's and children's satisfactions than to their own.

In this chapter, we look at how the institution of motherhood constricts mothers' sexuality. We then turn to feminist theorists whose ideas about the erotic expand far beyond a narrow, genital sexuality. These ideas pave the way for our exploration of maternal eroticism. Next we examine breastfeeding as a concrete practice through which mothers' pleasures are often denied and sometimes reclaimed. In the final section, we present ideas about the mother-child relationship as a romance, a relationship of playful delight, mutual attunement, emotional intensity, and diffuse eroticism. We thus challenge the taboo that keeps us from thinking of mothers as enjoying an erotic relationship with their children, a relationship of physical as well as emotional intensity.

This chapter was written by Mary F. Rogers and Susan E. Chase.

Spiritual Mother, Sexy Wife

Like other theorists of women's sexuality, Simone de Beauvoir made much of the fact that the Virgin Mary "knew not the stain of sexuality." More generally, Beauvoir traced the spiritualization of women to the emergence of Christianity in Western societies, which made wives and mothers "the soul of the house, of the family, of the home." Indeed, women become "the soul of such larger groups, also, as the city, state, and nation."[1] Some nineteenth-century feminists contributed to this spiritual idealization of women by using it to fight for the expansion of women's rights. While arguing "for equal opportunity in education and employment and for equal rights in property, law, and political representation," they maintained that "women would bring special benefits to public life by virtue of their particular interests and capacities," namely, their superior moral character.[2]

Later, sexuality and reproduction became increasingly separate among modern Westerners, and "individual pleasure [became] a primary sexual goal." Yet women "remained more closely linked with reproduction, while men experienced greater sexual autonomy."[3] The persistent association of women's sexuality with their reproduction left them culturally positioned as sexual objects and reproductive instruments rather than as sexual and (sometimes) reproductive agents. Sexual liberalism did gradually widen women's opportunities for sexual expressiveness within marriage, but it left intact wives' relatively passive sexuality as well as the subordination of their needs and desires to those of their husbands and children.

Throughout the twentieth century that situation never fundamentally changed. Neither the so-called sexual revolution nor the emergence of second-wave feminism in the 1960s shifted sexual norms toward gender equality, even though more than a few feminist initiatives aimed in that direction.[4] Mothers' increasing labor-force-participation rates and high divorce rates did not shift them either. Nor did advances in contraceptive technologies equalize women and men sexually. Overall, American culture had no strong discourse of women's sexual desires.[5] Yet post-1960s American culture revolved around the "commercialization of sex and the sexualization of commerce," which guaranteed "a visible public presence for the erotic." John D'Emilio and Estelle Freedman observe that "exploitable as it was for profit, sex had become resistant to efforts at containment that failed to address this larger economic matrix."[6] In only one institutional arena did the containment of sex persist. The institution of motherhood remained a desexualized stronghold undercutting women's sexual agency.

What all of this means, among other things, is that sexuality, sexual passion, and eroticism continue to be defined mostly in male-centered ways. Without any established discourses of female sexual desire, sexuality remains a tangle of meanings, desires, and experiences understood mostly in boys' and men's terms. At best, women's sexuality gets seen as different from or other than men's. When motherhood is added to the mix, sexuality disappears as a vibrant, significant dimension of women's lives.

Consequently, mothers who present themselves as sexual or sexy are deemed "bad" mothers. Rock star Courtney Love's "transgressive style of mothering" is illustrative. Her "most damaging activity as a mother is her refusal to deny her sexuality." On top of everything else (including her stagediving), Love "uses her 'bad' mother persona in the same way she uses her 'bad' girl persona." By dramatically rejecting the "normative image of a mother as desexualized or asexual," Love defies cultural mandates to choose between maternity and sexuality.[7]

Sometimes the limitations on mothers' sexuality are downright punitive. Many lesbian mothers have lost custody of their children and had their visitation rights restricted for no other reason than their sexual orientation. Ellen Lewin notes that both lesbian and heterosexual mothers often respond to the ever-present fear of losing their children with "strategies of appeasement," which include "keep[ing] a low profile (particularly if they are lesbians or are living with a lover), abandon[ing] claims to marital property and to child and spousal support, and compromis[ing] on such issues as visitation." Some women bar lovers from their homes so that their children, and especially their ex-husbands, will not discover that they have the audacity to have a sexual life.[8] The stress of living such a compartmentalized life can be extreme. Moreover, it's hard to imagine that this deception is in children's best interest. But such contortions are a direct result of the stubborn wedge our society has driven between motherhood and sexuality.

Unmarried mothers' sexuality is under the watchful eye of the state in other circumstances as well. In her study of welfare policy in several Wisconsin counties, Renee Monson notes that unmarried mothers who receive welfare benefits must cooperate with the child support office's attempts to establish paternity so that fathers can be forced to provide support. If they don't cooperate, their benefits could be cut. Mothers' sexual activity is a central issue in the process: "Two questions about her sexual partners and practices are necessary to meet the minimum legal requirements for starting a paternity action against a man named as the sole alleged father: whether she had sexual intercourse with the alleged father during the conceptive period [the two-month period eight to ten months prior to birth or her due date] and whether she had sexual intercourse with any other man during the conceptive period."[9] While this information may help to establish paternity, the overall process is invasive and biased. First, women are sometimes asked for information irrelevant to establishing paternity, such as the exact location where sexual intercourse took place (287). Second, alleged fathers are not usually asked about their sexual behavior. When men are asked about sexual matters, "the woman's veracity and sexual practices [are] almost always at issue" (285). Third, women's ability to protect their sexual privacy varies by social class. Women not on public assistance could "choose whether to cooperate with the state's efforts to establish paternity; in effect, they could use their economic status to 'purchase' their sexual privacy and autonomy, but women who received AFDC or MA could not" (292). Such policies force economically disadvantaged mothers into at least an economic relationship with the child's father, whom they may have worked hard to extricate from their lives.[10]

As these examples illustrate, thinking about mothers as active sexual persons is difficult in a culture that largely reduces women's erotic lives to genital heterosexuality sanctified by marriage. Yet such thinking is essential if we are to make discursive space for the lived experiences of all mothers, especially those that come across as perverse, weird, or unintelligible. Many people, for instance, may find it hard to make sense of, let alone accept, the lifestyles of the African American teenage mothers whom Sharon Thompson studied. These mothers took some pride in the "entertainment and support" they were able to squeeze out of the "meager resources that came their way." While they protected themselves against sexual exploitation, they did their best to "get and keep the pleasures of sex and romance" in their lives. Even though their "triumph is marginal and unstable," it speaks to an insistence on having a sexual life alongside a maternal one.[11]

So obstinate is the divide between motherhood and sexuality that contemporary feminists have sometimes contributed to it (see chapter 1 on cultural feminism). Jane Flax notes that "[i]n the 1980s a curious dynamic emerges in feminist discourses: the more the maternalist dimension of femininity is valorized (and homogenized), the more sexuality is disowned, deconstructed, projected outward or made an effect of the action of others."[12] Under those circumstances women's agency was seen as residing in "maternity or nowhere." In Flax's judgment such feminist discourses reclaim women's agency, at least moral agency, by contrasting motherhood with female sexuality in patriarchal societies: "Sexuality may be exploited, distorted and misshaped by patriarchal power and heterosexuality, but maternity is portrayed as a relatively free space for the constitution and expression of female virtue" (149). In the process, sexuality disappears; "it is nowhere to be found, for example, in Ruddick's description of maternal practices" (150).

Eros Reclaimed and Redefined

Two feminist theorists have offered particularly powerful lamentations about this state of affairs. Both Starhawk and Audre Lorde affirm the erotic and urge that women reclaim and deploy its power. At the same time they lay grounds for rethinking the erotic. Like other feminists considered in this chapter, they help us move past male-centered, dualistic perspectives that treat our erotic lives as narrowly sexual and readily separable from other aspects of our lives.

Insisting that "our capacity for pleasure has a value in and of itself," Starhawk "affirm[s] pleasure, variety, diversity, fluidity, as sacred values worth struggling for." She says that erotic energy "holds the universe together."[13] Lorde comes close to that same conclusion. She emphasizes that etymologically eros is "the personification of love in all its aspects—born of Chaos and personifying creative power and harmony." In the opening paragraph of her essay "Uses of the Erotic: The Erotic as Power," Lorde treats the erotic as a "resource within each of us that lies in a deeply female and spiritual plane."[14] By linking the erotic with the spiritual from the start, Lorde opens up theoretical space for understanding the cultural wedge commonly driven between motherhood and sexuality.

Lorde enlarges that theoretical space by incorporating attention to oppression, too. She argues that "every oppression must corrupt or distort those various sources of power within the culture of the oppressed that can provide energy for change. For women, this has meant a suppression of the erotic as a considered source of power and information within our lives" (53). Not surprisingly, Lorde means by the "erotic" a great deal more than what we do. She centers the erotic on "how acutely and fully we can feel in the doing." Lorde thus resists perspectives that make spirituality a "world of flattened affect" (54, 56).

Lorde rejects the dualism not only between the erotic and the spiritual but also between the spiritual and the political, thus putting a provocative twist on the feminist shibboleth "The personal is political." She writes, "The dichotomy between the spiritual and the political is also false, resulting from an incomplete attention to our erotic knowledge. For the bridge which connects them is formed by the erotic—the sensual—those physical, emotional, and psychic expressions of what is deepest and strongest and richest within each of us, being shared: the passions of love, in its deepest meanings" (56).

For Lorde, the erotic is the arena of sensual experiences intense enough to evoke deeply physical, emotional, and self-expressive feelings all at the same time. Lorde's erotic thus parallels Roland Barthes's *jouissance*.[15] At least momentarily, the erotic blends intense experiences of transcendence and embodiment. One becomes one's body while flying beyond it. All the while, one feels powerfully and deeply. Lorde urges women to attune themselves to such feelings and the experiences evoking them: "To refuse to be conscious of what we are feeling at any time, however comfortable that might seem, is to deny a large part of the experience, and to allow ourselves to be reduced to the pornographic, the abused, and the absurd" (59).

Many women give in to the temptation to shortchange the erotic by denying their full feelings because intense feelings can seem self-centered, if not narcissistic. For mothers, in particular, norms about what one should and should not feel are well developed and widely promulgated in Middle American society. Above all, these norms downplay or even deny any erotic connections between mother and child. Cultural imagery revolves heavily around the chaste mother and the innocent child, while presupposing that chastity and innocence are incompatible with erotic experiences. The erotic gets relegated to the sidelines of social life, compartmentalized as a role- or situation-bound set of experiences rather than a continual source of energy and pleasure. Such imagery lays grounds for maternal guilt, shame, and ambivalence in the wake of richly sensual and sometimes erotic experiences of one's child(ren).

Cultural imagery can narrow the field of one's possible experiences by providing no respectable space for certain experiences and by withholding the vocabulary necessary for articulating such experiences. In Judith Butler's terms, not all experiences are "culturally intelligible."[16] Some experiences get rendered strange, obscene, or otherwise beyond the pale of what is acceptable or at least tolerable. Along the same lines, Flax notes, "What can appear as sexuality [or eroticism] depends upon complex networks of disciplinary practices."[17] Put differently, what one can readily experience as erotic depends heavily on what one's cultural community authorizes as "erotic." If it mandates that some experiences preclude eroticism, then most members will be disinclined to understand those experiences in erotic terms and others will feel uneasy or guilty for experiencing the erotic where it is culturally outlawed.

Let's look at a nonthreatening example. Alison Hawthorne Deming centers her essays on the "eros of place."[18] With that phrase she points to the sensory richness in the places that feel like home to her—the color and feel of the soil, the gurgling of a waterway, the raucous chatter of birds, the shafts of sunlight that find their way through clouds, trees, and patchy fog. These riches transport Deming in the ways that Starhawk and Lorde describe as erotic, yet most of us find it difficult—perhaps impossible—to think seriously about the erotics of trimming rose bushes in one's yard, of waking up to birdsong on a spring morning, or of gazing at and listening to the trees that beautify one's everyday world. The erotic is siphoned off from our everyday lives to such extremes as these.[19] We are not claiming that all such experiences are erotic. We are suggesting that sometimes such experiences affect us powerfully enough that we feel transported and fulfilled in unutterable, momentary ways.

Sally Hacker provides another example. Theorizing in much the same fashion as Starhawk and Lorde, she argues that modern "technology involves a strong sensual and erotic dimension." It has become "a passionate project for many of us"—so much so that Hacker deems it "important to explore relationships between technology and eroticism." All the while, she assumes that

"Whoever captures and defines erotic energy, a source of great social power, has more than an edge on the rest."[20]

At this juncture Adrienne Rich's theorizing is helpful:

> In arguing that we have by no means yet explored or understood our biological grounding, the miracle and paradox of the female body and its spiritual and political meanings, I am really asking whether women cannot begin, at last, to *think through the body*, to connect what has been so cruelly disorganized—our great mental capacities, hardly used; our highly developed tactile sense; our genius for close observation; our complex, pain-enduring, multipleasured physicality.[21]

Rich goes on to describe an embracing eroticism:

> We know that the sight of a certain face, the sound of a voice, can stir waves of tenderness in the uterus. From brain to clitoris through vagina to uterus, from tongue to nipples to clitoris, from fingertips to clitoris to brain, from nipples to brain and into the uterus, we are strung with invisible messages of an urgency and restlessness which indeed cannot be appeased, and of a cognitive potentiality that we are only beginning to guess at. (290–291)

Rich's stance presupposes "an inexorable connection between every aspect of a woman's being and every other" (291). Like the other feminists whose ideas we have considered, she rejects compartmentalized eroticism. For her, body and mind are as inseparable as sensuality and spirituality. Rich thus stands in the company of Beauvoir, Starhawk, Lorde, and the others. So, more recently, does Greta Gaard who sees eroticism not only in sexuality but also in "sensuality, spontaneity, passion, delight, and pleasurable stimulation."[22]

Some feminist theorists are thus reclaiming the erotic. They enlarge its meanings so that that sphere of experiences is less narrowly sexual and masculinist.

Maternal Eroticism

We need this enlarged definition of the erotic if we are to understand the joys and fulfillment that motherhood holds for many, perhaps most, women. We also need this expansive eroticism if we are to resist the maternal guilt and shame that so often impinge on women's relationships with their children. Perhaps predictably, depictions of mother-child eroticism sometimes show up in novels, cultural forms that provide relatively safe space for expressing and exploring experiences relegated to the margins of culture. In Arundhati Roy's *The God of Small Things*, for instance, the mother, Ammu, is wakened from a nap by her twin children, Estha and Rahel. They lie together on Ammu's bed, singing with the radio and talking about "afternoon-mares" (as opposed to nightmares) and other matters. Roy writes,

> In the afternoon silence (laced with edges of light), her children curled into the warmth of her. The smell of her. They covered their heads with her hair. They sensed somehow that in her sleep she had traveled away from them. They summoned her back now with the palms of their small hands laid flat against the bare skin of her midriff. Between her petticoat and her blouse. They loved the fact that the brown of the backs of their hands was the exact brown of their mother's stomach skin. "Estha, look," Rahel said, plucking at the line of soft down that led southwards from Ammu's belly button. "Here's where we kicked you." Estha traced a wandering silver stretchmark with his finger.[23]

The children query their mother about their birth and her stretchmarks. Gradually,

> Between them they apportioned their mother's seven silver stretchmarks. Then Rahel put her mouth on Ammu's stomach and sucked at it, pulling the soft flesh into her mouth and drawing her head back to admire the shining oval of spit and the faint red imprint of her teeth on her mother's skin. Ammu wondered at the transparency of that kiss. It was a clear-as-glass kiss. Unclouded by passion or desire—that pair of dogs that sleep so soundly inside children, waiting for them to grow up. It was a kiss that demanded no kiss-back. Not a cloudy kiss full of questions that wanted answers. (211)

Rarely do expressions of maternal eroticism show up in nonfictional accounts, such as in Lynda Marín's narrative, which follows this chapter.[24] Feminist philosopher Iris Marion Young offers another example. She tells how she began breastfeeding her child while sitting stiffly in a chair. She felt "efficient and gentle" doing that "mother work." Gradually, though, she found herself "drowsy during the morning feeding" and says that she decided to go

> to bed with my baby. I felt that I had crossed a forbidden river as I moved toward the bed, stretched her legs out alongside my reclining torso, me lying on my side like a cat or a mare while my baby suckled. This was pleasure, not work. I lay there as she made love to me, snuggling her legs up to my stomach, her hand stroking my breast, my chest. She lay between me and my lover, and she and I were a couple. From then on I looked forward with happy pleasure to our early-morning intercourse, she sucking at my hard fullness, relieving and warming me, while her father slept.[25]

Young expresses what often remains unexpressed and even inexpressible among those mothers whose experiences are similar to hers. Middle American culture stymies such expressions, sometimes even the recognitions they presuppose.

Barbara Katz Rothman notes the absurdity of this state of affairs:

> If we were to recognize the continuity, the continuing connection between a mother and her fetus/baby, we would not destroy their intimate rhythm. . . . But American mothers are specifically told not to take the baby to bed. We try to avoid intimacy, any hint of sexual intimacy, in the most profoundly intimate and essentially sexual of experiences. We ignore the fact that the baby has been sleeping in its mother's bed, and in its mother's body, all along.[26]

Roy, Young, and Rothman articulate the joy, pleasure, and intimacy that many mothers feel as they snuggle and play with their children. But these feelings are sometimes tinged with guilt, shame, and ambivalence. These feelings are surely promoted by the cultural invisibility and unintelligibility of maternal eroticism. They may also reflect the ugly specter of sexual abuse that lurks in the margins of any discussion of sexuality. It is important, then, to distinguish clearly between the erotic enjoyment of the mother-child relationship that we articulate here and the sexual exploitation of children. As illustrated by our examples, the pleasure and delight are not the mother's alone, but are deeply shared. Most children love physical intimacy with their mothers and others they love. Many children want more than they get. When adults respect children's boundaries (it's always ok for a child to say no to touch of any kind, just as it's ok for an adult to say no to touch of any kind from another adult), children learn respect for their own bodies as well as others' bodies. They also learn to trust those adults who use their greater power in children's best interest.

Child abuse, including sexual abuse, betrays a child's trust and violates his or her personhood. Like everyone who cares about children's well-being, we are deeply disturbed by its extent in our society, a topic we address in chapter 8. At the same time, we argue confidently that the mother-child eroticism we address here is an utterly distinct phenomenon from child abuse. To be sure, in everyday life, there are moments when boundaries need to be drawn, as Lynda Marín discusses in narrative J. Yet embracing that responsibility is completely compatible with embracing the pleasure, delight, and transcendence that belong to eros in the mother-child relationship.

Breasts, Breastfeeding, and Women's Pleasures

One way to theorize the dense connections we are exploring is to turn to mothers' experiences of breastfeeding. That turn will accomplish at least two things. First, it will give us an array of concrete experiences to consider that are central to many women's first months of maternity. Second, it will give us grounds for exploring women's diverse experiences of the same set of practices.

Pam Carter, who has done a lot of research on breastfeeding, notes that women's breasts "sometimes seem to have a life of their own."[27] Young has theorized along those lines by contrasting the fluidity of women's breasts with "the firm and stable objects that phallocentric fetishism" promotes in hegemonic cultural imagery. Young observes that braless breasts "are not objects with one definite shape, but radically change their shape with body position and movements. . . . Many women's breasts are much more like a fluid than a solid; in movement, they sway, jiggle, bound, ripple." Young goes on to emphasize that "phallocentric culture tends not to think of a woman's breasts as hers."[28] In this cultural context women's breasts are for men's pleasure, at least visually, and for children's first feeding.

Susan Bordo points out that the public image of feminists as "bra burners" reflects our society's uneasy recognition of "the deep political meaning of women's refusal to 'discipline' our breasts, culturally required to be so exclusively 'for' the other—whether as instrument and symbol of nurturing love, or as erotic fetish."[29] One sure sign of that cultural constriction around women's breasts is reactions to visible nipples. As Young notes, "Nipples are indecent. Cleavage is good—the more, the better—and we can wear bikinis that barely cover the breasts, but the nipples must be carefully obscured. Even go-go dancers wear pasties. Nipples are no-nos, for they show the breasts to be active and independent zones of sensitivity and eroticism."[30]

But nipples may also be no-nos for a second big reason, namely, their centrality to breastfeeding. Nipples point emphatically to the "apparent contradiction between breasts for feeding babies and breasts as symbols of sexuality."[31] As Young observes, "To be understood as sexual, the feeding function of the breasts must be suppressed, and when the breasts are nursing they are desexualized."[32] A good example is a draft document of the World Alliance for Breastfeeding Action that emphasizes how "breastfeeding empowers women and contributes to gender equality," thus implying a fundamentally feminist stance. Yet this document furthers the opposition between erotic breasts and maternal breasts by asking how breasts got "defined as sex objects for male pleasure *rather than* as the source of food and comfort for children. The sex industry and beauty industry have succeeded in objectifying women's breasts through media and advertising."[33] Excluded from this either/or setup (breasts are either for men or for children) are women's experiences of their breasts, including those that accompany breastfeeding.

Other advocates of breastfeeding also marginalize women's experiences, perhaps inadvertently. In *Milk, Money, and Madness*, Naomi Baumslag and Dia L. Michels examine "breastfeeding attitudes, customs, and practices of people over time, all around the world."[34] Yet on the question of women's experiences, they equivocate. On the one hand, they embrace the pleasurable relationship between mother and child embodied in breastfeeding: "breastfeeding is not only a woman's right and an infant's best start, but . . . it can also be a delightful experience for both mother and baby that is as beneficial physically as it is emotionally" (xxxi). On the other hand, they dichotomize maternity and sexuality: "Many men and women confuse breastfeeding with obscenity since the breasts are such a key aspect of female sexuality. This issue tends to go away as women gain confidence in, and respect the importance of, breastfeeding. They not only discover that very little of the breast needs to be exposed in order to nurse, but they also alter the image of their own breasts from being sexual organs to being magnificent feeding vessels" (xxx).

We understand why breastfeeding advocates sidestep women's experiences, particularly the topic of sensuality or eroticism in the mother-child relationship. Baumslag and Michel's primary aim is to document the physical benefits to mother and child in a worldwide context where more than a million infants die each year because they haven't been breastfed and because their mothers have no reliable, long-term access to safe water, baby formula, and postnatal health care (154). They demonstrate how breastfeeding has been eroded throughout the twentieth century, especially in developing countries, by the profit-driven practices of multinational infant formula corporations. In this shameful context, it makes sense that breastfeeding advocates would favor the culturally intelligible discourse of health benefits rather than the marginalized discourse of maternal eroticism. By using the former, they are much more likely to be heard, to have an impact. Nonetheless, the silence of breastfeeding advocates about women's experiences further shows how difficult—how culturally risky—it is to talk about maternal eroticism.

Feminist theorists' ideas about maternal eroticism make the apparent contradiction between breastfeeding breasts and sexual breasts seem like a woeful oddity. That lesbian sex often involves "nipple sexuality" suggests that the eroticization of women's breasts is probably no patriarchal plot.[35] The de-eroticization of breastfeeding mothers' breasts may be, however. Culturally de-eroticizing breastfeeding breasts means that overall women's breasts properly belong to someone else, namely, men and children. Women's breasts come to be defined by their other-centered functions. As eroticized objects, they give pleasure to men, at least visually; as de-eroticized instruments, they feed infants and young children. Both cultural constructions ignore how the breasts "shatter the border between motherhood and sexuality. Nipples are taboo because they are quite literally, physically and functionally, *undecidable* in the split between motherhood and sexuality. One of the most subversive things feminism can do is affirm this undecidability of motherhood and sexuality."[36]

We aim to do that sort of affirming. Instead of asserting anything definite and clear-cut, then, we affirm the diversity of experiences mothers have of their bodies while breastfeeding, and we explore how that diversity might be theorized. We begin by affirming with Carter that "women find breast feeding complex" and that feminists "should not try to pin down the truth of breastfeeding."[37] The better starting point is to appreciate that most of the women in Carter's study "found it difficult to name and evaluate the sensations that arose from breast feeding. Attempts to explain them were a sometimes uncomfortable mixture of feelings that 'belong' to mothering and feelings that 'belong' to sex."[38] While bottlefeeding "seems straightforwardly to do with feelings about successful mothering and the pleasure of doing the job properly," breastfeeding "arouse[s] strong feelings" that range from extremely positive to "entirely negative." Carter found that breastfeeding mothers' "positive feelings were sometimes 'motherly' and occasionally sensual." Few of the women "were able to express sensuality in positive terms." These maternal reports imply to Carter that the "language of motherliness" is a more comfortable resource than the "language of sensuality" for talking about the pleasures of breastfeeding.[39]

Carter concludes that cultural discourses and norms restrict how these mothers can talk about their breastfeeding experiences. Like the restricted cultural imagery of the erotic, there is no discourse for speaking about the full range of experiences breastfeeding women have. Their reports point to how

> sexuality for these women is inevitably connected with the ways in which their bodies are routinely talked about, looked at, examined and represented. The contradictions which they express and the ambivalence which they show, however, suggests . . . that there is more to this than a simple rejection of sexuality as "nasty and dirty." There are "places," "times," "situations" when women "enjoy" aspects of child bearing and breastfeeding and their own and other women's bodies, although it is often difficult for them to find a language in which to express this. (148)

Even the "experts" on breastfeeding face this linguistic challenge. In the advice literature on nursing Carter found that

> [t]he written texts . . . are almost constantly troubled by the demon of sexuality. Various strategic devices to manage this interloper have been adopted. One is to studiously ignore it. A second is to treat the idea that breastfeeding is sexual as a false Western idea. A third is to appropriate breastfeeding as a heterosexual activity. (135)

Those using the third strategy are "preoccup[ied] with the place of breasts and breastfeeding in the overall map of sexuality." Their concern is heterocentrist, however; they focus on how breastfeeding affects rates and experiences of heterosexual intercourse or how it can "accommodate what are assumed to be normal heterosexual relations" (137).[40]

Sociologist Cindy Stearns has studied how breastfeeding women experience and negotiate nursing in public. She found that they "uniformly emphasized the importance and/or necessity of learning to breastfeed discretely," by which they mean concealing the breast, especially the nipple. Many women spoke proudly about the invisibility of their public breastfeeding.[41] A major problem women associate with public breastfeeding is the gaze of male strangers. Many women are also concerned about how to breastfeed in the company of male family members, particularly fathers and fathers-in-law. Often, both parties feel awkward, so some women avoid that situation altogether. Like Carter, who emphasizes women's lack of a language for expressing their feelings, Stearns found that "many women could not articulate why they felt it was inappropriate to nurse in front of particular men but would say it just didn't feel right" (316, 317).

Some women deal with the cultural tensions embedded in public breastfeeding by defining it explicitly as an asexual act. One twenty-four-year-old mother stated: "I don't get turned on when I'm nursing my daughter. . . . It's like taking a bottle out of my diaper bag and giving it to her. In my eyes there is no difference. Milk is milk" (318). Stearns concludes, "As long as women's breasts are defined exclusively as 'for the other,' women will likely feel the need to negotiate their breastfeeding carefully. And, few women may even choose to breastfeed at all because of consequent fears of embarrassment and censure that come from defining breasts as only sexual and the act of breastfeeding as private behavior" (323).

Indeed, in the last several years, fourteen states have passed legislation stating that public breastfeeding is legal and should not be treated as public nudity. While public breastfeeding is not illegal in the remaining states, the very need to clarify its legality highlights our society's deep discomfort with it.[42] As Stearns notes, that discomfort results in a further imposition on breastfeeding women: "To be expected to hide breastfeeding is to hide much of the early work of mothering" (323).

Given these difficulties—not to mention the obstacles involved in trying to combine breastfeeding with full-time employment, it is not surprising that just over half of American mothers breastfeed their babies at birth. At six months, only 20 percent do, and when their children reach one year, only 6 percent still do.[43] Mothers who breastfeed older children, especially children who have learned to talk, are thought to have questionable motives. "Was the mother still breastfeeding because she could not 'let go' and did this thwart her child's need for independence? Was a woman breastfeeding for her own sexual and/or emotional needs as opposed to the child's?" Stearns notes that many women who breastfeed older children develop strategies for managing others' suspicions. Some restrict nursing to private settings; some develop "code words" for talking to their child about nursing.[44] Women committed to long-term breastfeeding thus find ways to resist the cultural sanctions against it. We need to push further, however. If we are to grant mothers full subjectivity, why shouldn't a mother's desire be one legitimate criterion for continuing breastfeeding? As Young indicates, "weaning is often a loss" for mothers.[45] What typically gets lost is not closeness per se, but a physical intimacy that mother and child will never again have. What gets left in the mother-child past, then, is profoundly physical and sometimes erotic, even sexual.

Robbie Pfeufer Kahn advocates nursing until a child is old enough to participate in the weaning process. She proposes that weaning can be negotiated, with both mother's and child's desires taken into account rather than pitted against each other. For example, Kahn describes how she and her son, Levin, settled their nursing relationship when he was three and a half. One afternoon when Levin mentioned another child who had just learned to walk, Kahn talked about how Levin was growing, too, and she expressed her own desire to stop breastfeeding now that he was an "older kid."

> That night I lay down with Levin by candlelight, as we often did. Looking by turns at the ceiling and at me he talked about how he wanted to stay up later at night now that he was "an older kid." . . . The direction of his conversation, like his glances to the ceiling, was up and away from the present. At one point . . . I couldn't tell if he was expressing a regret about stopping nursing so I asked, "How do you feel about stopping nursing?" Levin said, but not without a certain gentleness, "Oh I don't mind about that." . . . Although Levin probably doesn't remember our conversation, I wonder whether it isn't easier for a child to wean when the child participates in the decision. Perhaps the maternal body does not seem so remote and unretrievable as it might when weaning occurs before a child can easily and verbally communicate needs and wishes. I benefited from the language exchange too.[46]

What, then, constitutes a feminist approach to breastfeeding? The starting point is to look beyond the culturally dominant meanings of breasts as either sexual objects for men's pleasure or de-eroticized objects for nurturing infants. As several researchers suggest, we need to understand women's own experiences, needs, and desires more fully in relation to breastfeeding, acknowledging all the while that women's experiences are deeply conditioned by cultural constraints. Linda Blum, for example, points out that working-class African American mothers tend to reject breastfeeding because of its association with animal sexuality, an association that historically has been used to degrade black women's bodies.[47]

Following Barbara Sichterman, Young suggests that one radical approach would be to "shatter the border between motherhood and sexuality," in part by "pointing to and celebrating breastfeeding as a sexual interaction for both the mother and the infant."[48] Recognizing that feminists are torn over "whether to identify breastfeeding as a unique and important aspect of female sexuality," Carter "argue[s] that women have had to understand their breastfeeding experiences within an increasingly sexualized discourse" wherein we cannot determine whether or not "breastfeeding has an intrinsic meaning beyond the social relations and contexts in which it takes place." So its meanings "can, and should, remain an open question."[49] At the same time we should keep in mind that treating it "as [simply] natural disguises [its] complexity."[50]

Carter's stance seems reasonable, if not unavoidable, given the diverse influences on and meanings of breastfeeding. Our main concern is that no mothers' experiences of breastfeeding be written off as silly, perverse, or odd, especially when they involve erotic or sexual feelings. Silence about experiences of breastfeeding is detrimental enough; dishonesty about them is worse. Sadly, we recognize the pressures to be dishonest that breastfeeding mothers often face. Lauri Umansky reports, for instance, that Karen Carter lost custody of her child for a year after she called a hotline about getting aroused while breastfeeding.[51] Carter's is a 1990s story, not a Victorian one.

The Mother-Child Romance

Whether they breastfeed or not, many mothers and their children delight in one another's company and in the bond they forge with each other. It takes no stretch of the imagination to think of mothers and children as sometimes "in love" in the sense of sheer delight and mutual attunement.[52] Sometimes men also express this feeling. George Ritzer dedicates his book *Enchanting a Disenchanted World* to his grandson with these words, "Falling in love all over again."[53] Such experiences point to a (grand)parent-child romance. As a modern Western array of experiences, romance is not foremostly sexual. At most, it is parasexual, revolving as it does around appearances, anticipations, delight, and wonder.

We mean by "romance" the type of relationship and range of experiences implied by the romance genre in modern Western literature. Among its central characteristics, according to Barbara Stern and Morris Holbrook, is a heroine as its main character. Mother-as-heroine is a common cultural rendering, which tilts mother-child relationships toward the romance. The romance also idealizes sexuality and intimacy along chaste lines, which glorify courtship and premarital love over sexual activity. For the most part, mothers are allowed—even encouraged during some historical eras—to be "crazy about," "utterly devoted to," and even in some sense(s) "in love with" their young children, which again parallels traditions of romance. Stern and Holbrook emphasize that fantasy also weighs heavily in romances. "Happily ever after" wins out; suffering is short-lived; clear, sincere communication solves problems intractable in the real world. These thematic ingredients of the generic romance resonate with commonplace dreams mothers harbor for their children—safe and surefooted, even happy, arrival into adulthood; limited pain and suffering; and open, productive communication that prevents problems from getting out of hand.

Another characteristic of romances is their emphasis on consumption. In romances consumer goods "defin[e] the good life . . . and the dialog is replete with consumer references."[54] Ellen Seiter, among others, emphasizes how in societies like ours "parenthood is always already embedded in consumerism," with "women and children . . . blamed by scholars—most of them men—for their interest in shopping and consumer goods."[55] Except in the most impoverished circumstances, American mothers and their children are often joined together around activities and issues of consumption. Theirs is a relationship anchored in all the possibilities of the romance.

Here Georg Simmel's theorizing about flirtation is helpful. Like romance, flirting need not be sexual. Above all, it entails playing with possibilities, especially the alluring ones implied in the Perhaps. In formulating the "charms of . . . the Perhaps," Simmel theorizes what most mothers already know.[56] "Maybe" or "perhaps" are among the most tantalizing, promising words children hear. In mother-child dialogues around "maybe" or "perhaps" would seem to lie what Simmel points to as nonsexual but nonetheless heady experiences of flirtation.

During the middle decades of the twentieth century, psychoanalysts advanced the idea of a romantic bond between mother and child in terms of a "libidinal motherhood." Barbara Ehrenreich and Deirdre English summarize this "mother-infant love affair":

> The libidinal mother would rejoice in pregnancy and breastfeeding. She would seek no richer companionship than that of her own child, no more serious concern than the daily details of child care. She instinctively needed her child as much as her child needed her. She would avoid outside commitments so as not to "miss" a fascinating state of development or "deprive" herself of a rewarding phase of motherhood. No longer would motherhood be reckoned as a "duty." . . . Instead, mother and child could enjoy each other, fulfilling one another's needs perfectly, instinctively.[57]

Ehrenreich and English describe the maternal dimension of what Betty Friedan called the feminine mystique, in which women's fulfillment and pleasures are culturally constructed as child-centered and home-based.[58] Along with many other second-wave feminists, they criticize this version of the mother-child romance as unduly restrictive for mothers.

By the late 1970s feminists began to reshape the traditional psychoanalytic perspective by taking into account mothers' subjectivity as well as women's subordinate social position. Nancy Chodorow, a psychoanalyst and sociologist, has been most influential along these lines. In *The Reproduction of Mothering,* she focuses on the intense emotional bonding that often occurs between mothers and their children. Chodorow argues that in American society women commonly try to satisfy their emotional needs with and through their children.[59] Her framework revolves around the gender-differentiated psychic structures whereby girls typically learn other-orientedness and interdependence while boys typically learn self-orientedness and autonomy. These gender differences make it unlikely that (heterosexual) women can experience the same emotional richness with men as they can with their children (as well as with other women). Thus, Chodorow's framework imbues the mother-child relationship with terrific romantic potential.

Jessica Benjamin, a feminist psychoanalyst, has also had an enormous impact on conceptions of the mother-child relationship. She invites us to envision a mother-child romance that does not deny mothers' needs and desires. "It must be acknowledged that we have only just begun to think about the mother as a subject in her own right, principally because of contemporary feminism, which made us aware of the disastrous results for women of being reduced to the mere extension of a two-month-old."[60] As an alternative to the claustrophobia of "libidinal motherhood," Benjamin emphasizes "intersubjectivity" and "mutual recognition" between mother and child:

> The mother addresses the baby with the coordinated action of her voice, face, and hands. The infant responds with his whole body, wriggling or alert, mouth agape or smiling broadly. Then they may begin a dance of interaction in which the partners are so attuned that they move together in unison. This early experience of unison is probably the first emotional basis for later feelings of oneness that characterize group activities such as music or dance. Reciprocal attunement to one another's gestures prefigures adult erotic play as well. (173)

Benjamin theorizes the rhythmic, playful attunement of mother and child as the foundation for positive, healthy relationships throughout life. It is not the same thing as adult sexuality, but it is part of a continuum of pleasurable, loving ways of relating that include adult sexuality. While conventional psychological theories treat child development in terms of individuation and separation from the mother, Benjamin contends that independence and connection are both present at each stage of the relationship. In this scenario, a mother has room to develop other aspects of her identity, and a child learns how to relate through mutual recognition (rather than either domination or subordination). By beginning with intersubjectivity—a concept resonant with many mothers' experiences with their children—Benjamin makes room for understanding love in its various forms throughout the life course.

In "Lessons of the Milk," Kahn implicitly illustrates Benjamin's ideas. There she describes how her relationship with her son, Levin, developed as he grew up. At fourteen, Levin decided to live with his father, from whom Kahn was divorced. During this difficult time for both mother and son their attempts to connect seemed to fail.

> After a dark period . . . I realized that if I let my son see me when *he* felt like it, we would recover ourselves. . . . Sure enough, once I adopted the new (but, really, old) strategy (for what is this arrangement but the nursing rhythm conducted on a larger cycle of time and transposed onto a different spatial relationship of the body?), . . . we settled into a peaceful routine. . . . Invariably when we got together a time came when he returned to me to lean against my shoulder or to hold my hand for half an hour as we watched a movie . . . or to lean against my knees at a dog show.[61]

In this situation, Kahn gave her son what he needed (space) in order to reconnect with her. At other times, he orients to her needs. "As I age, when on occasion we touch, I feel him nurturing me." Over the years, Kahn and her son develop new routines and negotiate anew their departures and reconnections. "As the years stretch out like a bright ribbon from his early childhood, as each change comes over his life and mine . . . we find our way back to one another, always in a new way but always with the old imprint of the language of birth" (377). By "language of birth" Kahn means the nurturance and mutual recognition that can begin with birth and continue through nursing and beyond.

The bond of love that Benjamin and Kahn describe is what most mothers probably hope for with their children, a bond that grants both mother and child full subjectivity within their connectedness. Yet the romantic attachment characterizing this relationship—mutual attunement, emotional intensity, playful delight, diffuse eroticism, departures and returns—remains an underreported and underrecognized dimension of many women's mothering. In addition to the division between motherhood and eroticism that we have already discussed, our society's focus on individualism makes it difficult for many mothers and children to acknowledge and put into practice the deep feelings they have for each other.

We should not be surprised, then, when adults yearn for reconnection to their mothers' maternal bodies. Drawing on one of Tolstoy's biographies, Kahn notes that a few years before he died, the great writer longed for his mother's touch.

> Felt dull and sad all day. Toward evening the mood changed into a desire for caresses, for tenderness. I wanted, as when I was a child, to nestle against some tender and compassionate being and weep with love and be

> consoled . . . become a tiny boy, close to my mother the way I imagine her. Yes, yes, my Maman. . . . She is my highest image of love—not cold, divine love, but warm, earthly love, maternal. . . . Maman, hold me, baby me! All that is madness, but it is all true. (361)

Kahn interprets this longing in light of Tolstoy's loss of his mother before he was two years old. But she also suggests that many Americans are deprived of maternal touch because "U.S. culture, so intent on human development through individuation and separation suppresses the maternal body in its childbirth and breastfeeding practices" (361). On the question of how adults, "deprived of maternal touch, satisfy unmet longings," Kahn contends that "some men are consoled by looking." Then she quotes a colleague:

> Myla Kabat-Zinn . . . asked rhetorically, "What are the full breasts in *Playboy* magazine full of?" As any nursing mother knows, only milk could naturally provide such voluptuous breasts on all of these women. The silicone implants the women are most likely full of are mere substitutes for what is really wanted and ironically often prevent breastfeeding. (362)

These provocative ideas bring us full circle, back to the question of motherhood and sexuality addressed at the beginning of this chapter. Kahn suggests that the fetishized breast in American culture—the breast sexualized for men's pleasure—may represent the maternal breast denied, or more generally, the maternal body denied. This insight can not be acknowledged, at least consciously, because mother and *Playboy* model are culturally opposed images of womanhood. However, the most significant implication of this insight is that denied access to the maternal body helps to produce the dichotomy between motherhood and sexuality in the first place. In a society where mothers and children feel guilty and ashamed about the pleasures they derive from their relationship—and so curtail those pleasures—children become adults who are psychologically primed to deny mothers full subjectivity. They become adults who are horrified at the thought that their mothers have a sexual life, adults who can not imagine eros in anything other than narrowly sexual terms, adults who don't know what to do with the intense feelings they have for their own children. Yet the desire for connection persists and seeks fulfillment in other ways.

To put this in positive terms, all of us would benefit—children and adults, men and women—if our society recognized mothers as sexual beings, embraced an expansive understanding of eros, celebrated maternal eroticism, valued the emotional and physical pleasures of breastfeeding, and made room for expressions of mother-child romance over the life course. All of us would benefit, including the children who grow up to become mothers.

NARRATIVE J

Mother and Child: The Erotic Bond

Lynda Marín

No one is prepared for becoming a mother even though the world is full of discourse on the subject. I became a mother at thirty-eight and by then I thought I knew a few things. I knew for a fact that I would never be adequately prepared, for instance, and that I would just do it the way every other woman probably had, the best way I could. Right from the beginning of the pregnancy I felt myself initiated into the realm of the best-kept secrets. No one had ever mentioned, for instance, the tingly little cramps just over the pubic bone that set in almost immediately with a first pregnancy and raise the fear that just when you'll need those very muscles to be strong they seem to be giving out. Many months after the birth of my son, a mother of three told me they're called round ligament pains.

The best-kept secrets pile up around the subject of childbirth, post-partum "depression," and the first twelve months. My son was born prematurely and so I encountered a whole other set of secrets no one thinks she'll need to know until she does. I remember, though, being determined, as I had heard other women say they had been, to not forget a thing, to document every private discovery, every hidden event. But denial, displacement, and cultural mandates for self-effacing motherhood aside, there are compelling logistical reasons why new mothers keep the secrets. They are too exhausted, disoriented, and busy for the most part to be recording them all, and by the time they aren't (do I really believe such a time arrives?) the vagaries of memory commit those secrets yet again to the farthest outposts, the silent margins that delimit the discourses of mothering. And so I have failed, like so many other mothers, to resist the inevitable. Most of the best-kept secrets of pregnancy and early motherhood lie buried safely within me shimmering just out of reach in some vast and timeless collective.

But that is not that. Other secrets replace them, take up the present moment, carry thornier implications. A secret that compels me now, that has increasingly gained complexity in the last two years, has to do with the erotic bond between my son and me. That the bond is an erotic one is not in itself a secret. This is the secret

From Mother Journeys: Feminists Write about Mothering, *edited by Maureen T. Reddy, Martha Roth, and Amy Sheldon. Spinsters Ink, 1994. Available from Spinsters Ink, 32 East First Street #330, Duluth, Minnesota 55802. Reprinted by permission.*

upon which Freud founded psychoanalysis as we know it—that the child has drives that are sexual and that the first objects of those drives are its parents, most initially its mother('s body). But what we do with that bit of psychoanalytic insight is what we seem so bent on keeping hidden.

Alexander likes to say he is "four-and-three-quarters." I got plenty of warning about this age, about the intensity of the little boy's attachment to the mother and his Oedipal struggle to possess her entirely for himself. Numbers of women friends with boys assured me that their preschool age sons really do propose marriage to them, intercept their affectionate gestures intended for spouses or lovers, and lavish them with tender phrases and caresses. How dear, I thought. And how poignant the necessity of redirecting these most passionate expressions of desire. Nevertheless, that is exactly what our culture requires, however mediated by our various ethnicities and classes, in order that the boy child identify finally with the other, the father, the law, to take up his place in culture as a man. And while I am ceaselessly rewriting culture's script for men, I recognize my limited power in this arena. I have one son whom I would wish to become an unusual man, a man who resists his gender identity enough to grapple always with the rigors of self-reflection and the complexities of social construction. But seeing no other alternative (how many androgynes do I actually know?), I would wish him still to identify as a man. So it was with a sense of forewarning and purposefulness that I imagined myself meeting Alexander's first dramatic displays of Oedipal conflict. This sense was nurtured by not only the content but the tone of all those conversations I had had with mothers, the books I had read, the films I had seen. My position always seemed clear. I was the figure who must nurture and assist my son through this difficult attachment/detachment maneuver to/from myself.

But no one had really ever told me, in a way I could hear at least, what it might feel like to be the mother in the Oedipal conflict. Indeed of the three key characters in the Greek myth of Oedipus, Jocasta's experience is least described. Upon discovering that she has had four children with her son Oedipus, we are told, she hangs herself. That, of course, is the best way to keep a secret forever. Still, it seems mothers do something equally silencing in the day-to-day way we do not speak of our erotic feelings toward those most desirable of objects, our children. We say our kids are cute, of course, or beautiful or remarkable, and we endlessly detail their behaviors and idiosyncrasies, but rarely do we acknowledge the erotic component of our own feelings in these observations of them. I say "rarely" because just today, when I was trying to explain the topic of this essay to a friend with a six-month-old daughter, she said simply, "It's the most erotic thing *I've* ever felt. You know it's no joke about pretending to eat her right up. I really do want to. It's just uncontainable, this desire. But what can I do? I can't have sex with her. Although nursing takes care of that." That's right, I thought. The physical intimacy of early infancy does mediate those drives in the parent, does "take care of" the uncontainable desire in a way that can't occur at the Oedipal stage. Now that my son is nearly five, I do not have access to his body in the same ways I did when he was younger, nor does he have the same access to mine. I have to ask permission now to clean out his ears, help blow his nose, or make one last wipe after he gets off the toilet (could I ever have imagined such a thing in the midst of all those diaper changes?). And he knows better now than to try and pinch my breasts—"fondle" is, of course, much more like it, but language allows him the same diversionary tactics I use.

In fact, language is the very intervention in our children's developmental process that requires us to come to terms with the erotic energy that infuses our love for them (the developmental process I am referring to is here marked by the Oedipal stage—a crucial step in attaining gender identity that boy and girl children experience quite differently but whose name suggests its emphasis on the boy child's experience). But it is also language that foils our expression of that eroticism. When my son wraps his arms around my legs, sighs, and says, "Mommy, I want to have a baby with you," a number of things inevitably occur in me. The impossible tenderness of the moment is followed by the need to say something. "You do?" I say, stalling for the right response (and noting that last year he wanted to *be* me). I could extend the fantasy toward the realm of the practical and avoid the more problematic implications by asking what he'd do with a baby. Would he like to dress it and feed it and change diapers, etc. But I know that has nothing to do with what he wants. I could redirect the fantasy to include his father, and suggest that what he might like is a sister or brother, but that, I am sure, is not what he is talking about in this moment. I could "reality adjust" him in the service of heterosexuality by assuring him that one day he will marry someone he loves and have a baby with her. But now, far from being a comfort, this assurance will not alleviate the anxiety he must be feeling. After all it was just a short time ago that, lying next to me one morning, staring blankly at the ceiling, he sang a wandering little song that went, "Oh, mommy, I love you so much I don't know what to do." *Good grief, Charlie Brown*, I thought to myself in a voice I use when were playing sometimes, *I feel the same way about you.* The truth is just that simple and just that complex, too.

I remember a specific moment, a "where-it-all-began" moment when I glimpsed the enormity of language's intervention in the continuum of desire that contained us both. We were in the kitchen and he was two. He had been saying lots of words for a long time, so I had passed beyond the wonder of yet another new one but was enjoying tremendously his pleasure in stringing them all together, his various forays into meaning. "Mommy!" he said, "you want a cookie." And as if my brain were wired through his, I indeed felt hunger for a cookie, as if he had only "read my mind." In the time it took to hand him the cookie, a lot happened. I realized that we had been operating like this for a long time, that the boundarylessness between mothers and preverbal children did not simply shore up with the onset of language but rather found ways to persist inside it. This was the first time I had ever noticed in nearly a year of his acquiring language that he had never used the word *I*. I had been hearing *I* for all those *yous*, and not just by mentally exchanging pronouns but actually registering his desire in my body (what power in a pronoun!), feeling it come up against my often different desire, and finally assigning the conflicting desire to him. Not surprisingly, it was around this time that I noticed other people in the family helping him to make the distinction between *I* and *you*, something that is actually very difficult to explain due to the nature of pronouns themselves, i.e. "Oh, you mean *I* when you say *you*. No, I know you don't mean me, you mean you, but you need to say *I* when you mean you," etc. I left it to the others. I was in no hurry to give up what might be the last vestiges of some of the most compelling commingling I have ever felt.

But the leaving it to others felt like a secret I ought to keep. No one likes the idea that a mother enjoys the boundarylessness of relation with her child. That pleasure suggests too intimately her own regressive, infantile underpinnings. More than anything, we need a mother to be an adult. We want to believe that all her own early polymorphous pleasure has now been securely organized around her genitals and directed toward her adult sexual partner. We like to think of a mother's delight in the softness of her child's skin, the firmness of its body, the familiarity of its smell, the singularity of its voice, the sweetness of its breathing as something quite separate from a woman's delight in the body of her lover. We like to make a clear distinction between motherly affection and female passion. If there were not a clear distinction, what would stop mothers from engulfing their children forever in their own hedonistic designs? What hope would culture have?

But what if one of the best-kept secrets is that there is no distinction, really, between motherly affection and female passion? Or rather, that we practice this same love, this erotic energy continuous with our early attachment to our own mother's (or her substitute's) body, in tirelessly deliberate and mediated ways. And we do this exactly because of the lack of boundary between ourselves and our children, exactly because our children are never entirely other. This is the positive side of the narcissistic attachment to children for which mothers are so often criticized. Never is it more clear than with our own children that what we do unto them, we do unto ourselves. If we support their independence and self-reliance, we inevitably gain more freedom and time for ourselves. If we honor their individual expression and spirit, we usually get respected in return. And if we burden them with guilt and shame, we can count on being plagued with those same feelings about ourselves and our parenting. Since the feedback loop is almost immediate, we learn early how to mediate the merging of desire (ours, theirs, and whatever overlaps), how to negotiate the tangle of erotic drives that constitutes the bond between a mother and a child. The other thing we learn is not to talk about it.

Alexander likes to cuddle a lot. *A lot*. I remember hoping before he was born that he would be an affectionate child because I like to cuddle, too. An astrologer friend assured me in the hospital that his early birth in the sign of Cancer would predispose him to strong emotions and an affectionate nature. For the first year, of course, there's no telling. Five months of colic, followed by teething and developmental anxieties, made it almost impossible to discern what sort of little person he would become. I only know I seemed always to be holding him and always on the lookout for another pair of willing arms. By the second year, though, the astrological prediction seemed to be bearing itself out. And what really confirmed it was the language that began to accompany his affectionate gestures. I can rarely turn down invitations like "I need to cuddle with my soft sweet mommy."

By now Alexander's cuddling is a highly developed art. It begins early in the morning when he appears in my room holding Orker the seal, slips into bed beside me, and coaxes one of my sleepy arms around his middle. This is complicated. On the one hand, I resist. I am never ready to be awake. On the other, I am endlessly grateful that here he is whole in body and spirit, in all his morning good cheer, and almost calm enough to let me pretend to myself that I am resting a little while longer. It's a count-my-blessings kind of moment, and then some. "Mommy," he says, after about ten or fifteen minutes, "let's be animals." This has been going on for as long as I can remember (perhaps this is what replaced nursing so long ago). He is the baby elephant, bird, snake, fish, seal, horse, dog, or kitty, and I am the mommy of the same species. We go looking for food, we have adventures, we don't get caught, we return home where we cuddle, of course. Sometimes he just collapses against me, his face pressing down on mine, and I breathe him in, breathe him out. Sometimes in these moments he says how much he loves me, but most of the time he is talking to himself, or singing, or just staring off. If his dad tries to enter in, Alexander always pushes him away, even though at other times he is quite loving with him. Then suddenly he will disappear under the covers all the way to the foot of the bed. After a lot of tossing and giggling he reappears, naked, having left his pajamas somewhere down at my feet. He presents himself with noisy fanfare, giddy with his own power. He is delighted by his nakedness and, I sense, by something like defying an assumed prohibition. For although nudity is commonplace in our family, he seems to sense that he's on some kind of an edge. He turns his skinny backside to my front and we lie like spoons, half-moaning half-humming an exaggerated "Yummmmmm." The sensuality of this moment that we have constructed almost takes my breath away. For the short time that we snuggle like this, I feel as close to perfectly happy as I imagine possible.

Most of the time I'm the one to say we've got to get up, to eat, to dress, to go to school, etc. But when I can't marshall the forces, or when I am lulled into overtime by the pleasure of our play, I sometimes begin to feel uncomfortable. "OK, I'll be the mommy bird and you be the baby and you cry and I'll feed you. Here, nurse the mommy," he says, pointing to his tummy. And although I'm tempted to kiss that spot as a way of playing along (I can't even imagine pretending to nurse him—here a taboo is in full force), I often hear myself responding with things like, "No, I'm sleeping now," or "Yikes, I fell in the river." Nevertheless I let the game go on. I am, of course, partly curious to see how he plays out being the mommy (she's always good at finding food and fighting off hunters). Now suddenly he's the baby and wants to nurse. I laugh him away, but he insists and pretends to grab for my breast. "Cut it out!" I say partly laughing because he's laughing, but partly serious, too, and in this moment thinking quite concertedly about where the boundaries ought to be. "OK, OK," he says, seems to stop, and then dives towards my chest, kissing me on the clavicle. That he kisses me takes me aback. I see that he does the same thing I do—that he doesn't really pretend to nurse either, that he opts for that more adult vestigial gesture of nursing, the kiss. And, like someone who suddenly realizes she is witnessing an historical event in the making, I think IT IS HAPPENING RIGHT NOW. In this moment, unlike any other that I have known, I am actually the mother and the woman, the original object and its displacement. This is the impossible conjoining that patriarchal and heterosexual culture so labors to veil, to mystify, to interdict, which I can hardly hang on to long enough to mark before it passes imperceptively like water into air.

What, I wonder in moments like these, would I do if he were a girl (or if I had a second child and no time for this sort of play)? Would a daughter his age and I even be playing these games? Or would our games be more informed by the kinds of power struggles that ordinarily accompany a girl child's efforts to separate out who is who in the selfsameness of mother-daughter gender? But just say that we did play mother-and-baby games as part of our morning ritual, would I feel the same ambivalence at the same turns? Would I wonder for a moment about our nakedness together? Or about the appropriateness of the game? My sister-in-law has been saying tactfully for a long time now that "most mothers curtail access to their body to their boy children at this age." She is a psychotherapist and a sensible woman/mother, so I take her advice to heart. But she is also, I always tell her, a white, middle-class American. Many people of other cultures and classes don't operate with these same taboos, and anyway I don't want my body to become distant, mysterious, and only, therefore, an object of frustrated desire. I want a woman's body to be a real thing to him, with its various characterizing features and quirks, cycles and stages. She reminds me, though, and I acknowledge also, that Alexander is growing up in this culture in a predominantly white, middle-class family. But, I ask her obliquely, what woman in her right mind wouldn't want to resist that institution and remold its membership? And how better to do it than with our bodies, the most split-off and thereby suppressed/oppressed instruments culture has at its disposal? And that brings me back to erotic love and its power in the mother-child relationship, because all those normative steps to desexualizing the child's attachment to his/her mother's body are predicated on a split between mother and woman that is culturally required but personally mutilating for both mothers and children, a category that finally includes everyone.

I see that what I am holding out for, in these borderline experiments in erotic love with my son (the wording is so sensitive here, and nothing that I can think to say is quite what I mean), is a rewriting of sexuality as I know it. It is not a free-for-all kind of sexuality that powered the imagination of the "sexual revolution" of the '60s and '70s but left us, men and women, just as split in ourselves as ever. It is an inclusive kind of sexuality that recognizes itself basically everywhere. It is not so scary in its infantility because it's just as much a part of adulthood, too. And if we were to recognize that kind of sexuality much more intimately in ourselves all the time (since it's operating there all the time anyway), we would have to pay it close attention, to be careful and caring with it. I imagine our having to add lots of new words to our language to describe it in its multiple manifestations in any interaction, fantasy, work of art, etc., in much the same way we have thought Inuit peoples to have so many words for snow. But I recognize that as innocently as I try to cast it, it's a sexuality that would not support life on the planet as we know it, that is, would not support social hierarchies, multinational corporations, a free market economy, racism, colonization, or any other of the problematic realities that depend on our ability to split off what's safe and good (mother) from what's desirable (woman).

Last year Valorie (a dear friend and second mother-figure to Alexander) and I took him to the Women's Music Festival. It is an all-women's event, four days of music and sun, hikes and swimming, workshops and food. Boy children ten years of age and under are also allowed. When we got inside the festival grounds, I was amused by the first truckload of women passing by laughing and waving, their bare breasts jouncing to the bumps in the road. They were acting out, I thought, taking every opportunity to do what is everywhere else forbidden. But I didn't blame them. By the next day I didn't blame myself either. In the afternoons the large swimming pool filled up with bodies of every imaginable size, shape, and texture. Mothers, children, lovers, friends towel-to-towel along the steamy concrete deck, dipping in and out of the brisk water. All those naked bodies so happily commingling in the security of our shared gender. Was it erotic to be there? Of course it was. It was magnificently, luxuriously, ubiquitously so. And yet we were as orderly as any other crowd, waited in long lines for dinner and almost as long ones for showers, had regular conversations, and helped each other out in small, immediate ways. I don't remember ever seeing any overtly genital sex acts between women there, although the atmosphere was clearly sexually charged. In fact I felt more comfortable and secure in this crowd than in any other I'd been in.

No surprise, much of that comfort had to do with Alexander, that he was in as safe a place as he could possibly be, all those women/ mothers with an eye and an arm out, just in case. I wasn't surprised either that the other children there seemed less competitive, more trusting, and, interestingly, more independent than many kids I've had occasion to know. But I was surprised at my sense of relief when, dropping Alexander off at the festival daycare center, I felt unambivalent pleasure at his fingers tracing my cheekbone and his "Goodbye, my dearest mommy lover." How often I have marked those kinds of goodbyes at his regular preschool with a vague anxiety about their possibly problematic implications. How often I have listened furtively to the way other children say goodbye to their mothers hoping to hear equally "excessive" endearments. And how often has the sensible mother within had to remind me that what really should be noted is how happily he says goodbye and lets me go. But what would it mean to never feel one moment of that ambivalence, to trust that this love I feel for my son is as good as it ever gets? What would it mean if I could openly and directly model all my other loves on this, my finest? When it was time to leave the festival, none of us wanted to go home. Alexander made us promise we would bring him back next year. Both Valorie and I got ready for reentry trauma, and we didn't have to wait long. Just twenty minutes down the highway we stopped for gas, minded our business, and, predictably, got harrassed by two drunk men until the tank was filled up.

"How would you feel if Alexander grew up to be gay?" a lesbian friend doesn't quite ask as we speak recently of things erotic and motherly. Or, I think to myself, sexually ambivalent or a cross-dresser or a fetishist, or—? These questions have crossed my mind before. I would be kidding myself to say it wouldn't matter, that whatever his sexuality I would accept it without reservation, remorse, guilt, or judgment. "It would be hard," his father says when I ask him the same questions. And I agree. Life is hard enough, and being "different" is that much harder. I'm already feeling sorry that he's having to deal with being left-handed. (I was left-handed, too, but the kindergarten teacher would have none of that.) On the other hand (the right one), to consciously guide him into the heterosexual model of masculinity feels abusive. Yet again, to *not* deliberately guide him in that direction seems at times equally injurious. Example: Alexander at his gymnastics lesson begs me for a leotard like the other kids have (the girls, that is). Here's one of those moments where I watch my conditioning vie with my resistance to it. I think "No," plain and simple, but I try out "Yes" for a fleeting second just to really test myself. After all, I might have been able to say yes just a year ago, but kids say things now to each other about haircuts and clothes and so I know a leotard is sure to bring him immediate censure, probably even from his teacher. Nevertheless, as I am feeling the absurdity of my own explanation to him, that boys and girls usually wear different kinds of uniforms for most kinds of sports (though I am hard pressed to answer his outraged "Why?"), I grind to a halt between what I know and what I want. "If you really want a leotard, you can have one," I tell him, "but you just have to know that someone might make fun of you because you will be different." "Never mind," he says. A week later after co-oping at Alexander's preschool, his dad reports that in the fantasy room Alexander got himself dressed up as a cowboy and then with equal enthusiasm donned an elaborate bride's costume and went through a double wedding ceremony with his friend Evin and another "couple." "How was that?" I ask his dad. "He made a beautiful bride," he says. And we both laugh and remember the evening before when Alexander had said to me at the dinner table, "OK, I'm the bride and you're the broom." "Groom," his dad said, "the man is the groom." "Oh," Alexander says, a little abashed, and then, "No, I want you to be the broom." "OK," I agree. A bride and broom seem likely enough in a domestic sort of way, but then again, if the broom can fly. . . .

On my desk sits a small photo of myself *circa* four "and-three-quarters." I retrieved it from my stepfather after my mother died thirteen years ago. It had been taken in Iowa where I lived with a foster parent who must have sent it on to my mother in California. I have often wondered at the self-possessed expression on that child's face, her legs crossed and her hands clasped squarely in her lap. It is one of the few photos I have of my childhood and it has become, by now, one of my most familiar images of myself. Recently, though, while late-night working on some translation at my desk, I saw that photo/myself anew. Who knows what triggered it. Perhaps it was *La Amortajada*, the text I was so feverishly unravelling, about a dead woman's dialogue with her split-off selves, or perhaps it was the residue of a drawn-out, difficult "good night" with Alexander, who that evening thought his bedroom too lonely to fall asleep in. Perhaps it was everything and nothing I could point to, but in any case it happened. I looked at the little girl in the photo and I felt such a surge of desire I must have stopped breathing. I wanted her entirely, to embrace her until she melted into me, to infuse her with all of myself, to enjoy the delicious intimacy of her little body as a day-to-day, minute-to-minute commonplace—her skin, her hair, her smell, her sound. I could almost reproduce her right then and there, a tangible, palpable child.

In a trying-to-make-sense-of-this effort I reminded myself that these were actually feelings I have for Alexander. And it did make sense that on account of family resemblance and age correspondence I had, at that moment, mapped the feelings I have for my actual child onto the photographic image that represents for me my internalized child. But the unmediated desire I felt for that small girl in the photo made me at least suspect that it might be the other way around. What I mean to say is what if, for a reason I can't presume to know, for a split second some of my psycho-social infrastructure slipped just enough to reveal another of the best-kept secrets: that all love whether it be for our children, our lovers, our work, our ideas, is fundamentally the same love, is first and last, coming and going, not even erotic but autoerotic? For isn't erotic love just a further development, a successful splitting off, redirecting, and renaming of that first continuous unbounded connection/pleasure we feel with our mother's body?

Of course, autoeroticism is not such a secret since we can find it strategically positioned, just as I'm suggesting now, in psychoanalytic discourse. The real secret, though, is how "ardorously" culture struggles to forget what eroticism actually is, where it comes from, and why it is absolutely everywhere all the time, especially and necessarily in a mother's love for her child. When we successfully forget that fact, as we require ourselves to do in the name of becoming adults, we severely limit the ways we can experience the connection/pleasure which originally nurtured us into life and which sustains our desire for life forever after. It seems evident that one of the reasons, for instance, that Western culture has so little regard, by and large, for what's left of natural life—for plants and animals and earth and atmosphere—is its successful endeavor to see itself as separate from all that life, to forget the connection/pleasure that informs our very being here.

So what *is* a mother to do? If I had never had a child, my task would be the same. I would still have that little girl internalized and her picture on my desk. I would still need to be parenting her, the child she is, the woman I am, the best way I know how. It's just that having Alexander confronts me more urgently to uncover the secret of what that best way is.

"Do you love me so much that you just have to close your eyes?" he asked me the other day when we were hugging. "Yes!" I said, surprised at his accuracy. "Me, too," he said matter-of-factly and patted my hand. But for whatever permission I am learning to give myself in honoring the erotic bond between us, I wonder still if it makes any difference. One morning recently he sits at the table eating cereal and crooning a love song to mother. Something about how wonderful and sweet I am and how much much much he loves loves loves me. "Goodbye," I interrupt him on my way out the door. "Can I have a hug?" The goodbye hug is a ritual. But this morning he doesn't even hear me. His eyes are so far off in his song that I hesitate to ask again, though I suppose that later on he'll think I didn't say goodbye. So I try once more. But it's no use. "I just love her so much my mommy," I hear as I leave the house. Tossing his car pillow into the backseat to make room next to me for my books and papers, I marvel at that other "mommy," that symbolic creature who, seemingly overnight, has exceeded and displaced me, and who, this morning, has him in thrall. I only hope, for all our sakes, she loves him as undividedly as she can.

CHAPTER 6

Pregnancy and Childbirth

When I was pregnant with my daughter, Marie, I wanted to hear the pregnancy and birth stories of anyone who would share them with me. I found (as anyone knows who has listened to even a few women talk about these profound life events) that women's experiences vary widely. Pregnancy can be expected or a surprise, easily achieved or long awaited, a source of joy or of anguish.[1] Pregnancy can be invigorating or exhausting, and often both over the course of nine months. A woman's appetites—including her sexual desire—may be enhanced or dampened. She may be nauseated for all, part, or none of the time. As a woman's body changes, so might her sense of self: she may revel in or be dismayed by her fullness.[2] In any case, her girth is hard to miss, which may change her relationships with others, including strangers who feel entitled to comment on or touch her body.

Once a woman has children, that circumstance shapes any subsequent experiences, physical and emotional, of pregnancy and birth. (A minor point: it's difficult to carry a toddler when one is nine months pregnant). If a woman has suffered a miscarriage, stillbirth, or the death of a child, pregnancy may evoke intense fear, as Kathryn March discusses in narrative L.[3] A birth mother who plans to surrender her child for adoption may feel confident, ambivalent, or distressed about her decision.[4] Many pregnant women feel that they have a relationship with the fetus they carry within them.[5]

In giving birth, a woman may be assisted by her partner, family, friends, midwife, doula (labor assistant), nurses, and/or doctors. She may feel supported or mistreated by those who attend her. Some women feel alone even if the room is crowded with people. A woman may experience labor as short, long, empowering, frightening, sensual, or painful, even unbearably so. She may moan, cry, scream, or attempt to stifle her voice in pain. Some women feel in control during labor, others feel out of control. Some feel that control is not what labor is about. Depending on how labor and birth go and on the baby's health, a woman may feel exhilarated and proud of her accomplishment. Or she may feel disappointed or even outraged about what could have been otherwise. Finally, the postpartum period can be a smooth transition to

This chapter was written by Susan E. Chase.

motherhood, an emotional and physical roller coaster, or a time of debilitating depression.[6]

In this chapter I look at the historical and cultural forces that have shaped women's experiences of pregnancy, and especially childbirth, in the United States. I begin with the centuries-old struggle for control over childbearing women's bodies. Then I explore contemporary feminist studies about women's experiences, particularly about how women accept or resist the medicalization of pregnancy and childbirth. I conclude with some specifically feminist ideas about women's maternal bodies. The history, empirical studies, and ideas presented in this chapter invite us to listen in new ways to the stories we tell, or hear other women tell, about pregnancy and birth.

The Struggle for Control over Maternal Bodies

Many scholars have documented the history of the medical profession's increasing control over childbirth during the last few centuries, as well as the women's health movement's reclamation of woman-centered, midwife-attended childbirth since the early 1970s.[7] Instead of attempting to review these complex histories, I focus on a few of the main points.

Women's Traditional Birth Practices

Until the twentieth century, high fertility rates meant that pregnancy, childbirth, and nursing made up a large part of most women's adult lives. In 1800, white women in the United States had more than seven live children on average; in 1870, black women had six or seven live children.[8] The constant possibility of miscarriage, stillbirth, infant death, and maternal illness or death also had a profound impact on women.[9] Through the first few decades of the twentieth century, women feared death from puerperal fever, an illness resulting from infection of the uterine lining, caused by unsterile technique.[10]

Traditionally, in the United States as in other areas of the world, childbirth was woman-centered and woman-controlled.[11]

> Within their own homes, birthing women controlled much of the experience of childbirth. They determined the physical setting for their confinements, the people to attend them during labor and delivery, and the aids or comforts to be employed. Midwives traditionally played a noninterventionist, supportive role in the home birthing rooms. . . . The other women attendants supported the midwife and the birthing woman. . . . Parturient women, who felt vulnerable at the time of their confinements, armed themselves with the strength of other women who had passed through the event successfully.[12]

Women felt vulnerable, of course, because of the dangers of childbirth. Yet historical evidence shows great variation in mortality rates across locations. Historian Laurel Thatcher Ulrich examined the diary of midwife Martha Ballard, who carefully recorded the 814 births she attended from 1785 to 1812 in rural Maine. None of the mothers died giving birth, and only five died in the following days. Newborn deaths were also rare; Ballard recorded fourteen stillbirths and five infant deaths shortly after birth. Ballard's mortality rates compare favorably with those of nineteenth-century physicians. For example, she had 1.8 stillbirths per 100 births compared to Dr. James Farrington's 3.0 stillbirths per 100 births between 1824 and 1859 in New Hampshire. Yet Ulrich notes that even Farrington's mortality rates, as well as those of other eighteenth- and nineteenth-century midwives and physicians, were much lower than those in other locations. Several British hospitals, for example, reported that one out of every thirty or forty women died from puerperal fever in the mid-1700s. Ulrich explains that "because Ballard was a part-time practitioner who delivered women at home and shared their postpartum care with nurses and family members, she had little opportunity to spread puerperal infection from one patient to another."[13] In addition to these environmental factors, the evidence from Ballard's diary suggests that her skill as a midwife was unsurpassed.

The Medicalization of Childbirth

In reviewing the history of maternity care, sociologist Barbara Katz Rothman notes that after forceps were developed during the seventeenth century, men started to get involved in live births and to challenge the authority of midwives. As the field of medicine professionalized, physicians excluded women practitioners, monopolized technology, especially forceps, and devalued the practical knowledge and experience of midwives.[14] In the United States, childbirth became almost completely medicalized by the middle of the twentieth century, as evidenced by the transitions from midwife-assisted to physician-controlled birth and from home to hospital birth. In 1900, 95 percent of births took place at home; 50 percent of birthing women were attended by midwives and 50 percent by doctors. In 1940, 55 percent of births took place in hospitals; in 1960, almost 100 percent did.[15] In 1980, midwives attended only 1.7 percent of births, and in 1990 only 1 percent took place at home. A resurgence of midwifery increased midwife-assisted births to 5.5 percent in 1994.[16] Nonetheless, the medical profession had successfully subordinated midwifery, depriving midwives of autonomy in their work. Even today, midwives must depend on physicians for back-up services in emergency cases, services that doctors have the power to grant or deny.[17]

Feminist scholars argue that, for the most part, the medicalization of birth has been detrimental to women and their newborns. In order to understand this argument, we must first address women's fears and desires concerning childbirth and the question of safety.

Women's Fears and Desires. Historian Judith Walzer Leavitt contends that over the course of the nineteenth and early twentieth centuries, many elite, white urban women in the North East welcomed the medicalization of birth: they invited male physicians into their homes to attend them along with their mothers, sisters, and friends. Because physicians, unlike midwives, had formal learning and the prestige that accompanies it, these advantaged women believed that doctors were more likely to protect them from the hazards of childbirth. Even as fertility rates declined (white women had an average of 3.5 live births in 1900; southern white farm women, almost 6; black women, more than 5), women continued to fear death. Their fear persisted because the risks were highest for first births and because maternal mortality did not decline as much as was expected with increased understanding of how to control infection.[18]

Even though they sought the services of physicians, privileged women maintained quite a bit of control over childbirth in the woman-centered world of home births. Birthing women and their female assistants could negotiate with the doctor and even refuse his orders. They could also ask him to leave.[19] Leavitt suggests that at this point many women felt they had the best of both worlds—women's birthing traditions and men's medicine; she also suggests that the historical record can be read otherwise. Not only did physicians' skills vary widely, but their training rarely included actual practice in childbirth. Moreover, whether because of physicians' training or women's expectations, or perhaps both, doctors intervened more than midwives did, at least sometimes to the detriment of women and babies. During the first half of the nineteenth century, physicians' interventions included bloodletting (thought to relax the muscles and aid labor's progress), drugs (opium or its derivatives), and forceps. At mid-century anesthesia and suturing perineal tears were added to the medical repertoire.[20]

During the first few decades of the twentieth century, Leavitt contends that many upper- and middle-class women welcomed the further medicalization of birth, this time in the form of hospitalization. Women did not anticipate, however, how radical the change would be, particularly the shift in the balance of power (190). In the midst of any rapid social change, of course, people do not understand fully the consequences of that change. "In hospitals, control moved to the profession, and birthing women found themselves 'alone among strangers' and unable to determine any parts of their birth experience" (206).

Why did advantaged women seek hospital care? First, they believed that scientific advances made hospital birth safer than home birth. Reality, however, did not support that belief. "In obstetrics [as opposed to other medical fields] it was more the image of science's potential, the lure of what science could offer, than any proven accomplishments that attracted women to the hospital." Contributing to the gap between belief and reality was the growing distance between lay people and medical professionals, who controlled technical knowledge (174). At the same time, women's social networks were declining, which made satisfactory home births much more difficult to accomplish than before. Greater mobility and urbanization prevented many women from gathering enough kin and friends to help not only with birth but also with the domestic responsibilities a birthing woman had to set aside (176). Thus, middle-class women who did not have household help may have welcomed hospital births as a relief from those responsibilities.

Other social factors contributed to the movement of birth from home to hospital after the turn of the century: hospitals for private-paying patients proliferated; modern nursing evolved, offering continuous observation and care in the hospital setting; increasingly structured medical education required a large supply of patients in one locale for student training; and the medical profession began to specialize, including the field of obstetrics.[21]

The Question of Safety. The historical record suggests that the movement of birth from home to hospital in the first few decades of the twentieth century did not improve maternal and infant mortality rates. Indeed, during the 1920s, when urban women flocked to hospitals for birth, their mortality rates increased as a whole, while rural women's rates decreased somewhat.[22] (Rural women were much more likely to give birth at home, well into the 1940s.[23]) In the United States. in 1910, there was one maternal death for every 154 live births and one infant death for every 8 live births. (Infant mortality rates include deaths up to one year; they do not include stillbirths.) Over the next twenty years, infant mortality declined to one death per 15.4 live births in 1930, but maternal mortality did not improve. In 1930, there was one maternal death for every 143 live births.[24] Notice that the maternal mortality rate for the women assisted by midwife Martha Ballard between 1785 and 1812—1 in 160 live births—was better than this twentieth-century mortality rate when about half of American women were giving birth in hospitals and well over half were attended by physicians. In 1950, the stillbirth rate was 1.9 out of 100 births; Ballard reported 1.8.[25]

Although they minimized their concerns in the popular press and women's magazines, physicians began to ask themselves "why modern medicine—showing its mettle so strongly in areas outside of obstetrics—could not control, within its own halls and by its own experts, the ravages of puerperal death." Dr. Joseph B. DeLee of the Chicago Lying-In Hospital, a strong proponent of medical interventions in birth, became one of the most vocal critics of his profession, blaming it for the deaths of thousands of women. Rather than abandoning hospital births, however, the medical profession examined its procedures and techniques. Finally, by the 1940s and 1950s, maternal mortality fell as a result of "increasing hospital regulation of obstetrics practices, antibiotics to treat infection, transfusions to replace blood lost by massive hemorrhaging, and prenatal care to identify many potential high-risk cases."[26]

It was these specific advances—not the transitions from midwife to physician and from home to hospital—that produced better maternal mortality rates than those of midwife Martha Ballard a century and a half earlier. Indeed, the rates declined dramatically in the second half of the twentieth century. In 1950, one in 1,200 women died for reasons related to childbirth. By 1994, there was only one maternal death for every 11,756 live births. In 1991, the stillbirth rate was one in every 137 births.[27] In 1996, there was one infant mortality in 138 live births, the leading causes of which were "congenital anomalies, disorders related to immaturity (short gestation and unspecified low birth weight), SIDS [sudden infant death syndrome], and respiratory distress syndrome."[28]

Do these statistics mean that the hospital became the safest place to give birth in the United States in the second half of the twentieth century? Although this has been a matter of great debate among midwives and physicians, there is evidence that midwife-assisted home births produce equal if not better results in terms of maternal and infant survival and health. After reviewing the empirical studies on this question, Henci Goer concluded that "[n]o study of planned home births of a screened population of women with a trained attendant taking proper precautions has shown excess risk." Furthermore, "Excellent outcomes with much lower intervention rates are achieved at home births," and "home birth becomes dangerous only when doctors and hospitals fail to provide backup services [in emergency cases]."[29]

A closer look at specifics might help here. Rothman summarizes the findings of a carefully constructed comparative study of 1,046 hospital and 1,046 planned home births, published in 1977. The women in each group were carefully matched in terms of age, number of previous births, economic and educational backgrounds, and risk factors. While the infant death rates were essentially the same for both groups, the hospital births had higher incidences of the following: maternal high blood pressure; shoulder dystocia (the shoulder getting caught after the head is born); postpartum hemorrhage; newborns requiring resuscitation; birth injuries to newborns (attributable to the greater use of forceps in the hospital); cesareans; episiotomies; and severe tears.[30]

If home births are as safe as or safer for women and newborns than hospital births, how do we explain the predominance of hospital births? Anthropologist Robbie E. Davis-Floyd suggests that "our cultural belief in the superiority of modern medicine [is so pervasive] that the very real risk-enhancing dangers of hospital birth are simply not culturally acknowledged." She argues further that "'Safety' is the disguise worn by technocratic ideology. The real issue in the home versus hospital debate is not safety but the conflict between radically opposed systems of value and belief."[31]

Before comparing these radically opposed belief systems, let me be clear about one thing: when feminist scholars contend that the medicalization of childbirth has been harmful to women and newborns, they are not suggesting that technology per se is the culprit. For example, the development of antibiotics for infections, blood transfusions for hemorrhaging, and safe procedures for cesareans in emergency cases are clearly in the interest of women and their babies. The problem, then, is not technology itself, but the medical profession's "monopoly of professional authority, of material resources, and of what may be called linguistic capital—the power to establish and enforce a particular definition of childbirth."[32] In our society, the medical model of childbirth constitutes what anthropologist Brigitte Jordan calls "authoritative knowledge," which "is persuasive because it seems natural, reasonable, and consensually constructed." Yet, "*the power of authoritative knowledge is not that it is correct but that it counts.*"[33]

The Medical Model of Birth vs. the Holistic Model of Birth

The medical model of birth includes technological, industrial, and patriarchal assumptions about maternal bodies and birthing processes. Within this model, the maternal body becomes an object, a machine whose functioning must be closely monitored. Labor is a mechanical process and the baby is the product. The obstetrician is the supervisor, manager, or skilled technician in charge of the body as machine. Because labor is a mechanical process, it can be standardized. Obstetricians determine the standards for "normal" birth such as that it should happen within twenty-six hours of the onset of labor. Labor pain is treated as a problem that can be solved through pharmaceutical intervention.[34]

The dramatic increase in cesareans over the last several decades in the United States can be read as the triumph of the medical model. In 1965, only 4.5 percent of births in the United States were cesareans; in 1990, 23.5 percent were. By the 1980s, even some physicians were questioning the high cesarean rates.[35] By 1995, the cesarean rate had dropped to less than 21 percent.[36]

The women's health movement, and under that umbrella, the holistic childbirth and independent midwifery movements, arose in the 1960s and 1970s in resistance to the medical model's industrial, technocratic, and patriarchal assumptions about birth. Like all social movements, the women's health movement has a complicated history. Feminist activists sometimes aligned and sometimes separated themselves from other social movements, such as the consumer movement, the counterculture movement of the New Left, La Leche

League, and the "natural" childbirth movements of Grantly Dick-Read and Ferdinand Lamaze (which began in the 1940s and 1950s). As midwifery re-emerged, debates proliferated (and continue to this day) about how it should be organized educationally, politically, and professionally. As alternative birth centers were created in response to feminist and consumer demands for more humane medical treatment, questions arose about whether these centers really provided an alternative to or just a more comfortable version of the medical model.[37] In any case, midwives' attendance at births began to increase: from 1.7 percent of births in 1980 to 5.5 percent in 1994.[38]

Feminist activists in the women's health movement developed and continue to work for a radical departure from the technocratic, medical model. Whether it is called holistic, home, or midwife-assisted, within this model the birthing woman is an active subject, her body is a healthy organism, and labor is a natural flow of experience. Mother and baby are an inseparable unit. The midwife is a nurturer who supports and assists the laboring woman. Rather than applying narrow criteria for normalcy, this model treats as normal a wide range of labors in terms of starting, stopping, slowing down, and speeding up. Labor pain is accepted as normal and best handled through mind/body integration and social support.[39]

Sociologist Robbie Pfeufer Kahn brings this comparison of the medical and holistic models to life through her analysis of two noteworthy texts: *Williams Obstetrics*, a major manual for obstetricians throughout the twentieth century, and *Our Bodies, Ourselves*, first published in 1970 by the Boston Women's Health Collective.[40] The latter remains a popular feminist self-help book accessible to a wide audience of women.

Kahn finds that *Williams Obstetrics* became increasingly technocratic throughout the 1970s and 1980s. For example, on the question of how labor begins, the 1971 edition states, "The factors regulating this highly synchronized sequence of events are obscure. In fact, the old adage, 'When the fruit is ripe, it will fall,' serves to summarize the extent of our knowledge of the causation of spontaneous labor."[41] Kahn interprets this statement as respecting nature and urging caution: "if you impose a time for labor, you risk prematurity—a baby that is not ripe." It also acknowledges the limits of human understanding and human control. In the 1976 edition, however, the nature metaphor is deleted and we read instead, "The cause of labor remains unknown. Several attractive theories concerned with the mechanism for the onset of parturition in the human, therefore, are to varying degrees still viable." Kahn notes that the replacement of the nature metaphor with scientific language shifts creativity from nature to humans (211–212).

Among many other changes in subsequent editions, Kahn discusses the "discovery" of the fetus as a "second patient." In the 1980 edition, *Williams Obstetrics* describes the new tools of fetal diagnosis and therapy as making this "the most exciting of times to be an obstetrician" (215). Kahn interprets this excitement about the fetus as a second patient in light of Western culture's elevation of the work of making durable objects over labor that "merely" sustains human life (214–217). The obstetrician is excited about using new diagnoses, therapies, and tools, then, because they give him or her something to make: the baby as a durable object (215). Many parents, of course, are deeply grateful for the life-saving and health-improving procedures that these new technologies make possible. Nonetheless, Kahn points to the relationships created and severed, not necessarily by the specific technologies themselves, but by the orientation obstetricians develop toward them. The treatment of the fetus as a second patient creates a new relationship between the doctor and fetus, which takes priority over the tie between woman and fetus, because of the obstetrician's "authoritative knowledge." At the same time, this approach ups the ante for obstetrical intervention.

Kahn is far from alone in her distress concerning this development. In chapter 2 of this book I discussed Bordo's critique of the language of fetal rights. She demonstrates that accompanying the development of distinct legal rights for fetuses is a parallel desubjectification of pregnant women. This is seen most poignantly in cases of court-ordered cesareans where the legal and medical systems construct the woman and fetus as adversaries. In such cases, pregnant women have fewer rights than all other persons in our society, whose bodily integrity is treated as inviolable. In no other circumstance have the courts required a person to undergo even minor bodily interventions, even when they could save a family member's life.[42]

Cindy Martin, a sociology graduate of my university, the University of Tulsa, shows how the medical model's desubjectification of pregnant women can occur in mundane interactions, not just in dramatic cases of fetal surgery or court-ordered cesareans. During her second pregnancy, Martin had extreme nausea. The clinic physician prescribed medicine, which did nothing to alleviate her symptoms.

> On my next visit to the clinic I had a different doctor [to whom] I reported the prescription's ineffectiveness and expressed some frustration about the virulence of my symptoms, *not* my pregnancy. I will never forget the doctor' response as he looked straight at me and asked "Don't you want this baby?" Before reading Bordo, I did not understand how that doctor could have so greatly misconstrued my frustration about symptoms and my concern that they were affecting my parenting skills with my 3-year-old son, with the premise that my second, *planned* pregnancy was an *unwanted* pregnancy. However, Bordo's proposal that as a maternal incubator a woman is de-subjectified may explain his view. I believe Bordo's statement best summarizes my experience: "in this culture the pregnant,

> poor woman (especially if she is of non-European descent) comes as close as a human being can get to being regarded, medically and legally, as 'mere body,' her wishes, desires, dreams, religious scruples of little consequence and easily ignored."[43]

Martin articulates how the doctor disregarded her needs, even her needs as a mother, a desubjectification process probably exacerbated by her status as a working-class Native American woman. Such treatment is comprehensible only when we understand that the medical model views a woman and her fetus as distinct beings with diverging needs. The obstetrical "discovery" of the fetus as a second patient contributes to this process.

Kahn's analysis of changes between 1970 and 1984 in *Our Bodies, Ourselves* shows that it took some time for the feminist critique of the medical model to develop fully, even in this woman-centered text. For example, the section on childbirth is the least radical part of the first edition. This partly reflects, Kahn explains, the ideological power and authoritative knowledge of the medical model. She confesses that even as a holistic childbirth educator, she did not truly believe that a holistic birth was possible until she witnessed one in 1976.[44] The 1976 edition of *Our Bodies, Ourselves* expresses skepticism of home birth, raising the issue of safety. It finally came out in favor of home birth in 1979. In that year's edition as well the text criticizes the overuse of cesarean births (333–334). By 1984, the text not only portrays the hospital as a place where "the climate of doubt" takes hold but also encourages women to create "a climate of confidence" (335–336). Kahn quotes the text:

> When you believe in your basic health and strength, in your ability to give birth in your own way, trusting yourself and the people around you to provide guidance and support; when your practitioners believe in you, bringing to the birth of your baby their cumulative experience of seeing many normal births and healthy babies, then you and they together create a climate of confidence. (335)

Not until the 1984 edition does *Our Bodies, Ourselves* include photographs that fully capture a holistic birth. Kahn writes:

> In one of them a laboring woman breathes out her baby—her lips are pursed and sensuously open. Her arms circle over her head to hold onto the person behind her; her body, which is in the center of the picture, is framed by four people who are leaning in toward her to help with the birth of her child. One person is ready to catch the baby, two others are holding her legs. Surrounded by support, she is at the center of the circle. The circle so repeated in this image—her rounded lips, her encircling arms, her round belly, the circle of helping persons—suggests wholeness, unity, and community. (338)

By contrast, *Williams' Obstetrics* moves in the opposite direction during the same years, not only in its language but also in its visual representations of birthing women. Beginning in 1976, "*all pictures of a normal, unimpeded course of labor and delivery*" are deleted (223).

I looked at the twentieth edition of *Williams Obstetrics*, published in 1997. In the chapter titled, "Conduct of Normal Labor and Delivery," the photographs show close-ups of the vagina and surrounding area of a woman who is apparently lying on her back (the lithotomy position preferred by obstetricians); they also show an episiotomy and then birth. In none of these photos, do we see the woman's face or even the rest of her body. Indeed, when I scanned all 1,381 pages of text, I found only one photograph that includes a woman's entire body and face. A pregnant woman of African descent with an "advanced degree of hydramnios" (an abnormal amount of amniotic fluid) stands rigid, staring out at the viewer as in a mug shot. This picture clearly objectifies her as a clinical specimen.[45]

Women's Experiences of Pregnancy and Childbirth

How has this struggle for control over women's maternal bodies shaped contemporary women's experiences of pregnancy and childbirth? To what extent do women embrace the medical model, the holistic model, or both? Do women of various races and social classes develop different relations to these models?

Pregnancy

Women who receive prenatal care from physicians and who have decent health insurance are likely to feel the impact of the medical model in the form of prenatal diagnostic technologies.[46] Ultrasound, for example, is a widely used, easily administered, painless procedure employed to determine the age, size, normalcy, and sometimes sex of the fetus. Judy Wajcman notes that many women actively seek this technology and find it exciting and informative because it adds a visual experience of the fetus to the physical sensations a woman already has. Nonetheless, she cautions that this and other diagnostic procedures contain hidden constraints because of the way they alter a woman's experience of pregnancy. "Rather than assuming a healthy baby barring evidence to the contrary, the new procedures are shifting attitudes toward a suspicion that the baby may not be all right—a doubt which, once sown, can only be satisfactorily removed by undergoing a series of tests." Pregnant women now have new worries, even while the chances of having a healthy baby are greater than ever.[47]

For example, if a blood test reveals readings indicating the possibility of neural tube defect or Down syndrome, obstetricians typically recommend the more accurate but more invasive (sometimes painful) amniocentesis. (Amniocentesis, usually performed between the fifteenth and eighteenth weeks of pregnancy, involves drawing out a small portion of amniotic fluid through a needle inserted in the abdomen.) My friend whose blood test revealed a possible fetal defect had to wait a torturous month for the right time for amniocentesis (the needle must not go through the placenta) and for the results (it takes about two weeks for the amniotic fluid to be cultured). She was greatly relieved, of course, when the fetus was finally declared normal, but an inaccurate diagnostic procedure was the source of a great deal of stress in the meantime. Moreover, while waiting, she discovered that in order to have a second-trimester abortion (a choice she would have made if there were a fetal defect), she would have to travel out of state for a three-day stay. Not an easy feat for an employed mother of a two-year-old, even one who is partnered, can afford to pay for travel and hotel, and whose insurance would cover the procedure. Of course, if the fetus had had a genetic defect, my friend ultimately would have been grateful for the more accurate diagnostic test. Nevertheless, there is something askew in our society when a diagnostic technology designed to allow women to abort genetically "abnormal" fetuses coexists with laws and policies that make such abortions difficult to get.

Anthropologist Rayna Rapp interviewed a racially and economically diverse sample of more than seventy women who received genetic counseling during their pregnancies. Such counseling is offered to women whose genetic histories place them at risk of a wide range of genetic defects or conditions, and it is usually required before amniocentesis is performed so they will be informed of its risks and benefits. She found that most middle-class women, the majority of whom were white, accepted the idea that amniocentesis is a valuable scientific technology, making statements such as "Science is there to make life better, so why not use its power?"[48] By contrast, she found that working-class African American women were much more likely to reject the scientific language of prenatal diagnosis. Even in choosing to undergo amniocentesis, black women who had grown up in the rural South had nonmedical reasons for accepting the procedure and they used dreams and visions and other meaning systems for interpreting their pregnancies (31–32). For example, a twenty-seven-year-old hospital orderly told Rapp about this recurrent dream:

> So I am having this boy baby. It is definitely a boy baby. And something is wrong, I mean, it just is not right. Sometimes, he is missing an arm, and sometimes, it's a leg. Maybe it's a retarded baby. . . . I tried to get that test to make peace with that dream. . . . The whole thing was going back to the dreams . . . just so's I could say, "this baby is the baby in the dreams" and come to peace with it. (32)

Rapp also interviewed forty women who were informed through amniocentesis that their fetuses had serious disabilities. Only two of these women chose to continue their pregnancies after receiving this information.[49] Reflecting on the dilemma posed by amniocentesis, one woman stated:

> I was hoping I'd never have to make this choice, to become responsible for choosing the kind of baby I'd get, the kind of baby we'd accept. But everyone—my doctor, my parents, my friends—everyone urged me to come for genetic counseling and have amniocentesis. . . . They all told me I'd feel more in control. But in many ways, I feel less in control. It's still my baby, but only if it's good enough to be our baby, if you see what I mean. (217)

Rapp is concerned that the use of amniocentesis as a standard procedure encourages an image of women as quality-control agents on a reproductive production line (217). To the extent that women think of their fetuses as good or bad products and their bodies as effective or defective machines in the production of those products, they accede to the technocratic model of pregnancy and birth. Along the same lines, Rothman points out the contradiction women face when they are asked "to think about the needs of the coming baby, to fantasize about the baby, to begin to become the mother of the baby, and yet to be willing to abort the genetically damaged fetus. At the same time. For twenty to twenty-four weeks."[50] It is clear that many women want the information offered by these technologies, yet they also suffer from the consequences of having it.

Anthropologists Carole H. Browner and Nancy Press look at other aspects of pregnant women's experiences. Interestingly, they find that women frequently resist physicians' recommendations concerning diet and exercise, as well as their recommendations in situations such as threatened miscarriage. Whether women heed their doctors' advice depends on how it fits with or contradicts their personal interpretations of their bodily changes as well as how practical that advice is given their particular life situations.[51]

Childbirth

During pregnancy, women spend only a small portion of their time in the presence of medical professionals. For most of labor and birth, however, the majority of women are directly supervised by medical professionals.

Anthropologist Emily Martin finds that social class shapes how women respond to the medical model during labor. Among her racially and economically diverse group of interviewees, twice as many middle-class women as working-class women spoke of themselves as active in the birthing process. However, middle-class women's self-assertiveness—their apparent defiance of medicine's attempt to control them during labor—turns out to be a form of self-control. Specifically, middle-class women exert control over their bodies in the public space of the hospital. By contrast, Martin suggests that what may look like a relative lack of resistance to the medical model among working-class women can be interpreted as a rejection of both medical and middle-class norms of composure during labor.[52]

Martin develops these ideas by listening to how women talk about their vocalizations during labor. Most of the middle-class women who mentioned their voice felt that yelling and screaming represented a shameful loss of self-control. More than half of the working-class women, however, did not condemn themselves for being noisy, even when the medical staff treated them as refusing to cooperate and to be good patients (305–306). Martin interprets this difference as suggesting that working-class women may be more in touch with their bodies and the natural processes of birth than middle-class women. Yelling can be heard as an expression of intense pain rather than as a loss of control (307).[53] When women are so concerned about controlling the sounds they make, they may ignore those aspects of the birth process that are more physical and less controllable. "Working-class women more readily articulate precisely these kinds of experiences: I am in pain; this hurts; it is enough to make me scream; I am not really in control of this situation, *and no one could be*."[54]

Martin suggests that for white middle-class women, resistance to the medical model may take the form of waiting as long as possible to go to the hospital in order to slow down the labor clock. Working-class women of any race may have the added burden of struggling to pay for their prenatal, birth, postpartum, and infant medical care. As hourly-wage workers, they are also less likely than middle-class women to have adequate "sick" leave. Working-class women of color, however, may also have to deal with mistreatment, including the withholding of information, on top of the rest. Indeed, Martin heard a disproportionate number of stories of poor treatment from working-class African American interviewees (154–155).

Let's turn again to my former student, Cindy Martin, as she reflects this time on her first labor, which took place at an Indian Health Services hospital.

> My first labor was very long and painful, and it became even more difficult as I was unable to obtain even a mere estimate from the medical staff as to what stage I was in throughout the entire process. As my labor became more drawn out and increasingly painful, I became more insistent about knowing whether I was progressing or not, and if I had or hadn't then what did that mean? The standard response I would receive after each "progress" exam was either, "Oh you're about the same" or, "Oh you're coming along." As I would become even more insistent and try to convey how this information was essential to my pain management and even more importantly, my self-control, I would be given a plain annoyed look and then told how pain was "just part of it" or that "babies come when they want to come"

> and that "these things just can't be predicted." When I began to cry, primarily because of stress, one nurse stated, "Well, that's what you teenagers get." On the surface it would appear as a comment expressing a general disgust of teenage pregnancy. However, it proved to be an illustration of Bordo's description of "the mediating racist image . . . of the promiscuous breeder, populating the world irresponsibly, like an unspayed animal." After my husband told her that we were well beyond the age of consent, she retorted, "Well, I still don't know what it is you people expect." I do not think [her racism/classism] could be much clearer.[55]

Martin presents herself as attempting to be a good patient by using the language of the medical model. She refers to the stages of labor, the progress of labor, and pain management. She expresses the need for this information in order to maintain self-control. But her efforts to cooperate were for naught. Paradoxically, she suggests that the medical staff used the language of holistic birth ("babies come when they want to come," "these things just can't be predicted") as a method of withholding information and exerting control over her. Finally, at least one nurse's racist and/or classist attitude emerged undisguised. Although Martin doesn't tell us much about her vocalizations—how loudly she demanded answers to her questions or how loudly she cried—she was clearly perceived as a bad and undeserving patient.

I was deeply moved by this story. Giving birth in a private hospital in a nearby city a few years later, I felt respected by the medical professionals who attended me. Protected by my social class, my race, and perhaps by the presence of the doula my partner, John, and I hired to assist us, my labor experience, although long and difficult, included none of the mistreatment Cindy Martin describes. Indeed, I emerged from my birth experience with a great respect for nurses, who do the majority of labor assistance in hospitals.

Davis-Floyd decided to study women who have options, who have the economic resources to pay for private obstetricians and private childbirth classes rather than having to rely on public clinics or hospital-sponsored classes. Of the one hundred white middle-class women she interviewed about their birth experiences, eighteen percent believed fully in the technocratic model, that doctors rather than mothers accomplish birth. These women "perceive[d] the processes of labor and birth as bewildering and frightening and wish[ed] for their labors to be made as reassuringly mechanical as possible." Six percent of the women gave birth at home, fully accepting the holistic model of birth. These women experienced birth as a natural aspect of womanhood or a spiritual process of growth, and they embraced their biological processes.[56]

Davis-Floyd calls the largest and remaining group in her sample the "women-in-between." The majority of these women entered the hospital wanting to give birth without interventions, but ended up being satisfied with heavily technocratic births. She suggests that they were not upset by this turn of events because the rituals of hospital birth reinforced their deep belief in their inadequacy as birthgivers (219–227). Nonetheless, some of the "women-in-between" partially resisted the technocratic model, either by managing to give birth with relatively few medical interventions or by reinterpreting interventions as serving their desires and needs (208–219). In addition, a few women were deeply distressed by their highly medicalized births because they believed they should be able to give birth without intervention (227–240).

Overall, Davis-Floyd found it surprising and disturbing that most of the women she interviewed—70 percent—"either accepted, demanded, or merely did not mind the eventual complete application of the technocratic model to their births." How could that many women be comfortable with technocratic birth when so much research concludes that it is neither physically healthy nor psychologically empowering for women (281–282)? The first part of Davis-Floyd's answer is that most white middle-class women today believe deeply in the value of the medical model. "To ask why women want technocratic births is, in a broader sense, to ask what technocracy has done for women that they should value it so. The answer to that question seems clear: in the early years of this century technology began to give women the power to expand beyond the 'natural order' that made many of them, in an industrializing society, appear to themselves to be slaves to their biology" (282).

Davis-Floyd's answer returns us to the broad historical and social forces that shape what appear to be individual women's choices: the cultural devaluation of nature, women's bodies, and the practical knowledge women have of their own bodies; the professionalization of medicine; the authoritative knowledge of science; and the industrialization of society. These social forces intersect to make medicalized birth appear to most women to be the most logical "choice." This is especially true for privileged women who have access to the "best" that the medical profession and science have to offer.

Davis-Floyd offers an even deeper answer, however. When women accept the technocratic model of birth, even when it devalues them, they are acting much like Americans in general, who routinely engage in actions that are detrimental to humankind and the well-being of our natural environment: eating processed foods that are stripped of natural nutrients; poisoning groundwater supplies with pesticides; packing landfills with reusable objects made of nonrenewable materials; polluting rivers, lakes, and oceans with chemicals; and releasing enough chlorofluorocarbons into the earth's atmosphere to threaten the protective ozone layer (283–284). While these actions make no sense from a holistic, life-enhancing point of view, they make perfect sense within the technocratic model, "which holds that whatever predicaments our technocratic ideology gets us into, our technological skills will get us out of" (284).

I am fully convinced by Davis-Floyd's historical, social, and cultural explanations of why most women accept the medical model. At the same time, I think we need to take into account the immediate social context in which women give birth. Sociologists Bonnie Fox and Diana Worts do just that. Their interviews with forty first-time mothers in Toronto reveal that women who had solid, ongoing support, especially from their partners and mothers, were most likely to resist medical intervention during labor and birth, and least likely to suffer from postpartum depression. Most importantly, such support helped women to endure intense labor pain. By supportive partners, Fox and Worts mean those who were not only helpful during labor and birth but also could be expected to share responsibility for parenting and domestic life after the baby's birth. Women who had no realistic expectation of such support were much more likely to welcome medical intervention during labor. Fox and Worts interpret this pattern in light of our society's treatment of mothering as a woman's privatized responsibility. Because that responsibility is too much for any one individual, women embrace medicalized birth as a substitute for social support in their immediate context. Until society makes a dramatic shift to shared or collective parenting, Fox and Worts suggest, many women will seek the limited and inadequate support they get from medicalized birth.[57]

Working on this chapter made me rethink my own birth experience. I wanted to give birth without medical intervention but working with a midwife was not an option under my health insurance. The closest John and I could get was to choose an obstetrician known for his noninterventionist approach, take a childbirth course with a Bradley teacher known for her holistic approach, and hire a doula for labor support. When the time came, I labored two days and three nights with no sleep and little food. My contractions were plenty strong, but my labor progressed very slowly. Finally, completely exhausted, I asked for an epidural. Several hours later, still stuck at seven centimeters dilation, my obstetrician told me I had no choice but a cesarean. By that point I was ready.

I was, and still am, confident that I did the best I could under the circumstances. I am grateful for the nurses' willingness to let me labor as long as I wanted to without intervention. (Again, I believe the leeway I was given may have been influenced by my social class and race, and by the doula's presence.) I am also thankful for my obstetrician's expertise and the technology that made a cesarean possible when I needed it. But studying the feminist critique of the medical model made me wonder what my birth experience would have been like under different circumstances. What if I had been at home, attended by a midwife, and not just two supportive people (John had little sleep during my labor and so was also completely exhausted; the doula had to leave at a certain point to care for her own children), but also by my mother, my sister, and friends who have been through childbirth themselves and who could take turns helping me? If solid social support enables a woman to endure intense pain, could it not also have helped me to endure exhaustion from such a prolonged labor?

I will never know, of course, whether my nine-pound baby really was too big for me to give birth myself (the official diagnosis) or whether in time I would have fully dilated. Furthermore, the image of me at home, surrounded by a legion of supportive people, is completely impractical in our contemporary society. I could not expect family and friends to take time away from jobs and domestic responsibilities to devote several days to my needs. Two hundred years ago, maybe, but not today. Yet this impracticality merely points us back to the contemporary organization of our society and its cultural priorities. Although birth is an epiphanal moment in many women's lives, our society is not organized in ways that recognize and value the birth process.

On another level, working on this chapter made me wonder whether I am one of Davis-Floyd's "women-in-between." I did want very much to have a holistic birth. Yet in the absence of practical, experiential knowledge of what that means (I had never attended a childbirth before my own), I found it impossible not to rely on the knowledge and expertise of the nurses and obstetrician. I have come to believe that trusting one's maternal body requires much than an intellectual critique of the medical model.

Living Within, Thinking From, and Trusting Maternal Bodies

It would be a mistake to view the women's health movement's holistic model of birth as creating a new rigid standard for birth performance. The feminist goal is to make holistic birth possible, not to condemn the "choices" individual women currently make under conditions that are far from ideal.[58] The aim is to change the ideological and social conditions under which most women currently give birth. I conclude this chapter, then, by outlining some pivotal feminist ideas about women's maternal bodies. I have already touched on many of these ideas because they are embedded in the feminist critiques of the medical model of pregnancy and birth, as well as in the research on women's actual experiences. I gather these ideas together here, and illustrate them with quotations in order to leave us with strong, provocative images of what it means to live within, think from, and trust maternal bodies.

The sheer physicality of pregnancy needs to be respected; it often shapes a woman's sense of self, her subjectivity. Philosopher Iris Marion Young:

> Pregnancy roots me to the earth, makes me conscious of the physicality of my body not as an object, but as the material weight that I am in

> movement. . . . In the experience of the pregnant woman, this weight and materiality often produce a sense of power, solidity, and validity.[59]

Pregnancy is an activity, not just a physical condition. Philosopher Sara Ruddick:

> Pregnancy is an active, receptive waiting that cannot be hurried. To call that waiting a "physical condition" . . . obscures the activity of waiting. . . . Active waiting has an intrinsic relational character. A birthgiver can take care of her fetus simply by taking good care of herself.[60]

Pregnancy is both a physical and social relationship between a woman and her fetus, a relationship of connection and embodiment. Sociologist Barbara Katz Rothman:

> The mother, as a social being, is responding socially to the experience of carrying her baby. . . . When a baby uses her bladder as a trampoline, the woman responds. She responds not only by making another trip to the bathroom; she responds socially, with annoyance, amusement, irritation, anger, sometimes even with pleasure at the apparent liveliness of the baby, and most often by the end of the pregnancy with a longing to end this phase of the relationship.[61]

The relationship between a woman and her fetus alters her subjectivity in ways that are unique. Barbara Katz Rothman: "The isolated, atomistic individual is an absurdity when one is pregnant: one is two, two are one." (89)

Childbirth is a process that has the potential to integrate a woman's mind and body, thus overcoming a duality and hierarchy so prevalent in Western culture. Anthropologist Emily Martin: "Why can we not see [birthing women] as engaged in higher-order activity? . . . Here, perhaps, are whole human beings, all their parts interrelated, engaged in what may be the only form of truly unalienated labor now available to us."[62]

If women were truly able to control the conditions of reproduction, most births would be very different than they are today. Emily Martin:

> If birthing is part of our river of life, part of an inward and outward journey, we would want it to occur where we live our lives, at home, surrounded by friends and family. If birthing is hard work, but work that is rewarding in the doing of it, then we would want to be given time, encouragement, and support to do it ourselves. If birthing is a profound, heightened experience involving deep (often ecstatic) feelings and perception of powerful forces in the world, we would want the experience, period. (159)

Martin's ideas offer a strong introduction to Barbara Katz Rothman's account in narrative K of her desire to give birth at home. Rothman wanted to control the conditions of her labor and she wanted to define birth as a natural rather than a medical process. Her story about the birth itself shows how empowering home birth can be and it shows that strong social support can make all the difference in a woman's birth experience.

Pregnancy and birth partake of natural forces that cannot always be and should not always be predicted or controlled. A deep respect for those natural forces requires moving beyond the desire for control.

For example, instead of being controlled, pain can be chosen. Anthropologist Robbie E. Davis-Floyd:

> It seems to be a fundamental assumption of Western culture that pain is bad. Perhaps we devalue pain so much because it, like birth, reminds us of our human weaknesses—our naturalness, our dependence on nature. Machines don't feel pain, so if we are going to be like them, neither should we. The physical—and conceptual—experience of pain, like the physical and conceptual experience of birth, grounds us in our natural selves.[63]

Respecting the power of nature and the limits of human control also means understanding the connections between birth and death. In narrative L, Kathryn March points out that "control" and "choice" are words that can marginalize the experiences of women who face infertility, miscarriage, stillbirth, or the death of an infant. She argues that American culture, with its focus on the joyfulness of birth, fails to offer adequate recognition of the grief that often accompanies pregnancy and childbirth. She implores us to hear women's stories of loss because loss is as integral as joy to women's lives.

NARRATIVE K

Childbirth with Power

Barbara Katz Rothman

Note: In 1973, during her first pregnancy, Barbara Katz Rothman sought and found an obstetrician who was willing to assist her in a home birth.

• • •

[My desire to give birth at home] had something very basic to do with control, power, and authority. At home, I would have them; in the hospital they would be handed over to the institution. I read arguments for home rather than hospital birth that spoke about privacy. For me it was less a question of privacy and more a question of authority. At home, nobody was coming in the door whom I did not choose to have come in. One doctor alone or a dozen assistants—they would all be there because I personally hired them, and I personally could tell any one of them to leave. I was willing to delegate control over my body to the doctor—more so then, in fact, than I ever would now—but it was only because I expected her to be making her decisions on the basis of what I thought of as "medical expertise," and not on the basis of "them's the rules," or of whatever is most convenient in an institution that's simultaneously processing umpty-seven baby-making women.

Besides the authority/control issue, there were other reasons. I was having a baby, after all, and not an appendectomy. It's a condition of healthiness, not of illness. At home I would be simply having a baby. At the hospital? You do not put someone in a hospital gown, place her on a hospital table under hospital lights, and affix little bracelets to her arm so that you can always tell whose baby is whose, and not create the image of "patient." A woman cannot view herself as healthy while all the external cues proclaim illness. At home I would go into labor and call the doctor, and eventually she would show up and eventually the baby would be born, and eventually the doctor would leave, and I'd be there, with the baby outside of me instead of inside. There would be a continuum, and I would always be me, my own self in charge of my own self. The hospital alternative meant that first I would go into labor and then we'd have to decide when it was "serious" enough for me to be driven to the hospital, to become a patient. From there on, I'd be processed through—in clearly demarcated stages—labor room, delivery room, wherever one goes there after, and then back home. So, it was partly a question of how the situation is defined, and again partly a question of control over self and situation.

But what about safety? How would I feel if something went wrong? There was something very interesting that I realized I had to deal with. Anything that went wrong was going to be my fault if I did it at home, or at least was going to be perceived as my fault. I had to take on that responsibility personally—I couldn't even share it with Hesch. It was my problem. If the child was born without arms or something, somehow it was going to be my fault for having had it at home. Logic or no, that was going to be in people's minds, and maybe even in the back of my mind.

It's a tricky question, maybe best dealt with through the sociology of knowledge, as to what we define as risk-taking behavior, and what as normal, acceptable behavior. One of the many doctors I talked to about home birth assured me that I would not have to go to the hospital until I was pretty far along in labor. And the one I was seeing had said that I could go home right after the birth if it was important to me. Now, things do sometimes go wrong early in labor, babies do sometimes die when they're two days old, women do sometimes hemorrhage twelve hours later—but those were acceptable risks, risks the doctors were willing to take. So it was never a question of risk or no risk, but of which risks.

That was never so clear to me as when I saw women who would never subject their babies to the risk of home birth leaving the hospital to drive home, without seat belts, holding their babies loose in their arms in the front seats of Volkswagens. I, on the other hand, with fears of a baby smashed on the windshield in a sudden stop, went out and purchased the best infant car seat made and bolted it into place before the baby was even born, so that if we had to transfer it to a hospital we would have safe transportation.

• • •

Appeals to the doctor about the beauty of the birth experience did not impress her. I'm not even sure that I myself was convinced on that level. But the issues of autonomy and control were good, solid, feminist issues she could relate to—it was, after all, the basic issue of a woman's right to control her body. She agreed because she was a good feminist. So, we were on.

Around three-thirty on a Tuesday morning, the week before my due date, I woke to find myself in labor. It must be awkward and make a person feel silly to go rushing off to the hospital on a "false alarm," but to bring the doctor to me if I wasn't really in labor was unthinkable. So I just stayed in bed, read the Times, polished my nails, made a list of things to get done, and sometimes tried to time the contractions. But I kept getting up to go to the bathroom and losing track.

By eight-thirty I decided it was time to get mobilized. I woke up Hesch and handed him the watch and the list (things like "make sure we have ice cubes, clean the bathroom, make the bed, sweep"—baby or no baby, we had company coming!). I left a message with the doctor's answering service that I was almost certainly in labor and called my mother and asked her to drop off the cushions she was recovering for my big platform rocker. She and my sister visited for a few minutes on their way to work.

I sat in my rocking chair while Hesch cleaned up. We found pretty music on the radio, and chatted and timed contractions. On Hesch's list (we are crackerjack list makers) he noted that at eleven o'clock I was looking happy and self-satisfied, beginning to feel an outward, downward thrust to the contractions. But by eleven-thirty he noted that I was looking decidedly uncomfortable.

The doctor had returned our call and told Hesch to remind me that it was really going to hurt. It helps us to understand what is going on anatomically when we speak of "contractions" rather than "pains"; but the contractions of labor are painful, and I guess it's easier to deal with them if your expectations are realistic. So I wasn't frightened or worried, and knew perfectly well what was happening, and started using the breathing techniques I had been taught. By then my mother had left work and was sitting in my room looking at me—compassionately. I didn't think I would be able to deal with it all in a grown-up, sensible way with her there, but would revert to being a little girl with a bellyache who wanted her mommy to make it all go away. So, my mother left me alone with Hesch.

If I had been going to the hospital, that is probably the point at which we'd have gone. Contractions were strong and occurring every three minutes. I was still sitting in my chair, with Hesch sitting opposite me and very gently rubbing my belly, when the doctor arrived, at around two o'clock. By then we had given up timing, no longer able to sort out the pain into separate contractions. The doctor timed the contractions at two and a half minutes, with ten-second rests, and told me I could expect a "horrendous but short" labor. She also asked if I drank, and when I said yes, had my mother send up some gin. She examined me again about an hour later, and thought maybe it wasn't going to be such a short labor after all, and decided to go to the drugstore for Demerol. I never had to use it. By the time she got back I was making real progress.

All afternoon our family had been arriving, one by one. My mother sat tensed at the bottom of the stairs while Hesch's mother compulsively cooked chickens. Father and siblings sat around. When I cried out during a particularly painful examination, the doctor went out afterward to explain to them that I was okay—and came back with the message that they were all bearing up well.

Sometime after four o'clock, I entered the phase of labor called transition, in which the last few centimeters of dilatation takes place, the cervix opening up completely to let the baby come through. Birth-preparation classes warn that it is the most difficult stage, but for me it was an incredible relief. The contractions may have been more painful—I really don't know—but they started sorting themselves out into separate entities, maybe ninety seconds on and sixty off. Again, I'm not sure. But they did have peaks and, blessed be, valleys. Hesch (who never moved from his seat opposite me) suggested I deal with the contractions by using two pants and a blow. That was the smartest thing I've ever heard in my life. I was impressed by how clever and insightful he was—it sounds silly, but that's just the way I felt: how clever an idea. That, I gather, is what they mean when they say you need strong direction during labor.

I'd read that women get a "second wind" once they're fully dilated and ready to begin pushing the baby out, and it was certainly true for me. Pushing was the strangest, and in some ways the nicest, sensation I've ever had. I could actually feel the shape of the baby, feel myself sitting on the head as it moved down. The doctor said I looked comfortable enough on the chair, and I didn't have to get to the bed if I didn't want to. At the time, the thought of moving, especially from a good, comfortable, well-supported seated position, to flat-out on a bed, seemed ridiculous. So there I was, on my rocking chair, with my feet up on two little kitchen chairs, with Hesch on one side and the doctor on the other, and pushing like crazy. It was like moving a grand piano across a room: that hard, but that satisfying, to feel it moving along.

The doctor asked if there was a mirror around. I said "Skip it," I didn't really want one. Hesch read my mind and said that there wasn't a lot of blood and that I looked fine, and sent down for a mirror.

Eventually the doctor said I could have the baby in two pushes with an episiotomy (the small incision to widen the birth outlet), or maybe ten pushes without. I said no thanks. I thought, hell, I still wasn't sure it was happening; maybe I could accept the reality of it given the few extra minutes. I really needed the time to prepare myself, as with the last-second cramming before the exam booklets are passed out.

Hesch said my mother wanted to come in. For a moment, I wanted to say no but realized that was just too selfish, that I was fine now. I said to send her in. My mother-in-law came in shortly afterward. It didn't take me ten pushes, just five. I heard noises coming out of my throat that I couldn't believe—like the soundtrack of a horror movie, but I had no time to laugh. And then I felt myself sitting on the head, felt myself opening, felt the head push through: a beautiful, total sense of opening and roundness. The shoulders seemed big, and the shape was less comfortable than the symmetry of the head. And then—slurp, wriggling, warmth, wetness, and there was a baby. He was up in the air, upside down, the doctor holding him over me. The longest few seconds in the world passed, and then this gray-blue thing became alive and pink and breathing. The doctor handed him to my mother. I kept reaching out for him, but my mother was too dazed to move. I watched the cord being clamped and cut, and my baby, my son, Danny, was suckling by the time the placenta was out.

After maybe five minutes I stood and spilled blood all over the floor, and my mother walked me to the shower. As much as I had needed Hesch's support before, I felt the need for mothering then. I got the shakes—part physical, part emotional reaction, I guess. She bundled me up so that I was warm and, helped me put on a sanitary napkin—it was like the first time I got my period and was initiated into all the mysteries. Once I was changed and back into the rocker, and Hesch and his mother had cleaned up the blood that had spurted from the cord, the whole world was in my room. Brothers and sisters and parents; suddenly, aunts and uncles and grandparents. They brought with them champagne and flowers and a teddy bear and a silver spoon, and looks of wonderment and love. It was the best birthday party I had ever been to. I had another gin and tonic and a chocolate malted and champagne all at once, while everybody ate dinner. We'd been smelling my mother-in-law's garlicky chickens for hours.

As much as I had wanted it, I don't think even I had understood how good it can be to have a baby at home. I never really was a "patient." I wasn't in bed; I had my contact lenses in throughout (only the myopic can understand what it means to remain in touch with the world visually); I gave birth, freely and consciously—I was not *delivered.* And my baby and I were surrounded by love, not efficiency. Images pass through my mind—my mother-in-law helping me get my breast out of my nightgown and to Danny; my brother, carrying a big plastic garbage bag down from the bedroom, singing "afterbirth" to the tune of "Over There"; my mother and Hesch trying to clean up the meconium (the baby's first bowel movement) in the middle of the night without waking me. I am sure there are more efficient ways to do these things—but who needs them?

The pediatrician came the next day to examine the baby. She kept telling us we were crazy. The baby looked big and healthy (he was eight pounds, five ounces, and had been a nine-plus on the Apgar newborn scale of ten), and I looked good, dressed and walking-around, up and down stairs; but still we were crazy.

• • •

NARRATIVE L

Childbirth with Fear

Kathryn S. March

When we talk about reproduction, our language, especially as feminists, is about "choice": the freedom to parent, or not to parent. My own experiences have been more constrained. I have struggled to find the words to talk about them, without much success. These are things we do not talk about. Clinically, they are called "childbearing losses"—infertility, miscarriage, stillbirth, and neonatal death, among others. These losses touch many more people than any of us believe. Still, we are collectively silent.

• • •

I began to see life through my cervix darkly, when, in 1971, I was among the first to get a Dalkon Shield IUD. As happened to so many others,[1] an infection nearly cost me my life. As young women concerned about *not* getting pregnant then, few of us realized that the very device we chose to get control over our bodies could take it away further. Each woman's experiences vary but, for most of us, "control" was lost with those first embarrassing unpredictable menses. For those of us who live in women's bodies, the issue of control is not the same issue it is for those who do not. If anything, pregnancy and childbearing are the prototype for absence of control.

I had a tubal pregnancy in 1973, followed by four laparotomies and numberless other infertility treatments between 1979 and 1981. Major surgery in 1982 tried to fix the then-remaining tube, and was followed by increasingly aggressive hormonal interventions. We went into an *in vitro* program in 1985, but I found myself pregnant, in a nontreatment cycle, only to lose that child, starting with placental separation and hypoxia at his birth and then in daily medical and legal machinations for

From Mother Journeys: Feminists Write about Mothering, *edited by Maureen T. Reddy, Martha Roth, and Amy Sheldon. Spinsters Ink, 1994. Available from Spinsters Ink, 32 East First Street #330, Duluth, Minnesota 55802. Reprinted by permission.*

the six months of his sadly compromised nonlife. A second *in vitro* program in 1986 was disrupted when again I was pregnant; it was in and destroyed the other tube. More recent attempts in 1988–89 at *in vitro* progressed farther, but there were no more babies.[2] I spent all my early adult years, then, alternately enjoying the wider vistas of childfreeness and obsessed with my ever more constricting childlessness.

Instead of loss of "control," however, what I felt was failure. I was schooled early in responsibility: first, as the oldest and only girl child; then, later, as a feminist eager to chart my own life course. Perhaps because in most respects I have been successful, my inability even to foresee, let alone forestall, my varied reproductive disasters was an unexpected insult. Never, and in no other matter, have I felt so worthless. Especially having cast the issue of mothering as a "choice," I had no shelter from the double blow of neither being a mother, nor having chosen *not* to be one.

I always knew I wanted children. But I wanted many other things as well: a loving partner and a job I loved. I resented the polarity presented by popular wisdom and my mother—that you had to choose between having children and having meaningful work if you were a woman. Even though I tried to be realistic about my inadequacies as a superwoman, I hoped that, especially if you had a partner who shared your desires and if, together, you were willing to make endless compromises, it didn't have to be an either-or decision. Imagine my consternation: I thought the problem in redefining mothering was juggling family and work without too much personal or professional damage; instead, *not* having a family extracted a devastating toll on both counts.

But the terrible irony of all my efforts to understand what had happened to my body, and why willpower couldn't make babies, or make them whole, or how to move beyond my grief and anger is this: there is often nothing there to understand. It is, all too often, a gratuitous lesson in bad luck. Slowly, I am coming to accept that there is no sense to be extracted from the senseless. To be unlucky is, however, unfashionable, in this era of planned pregnancies and a woman's right to decide. As an explanation, it helped assuage the guilt and blame, but not the feelings of failure, anger, jealousy or fear. I was at loss again, buffeted by unfamiliar political currents. We—feminists and not, alike—are encouraged to think of childbearing as the most natural thing in the world. Childbirth without fear is the idiom of our generation. It is not mine: my births and non-births have been all wrong; mine is very much childbearing with fear.

Uneasily, I have tried to set my fears aside. And I tried to return to my work as an anthropologist of women's worlds and gender. I have been working on a book based on women's life stories and songs from the other side of the world, in Nepal. Childbearing figured importantly in the telling of their lives, but their tales were not at all like those of women I knew here.

Most of the birth stories I'd heard in the United States danced around a maypole of joyful images. . . .

Not so the accounts from women I met in the course of my anthropological work in Nepal. They expected to face suffering and death in birth. One life history I recorded came from a woman . . . in her ninth month with her third:

> It's a personal plague, this illness, this childbearing. . . . Some others have no trouble; I, I have a lot. . . . a lot of hardship. That's all you can think about. You know you are pregnant and then as soon as you are pregnant, that's all you can think about . . . hardship. All night long, worry and suffering come to mind. You try to sleep, but you can't.
>
> [She began to cry softly, but held tightly to my hand and continued talking.] You try to do your work, but you can't. Others speak to you sharply; they scold you. You think about it and only anguish comes into your mind. It's your own personal anguish. It's very hard. . . .
>
> [Very deliberately] I wonder how it will be for me: if what's inside me is a source of grief and trouble, how will I survive? What might happen? That's what comes to me now. I don't think about anything before now, or anything that might come after. At any other time, it wouldn't bother me, but when I'm this way and can't do anything . . . When I'm this way and can't do anything and get scolded, my heart-and-mind is pained; I feel like crying. I feel like crying, and I cry. I even cry when it comes time to go to sleep. . . .
>
> [Pausing] Maybe I'll die. Or maybe I'll live. How will it be? What will happen to me? That's what comes to me now; that's what's in this heart-and-mind of mine. . . . My heart-and-mind hurts! I hurt and a crying need overcomes me and then I cry. I cry.

• • •

The difference between [birth stories in the United States and Nepal] is not statistical. Or at least it is not just that. Infant and maternal mortality are high in countries like Nepal, but they have not vanished from the medical landscape in the United States.

• • •

It is not just, then, that other women are more likely to suffer childbearing losses than their American counterparts are. It is that, regardless of the individual experiences of women in either country, my overseas friends (however counterproductive it may sound to us), surround their contemplation of childbearing with shared and loudly voiced expressions of fear. We, on the other hand, collectively want to think of childbearing without fear so we surround ourselves with a discourse of joy. We can presume (although, of course, never know) that women everywhere experience about the same range of pains and pleasure coming from childbearing, children and mothering. What is different is how we express that range. What they talk about easily, we cannot. And vice versa.

American expectant parents arm themselves with lollipops for labor, worry about whether there will be enough light in the delivery room for their cameras, and stock up "baby on board" signs almost as soon as they set aside their diaphragms. Our newspapers discreetly withhold announcements of births that are, or are soon to be, deaths. Miscarriages are mentioned only in whispers. And infertility is not mentioned at all.

Quite conversely, the women and their families that I came to know through my field research publicly bewail infertility, repeat miscarriages, hard births, and deaths in and near birth. They are, in many respects, collectively unable to give voice to the joys that are potentially there for them, too. Where they are distressed by the ways in which their childbearing fears loom so large culturally, we have been deceived by our shared faith that chosen childbearing is always happy.

Nowhere are we so deceived as in our own childbirth education. I never got to take my "birthing kit" with me when I rushed to the hospital spouting blood, but its irrelevance was waiting for me—lollipops, camera, warm socks, focal point, and all—when I came home. Two of the couples in our childbirth education class lost babies, ourselves to placental abruption and another to prematurity with fatal birth defects. All that we had learned in class seemed to me afterwards like so much disinformation. Nothing had ever been said about babies born dead. Or dying. Or unformed for life.

When our childbirth educator came to see me sometime after the delivery, I asked why all the "birth reports" she had shared with us had been without trauma. Where were the thousands of stillbirths, birth defects, and neonatal deaths? She—a bright, blond, long-legged mother of three handsome births—agreed there was a problem: she worried what effect the news of our disasters would have on the remaining members of the class. I worry more what the effect of such classes is on those of us whose experiences do not fulfill their cheery expectations.

• • •

Seeing the difference in how childbearing losses and fears are expressed in different cultures has been, for me, almost a revelation. In the U.S., I have many good, deep and dear friends. Family, too, is always there in support and love. Indeed, without their encouragement and affection, I surely could not be writing as I do. But talk—the kind that shares knowledge, validates experience, and understands the struggle to heal—is missing. People "don't know what to say." The few who come forward to talk about the ordinary and the terrifying without melodrama are cherished. The irony, of course, is that our general silence binds each new victim in its ever-widening conspiratorial circles.

When I returned to my original fieldwork in Nepal, I found a completely different interplay of talk, experience and emotion. In America, for example, ask anyone how many children they have and you will hear about Liz, who's eleven, and Johnny, who's five. About living children, in other words. When women talk at parties about their pregnancies, difficulties are only a vaguely humorous subtext on successful outcomes. The words of the women of my work re-count their children very differently: they include all births, near births, still births, and deaths. "Seven children have come to me," said one friend, "the eldest daughter I still have today; the two sons born after her died, one was born dead and the other died after he was big;

then came the son I still have who is now grown; last are my two little daughters I still have, but in between them was the 'half-trail' [miscarried] baby I lost."

Hearing these women talk, I came to recognize some of the characteristics of my situation: the night sweats, the forgetting to breathe, the inability to complete sentences, the fatigue, the anger, the increased (not lessened) desire for more children, my monochrome vision and the general two-dimensional flatness to the world, the sense that time had stopped still, the fear that my own ill fortune could be contagious, the need for physical contact.

Their discussions of infertility, childbearing trauma and death, however, did not extend to understanding the special ironies of cosmopolitan medical practice with regard to our birth son's death or our many infertility treatments. They talked about death and infertility openly, but they could not know how uneasy American medicine is about death and unbirth—each in its own way ultimately beyond the scope of the miracles of modern science.

It was among these Nepalese friends that I was fortunate to learn answers to the many questions I didn't even know how or whom to ask at home: how long would my breasts continue to produce milk? why do I fall asleep only to wake up violently three hours later? how long was it before you stopped crying every day? what did you do when others got angry with you? how did you keep from hurting your other children? how did you interact with others and their children, especially those who are the age yours would be?

• • •

I chuckle to imagine how these women's stories would chill American conversations. Cocktail party question: 'When did you say that the new highway was built?' or 'When was it that the old barn burned?' Answer: 'Just before Mary was born,' or 'When I was pregnant with Ted,' but not 'Oh, that was the summer I had my third miscarriage,' or 'When my only son was dying.' Those of us who have lost pregnancies or children tell time by them, too; but we have learned to keep them to ourselves. To bring them up would redefine any conversation as a highly-charged encounter session. Even people who have experienced similar losses share only the general fact that they, too, have felt a similar pain. We do not talk about specifics. And we definitely do not talk about them over breakfast, on airplanes, or at parties.

• • •

Our individual and collective denial of the place of fear in childbearing puts us all at a dreadfilled risk. Put bluntly, it seems obvious: how could we ever have imagined that reproductive choice, self-confidence, or freedom from fear would conceive children and deliver them up whole? For those of us whose fears are not realized (who maybe birthed healthy children, more or less easily), even the ghost of fearfulness is cast aside because it was "wrong" in not accurately foretelling disaster. For those whose attempts to overcome our fears still did not see good results, the realized fear that others continue to deny leaves us horribly alone, confused and unable to reach out even for solace.

It is not, however, the fears themselves that we need to set aside, but our fear of talking about fear. In childbearing, whether from the charged perspective of modern professional womanhood or from distant rural lifeways, bad things will happen to many of us, whether or not we are brave. To silence our fears denies the special poignancy and very human vulnerability of childbearing, in which happy endings are separated from sad ones by chance as much as will.

Notes

1. Including at least the 330,000 who have filed a class action suit against A.H. Robins, manufacturers of the Dalkon Shield IUD.

2. Lest this tale seem one of unremitting woe, I must also say that, after the long dying of our birth son, and with support of family and friends, I travelled abroad as soon as I reasonably could, both to complete some research that had been started long ago and to pursue adoption. Our son was almost four when he came to us and is now an energetic, courageous eight-year-old. A year and a half after he made us a family again, we went abroad in search of a second child. Our daughter was seventeen months when she came to us. She and her story are completely different from her brother's, but today she charges through life with all the physical and verbal gusto that should mark any four-year-old. She and her brother have very different personalities and, undoubtedly, possibilities, but together they bring us the joy and chaos that we had been seeking. And more. I don't include them in this story more fully only because this paper is about how we come to terms with childbearing sorrows, not the pleasures in parenting—which they are.

CHAPTER 7

Family Making and Reproductive Technologies

While researching this chapter, I visited the website of Creating Families, Inc. Like infertility clinics and other sites of "reproductive medicine," Creating Families deploys a distinctive, dehumanized vocabulary. Couples (and individuals sometimes) arrive at such sites after having been diagnosed as infertile. They may need not only the services of medical personnel for such procedures as in vitro fertilization (IVF) but also the assistance of sperm donors, egg donors, surrogate mothers, or surrogate gestational carriers. This last phrase refers to a woman pregnant with a fetus to whom she has no genetic connection. Instead, one or both members of the "commissioning couple" has that connection with the child-to-be. Infertile people may still try to adopt a child, but today their options also include embryo adoption involving the frozen leftovers of others' reproductive efforts.

Creating Families, Inc. crowds its Web site with information that left me reeling. That cognitive vertigo matched what I had felt weeks earlier when I launched this research with readings about the ethics of assisted conception in all its dazzling, growing variety. How could I do justice to a topic so at odds with most people's ideas about family making? In the end I decided to begin with the lived experiences of those yearning to be parents who learn that their bodies will not readily cooperate in that endeavor. I begin, then, with the phenomenology of infertility, which focuses on the kinds of consciousness and experiences associated with infertility in American society today. All the while, the actual voices of infertile people, especially women, remain mostly absent here. The narratives at the end of this chapter serve as a preliminary corrective to that absence but cannot erase it. Sadly, infertile women's voices are still not usually heard, even in feminist analyses.[1]

The Phenomenology of Infertility

Over a million Americans are treated for "infertility-related problems" each year at a cost of roughly $1 billion. Paul Lauritzen and his wife were two of those people. As he emphasizes in *Pursuing Parenthood: Ethical Issues in Assisted*

This chapter was written by Mary F. Rogers.

Reproduction, widespread "intervention in the reproductive process . . . reveals the importance of the values and interests at stake here."[2] This part of the chapter aims at illuminating how those values and interests affect infertile people, whose experiences are profoundly personal as well as substantially cultural. Their experiences are about personhood as well as parenthood, identity as well as family, choices and constraints as well as relationships and technologies.

"Ambiguity" may be the key to understanding experiences of infertility in societies like ours. As Margarete Sandelowski shows to great effect, infertility is ambiguous in multiple ways. First, "it is a condition of *not yet* achieving or maintaining a viable pregnancy." Temporally, infertility is anchored in waiting[3]—waiting to see whether or not a pregnancy eventuates without medical intervention, waiting to see whether or not a medical procedure "worked," waiting to see whether or not a pregnancy can go full term. Thus, infertility can seem like a "tentative condition" until all one's options have run out. Yet the time-consciousness of infertile people is more complex than that.[4] As Sandelowski notes, it often involves anxiety both "about time running out and time wasted in pursuit of parenthood" (178).

Second, infertility comprises ambiguous prospects. Its not-yet character has a parallel in its in-between status. As Sandelowski observes, "infertile couples are neither absolutely capable nor incapable of procreation" (11). Their "state of in-betweenness" (92) lands them in a gray area where the possibilities of parenthood beckon, but the odds are against them. Given the diverse technologies available today, people can resist the in-between, commit to the not-yet, and struggle against infertility as long as their resources permit. Pressures to do so may be on the rise in American and other societies where the supply of infertility services may be outpacing the demand.

Third, as Sandelowski points out, infertility is ambiguous in its mix of physical and psychological elements. It originates "with the desire for, rather than with the inability to have, a child" (19). In other words, those of us who may be physically infertile but who never wanted a child enough to act on that desire are unlikely to have *experienced* infertility. By contrast, finding that one's own or one's partner's body poses some impediment to fulfilling one's desire for a child makes infertility an unsettling condition, comprising an ambiguous amalgam of psychological as well as physical challenges.

Fourth, infertility is ambiguous in terms of treatment. Even though it is a medicalized phenomenon overseen by experts in reproductive medicine and therapy (as well as the law), infertility's treatment is usually far from clear-cut. Infertile people face expanding options that can even intensify their desire for a child.[5] Among the experiences of some infertile individuals, then, is uncertainty about how much their reproductive desire comes from them and how much derives from infertility experts offering encouragement, statistics, and other grounds for heightened expectations. Elizabeth Bartholet, the author of narrative M, reports, "In the nearly ten years that I struggled with infertility, I spoke to dozens of different doctors, nurses, administrators, and social workers. . . . No one ever asked me to think hard about what I was doing and why. No one ever advised me to seek counseling to deal with my feelings about infertility. No one ever suggested that I consider adoption as an alternative to further treatment or proposed ways to find out more about adoption."[6]

Finally, infertility is ambiguous in its outcome. It "ends" when the infertile individual decides so. It may result "in childlessness, in fewer children, or in . . . having children only after a delay," often involving medical treatment or some other intervention.[7] That infertility typically has unpredictable results in part reflects the growing choices available to those with the financial and psychological resources to pursue extended treatment.

Choice is as central to experiences of infertility as ambiguity is. As assisted conception becomes more diverse, infertile people face multiple decisions where once they had no practical alternatives at all.[8] Lauritzen emphasizes the pressures on infertile people to turn to technologies; "they become difficult to avoid." Thus, some infertile people face "inescapable but unwanted choices" as reproductive technologies proliferate. They may feel, as Lauritzen did, that they "should at least try it, if only once." After all, Lauritzen concludes, to reject the reproductive technologies means "to accept responsibility for one's childlessness."[9] Not surprisingly, women pursuing pregnancy through IVF typically report that "they 'had to try'" it.[10] Moreover, once individuals begin treatment, they often feel the "obligation to keep trying," which "is powerfully reinforced from the outside."[11] Infertility specialists encourage keen determination, which they take as evidence of one's suitability for treatment. The rapid proliferation of new twists on extant approaches also heightens the possibility of getting trapped in treatment. Sometimes "publicity about new technologies can open the old wounds of those who truly felt that they were done with trying."[12]

Thus, reproductive choice is often painfully difficult for infertile individuals.[13] As consumerist as it is medical in nature, such choice carries the same fate as all choosing: it is powerfully constrained by one's life circumstances as well as other factors. Ultimately, for example, physicians determine who gets accepted for treatment as well as which "treatment regimen" is best. If a patient objects or holds back, she may be seen as uncooperative and thus compromise her treatment status, at least slightly.[14]

Although "choice" figures prominently in popular and professional discourses about infertility, little is said about how choosing may get particularly wrenching when two people are typically involved.[15] Imagine that a wife and her husband differ markedly in their desire for a child, especially a child genetically connected with one or both of them. Imagine what ensues when that couple finds they cannot readily bring a child into the world together. Usually, only one of the individuals is diagnosed as infertile. Think about the challenges that eventuate when that person is also the partner less committed to having a child. Yet reproductive medicine has been institutionalized with the *couple* as the patient, in effect, not solely the individual whose body is somehow at reproductive issue. Also pertinent is the typical circumstance that the couple rarely consists of two equally advantaged partners. This bare-bones scenario conjures up all the complexities of reproductive choice when choices typically have to be made by two people unequally motivated, unequally problematic in the reproductive process, and unequally advantaged in society at large.

Sandelowski, among others, sees problems in thinking of the "patient as more-than-one." Of particular concern to her are the "unequal relationships of power that actually exist among the individuals who compose the unit of care." Similarly, Caroline Whitbeck notes that assisted conception often requires these unequal partners "to engage in new and unfamiliar negotiations with one another."[16] In addition to all else, their negotiations must somehow take into account the greater intrusions the wife and prospective mother will experience with most technologies or the greater displacement she may experience with options such as contract (or "surrogate") motherhood.

Usually, the husband and prospective father has a stronger preference for a child genetically connected to him than the wife and prospective mother has. Judith Lasker and Sarah Borg, among others, report that "[m]any women told us they would be happy to adopt but that their husbands wanted a genetic connection." Lasker and Borg conclude, "It is for the men that many women are pursuing a pregnancy, to have 'his' child."[17] Sociologist Judith Lorber sees that situation as laying the grounds for a patriarchal bargain that many wives ultimately make. Such a bargain involves trying to maintain one's relationship and have a child "within the constraints of monogamy, the nuclear family structure, and the valorization of biological parenthood, especially for men."[18]

Besides the constraints on choice that typically come with couplehood are those that come with other life circumstances. In the United States only individuals who are at least solidly middle-income and those who have medical insurance have any reliable access to assisted conception and other reproductive technologies.[19] In addition, most infertility clinics restrict their services to married heterosexual couples. Creating Families, Inc. is an exception. Its Web site announces its willingness to work with single women as well as lesbian and gay couples. Race also serves as a constraint, at least indirectly. Just as sexual orientation and marital status are statistically associated with one another, so are race and social class in American society. Even though infertility among black wives is perhaps 150 percent greater than among white wives, the former group less often uses reproductive technologies. Cultural values may interplay with economic constraints to yield that pattern. More than women in other classes and racial groups, for example, "[m]iddle-class white women . . . experience infertility as a frustrating foreclosure of choice; they seek to regain personal control . . . through medical intervention." At the same time, however, "[e]ducated, affluent women of all racial backgrounds have similar rates of childlessness," suggesting that in the higher reaches of the middle classes racial differences among prospective mothers decrease.[20]

All the while, the emotional toll of involuntary infertility tends to run extremely high. Women, more than men, "express the pain and isolation of childlessness." Many anguish over their state, experiencing childlessness as no "mere disappointment" but "a loss akin to the death of a loved one."[21] Linda Lacey accounts for these painful experiences in terms of "the bond the intentional [or prospective] mother feels toward 'her' child."[22] Perhaps only their extreme pain makes some individuals' extensive use of reproductive technologies understandable at all to (presumptively) fertile and voluntarily childless individuals.

Coming to terms with the pain of infertility typically involves a diagnostic phase, a treatment or non-treatment phase, and a "comeback" phase. For most, the diagnosis of infertility comes as a shock. Facing the news of one's prospective "genetic death"—that one might not be an active member of the gene pool—people often react with disbelief.[23] Lasker and Borg found that infertile individuals often feel "as if they have been struck by a natural disaster" or "hav[e] a chronic illness." Alternatively, they may feel "condemned to a life sentence walking a treadmill."[24] As the narrator of *My Year of Meats* puts it, "involuntary infertility . . . kills your sense of a future."[25]

The next phase begins with the decision whether to seek treatment or some reproductive alternative. My concern lies chiefly with those who fight their infertility. Sarah Franklin has found that desperation functions as "the primary frame of reference within popular representations of infertility." From the infertile people in their study, Lasker and Borg often heard "words of desperation, of willingness to endure any pain or expense, even to risk one's life, all in order to have a child."[26] Lasker and Borg compare some infertile people's quest for parenthood to a "terminal cancer victim's quest for a cure" (11).

Besides desperation, some infertile people feel a sense of shame and failure. Thus, as Sandelowski reports, some try to "pass as voluntarily and uncaringly childless."[27] As the treatment phase continues, some adopt a "self-protective waiting-to-fail standpoint developed after years of failure" (175). All the while many of their friends and relatives do not even suspect what they are withstanding. Sandelowski found, for example, that "a typical infertility story was the baby shower that women were either forced to give or to attend for the sake of a pregnant relative or friend" (81). Not surprisingly, envy is also common among infertile people. They find it hard to look with equanimity on people who appear to face no big obstacles to having children.[28] That infertile people have their own national self-help group, Resolve, Inc., is understandable.[29]

The final phase of experiencing infertility is the comeback phase. This label comes from Sandelowski who delineates all the "comeback work" individuals do in the aftermath of infertility.[30] Facilitating such work is the construction during the treatment phase of a personal calculus of pursuit (95) whereby individuals decide how much money and effort they are willing to expend in pursuit of parenthood. For some, comeback work begins when money runs out, emotions are frayed, or physical hardships weigh too heavily. Even for those released from treatment by the arrival of a daughter or son, though, comeback work may not be taken up easily. One impediment is the "uncertainty and ambivalence couples ha[ve] about having additional children" (233). A less obvious impediment for many couples is the sheer drain on their psychic resources. As Lisa Sowle Cahill puts it, "Many of the veterans speak of profound personal humiliation as the intimacy of their sexual and procreative capacities is invaded and their person is objectified into a set of body parts and reproductive processes."[31]

Women, in particular, are likely to feel that way. A brief look at in vitro fertilization illustrates how much—never mind how painfully—their bodies are manipulated to produce a viable pregnancy. As Robyn Rowland emphasizes, "the practical experience of IVF is more complicated" than typical portrayals of it. For one thing, if the wife's eggs are used, she is usually "superovulated" using fertility drugs and then her eggs are "harvested" through laparoscopy, which sometimes involves general anaesthesia. Embryo implantation is the next big step.[32]

The husband's sole physical duty is to ejaculate into a container after masturbating. The wife's everyday life, by contrast, gets invaded in multiple ways. Lauritzen summarizes: "After hysterosalpingograms, endometrial biopsies, tubal insufflations, drug regimens, and surgeries—all done before IVF—it is little wonder that some women who have gone through IVF report feeling like a piece of meat."[33] It is little wonder either that "the rigors of repeated invasive techniques and hormonal hyperstimulation on women and the associated culture of perseverance have been much criticized."[34] Yet as Lila Abu-Lughod reports in narrative N, IVF sometimes makes maternal dreams come true. Her own experiences led her to affirm that "women might experience this technology positively" despite its invasive, painful character.

Most people have no more idea of IVF's ins and outs than they do of the agony often associated with involuntary childlessness. Atop all else they have to deal with, infertile people commonly face harsh judgments from people who are at least presumptively fertile and people who are childless by choice. Those who pursue genetic parenthood may also get negative reactions from adoptive parents.

Given world overpopulation and rapid population growth in most of the world, the first judgment many people make about infertile people pursuing costly treatment is irresponsibility. Another common reaction is that they brought their situation on themselves by having given priority to other matters, especially career.[35] Lauritzen cites a rhetorical strategy often used against infertile people. Their desire for a child is presumptuously pitted against need, as if something like IVF were "a sort of rhinoplasty for the ego."[36] Other common reactions apply, in particular, to women. Often infertile women seeking to have a child are seen as unenlightened or unliberated. Others are seen as too old for reproductive assistance such as IVF.[37]

A final reaction that infertile people often face is that they should adopt a child. Yet Lasker and Borg found that most infertile couples had seriously considered adoption or were already on a waiting list to adopt a child.[38] For some infertile individuals, including the author of narrative Q, infertility treatments do happily eventuate in adoption. Bartholet says, "I got lucky. I ran out of money. IVF treatment was excluded from health insurance coverage during this period, and I had cursed my fate and timing, as it seemed likely that the exclusion would eventually be eliminated. I had been paying the going price, $5,000 for a full treatment cycle. I had about run through what savings I had."[39]

Predictably enough, Sandelowski found that a major theme among infertile women was the "lack of understanding and sensitivity" they faced. Lasker and Borg note the sense of isolation that crops up among infertile people. Especially vulnerable to feeling isolated are those couples grappling with secondary infertility, that is, those who already have one or more children but have failed to conceive a child after trying for at least one year. About 60 percent of infertile couples fall into this category, which seems even more misunderstood than primary infertility.[40]

Yet harsh judgments, insensitivity, unsolicited advice, and sense of isolation do not keep infertile couples from seeking treatment. Although the percentage seeking treatment is unknown, it is undoubtedly growing as medical insurance begins covering some amount and kinds of treatment and both the options and the awareness of those options increase. Like many people, I had thought that the "new reproductive technologies" and "reproductive medicine" are new. In fact, infertile people seeking treatment are entering a well-established arena. As Margaret Marsh and Wanda Ronner indicate, "[t]he medicalization of infertility began almost two centuries ago."[41] To that phenomenon we now turn.

Assisted Conception

The two most common forms of assisted conception are in vitro fertilization and artificial insemination. In vitro fertilization, the core procedure among reproductive technologies, is more than fifty years old. The first successful IVF was reported in 1944, when John Rock and Miriam Menkin published their work in *Science*. (Rock had launched one of the country's longest-lived infertility clinics in 1926.) By 1978, the first known IVF baby, Louise Brown, was born in England. By now, conventional IVF using a wife's ova and her husband's sperm has nearly become routine.[42]

Yet IVF is no simple treatment, as we saw, and its effectiveness is limited. Lasker and Borg report that a pregnancy, however brief, counts as a "success" in IVF programs and that fewer than ten percent of IVF couples end up having a baby. Moreover, they cite one survey indicating that one-third of American IVF clinics have never had a single successful birth of an IVF baby. IVF "successes" include miscarriages, and Lasker and Borg report that up to half of IVF pregnancies end that way.[43] Even though the American Society for Reproductive Medicine requires certified clinics to publish success rates, that requirement means little as long as measures of success remain unreasonably generous.

Despite IVF's dubious success rate the "test-tube baby" has become "the icon of reproductive technology." In fiction and other texts such as advertising, "babies in bottles" are a central image rendering the womb "a see-through container."[44] Such images anticipate the emergence of ectogenesis, the "total growth of embryos outside of women's bodies." In other words, IVF anticipates IVG, or in vitro gestation, a reproductive technology on the horizon. While IVG would add another alternative to people's reproductive options, it might endanger abortion rights since fetuses could be sustained outside any woman's womb. Moreover, IVG could make conventional pregnancy seem inferior, because of the latter's greater risks.[45] Finally, IVG might be marketed to whoever prefers to bypass pregnancy on the way to parenthood.

Like IVF, artificial insemination is scarcely new. Its known history in the United States goes back to J. Marion Sims's experiments during the 1860s. Not until 1934, however, did it become known to the public when, after artificial insemination by donor (AID), Lillian Lauricella gave birth to twins. In 1937, a paper on "test-tube babies" appeared in the *Scientific American*. Mass media attention to AID continued into the next decade. In 1942, for instance, *Harper's* carried a feature on it, as did *Newsweek* in 1943. By 1960, roughly fifty thousand children had been born as a result of AID.[46]

More acceptable to most people than artificial insemination by an anonymous donor, it would seem, is artifical insemination by husband (AIH), the least expensive, least complex form of assisted conception. AIH might be used when the husband cannot sustain an erection or is physically incapable of coitus at all. It is sufficiently simple that Lasker and Borg found many couples who "wish they had done it at home" rather than go to a doctor's office or clinic. Indeed, Lasker and Borg say, "Some physicians will teach couples how to do this if they ask."[47] For many couples, though, AIH is not an option due to the husband's lack of sperm or problems with their volume, quality, or motility. Other couples try AIH with no success. AID has a higher success rate—about 60 percent, as opposed to about 25 percent for AIH.[48] Most donors are medical residents or students who are paid for their sperm, but the donor can be just about anybody meeting the requirements of any of the four hundred or so sperm banks in the United States. In the extreme, thanks to the cryopreservation of sperm, it might even be one's dead husband: By 1994, eight American women were known to have had doctors take sperm from their husbands' bodies during autopsy for possible later use.[49] Indeed, "retrieving sperm from the dead is now so common that the American Society for Reproductive Medicine has developed a protocol, 'Posthumous Reproduction,' for dealing with it."[50]

Finally, self-help approaches to artificial insemination are more widely known today. Colloquially known as "turkey baster methods" of insemination, these are attractive to some lesbians as well as to other women who want to know the father of their child but want to bypass both intercourse with him and the regimen and expense of infertility clinics. The narratives of such women are rich and illuminating.[51]

Of all the forms of artificial insemination, AID is the most controversial. Apart from issues about anonymous fathers, some people object to the secrecy widely associated with AID. Lasker and Borg report that most medical personnel "strongly encourage their patients to keep AID a secret from everyone." These experts think even the children of AID should not know the circumstances of their conception.[52] Yet people's reservations about AID pale in light of their resistance to contract (or "surrogate") motherhood. We turn now to that "collaborative" arrangement.

Collaborative Reproduction and Reproductive Conundrums

Evocative as it is of anxieties about the commodification of life in the reproductive marketplace, surrogacy poses painful reproductive conundrums. Nonetheless, it remains a family-making option, especially in the United States where it is neither illegal nor intensely regulated. It also remains vivid in the public imagination after the publicity about Mary Beth Whitehead, Baby M, William Stearn, and Elizabeth Stearn in the 1980s.

Contractual reproduction comes at a precious cost. For example, the Surrogacy Parenting Center of Texas, based in Austin, charges $10,500 "to provide the [commissioning] couple with a qualified surrogate mother." This fee includes screening candidates for surrogacy, matching one with the couple, and contracts between the couple and their reproductive collaborator. Roughly half of this nonrefundable fee is paid when the contract is signed, with the other half paid three business days before the couple meets the woman who will hopefully bear them a child. In addition, the couple must come up with $10–13,000 that the company will disburse in monthly payments to the surrogate "in exchange for her time, inconvenience, discomfort and services." Other reimbursable expenses include (in some instances) child care when she goes for medical appointments or counseling, mileage for those trips, an "ovulation predictor kit," and maternity clothes (up to $750 worth). There is also a fee for her medical insurance, which varies depending on what her current insurer (if she has one) covers. Further complications bring further costs. Surrogacy is aimed primarily at heterosexual couples in which the husband is fertile and the wife is not. Sometimes the wife produces eggs that can be fertilized but is incapable of a viable pregnancy. In such a case, the Surrogacy Parenting Center of Texas estimates the couple's overall cost at $23,825 plus the costs for IVF and medications. When a donor's eggs are needed, the estimated costs rise to $26,825 plus the costs for "egg retrieval," IVF, medications, and "possible short-term counseling for the donor."[53]

Like artificial insemination, surrogacy has been around a long while, particularly in the form of "coerced" surrogacy commonly imposed on female slaves.[54] Another form is altruistic surrogacy, which is voluntary but involves no monetary payment. Throughout the ensuing discussion, depending on the context, I use "contract mother," "birth mother," or "genetic mother" to refer to surrogates. Just as "test-tube babies" come from mothers' wombs and are thus misnamed, so are "surrogate mothers."[55] The directors of three surrogacy programs told Lasker and Borg that they prefer contract mothers who already have children of their own. They also prefer that contract mothers be married, since "a husband may be valuable for support," and a contract mother may more readily "give up a baby because it is not her husband's."[56]

Surrogacy programs vary in how they treat the relationship between the contract mother and the commissioning couple. Some programs forbid such a meeting, while others require it (79). Given the money and emotions involved, one supposes that at least a few programs leave that option open. In any event Lasker and Borg found that "couples seem more interested in anonymity than the surrogates," if only because of their "uncertain[ty] about what part a known surrogate mother should play in their lives" (79). For their part, contract mothers want more counseling available and more attention to the "feeling of loss" they often experience (89). That feeling represents the core of the conundrum that contract motherhood poses for many people, including feminists. As Barbara Katz Rothman emphasizes, "A baby enters the world already in a relationship." Pregnancy is that relationship.[57]

Unlike other pregnant women, a contract mother is often seen as "no more than a sort of carrier or environment" for a fetus that will by contract become the commissioning couple's child.[58] In other words, that couple usually cannot be expected to give the contract mother's feelings much practical priority. The fetus inside her is their paramount concern, and they may be hard pressed to experience its prospective birth mother as a person entitled to their full consideration.

In its traditional form surrogacy involves artificial insemination using the sperm of the husband of the commissioning couple. As we saw, though, the wife of the commissioning couple may contribute the eggs, or an anonymous donor may be their source. These latter instances eventuate in gestational surrogacy via IVF. "Mother" does not much appear in texts about gestational surrogacy. Instead, these contract mothers are commonly called "surrogate gestational carriers" or "gestational carriers."[59] A gestational mother's position within "existing relational precedents" is sorely ambiguous.[60] Her very motherhood is sometimes challenged. One court case involved a gestational mother named Anna Johnson petitioning the court to recognize her maternity. Katha Pollitt reports,

> On October 23 [1990], in Orange County, California, Superior Court Judge Richard Parslow decided that the rightful mother of Baby Boy Johnson was not Anna Johnson the black "gestational surrogate" who, for $10,000, carried him and birthed him, but Crispina Calvert, the wombless Asian-born woman who provided the egg from which, after in vitro fertilization with her (white) husband's sperm and implantation in Ms. Johnson, the baby grew.

Pollitt notes that "Judge Parslow ruled that genes make the mom, as they do the dad." His ruling regards Johnson as a "home" or an "environment." Pollitt goes on,

> One wonders what Judge Parslow would make of a headline two days later. "Menopause Is Found No Bar to Pregnancy" announced the *New York Times*, reporting that doctors had succeeded in making six prematurely menopausal women pregnant by implanting each with donated eggs fertilized in vitro with her husband's sperm. By Judge Parslow's reasoning, of course, those women are merely foster mothers, homes and environments.[61]

At the time Ms. Calvert was a nurse; Ms. Johnson was "a sometime welfare recipient, single mother and low-paid worker at [Ms.] Calvert's hospital" (103). Underscoring the class inequities between the two mothers, Pollitt writes,

> "You wave $10,000 in front of someone's face," said Anna Johnson, "and they are going to jump for it." By "someone," Johnson meant women like herself, shuttling between welfare and dead-end jobs, single, already supporting a child, with a drawerful of bills and not much hope for the future. (103)

Then, too, racial and marital inequities divide these women. Pollitt argues that gestational surrogacy may often exploit black women, if only because "their visible lack of genetic connection with the baby will argue powerfully against them in court" (103). In Pollitt's view Johnson got treated as if her pregnancy were only "biological baby-sitting," as if "the fertilized egg already is a person; she's only caring for it, or housing it, or even (as one imaginative federal judge recently wrote) holding it captive" (105). Yet Johnson sought only visitation rights, not custody (104).

In "Contracts and Apple Pie: The Strange Case of Baby M," Pollitt tackles the ethics of surrogacy by challenging the common rationales for it.[62] Her discussion centers on six points that lay bare the issues involved in assisted reproduction, the issues guaranteeing soul-searching conundrums for some long while to come.

Pollitt's first point is that "surrogate mothers" are not surrogate mothers. Motherhood concerns the "relationship of a woman to a child, not to the father of that child and his wife." One might argue, then, that the "woman who contributes egg and uterus functions more as a substitute *spouse* than as a substitute *mother*."[63] If that distortional two-word phrase is to be used at all, the wives in commissioning couples are the "surrogate mothers" in conventional surrogacy arrangements. As Pollitt emphasizes, they usually have neither a genetic nor gestational bond with the child they adopt, who is, however, their husband's biological child (66). In the end "surrogate mother" discounts pregnancy, which brings us to Pollitt's next point.

Second, that a client husband provides sperm and becomes a biological father does not make him equivalent to the woman who contributed the eggs as well as the gestation and birthing (conventional surrogacy) or the gestation and birthing (gestational surrogacy). Nevertheless, American courts tilt toward ruling in effect that his genetic material outweighs the conventional contract mother's or the gestational contract mother's pregnancy and birthing. Such stances ignore the relationship that pregnancy usually entails.

As adoptive parents and their children well know, biological and social parenthood do sometimes diverge. Today biological motherhood is increasingly divisible as well as increasingly cut off from social motherhood: "An older woman's fading egg, and the chromosomes it enfolds, can be rejuvenated through the addition of the rich, viscous cytoplasm from a younger woman's egg. If that chimeric gamete is then fertilized and transferred into the womb of a third woman for gestation, the resulting child can claim three biological mothers: the chromosomal mom, cytoplasmic mom and gestational mom."[64]

Exploring the ramifications of maternal divisibility, Michelle Stanworth first notes that "Women's legal and moral claims to children rest on two bases: first, their day-to-day responsibilities . . . and secondly, the fact that children are born to them. The latter claim reflects not so much a mother's genetic input to the child as the commitment involved in pregnancy and birthing." Stanworth goes on to note that moves to emphasize genetic parenthood over "real parental commitment, would work decisively to the detriment of women." In her judgment such moves are already under way: "The eclipsing of the pregnant woman's part in child-bearing is . . . a striking feature of discussions of the new conceptive technologies"; "it is precisely the significance of her pregnancy which the terms of the discussion deny."[65] Such denial is built into court decisions such as Judge Parslow's, too. Rothman also decries the trends at work: "If we believe that the *real* mother is the egg donor and the surrogate is the 'host,' the 'rented womb,' then the importance of genetic parenthood—the importance of *fatherhood*—is underlined."[66]

Rothman's point about fatherhood is well taken. Since a man's contribution to reproduction is narrowly genetic, any trend toward giving greater weight to genes gives greater weight to biological fathers' rights relative to genetic, gestational, and even social mothers' rights. In addition, the more that pregnancy and birthing are marginalized as assisted reproduction becomes more diverse, the more birth mothers seem like little more than a reproductive medium or "reproductive object."[67]

Third, contract motherhood is not necessarily an arrangement whereby infertile women can become social mothers. Pollitt insists that contract motherhood is, above all, a means whereby men can become biological fathers independent of their wives' reproductive capacities or even their wives' reproductive intentions or desires (68). Even though some people regard contract motherhood as the counterpart of AID, the parallels are narrowly genetic.[68] As Sara Ann Ketchum emphasizes, "The position of the man seeking a contract mother is the opposite [of the woman seeking AID]; he chooses a birth mother and the wife does not have to consent to the procedure (although the mother's husband does)." Moreover, says Ketchum, *contract* motherhood requires something AID does not, which points to "the differences between pregnancy and ejaculation."[69]

In any case, contract motherhood lets men—married or not—become biological fathers independent of any woman except the contract mother. In Los Angeles, at least one surrogacy center caters to gay men. There is no reason to expect that all its clients are gay. They could just as well be straight men whose nonmarried status virtually bars them from most infertility clinics. For now, the main point is that contract motherhood may sometimes have nothing to do with infertility.

Fourth, Pollitt dissociates contract motherhood from reproductive technologies. Contract motherhood itself, she emphasizes, is a "maternity contract," not a technology. What is "new" about it is that it denies women rights to their children that are historically recent as well as hard won (67). Fifth, Pollitt sees no connection between contract motherhood and a woman's right to control her own body. The issue is not whether a woman can get pregnant and give birth for any reason she chooses. Instead, the paramount issue is whether she can be legally required to turn that child over to its father (67). Pollitt notes, too, the legal paradox wherein a woman may rent her womb (contract motherhood) for nine months but not her vagina (prostitution) for even nine minutes (63). Some thus think of contract motherhood as "reproductive prostitution" (69) since it involves some of the same realities as sexual prostitution.[70]

Finally, Pollitt emphasizes that "surrogate" arrangements deny the contract mother the "protection she would have if she had signed nothing" (77). As Susan Ince sums it up, "[C]ontrol by contract" is crucial in surrogacy arrangements. Significantly, the typical contract is not akin to a preadoption contract. For one thing, preadoption contracts are extended to women who are already pregnant and planning to give birth. Then, too, preadoption contracts usually let the mother change her mind about giving up her baby.[71]

Overall, contract motherhood may pose many more problems than it solves. While collaborative reproduction might appeal in principle to most feminists, in practice little person-to-person collaboration usually goes on among the biological father, biological and/or gestational mother, and the father's wife.[72] Again, the language at hand seems to misname and distort the actualities involved.

Feminism and Reproductive Technologies

Susan Chase observes that "reproductive technologies have absorbed an enormous amount of feminist attention." She speculates about why feminists give these issues close attention. One reason may be that these "technologies" powerfully illustrate the distinction, long noted among feminists, between biological and social motherhood. Another may be that men mostly create and oversee them and may be seen as tailoring them to their own priorities. Then, too, these technologies are ever changing and thus invite continual attention.[73] Another reason for such resistance may be the regulatory vacuum around reproductive technologies in the United States. Lori Andrews indicates, for instance, that "in England, . . . the Human Fertilisation and Embryology Authority, a government agency, passes judgment on which fertility techniques are beyond the pale. They have nixed human cloning, creating babies from eggs from aborted fetuses, and using dead men's sperm without their prior consent. In the United States we have no such deliberative body."[74]

While some feminists—Shulamith Firestone and Donna Haraway, for example—see reproductive technologies as possibly liberating women, most seem to resist them.[75] In fact, feminists have formed at least one organization for that purpose: the Feminist International Network of Resistance to Reproductive and Genetic Engineering (FINRRAGE).[76] A swift look at their resistant or at least critical stances may be an instructive way to end this chapter.

Sara Ann Ketchum disallows even altruistic surrogacy: "If children are not property, they cannot be gifts either." Lauritzen regards altruistic surrogacy as "less clear" than contract motherhood, about which he concludes: "Because surrogacy requires a mother to attempt to maintain an emotional distance from the fetus she carries, because it demands that she regard the child as belonging only to the biological father and his spouse, and because it treats her relationship to the child as parasitic upon her agreement with the biological father, surrogacy is fundamentally in conflict with the commitment to care that is at the heart of responsible parenthood." Christine Overall's position is not unlike Lauritzen's. Contract motherhood "should not be legalized," but those who enter into " 'surrogacy' arrangements, especially women who are recruited into them, should not be subjected to criminal prosecution." "Middlemen" should be, however. Laura Purdy's position is more open ended. She remains unconvinced that contract motherhood should be prohibited but does support its regulation "so as to protect the interests of the women who participate."[77]

Contract motherhood and today's reproductive technologies raise broad questions about people's right to reproduce. Like most human rights, that right is, of necessity, limited and nonabsolute. Above all, "What is protected legally and morally is the right to exercise a capacity, not the securing of the end of that capacity." One might think of weak and strong senses of this right: "The weak sense . . . is the entitlement not to be interfered with in regard to reproduction or prevented from reproducing. . . . in its strong sense, the right to reproduce would be the entitlement to receive all necessary assistance to reproduce."[78]

The strong sense of the right to reproduce is sharply at issue in many societies today, although the weak sense is at issue among poor women, "older" women, and women with certain disabilities. The strong sense of this right most stimulates the marketing of reproductive goods and services. Infertility clinics and pharmaceutical companies as well as genetic and other counselors are key players, and their playing field is growing by leaps and bounds. Membership in the American Fertility Society (formerly the American Society for Reproductive Medicine) tripled between 1974 and 1995, growing from 3,600 to 12,000 members.[79]

Marketing reproductive goods and services is not unlike marketing anything else, it seems. Glowing, reassuring language predominates in companies' materials. The Surrogate Parenting Center of Texas (SPCT), for instance, is "proud to be a leader in this age of miracles." It claims to "carefully orchestrate the most delicate details for surrogates and prospective parents." (The "surrogate" herself is not considered a "prospective parent.") In a particularly revelatory statement, the SPCT says that its "staff works full time to protect the goals of our clients and the future of surrogacy," which is of course its source of income.[80]

Given the nature of markets, where consumer demand usually shapes what is available, Michelle Stanworth, among others, sees a New Eugenics at work in the burgeoning reproductive marketplace.[81] With maternity divisible and technologies being continually refined, affluent people can just about get the baby they order. As Barbara Katz Rothman argues in *The Tentative Pregnancy*, what is at hand is the commodification of life.

That commodification centers on women and babies. In the end the reproductive marketplace is as gendered as reproduction itself. Its primary marketers, practitioners, and experts are men, yet its primary targets of manipulation and commodification are women. Women's voices—especially those of infertile women and gestational mothers—are scarcely heard at all in this marketplace. At the same time, women's unique contribution to human reproduction is more and more in jeopardy with ectogenesis on a horizon that may not be at all distant. As Michelle McCaffery puts it, "Woman/mother has become . . . a non-subject superseded on the one hand by the renewed rise of paternal rights and on the other by the explicit separation of the fetus from her." In a nutshell, says Sarah Franklin, "fathers, fetuses, and embryos acquire new reproductive rights"; mothers do not.[82]

Perhaps this chapter should end where it began, with the experiences of infertile people. Narratives that follow this chapter illuminate the diffuse challenges of coming to terms with one's infertility; both disclose the personal pain and intrusive processes that are often woven into women's experiences of infertility. Elizabeth Bartholet and Lila Abu-Lughod also show us, however, that grappling with infertility need not be at all self-defeating. They show us that reproductive alternatives and reproductive technologies, respectively, can yield unutterably precious outcomes despite the long, hard road a woman usually has to travel to arrive at those uncertain destinations.

NARRATIVE M

Adoption Rights and Reproductive Wrongs

Elizabeth Bartholet

• • •

I believe that the concept of reproductive rights should be expanded to include adoption rights—the birth mother's right to give up her child, the infertile woman's right to parent a child who has no parent, and the child's right to a home. The twin stigmas that surround adoption and infertility today shape and constrain choice in ways that promote a traditional understanding of women's roles. We condition the infertile to obsess over treatment options rather than consider adoption, and we condition birth mothers to feel that it would be "unnatural" to surrender their children for others to raise. "True" women are supposed to be fertile, get pregnant, give birth, and raise the resulting children.

But adoption rights are sometimes seen as being in conflict with women's rights to control their reproductive lives. This is, in part, because anti-abortion forces have pushed adoption as the *only* appropriate route for a woman who does not want or feel able to raise the child she is carrying. They have helped create the impression that to be pro-adoption is to be anti-abortion, but there is no necessary inconsistency between abortion rights and adoption rights. We should not let abortion opponents hoodwink us so easily. Women should be free to choose whether to carry a child to term or to abort, and also free to choose whether to raise a child or give it up for others to raise. True reproductive freedom includes all these choices. The anti-abortion forces purport to be adoption's friends but they have not proven true friends. Their adoption advocacy has not extended beyond the abortion decision point. They simply use adoption as a club to wield in their abortion battle. And this is entirely understandable, because a real commitment to adoption rights would help free women from the traditional role anti-abortion forces generally promote.

A more fundamental concern is that adoption rights for the infertile may mean constraint and exploitation for the birth mother. Many feminists and others committed to liberating oppressed groups worry about adoption's potential for exploitation. Adoption does, typically, involve the transfer of children from those who suffer various forms of deprivation to those who are relatively privileged. Poor birth

From Power and Decision: The Social Control of Reproduction, *edited by Gita Sen and Rachel C. Snow. Cambridge: Harvard School of Public Health, 1994, 177–184. Reprinted by permission of the author and editors.*

mothers give up their children to well-off adoptive couples; Third World nations give up their children to the industrialized Western nations; black and brown people give up their children to whites. To a significant degree, this is the pattern that adoption takes.

But adoption does not cause the situations of socio-economic disadvantage that result in some people and some groups and some countries producing children for whom they are unable to care. It is a symptom. And while it is of course true that justice requires new efforts to correct the conditions that make it so hard for some women to care for their children, adoption should not be seen as inconsistent with such efforts. Children are often termed "precious resources," but it does not make sense to think of them that way. Giving up children, like deciding to abort, may be the best choice among the options available at a particular point in time. Children deserve to be treated as human beings with their own entitlements, rather than as resources in which adult individuals and communities have a property interest. From the children's perspective, being given up may mean being given the opportunity to grow up in a nurturing home.

Adoption is now stigmatized and regulated in ways that unduly limit women's life opportunities. Birth mothers are conditioned to think it "unnatural" to surrender children for others to raise even when they are not themselves in a good situation to raise these children. The infertile are conditioned to think of adoption as a last-resort parenting option, and of infertility as a form of disfigurement that needs repair. They are encouraged to pursue reproduction at all costs, with the costs for women and society rising ever higher as reproductive technology expands the infertility treatment horizon.

We need to recognize that adoption generally works to expand life opportunities for birth mothers, for the infertile, and for children in need of nurturing homes. It would work even better if we were to eliminate the stigma and reform the restrictive regulation that shapes adoption as we know it today.

One Woman's Journey through Infertility to Adoption

In the fall of 1985 I flew from Boston to Lima, Peru, to adopt a four-month-old child. Some eighteen years earlier I had given birth to my first child. During the last ten of these intervening years I had struggled to give birth again, combating an infertility problem that had resulted, as is often the case, from my use of a contraceptive device.

I had been married when I produced my first child, but divorced when he was just a few years old. Some years later I decided that I wanted more children, regardless of whether I was married. But I found that I was unable to conceive.

I subjected myself to every form of medical treatment that offered any possibility of success. I had operations to diagnose my problem, I took fertility drugs and charted my menstrual cycles and my temperature, and I had sexual intercourse according to the prescribed schedule. I had surgery to remove scar tissue from my Fallopian tubes. And I went through in-vitro fertilization (IVF) on repeated occasions in programs in three different states. As a single person in my early forties, I was officially excluded from every IVF program in the United States that I was able to find out about. Almost all had a maximum age of forty, and all limited their services to married couples. But I was determined. I begged my way into programs that were willing to consider bending their age rules, and I presented myself as married, with the help of a loyal and loving friend who was willing to play the part of husband. Not being used to a life of fraud, I spent much of my IVF existence terrified that I would be discovered.

I wanted to have another child, and I was obsessed with the need to produce it myself. But IVF did not work for me, and I moved on to adopt.

The adoption experience changed me profoundly. It changed my life and my thinking about life. It changed my understanding of parenting and my view of the law, even though I had been a parent and a lawyer all my adult life. And it changed the focus of my professional energies, because I found myself intensely interested in what I had lived through during my struggles to become a parent, and deeply troubled by the way society was shaping parenting options and defining family.

It was, of course, to be expected that adoption would change my day-to-day life. I went back to Peru in 1988 and adopted another infant, and so am now the mother of two young children. My days start with small warm bodies crawling into my bed, my floors are covered with miniature cars and trucks and Lego pieces, my calendar is scrawled with the kids' doctor appointments and play dates. All this is familiar from twenty years ago, as are the middle-of-the-night coughing fits, the trips to an emergency room to stitch a bloody cut, and the sense that there is not enough time to fit it all in.

But I could not have expected these two particular magical children. I could not have predicted the ways in which they would crawl inside my heart and wrap themselves around my soul. I could not have known that I would be so entirely smitten, as a friend described me, so utterly possessed. And I could not have anticipated that this family formed across the continents would seem so clearly the family that was meant to be, that these children thrown together with me and with each other, with no blood ties linking us together or to a common history, would seem so clearly the children meant for me.

The process I went through to form this family affected my understanding of many issues that I had dealt with during my lawyering life. I had, for example, thought of the law largely in terms of its potential for advancing justice and social reform. In the adoption world, I experienced the law as something that functioned primarily to prevent good things from happening. You need only to step through the door of this world and look around to realize that there are vast numbers of children in desperate need of homes and vast numbers of adults anxious to become parents. It seems overwhelmingly clear that efforts to put these groups of children and adults together would create a lot of human happiness. But the legal systems in the United States and other countries have erected a series of barriers that prevent people who want to parent from connecting with children who need homes. So, for example, the legal system helped push me away from considering adoption during all those years I pursued infertility treatment. And for five months in Peru, the legal system required me to live through the peculiar form of torture reserved for foreign adoptive parents. Having made my way through the adoption barriers to find Christopher and Michael at the end, I can have no personal bitterness. I came out where I feel I belong. I am also glad that I had the opportunity to come to know and love the land in which my children were born. But I am deeply conscious that the huge majority of people who would delight in the opportunity to parent some of the world's children will not be able or willing to make their way through the barriers that the law has set in their path. The myth is that the legal structure surrounding adoption is designed to serve the best interests of the child. Actually experiencing the system as an adoptive parent shattered this myth for me.

Adoption transformed my feelings about infertility and my understanding of what parental love is all about. For years I had felt that there was only one less-than-tragic outcome of my infertility battle, and that was to reverse the damage that had been done to my body, the damage that stood in the way of pregnancy. I had felt that there was only one really satisfactory route to parenthood, and that was for me to conceive and give birth. I had assumed that the love I felt for my first child had significantly to do with biological connection. The experience of loving him was wrapped up in a package that included pregnancy, childbirth, nursing, and the genetic link that meant I recognized his eyes and face and personality as familial. Adoption posed terrifying questions. Could I love in the same way a child who had not been part of me and was not born from my body? Could I feel that totality of commitment I associated with parental love toward a child who came to me as a baby stranger? Or did the form of attachment I had known with my first child arise out of the biological inevitability felt in the progression from sexual intercourse to pregnancy to childbirth, and out of the genetic link between us?

I discovered that the thing I know as parental love grows out of the experience of nurturing, and that adoptive parenting is in fundamental ways identical to biological parenting. I have come to think of pregnancy and childbirth as experiences that for me were enormously satisfying but that seem of limited relevance to the parenting relationship. I do not see biological links as entirely irrelevant to parenting, but neither do I see an obvious hierarchical system for ranking biological and adoptive parenting. There are special pleasures involved in parenting the child who is genetically familiar, and there are special pleasures involved in parenting the children whose black eyes and Peruvian features and wildly dissimilar personalities proclaim their genetic difference.

I can, of course, be seen as specially privileged by virtue of having experienced both kinds of parenting. It may therefore be hard for those who have never borne a child to identify with me. If, for example, there is some primal need to project oneself into future generations by reproduction, I have had the luxury of satisfying that need. But it does seem to me that not much is gained by leaving a genetic legacy. You do not, in fact, live on just because your egg or sperm has contributed to another life. It is unlikely that the anonymous sperm donor takes significant pleasure in knowing that his genes are carried forward to the next generation in the person of some unknown child wandering the earth. The sense of immortality that many seek in parenting seems to me to have more to do with the kind of identification that comes from our relationship with our children, and with the ways in which that relationship helps shape their being.

This is not to say that *becoming* a parent through adoption is comparable to becoming a parent through giving birth. I found many aspects of the adoption process terrifying or unpleasant or some combination of the two. It was an entirely unknown world to me, as it is to many. In addition, society has conspired to make adoption extraordinarily difficult to accomplish.

Adoption also involves choice on a scale most of us don't generally experience. You can't fall accidentally into adoption, as you can into pregnancy. You exercise choice down to the wire. Choice forces you to think about what you want and to take responsibility for the consequences of your decision. And the choice to go forward with an adoption means a lifelong commitment, which simply isn't true of most other choices that we make. If you make a mistake in choosing a house, a job, or even a spouse, you can get out of it. Few of those who consciously enter an adoptive parenting relationship would feel comfortable opting out of their commitment.

While choice is difficult and uncomfortable for most of us, there are obvious advantages for both children and parents in parenting that results from conscious choice. In the world of biological parenting, all too many children are raised by parents who neither planned for nor wanted them, and the evidence shows that this is problematic for both the parents and the children. As a parent, I found that one of the gratifying aspects of the adoption process was the satisfaction that came from the sense that I was exercising choice and taking control over my life. Although adoption has been made far more difficult and more frightening than it needs to be, adoptive parenting is an achievable goal, at least for those with the time, energy, resources, and will to pursue it. When I wasn't in the depths of despair and depression in Peru, I relished the Wonder Woman role I had cast myself in, and delighted in my ability to overcome seemingly insurmountable obstacles. The contrast with the infertility struggle is compelling. If your goal is to have a biological child, there is no way that you can take control. No matter what you do or how long and hard you try, there is a good likelihood that you will fail. If your goal is to become a parent, you can do it through adoption. There may be a thousand obstacles, but you can triumph over them.

Current policy with respect to parenting options reflects a powerful bias in favor of biological parenting. As a society, we define personhood and parenthood in terms of procreation. We push the infertile toward ever more elaborate forms of high-tech treatment. We are also moving rapidly in the direction of a new child production market, in which sperm, eggs, embryos, and pregnancy services are for sale so that those who want to parent can produce a child to order. At the same time, we drive prospective parents away from children who already exist and who need homes. We do this by stigmatizing adoptive parenting in myriad ways and by turning the adoption process into a regulatory obstacle course. The claim is that no children are available for adoption, but the fact is that millions of children the world over are in desperate need of nurturing homes. The politics of adoption in today's world prevents these children from being placed in adoptive homes. My claim is that current policies make no sense for people interested in parenting, for children in need of homes, or for a world struggling to take care of the existing population.

Adoptive family relationships are often built on a foundation of human misery. Birth parents generally surrender children for adoption or abandon them because they feel forced to do so by poverty, discrimination or the chaos that results from war or some other disaster. Many of those interested in becoming adoptive parents feel forced to undertake this form of parenting by infertility. In an ideal world, we would eliminate the problems that force some to give up the children they bear and that deprive others of their fertility. But in the world in which we live today and will live tomorrow, adoption should be understood as an institution that works well compared to existing alternatives.

Adoption should not, however, be seen *simply* as a response to some of the world's problems. It should be understood as a positive alternative to the blood-based family form. A more positive construction of adoption would be liberating not simply for birth parents, or for the infertile who want to parent, or for the children who need nurturing homes, but more broadly. Adoptive families are different in some interesting ways from families based on a blood link. Understanding the positive features of adoption could open up our minds to rethinking the meaning of parenting, family, and community.

• • •

NARRATIVE N

A Tale of Scientific Pregnancy

Lila Abu-Lughod

• • •

"Our goal is to make you pregnant," the doctor had explained. . . . "Our success rates are the highest in the city. We average about thirty-three percent per three-month cycle." This kind of talk leads to a world of uneasy comparison. You look around the waiting room and wonder who will make the statistics. The woman next to you tells you she has fifteen eggs; yesterday you'd been told that you had five but that one was bigger than the others. "What does that mean?" you ask the busy doctor. "We'll see how they come along. If the others don't catch up, we'll have to cancel the cycle." You beg those little ones to grow.

Another woman tells you that this is her third try; last time she had to be hospitalized for ovarian enlargement. The next day someone tells you about her friend who had so many eggs she froze some. She became pregnant and had twins. Then her husband was killed in a car accident. Now she wants to thaw her other eggs and have another child by him. A tough young woman in blue jeans cheerfully jokes with the nurses as they take her blood. She's been coming for a year. You listen in dismay as another recounts how she got pregnant after four tries and then lost her triplets. She and her husband couldn't stand the strain, so they took a break for two years. You also look around at some of the women and think they're just too old.

All these women are surely bringing down the percentages. You think, with some secret pleasure, that this means your own odds as a first-timer are that much better. You keep talking to your friend and colleague, the one who told you about this clinic and who became pregnant on the first try. She barely seems to remember the anger and frustration you feel, or the uncertainty. She encourages you and tells you what will happen next. You compare notes about the waiting-room experience and tell her what an interesting anthropological study it would make, if only you didn't feel so much hostility to the money-making production line the clinic creates that all you want to do is escape—as soon as you no longer need their services so helplessly.

Retrieval is the clinical term for the procedure of removing your ripe eggs from the ovary to be fertilized outside your body. You go to the hospital for this, feeling perfectly healthy and afraid that when you wake up you won't be anymore. After

Adapted from "A Tale of Two Pregnancies," Lila Abu-Lughod, in Women Writing Culture, *edited by Ruth Behar and Deborah A. Gordon. Berkeley: University of California Press, 1995, 343–346, 349.*

being kept waiting, as usual, you are walked in your oversized nonskid slippers down corridors, into elevators, and then into an operating room. The room looks familiar from the slide show the nurse gave a few weeks earlier, and you feel less resentful at that two hours wasted in a session of elementary talk about IVF. (The session protects the IVF program by covering in simple language the complex material contained in the pile of consent forms you must sign.) The lights in the room are bright. It's a little cold. An intravenous feeder is put in your wrist, and the nurses talk to you reassuringly. You disappear. You wake up in the recovery room, people groaning all around you, some quite frightening with tubes in their noses. You want to get away but are too groggy to move.

As we were leaving the hospital, my husband and I bumped into one of the doctors. She asked how it had gone. I said no one had told us. Surprised, she went off to telephone the lab. She gave us the first good news: they had retrieved six eggs. She insisted that someone must have come to tell me in the recovery room but I had forgotten. I didn't believe her.

Then we waited for the telephone call our typed instructions said would come as soon as they knew the results. Five eggs had fertilized. One more success. As Sarah Franklin, one of the few feminist anthropologists to study IVF, has noted, the cultural narrative of conception has been rewritten by the infertility specialists so that conception is no longer the natural result of intercourse but a scientific and technological achievement. The road to pregnancy is a complex obstacle course in which hurdles are overcome, one by one.[1]

The next step was what they call "the transfer"—from dish to womb. Back at the hospital, I sat on a simple wooden bench with the same women who had been in the surgical waiting room on the day of the retrieval. Everyone was a little nervous, but cheerful. This part wasn't supposed to hurt. To pass the time we chatted. One of the women asked if I remembered the blonde woman who had been there with us three days earlier. Yes. "Well," she whispered, "her husband was in there for an hour and a half and couldn't do it. So they had to rush me ahead of her in line for the retrieval." We giggled in a mixture of relief that our husbands had performed efficiently and embarrassment at the others' humiliation.

Finally, my turn. I entered the familiar operating room and climbed onto the table. The doctor was joking with the embryologist in the adjoining room. It had been a long day. Suddenly I saw something come into focus on the elevated television screen to my right. My name was typed on the screen, and there were my four fertilized eggs. The fifth, the doctor explained, had disintegrated. An assistant printed out the image on two polaroid snapshots, a general view and a close-up. I had imagined test-tube babies as little fetuses in jars, but these were just cells, clusters of overlapping circles sitting in a petri dish, like illustrations from a biology textbook.

The transfer only took a minute, with some joking about not dropping the catheter as the embryologist rushed from the lab to the table. I was moved onto a trolley and wheeled out, like the women who went before me, clutching my polaroids.

Abandoned together in a small, otherwise empty ward, we made conversation. One woman's companion helped us exchange our "baby pictures," all we might get for the $8,000 we had had to pay up front (I was counting the days until my insurance company would reimburse me; most of the women had no insurance coverage for IVF). The doctor had told us we could leave after fifteen minutes, but we all insisted on staying for forty-five—superstitious that if we stood up our precious embryos might slide out. One by one, we gingerly climbed out of bed and dressed. I took a taxi home, not wanting to risk the subway.

• • •

I could have viewed pregnancy as an alienation of my body by the medical establishment. But I thought of Donna Haraway, the feminist historian of science, who keeps insisting that it is dangerous for feminists, nostalgic for an organic wholeness, to condemn and reject science and technology. Such associations of the natural with the feminine have been essential to women's confinements to the body and the home; and such rejections of science leave it in the hands of others who may not have women's interests at heart.[2] In the late twentieth century the boundaries between inside and outside our bodies are more fluid. Are glasses to be rejected because they are not our natural eyes? So what if for two days a petri dish served as my fallopian tubes?

Still, I refused to believe the nurse who telephoned twelve days later to say my blood test was positive. I thought the IVF staff would fudge the results so they could publish articles in the medical journals and claim to be the best clinic in the city. Then they'd accuse you, the incompetent female body, of having lost the baby. I didn't believe I was pregnant until two weeks later, when I saw, on that familiar black-and-white television screen, the image of those tiny sacs, each with a twinkling star in it. Fetal heartbeats. Multiple gestation as they call it in the business.

• • •

My menstrual cycle had been suppressed by drugs, and it was too early for the other signs. I was dependent on the ultrasound scanner for my knowledge of pregnancy. I recalled Rosalind Petchesky's classic work on fetal imaging and the politics of reproduction. Rather than condemning, along with other feminists, the panoptic gaze the ultrasound technologies afford the male medical establishment or even the disembodiment of the fetus from the mother, demoted to a mere environment for this rights-bearing entity, she drew attention to the possibility that women might experience this technology positively. "How different women," she wrote, "see fetal images depends on the context of the looking and the relationship of the viewer to the image and what it signifies."[3] I couldn't help finding it reassuring to see on the screen to my right what was supposed to be inside me. I was so unsure of my babies that I worried about their having disappeared if I didn't see them every two weeks or so.

• • •

Notes

1. Sarah Franklin, "Making Sense of Missed Conceptions: Anthropological Perspectives on Unexplained Infertility," in *Changing Human Reproduction*, ed. Meg Stacey (London: Sage Publications, 1992), 75–91; and "Postmodern Procreation: A Cultural Account of Assisted Reproduction," in *Conceiving the New World Order: The Global Politics of Reproduction*, ed. Faye D. Ginsburg and Rayna Rapp (Berkeley: University of California Press, 1995), 323–345.

2. Among the articles in which Donna Haraway makes this sort of argument, "A Cyborg Manifesto," in her *Simians, Cyborgs, and Women* (New York: Routledge, 1991), 149–181, is probably the most powerful.

3. Rosalind Pollack Petchesky, "Fetal Images: The Power of Visual Culture in the Politics of Reproduction," *Feminist Studies* 13, no. 2. (summer 1987): 280.

PART

3

Mothering in Everyday Life

CHAPTER 8

Mothers and Children over the Life Course

Mothers' relationships with their children include innumerable worries, frustrations, and joys. As we all know, those relationships change as children grow up and as mothers grow older. In this chapter we explore just a few of the problems and pleasures that may arise between mothers and children over the course of their lives. Because attention is usually centered on mothers with young children, in this chapter we skip that phase and jump right to adolescence, focusing on mothers, daughters, and issues of sexuality. Then we zero in on the nightmare of incest and its ramifications for the mother-daughter relationship. After that, we consider the fantasy of "the perfect mother," which contributes to pervasive mother-blame in our culture. The challenges and gratifications of feminist mothering occupy us next, first in relation to daughters, and then in relation to sons. We close the chapter with a brief reflection on aging mothers and their adult children, especially daughters.

As we look at mother-child relationships under these particular circumstances and at these specific points in the life course, three persistent themes emerge. First, most mothers and children desire connection with each other throughout their lives, even though circumstances sometimes make that difficult to achieve. Second, both mothers and children struggle to accept that good mothers are not perfect human beings, that mothers have their own needs, desires, and flaws. Third, feminism can facilitate both connection and acceptance.

Mothers, Adolescent Daughters, and Sexuality

In American culture, adolescence is usually seen as a time when children separate themselves from their parents with a vengeance. Mothers, for their part, agonize over what to do about their children's seemingly bizarre, reckless, or antisocial behavior. Typically, mothers feel social pressure to stay out of the way. Kathy Weingarten takes issue with this construction of the mother-adolescent relationship, proposing "that mothers be treated as allies, not obstacles." This reformulation assumes that "adolescents want to retain positive

This chapter was written by Susan E. Chase and Mary F. Rogers.

connections with their mothers" and that "mothers of adolescents have compelling lives of their own and that their wishes to be involved in their adolescents' lives stem from appropriate concern, not inappropriate boundaries."[1] Like Jessica Benjamin, whose idea of mutual recognition we discussed in chapter 5, Weingarten affirms mothers' subjectivity and insists that differentiation is not the same as separation. She suggests that connections can be fostered throughout life, even in adolescence when children may most resist parents' authority.

Let's test this idea by looking at some empirical studies of adolescent daughters and their mothers. Three psychologists, Jill McLean Taylor, Carol Gilligan, and Amy M. Sullivan, followed twenty-six poor and working-class girls from the eighth to tenth grades. Coming from various ethnic and racial backgrounds, these girls were considered "at risk" of early motherhood and dropping out of high school. As eighth-graders, they exhibited "vitality and psychological brilliance," much like their more privileged counterparts in Gilligan's earlier studies. As the girls moved through the ninth and tenth grades, however, they began "a fight for relationship that often became dispirited as girls experienced betrayal or neglectful behavior and felt driven into a psychological isolation they and others readily confused with independence." Many of the girls described their relationships with their mothers as shifting from openness and closeness to wariness. While more advantaged girls also struggled with relationships during these years, the girls "at risk" had fewer resources to draw on when they faced difficulties.[2]

During adolescence, girls in general "are at risk for losing touch with what they know through experience." Several factors contribute to this risk. First, puberty may make girls' childhood experiences seem irrelevant to them. Second, our culture tends to devalue, idealize, or ignore girls' perspectives. And third, the strengths that girls develop when they are younger, including the ability to "name relational violations," now seem to threaten their relationships. The researchers found that a strong relationship with her mother or an other mother such as an aunt or teacher was most likely to protect a girl from psychological isolation and disconnection. When an adult woman invites a girl to speak freely and takes her voice seriously, a girl has a greater chance of developing in self-affirming ways, maintaining her vitality, graduating from high school, and avoiding early motherhood. Girls were able to talk most easily and openly with women who spoke from their own experience, who shared the positive and negative aspects of their own lives (4–5).

Yet such strong relationships are not always easy to achieve. The difficulty stems in part from the dilemmas adult women face. Mothers and other women involved in girls' lives often feel caught between the need to educate girls to fit in and the desire to encourage them to be themselves. Not surprisingly, sexuality tends to be the most difficult area for mothers and adolescents.

Just as a daughter is ready to explore her sexuality in one way or another, a mother worries more than ever about her daughter's vulnerability to exploitation and pregnancy (70, 95). Our society's sexism—the persistence of a double standard for men's and women's sexual behavior and the persistence of good girl/bad girl labels—complicates mothers' and daughters' attempts to develop positive attitudes and conversations about sexuality.[3] As girls register their mothers' fears, they begin to hide their sexual thoughts and feelings; they assume that if they speak openly, mothers will impose greater restrictions. This dynamic is particularly evident among Latina and Portuguese American mothers and adolescents because of cultural norms that severely restrict adolescent girls' sexuality.[4]

The researchers stumbled upon a major insight as they discussed among themselves the girls' reluctance to talk with their mothers about sexuality and pleasure. They realized that they (and other adult women) often restrain their own feelings of joy, pleasure, and exuberance around each other, in a kind of "good woman policing." Gilligan "observed that women seem more able to support one another's painful experiences than to join one another in pleasure" (96). The psychologists realized that they themselves—presumably well-adjusted, self-affirming, successful women—stifle eros in their relations with each other. It is no wonder, then, that adolescent girls learn to squelch their passions. They learn to do so not only from the culture at large and in specific settings like health education classes, which are unlikely to address girls' desires, but also in relationships with the women they love and depend on most.[5] If girls' joy and vitality are not to be squashed, they need adult women who allow them to speak freely and who help them to understand cultural assumptions about sexuality and eros in the broad sense.[6]

Taylor, Gilligan, and Sullivan found that as they move from eighth to tenth grade, African American girls are more likely than other girls to continue talking with their mothers, even about sex. Nonetheless, sociologist Elaine Bell Kaplan contends that teen motherhood often escalates conflict between poor African American adolescent mothers and their own mothers. Kaplan interviewed twenty-two teen mothers and nine of their mothers, the majority of whom were poor or working class. Contrary to the stereotype of black mothers condoning teen pregnancy, Kaplan demonstrates that the adult mothers strongly disapproved of their daughters' early motherhood.[7] This study provides a concrete example of how disconnection can occur between mothers and their teenage daughters under conditions of extreme stress for both.

The teenagers expected motherhood to offer them "some kind of control over their lives." Their mothers, by contrast, worried that their daughters' parenthood would endanger the limited control adult mothers had over their family life (429). Adult mothers' emotional and financial resources were already drained to such an extent that they found it nearly impossible to offer the supportive relationship Taylor and her colleagues say adolescent daughters need. Traditionally, in African American communities, extended families and friends have provided a system of mutual support and exchange of resources. But such a system is less available today, in part because many families are too poor to help each other. Indeed, only two of the teen and adult mothers spoke of a mutual exchange system on which they could rely (435).

In becoming teen mothers, daughters needed their mothers' support more than ever, and they found it difficult to understand the social and economic conditions underlying their mothers' lack of support. "Like all children, [teen mothers] felt their mothers were obligated to care for them, regardless of the mothers' own problems. . . . These teen mothers idealized the concept of 'a good mother' and became angry when their mothers didn't conform" (432). At the same time, adult mothers felt that their communities and the society at large held them responsible for their daughters' early motherhood (439, 441). Being blamed from all sides surely compounded the stress.

Teen motherhood does not always produce the trauma described by Kaplan. Teen mothers sometimes do just fine.[8] Even in Kaplan's study more than a quarter of the teens reported that their mothers remained supportive.[9] However, the circumstances of the majority of the families in Kaplan's study—chronic poverty; low wages; lack of an adequate social safety net; lack of a mutual exchange system; the absence of other supportive persons such as the teen mothers' fathers and the fathers of their babies—led teen mothers to depend heavily on their mothers, who were already emotionally and economically overburdened. Kaplan's study thus highlights a critical point made by Weingarten and Benjamin when they insist on attention to mothers' subjectivity: mothers' needs must be met if they are to meet the needs of their children.

Mothers, Daughters, and the Trauma of Incest

Father-daughter incest—at once unthinkable and all too common in our society—is another, quite different, situation in which daughters desperately need their mothers' help. It is also a situation in which mothers' desire to help their daughters is often thwarted by the trauma mothers themselves experience in such cases. Feminists have exposed the experiences and explored the recovery of daughters, who are clearly the primary victims in father-daughter incest.[10] In this brief section, however, we focus on more recent feminist attention to mothers in incest families.

In the United States, child sexual abuse by family members was not publicly recognized as a serious problem until the 1970s. Beginning with Sigmund Freud, traditional psychoanalysts often dismissed as fantasy children's reports of abuse by family members. Even when they believed children, they blamed them for being seductive and thus causing the problem themselves.[11]

In the last few decades, however, blame has shifted from the child to the mother. According to Judith Green, much of the psychological literature on father-daughter incest accuses mothers of colluding in the abuse, either by ignoring signs of it or by arranging it (for example, inviting the daughter into the marital bed). In addition, the mother's personality is often seen as defective. "Because of her immature dependency needs, the mother reverses roles with her daughter, creating wifely expectations for, and unconsciously delegating her sexual responsibilities to, her daughter." Note the sexism in the idea that a woman's relationship to her husband includes sexual *responsibilities*. Finally, the mother may be blamed for abandoning her child, either physically or emotionally, by getting sick, dying, having a baby, seeking fulfillment in activities outside the home, or working long hours or at night. This form of mother-blame clearly exhibits antimother and sexist ideologies.[12]

Feminist explanations of father-daughter incest usually look beyond the immediate family to the patriarchal character of our society, which accords men and male activities more value than women and female activities. This gender hierarchy often shapes family patterns by condoning men's dominance over women and children. Although empirical research untainted by mother-blame is still not extensive, some well-designed studies corroborate the feminist approach (329). For example, in her study of forty adult incest survivors, Judith Lewis Herman found that most of the daughters' families of origin "were conventional to a fault." They were churchgoing, financially stable, and appeared respectable from the outside. In these families "sex roles were rigidly defined, and male superiority was unquestioned. . . . Fathers exercised minute control over the lives of their wives and daughters, often virtually confining them to the house." In half the cases fathers backed their authority with violence that provoked terror in their families but was not severe enough to come to the attention of outsiders.[13] In this family setup, a mother may find herself in an impossible situation. With her husband controlling her physically, emotionally, and economically, she may have difficulty supporting her daughter if incest occurs.[14]

Green and others argue that more research is needed—specifically, studies of large numbers of families over long periods of time—if we are to understand fully which family characteristics are related to sexual abuse within families. An abusive childhood seems to create risk factors for committing incest in adulthood (especially for men, since most perpetrators are men). Rather than starting with the victim's family, then, it might make more sense for researchers to start with the perpetrator's family of origin (335–336).[15]

In addition to resisting knee-jerk mother-blame, feminist psychologists examine mothers' experiences in such cases and look for the conditions that help mothers support their daughters. When mothers become aware that incest has occurred, they typically experience intense grief, for themselves and their daughters. While many mothers feel rage toward their husbands, they may also grieve the loss of their spouse. "Upon disclosure, much of the mother's adult life is rendered meaningless: nothing was as it seemed—not herself, her relationships with spouse and children, her sense of family, her role, efforts, hopes, expectations. Some mothers develop a pervasive sense of failure as both parent and wife."[16]

A mother's trauma may be further exacerbated if her support system collapses, if, for example, relatives refuse to believe that incest has occurred. Despite the trauma accompanying the disclosure of incest, however, several recent studies indicate that anywhere from 44 to 78 percent of mothers consistently supported their daughters, taking action such as stopping the incest and/or separating from or divorcing their spouses (340–341). Clearly, mothers need to be supported if they are to give their abused daughters the support they so badly need. If mental health workers truly have the daughter's welfare in mind, they need to support the distressed, grieving mother and "focus more on how the mother can help her child after disclosure than on her possible contribution to the incest events" (342).[17]

Mother-Blame versus Mothers' Accountability

As we saw in chapter 2, mother-blame is a persistent theme in American culture. Feminist scholars interpret the tenacity and pervasiveness of mother-blame in all kinds of situations as a matter of unexamined, even unconscious, assumptions about mothers' role in our society. Specifically, "the fantasy of the perfect mother"—one who can fully protect her child at all times and who exists to fulfill a child's every need—is an infantile fantasy that some children carry into adulthood, in part because it is supported by our cultural ideologies. When the supposedly all-powerful mother fails to meet expectations of perfection, she is blamed with a vengeance.[18] The two sides of this coin—idealizing mothers and blaming them—sometimes infiltrate the perspectives of researchers as well as child welfare experts.[19]

The problem, of course, with "the perfect mother" is that she is not a real woman with needs, desires, imperfections, and a life of her own. The adult mothers in Kaplan's study and mothers in incest families—as well as mothers who are blamed for every other possible problem—are real mothers who are too often held up to unrealistic standards. Once again, the idea of mutual recognition surfaces as an alternative, a more realistic model of mother-child relationships. Scholars and experts of all kinds need to recognize mothers' personhood. Children need to recognize it too, in ways appropriate to their developmental stage. So do mothers. In her small-group work with mothers of young adolescent daughters, Elizabeth Diem found that the mothers were weighed down by the myth that they could be perfect mothers, always calm and giving. When they unraveled that myth, the mothers "gained emancipatory knowledge about their mothering and the importance of looking after their own needs."[20]

We contend that recognizing mothers' subjectivity in all its complexity does not mean excusing mothers from accountability for their actions (or failure to act in some cases). To the contrary, only when we fully recognize mothers as persons can we think clearly about the harm they sometimes cause their children. After exposing the "the perfect mother" as the fantasy she is, Nancy Chodorow and Susan Contratto called on feminists to take seriously acts of maternal violence. Writing in 1980, these feminist scholars pointed to a "moral paralysis" about mothers' violence in the feminist literature at that time. Feminists were outraged by violence against women and fought to protect women from the wife batterer and rapist. At the same time, some feminist writers on maternal violence focused so much on patriarchy as the cause and motivation of mothers' violence that they failed to oppose it strenuously and to fight for the protection of children who are its victims.[21] Nearly ten years later, bell hooks made a similar plea for attention to all forms of physical abuse, including that perpetrated by mothers.[22]

Along these lines, we need to protest abuse in the small proportion of incest cases in which mothers are the perpetrators. Approximately 4 or 5 percent of identified perpetrators of intrafamilial child sexual abuse are women. Like men, women are more likely to abuse girls than boys. But while male perpetrators act alone, most women co-perpetrate with a man.[23] Perhaps what we need to hear most in attempting to come to terms with mothers' violence is the voices of their children. Rose Stone is one such daughter who was sexually abused by her mother and several male relatives. Here she reflects on the effects of that abuse:

> In my adolescence and early twenties, my future-fantasies had me as a single mother of a single child. Even before I was able to be self-critical about it, I knew that my motive was to create a creature who would have to love me and would not betray or abandon me as I had been abandoned as a child. . . . Under camouflage of a crude feminist self-sufficiency . . . I would have duplicated the incestuous scenario emotionally if not physically. At the same time, the line of feminist poetry, "I am a woman giving birth to myself," gave me the heebie-jeebies because it evoked my mother's perversion of that concept: because she had given birth to me, I was her and consequently she could do whatever she wanted to me.[24]

While Stone considers herself a feminist, she feels betrayed when some feminists assume that women are natural allies and that women never hurt each other. Further, she is angered by the idea that patriarchy is always to blame for any harm a woman causes another woman. She argues that when feminists conceal problems among women, they reenact "the closed system of the incestuous family" (234, 235). The consequence of such secrecy in both cases is that someone is deeply hurt by the erasure of her experience. Like Chodorow, Contratto, and hooks, Stone makes room within feminism for protesting women's violence against children, as well as protesting those instances where mothers fail to act when they might reasonably have been expected to do something. If feminism implores us to see women—and mothers—as the complex human beings they are, then that process must include facing painful truths.

For Stone, the long healing process has led to new self-understanding and a new concept of feminist mothering:

> I know now that the child I wanted to have was myself, and I understand that line of poetry ["I am a woman giving birth to myself"] as giving me permission to do it over the right way. "Feminist mothering" has to do, precisely, with learning to stick up for myself and speaking my truth. (238)

Feminist Mothers and Their Daughters

We turn now to relationships between mothers who explicitly embrace feminism and their daughters. How do feminist mothers encourage daughters (as Rose Stone encouraged herself) to stick up for themselves and to speak their truths? How do their relationships make room for mothers' needs and imperfections?

Rose L. Glickman's *Daughters of Feminists* is an oral history based on interviews with fifty daughters of (nonfamous) feminist mothers. She found that half the daughters grew up in feminist families that look conventional in form and makeup but function along more or less egalitarian lines. Among these daughters Glickman was unable to find a single one who reported that her brothers were excused from "women's work" around the house. Still, when it came to sexual leeway, feminist families repeatedly favored their sons over their daughters, a circumstance that "irritates the daughters" to this day.[25] The widespread sexual double standard, which we saw adolescent daughters and their mothers struggling with earlier, seems to infiltrate even feminist families in ways that daughters feel acutely. This may be an area where feminist mothers can expect particularly rough challenges in putting their values into practice. As Harriet Lerner puts it, "Sex makes hypocrites of the best of us."[26]

Another double standard also tends to show up in the feminist families. This one, however, is far from widespread in society at large. Glickman found that "some daughters squirmed under a heavier weight of expectations" than sons. Both fathers and mothers urged daughters to cultivate their minds and to aim for professional achievement. They nurtured daughters' self-esteem and self-sufficiency, reinforced their worth as women, and stressed their equality with men. This was "the strongest common denominator in the daughters' formative years."[27]

The other half of these daughters of feminists grew up in what Glickman calls "mother families," where no husband or father was part of the household (32). Never-married, divorced, and lesbian mothers headed these families, whose main continual challenge was typically financial. Most of these daughters "did not regard their family arrangements as aberrations." Moreover, the daughters of divorced mothers fared best when their mothers "drew them into a strong feminist community." In fact, many of the daughters—whether their mothers were divorced or not—wax poetic about the feminist communities that helped them come of age as strong, secure women (36, 38). Despite the hectic, even harried, lives of their mothers, Glickman found that none of the daughters felt neglected as children or teenagers. Only two of them even came close to reporting such a sense (39).

Near the end of her analysis Glickman generalizes about these daughters of feminists in both family types.

> I can't be sure that the touching intimacy between the daughters of feminists and their mothers derives in some linear fashion from their mothers' feminism . . . Nor can I say that the determining factor in these relationships is the mothers' personal fulfillment in the world of work in addition to motherhood. . . . But it is certainly tempting to speculate that the characteristics of mothers who are proud to be women, and proud to be the mothers of daughters, are tightly woven into this fundamental and dynamic relationship. (143)

Overall, Glickman finds vibrant, rich bonds between these daughters of feminists and their mothers. She concludes, "For the daughters of feminists, the mothers are examples of what women can and should be" (145).

In narrative O, Rachel Clift describes how she came to respect her mother's feminism and to embrace feminism herself. A college student at the time she wrote this essay, Clift realizes that her earlier ambivalence about feminism was influenced by our society's denigration of it, and closer to home, by her father's jokes about it. Ironically, because Clift benefited from feminist accomplishments (her high school supported girls in many ways), she was unable to understand the continued need for feminism, and unable to understand her mother's anger. Facing sexism in college, however, encouraged Clift to join her mother in feminist struggles. Like the daughters Glickman interviewed, Clift realizes her mother has set a strong, courageous example for her.

Similar themes are played out in *The Conversation Begins: Mothers and Daughters Talk about Living Feminism.*[28] Each chapter in the book focuses on one feminist mother and, usually, one daughter; their accounts of feminist motherhood and upbringing are vivid and straightforward. A project of feminist mother Christina Looper Baker and feminist daughter Christina Baker Kline, *The Conversation Begins* includes mostly prominent feminist mothers or, in a few cases, prominent feminist daughters and their feminist mothers. Since the oldest of the feminist mothers (the novelist Tillie Olsen) was born in 1912, this volume's first-person narratives touch upon all the major issues and organizations associated with twentieth-century American feminism. Told from African American, Native American, Asian American, and Latina as well as European American points of view, the women's stories are illuminating and inspiring.

For the most part, the mothers tell about the juggling necessitated by too many demands on their time. Most of these feminist mothers had jobs; many had careers. Even those who pursued their paid work at home often recall being torn by needing to meet deadlines while needing to be accessible and responsive to their children. Barbara Seaman, who helped launch the women's health movement, now has some regrets about that work arrangement:

> I had three young children and a busy writing career, and I always said it was wonderful that I could do both working at home. Now I'm not so sure. It was very confusing to the kids. If I had to do it over, I would rent a room in somebody else's apartment and leave to work and then come back and be all there for them. (121)

Seaman's daughter Shira offers a complementary but forgiving perspective:

> It benefits children to have working mothers. Mothers who have no other interests besides their children can become overbearing and too involved. But to have your mother at home working when you are young and don't understand it can also be a problem. When I was growing up, there was never the sense that specific time was put aside for us. (134)

Mothering while pursuing a career outside the home is no less challenging, it seems. These feminist mothers often took their daughters to work with them. As Carol Jenkins, the NBC television news reporter puts it, her daughter Elizabeth "did not have a regular childhood with regular hours because I felt it was important for her to be with me" (268). Shamita Das Dasgupta, a founding member of Manavi—an organization combating violence against South Asian immigrant women—and an academic psychologist, generalizes what many of the mothers articulate: "I never wanted to separate life's pieces. Sayantani [her daughter] was part of me, like my arm. I couldn't stick my role as a feminist in one compartment and my role as a mother and wife in another. Everything flowed together" (319).

Integrating their life's commitments meant that many of these feminist mothers also took their children with them to meetings, demonstrations, and marches, thereby linking some of them with the feminist communities Glickman found helpful to the daughters she studied. Eleanor Smeal, former president of the National Organization for Women (NOW) and president of the Feminist Majority Fund, states, "You don't take time out to have children; they have to become integrated into your life" (193). Such integration characterized the motherhood of Letty Cottin Pogrebin, a founding editor of *Ms.* magazine. She recalls that when her consciousness-raising group "met at my house, my children wandered in and out of the living room and got a lot of love and attention from these radical feminists who were supposedly antichild and antifamily" (176). Some of the daughters of these feminists are carrying on this integrative tradition. Olsen's daughter Julie Olsen Edwards, for instance, found being with her children exhilarating, and she wanted to have their company as often as possible:

> I loved their play, their questions, their energy, the sheer sensuality of their bodies snuggled up against mine. I took them to the library, the museums, the parks. We sang together, danced together. They came with me to classes, lectures, parties. I was enchanted by their unfolding, their blossoming. (24)

These feminist mothers exude welcome forthrightness about the ups and downs of their mothering. Evelyn Torton Beck, a professor of women's studies and Jewish studies, points to the emotional demands she feels in connection with mother/daughter intimacy: "I would like more intimacy with Nina, but in truth I might well be overwhelmed if she shared more of her feelings, especially if she was in pain" (110). Roxanne Dunbar, who launched the Female Liberation Front in the late 1960s and is now a professor, gave up custody of her daughter Michelle under terrific emotional and financial duress. Today this feminist mother sees her daughter as having two mothers, with Dunbar "always the shadow" who "became a kind of angel on her shoulder, giving her things without demanding of her." Dunbar concludes her maternal story this way:

> I call myself an errant mother, but I have given her unconditional love 95 percent of the time. That's not easy for me, nor perhaps for anyone. And though she is more critical than I sometimes wish, she is probably the only person who loves me unconditionally. Michelle is just about the most sensitive, smart, and just person I have ever known. Alas, I can take little credit. (162)

These mothers' high standards for themselves and their intense commitments make it seem that they are characteristically hard on themselves as mothers. Perhaps in the end most of them are like Paula Gunn Allen, the professor and writer who has illuminated Native American cultures through her work. She says, "It took a long time for me to understand that I am a good mother" (207). Like the mothers of young adolescent daughters in Diem's study—and like so many mothers in our society—these highly accomplished, confident women struggle to resist the perfect mother fantasy so embedded in our cultural ideologies and sometimes in our psyches. They struggle to accept that as people who are limited and flawed, they can still be good mothers. Their struggle, then, is like that of mothers in incest families and mothers of teenage mothers with perfect mother expectations to overcome. Indeed some of these feminists *are* mothers in incest families and mothers of teenage mothers.[29]

Most importantly, perhaps, these mothers seem to have respected their daughters' budding personhood and individuality, while working to maintain connection with them. Feminist journalist and public intellectual Barbara Ehrenreich captures the viewpoint undergirding such respect: "It's difficult to be a baby and a little kid, because you start out small and incontinent and dumb, and you don't know anything. It's easy to patronize or humiliate people in that condition, which is the traditional method of child-raising" (256). Like the other feminist mothers, Ehrenreich rejects that method. The reports of their daughters attest to the wisdom of doing so.

Reading *The Conversation Begins* gives one an abiding sense of how very secure most of these daughters felt in their relationships with their mothers, both then and now. Wendy Mink, daughter of former congressional representative Patsy Mink, says, "I knew that I was her first priority. If I needed her, she would be there" (61). Tessa Koning-Martinez, daughter of the civil rights activist Elizabeth Martinez, saw her mother as an "advocate mom" who "sided with" her (42). The daughter of Clarissa Pinkola Estes, who wrote *Women Who Run with the Wolves*, says, "I grew up secure in my mother's love. When I was born, her strong arms held me, and still to this day, deep inside me, I feel held by her." Tiaja Kaplinski Pinkola De Dimas Villagomes sums it all up this way: "My mother is my heart" (293). These adult daughters—secure in lives of their own—speak of a deep connection with their mothers as real persons, not "perfect mothers." In accepting their mothers' needs, desires, and limits through the ups and downs of their relationships, the adult daughters are able to recognize and thus be genuinely appreciative of all their mothers have given them.

Alongside strong maternal love is often a legacy of rituals and values that these daughters cherish. Abigail Pogrebin, for instance, says her famous feminist mother "loves celebration and ritual and making things beautiful. The family is so important to her, and it's the heart of who I am" (183). That legacy of cherishing family entails valuing household equality. Julie Olsen Edwards grew up knowing that her "parents were intellectual companions, comrades in their beliefs and causes. Dad's respect for Mom's intelligence, her capacities, her ideas, was a given in my life. It never occurred to me or to any of my sisters to be with men who expected to make the decisions, run the show" (22).

While these daughters clearly admire their mothers, sometimes they find their mothers' footsteps—their ideals, their achievements—huge and daunting. Mostly, though, they share their mothers' values. After talking with all these mothers and daughters (and more), Baker and Kline conclude, "For most of the mothers we interviewed, feminism was the tool that enabled them to dictate their own stories, reinvent their lives, and create more equal relationships. A measure of their personal influence and the influence of the women's movement is that generally the daughters share their mothers' values" (xxii).

Feminist mothers and their daughters have their problems, just as other mothers and daughters do. Yet *The Conversation Begins* supports the ideas we presented earlier in this chapter: Daughters thrive—they learn to stick up for themselves and to speak their truths—when they have strong relationships with adult women. Mothers' needs for support of various kinds and for lives of their own must be met if they are to mother their children well. And strong connections between mothers and children require mutual recognition of each other's individuality. Along with *Daughters of Feminists*, *The Conversation Begins* certainly debunks the stereotype that feminists are antimother. Both books offer powerful images of feminists loving their daughters and embracing the joys and struggles of mothering.

In narrative P, Barbara Hillyer reflects on what it means to be the feminist mother of a physically and mentally disabled daughter. In the first part of her narrative, written when her daughter was fourteen, Hillyer is distraught about the apparent conflict between feminism's advocacy of girls' independence and consciousness-raising and her daughter's inability to achieve either. In the second part of her narrative, written thirteen years later, Hillyer reflects on how she came to accept her daughter's limitations and, equally important, her own. At this point, she embraces a version of feminist mothering that gives ample space to her grief and struggles, as well as the particular relationship she has developed with her adult daughter.

Feminist Mothers and Their Sons

Feminist mothering presents particular challenges when it comes to sons. For one thing, our society treats mother-son relationships as requiring more distance than mother-daughter relationships. Penelope Sky recalls bursting into tears shortly after giving birth to her son, as she watched a group of men and young boys playing ball in the park:

> A premonition of loss engulfed me. I saw that as my son grew up, I would be cut out of his life automatically because of my gender. He would belong to other boys and men. I would be on the outside. It broke my heart to see that I was destined to be rejected by the person I loved most in the world.[30]

In addition, raising a boy to forswear conventional masculinity and its privileges is likely to arouse even greater resistance than raising a girl to slough off the limits of conventional femininity. As Carole Klein puts it, such mothers may find it hard to negotiate their way between "their love for a particular male child" and their resistance to and resentment of "male-supremacist society."[31] While feminist parents aim to undermine their son's gender entitlement, they may worry about the consequences of taking their sons too far off the path of "normality" and social acceptability.

Often the way out of any practical conundrum about how to raise a son starts with seeing that boys' and men's gender entitlement rests on the gender *dis*entitlement of girls and women. That cultural circumstance typically shapes the mother-son relationship as much as any other female-male bond. As Olga Silverstein and Beth Rashbaum observe, the mother-son relationship is often a double-edged sword; some aspects of the son's humanity get denied and some aspects of the mother's femininity get denigrated.[32] Specifically, sons' tender feelings often get stunted because those qualities, which mothers express and represent, are denigrated as "feminine." As Silverstein notes, being a "daddy's girl" is culturally acceptable, but being a "mama's boy" is not. She goes on:

> We're afraid that if we stop raising sons to be part of the patriarchal system, they won't survive. Well, in fact they *don't* survive in our system. We kill them in war, they die of early heart attacks, they kill each other in the streets. The notion that we're raising our sons to be aggressive so that they can survive is nonsense. It doesn't make any difference whether they have to be tough, hard-driving, and aggressive in business or in physical strength. The more aggressive, the tougher they are, the *less* they survive.[33]

All the while, though, cultural beliefs about effeminate, soft, sissy sons feed fears that parents will ruin their sons in the process of trying to make them balanced, fair-minded people. Here is another pernicious site of mother-blame. As Robyn Rowland and Alison Thomas point out, traditional psychoanalysis blames mothers who love and protect their sons "too much" and who fail to hand their sons over to male culture.[34] Patricia J. Williams notes that cultural beliefs about mothers as the source of effeminate sons particularly target single mothers. Her own experiences as the single mother of an adopted son have brought her up against the notion that "the fledgling male instinct will be crushed by an unchecked voodoo of single-mother sissification." When the single mother is African American, as Williams is, she faces race-specific venom along those lines. Her motherhood may instantly transform her into "the ruling Medusa archetype of Black Single Mother."[35]

Special cultural venom would also seem to be reserved for feminist mothers and even more for lesbian-feminist "single" mothers. Robin Morgan and Audre Lorde raised their sons in those respective statuses, and both offer practical wisdom about how to beat the cultural odds in such situations.

Morgan, the poet and feminist activist, cuts right to the chase: "If you are a feminist, the words 'It's a boy' preface one of the greatest challenges you'll ever know."[36] When Morgan had a son, she had no intention of raising a feminist prince, a man applauded for being more of a feminist than his partner or other women in his life. Still, she did want to raise a son who would be profeminist.

> With a son, you must somehow erode the allure of male entitlement and communicate a delicate double message: "Fulfill yourself to the utmost as a human being—but try to divest yourself of the male power that routinely accrues to you. Be all you can be as a person—but don't forget your automatic male advantages are bought at the cost of their denial to female people." If, as in my case, the son is European American, you try to communicate a comparable message about being white in a racist culture. (37)

From choosing a genderless name for their child even before knowing its gender to making up antisexist bedtime stories, from calling each other by their first names rather than by "Daddy" and "Mommy" to talking politics with their son, Morgan and her co-parent managed to raise the son they had hoped to bring to adulthood. She concludes: "Ultimately, it all comes down to love. Not the sugary kind; love fierce and creative enough to demand change—for ourselves, our children, and the planet. *That's* the 'mother love' I aspire to. And they've called me a man-hater for it. Ask my son if I am" (41; emphasis in original).

Lorde's son Jonathan was three and a half years old when she met her lover Frances, and he was seven years old when the two women began making a home together. Like Morgan, Lorde is adept at pinpointing the challenges of being a feminist mother to a son: "I am thankful that one of my children is male, since that helps to keep me honest. Every line I write shrieks that there are no easy solutions." Noting that "our sons must become men," she goes on to insist that they must be "such men as we hope our daughters, born and unborn, will be pleased to live among.[37]

As she saw it, Lorde's first task was "teaching my son that I do not exist to do his feeling for him" (74). Aware of how sharply boys' feelings are often curtailed, Lorde insisted on subverting that pattern. Moreover, as an African

American mother, she was determined to raise a son "who will recognize that the legitimate objects of his hostility are not women, but the particulars of a structure that programs him to fear and despise women as well as his own Black self" (74).

One day when her eight-year-old son came home crying, humiliated by bullies, Lorde resisted her impulse to lash out at his weakness. Instead, she held him and told him about her childhood fears when bullies taunted her.

> I will never forget the look on that little boy's face as I told him the tale of my glasses and my after-school fights. It was a look of relief and total disbelief, all rolled into one.
>
> It is as hard for our children to believe that we are not omnipotent as it is for us to know it, as parents. But that knowledge is necessary as the first step in the reassessment of power as something other than might, age, privilege, or the lack of fear. It is an important step for a boy, whose societal destruction begins when he is forced to believe that he can only be strong if he doesn't feel, or if he wins. (76)

Like Morgan, Lorde set out to encourage her son to become his very own self rather than some distortion of a human being shaped in the masculine mold. She decided that the main lesson for her son would be the same one she was teaching his older sister, Beth. She would teach him

> how to be who he wishes to be for himself. And the best way I can do this is to be who I am and hope that he will learn from this not how to be me . . . but how to be himself. And this means how to move to that voice from within himself, rather than to those raucous, persuasive, or threatening voices from outside, pressuring him to be what the world wants him to be. (77)

Feminist Parenting: Struggles, Triumphs, & Comic Interludes includes many personal accounts by feminist mothers and their partners of the challenges and joys of raising sons (and daughters).[38] In one narrative, Carolina Mancuso relates the lessons she imparted to her son, Sean, as he grew up. As a single mother, she taught him to cook at the age of five and gave him responsibility for one meal per week. She made sure he did his share of cleaning. She taught him to listen by listening to him, to be polite by treating him politely, to respect others by respecting him. She challenged well-meaning adults when they treated him as less than a person, for example, when they commented publicly on his thumb sucking as a toddler. She refused to discipline him by spanking him and she did not give him violent toys. She took his teacher to task when he punished boys by making them march at the end of the girls' line. Throughout her narrative, Mancuso offers a refrain: "*This young man, I said to myself, will not relegate cooking to a woman . . . will not depend on a woman to clean for him . . . will not be insensitive to other people's feelings. . . . is not going to be trained, however subtly, in violence. . . . must see men as gentle as well as strong and must not be threatened by women who are equally strong and gentle.*" Mancuso notes her doubts and fears in trying to raise a feminist son. But "when in his early 20s, his *compañera* thanked me for raising him the way I did, I breathed a sigh of relief."[39]

Lorde, Morgan, and Mancuso present feminist motherhood as a matter of having the personal courage to be themselves without kowtowing to commonplace expectations. They deploy the courage of their own individuality, among other things, to nurture their sons in the direction of a profeminist manhood. They offer powerful, inspiring examples of feminist mothers loving their sons while raising them to oppose male privilege.

Mothers and Their Adult Children

When their children are young, mothers spend countless hours noting changes in their daughters' and sons' bodies, minds, and spirits. When they are well into adulthood, daughters and sons spend more and more time noting the changes that overtake their parents. Our life cycles thus involve a grand inversion where daughters and sons become the watchers of those who once kept daily vigils over them. This typical, though not universal, circumstance means that mothers' relationships with their children shift gradually but profoundly over the typical life course. Adult daughters, in particular, are likely for some period of time to mother their mothers.

While we easily recognize "mothering" as an active process, Janneke van Mens-Verhulst offers the term "daughtering" to highlight an action-oriented approach to the role of daughter.[40] At root, perhaps, daughtering involves a "long goodbye to the mother as surrogate for godly care."[41] Like letting go of the fantasy of "the perfect mother," this involves coming to terms in one fashion or other with the full humanness of one's mother. It means dealing with, even accepting, her weak points as well as appreciating her strong points. At the same time daughtering includes shaping the terms of one's interdependence with one's mother. As we have seen, such interdependence is lifelong but varies dramatically across the life course in its mix of needs and desires. Often mother-daughter interdependence involves more than two generations, as the multigenerational family remains significant for many classes and racial-ethnic groups.[42]

Although adult daughter-mother relationships are often intimate, that is not always the case. For example, among the sixty working-class young adult daughters Pat O'Connor interviewed in London, she found that fewer than one-third described their relationships with their mothers as "very close." Even in those cases, closeness did not necessarily include intimate confiding.

At the same time, the majority of daughters felt that their relationships with their mothers were "highly identity enhancing."[43] Overall, it appears that daughtering involves a "complex sense of continuity and discontinuity" as the life course proceeds and daughters reach midlife.[44] Yet practical interdependence seems commonplace between adult daughters and their mothers. This may be particularly so with daughters whose elderly mothers live independently rather than relying on professionals for their daily care.[45]

In narrative Q, Judy Dothard Simmons gives us a forthright yet tender account of caring for her mother, a former teacher now afflicted with Alzheimer's disease. In this case, Simmons's mother is wholly dependent on her daughter (and for short periods, professionals) for her daily care. Simmons confesses her frustrations and even her rage as she tends to her mother's needs. (We hear echoes of the emotions mothers of young children sometimes feel.) She also expresses her grief as she watches her mother's mental abilities disintegrate. Like Hillyer, the author of narrative P, Simmons presents the painful realities of caretaking rather than sentimentalizing it, yet also like Hillyer, she acknowledges that she gains much from the relationship as well.

As all three personal narratives that follow this chapter show, the bonds between women and their mothers invite us to think about diverse matters, including personal growth for both mother and daughter, intergenerational differences, social change, and cultural transformation, as well as public policies about disability, aging, and care. That daughter-mother bonds can be so rich in their ramifications suggests that mother-daughter metaphors might well lead us to innovative, fruitful ways of grappling with life-course issues. As Mens-Verhulst, among others, points out, during the 1970s "sisterhood" provided the ruling metaphor for women's relationships with one another. By the 1990s interest had turned to the mother-daughter relationship as a metaphor for women's connections to each other. That shift expresses an awareness of how many practical benefits might accrue from thinking of women's interconnections in mother-daughter terms. Focusing on mother-daughter bonds might, for instance, "be helpful in understanding the dynamics between women in general not only in the family but also in the context of management, education, and therapy." At the same time mother-daughter metaphors position us to grapple with the "real and symbolic generational differences between women."[46]

Finally, another significant source of insight into mother-daughter relationships is daughters' narratives about losing their mothers. What they say in the aftermath of their mothers' deaths points to the dense ties that typically bind adult daughters to their mothers.[47] For example, in reflecting on their mothers' lives and deaths, Catherine Foote, Mary Valentich, and Leslie Gavel realized that unlike other family members, they "yearned to keep our mothers alive, if only as central characters in our stories." They suggest that grieving often includes coming to terms with how little one knows about one's mother. It may also mean trying to understand—rather than judge—her life choices within the particular time and place that she lived.[48] Mother loss can thus occasion feminist practice.

NARRATIVE O

I Am a Feminist

Rachel Clift

Feminism has always been a big part of my life, but it was not until recently that I was comfortable calling myself a feminist. My mother introduced me to the word and the movement gradually, as she discovered and embraced feminism for herself. However, I did not understand or respect the feminist movement. For many years, I feared the "F" word and felt ambivalent about my mother's dedication to women and women's issues. It was not until recently, after reading works by authors like Bell Hooks and Minnie Bruce Pratt, that I was finally able to understand my confusion and resentment toward my mother and the feminist movement itself. As I got older and more familiar with the movement, I slowly began to understand its significance.

My mother introduced me indirectly to feminism when I was quite young. I was about ten years old when she became depressed and angry over the loss of a job. She felt as though her only accomplishments were those of a wife and mother, and she realized she had creative energy and power she had never expressed before. She began to cry often, talking to my father about feelings I did not understand.

What lifted my mother out of her depression and encouraged her as a writer, I realize now, was feminism. She began going to women's conferences, including the huge one in Nairobi. She went back to school and began working as a consultant for health issues facing women in third-world countries. She pointed out sexism everywhere, all the time it seemed. I felt that feminism had made my mother an angry, outspoken person. Reactions from my father enforced my resentment. "Oh dear, here we go again," he would say with a roll of his eyes and a wink at my mother, as soon as she launched into a complaint about sexism in politics, on TV, or in the workplace. He meant no harm, and I always played along with his jokes; we both felt that it was too much. I realize now how we must have hurt her with our comments.

From Feminist Parenting: Struggles, Triumphs, & Comic Interludes, *edited by Dena Taylor, Crossing Press, 1994. Reprinted by permission of the editor and author.*

As someone who now completely advocates feminist issues, it has been a relief for me to realize that I was young, unaware, and steeped in patriarchal values. I saw my mother's commitment to feminism as her acceptance that she, as well as her women friends, were victims. I imagined her women's conferences as places where my mother and her friends would sit in a circle and discuss how they had been mistreated. I felt as though they were angry at being women, so I became afraid of feminism. I did not want to be angry or upset about who I was, and I definitely did not want to accept that I was destined to be a victim for the rest of my life, simply because of my gender.

As I got older and began to recognize sexism in the world around me, I still resisted embracing feminism because I was afraid I would be stereotyped by others. Throughout high school, however, I came to respect the ideology and my mother's dedication to it. I, too, felt it was important to end all forms of sexist oppression. My particular high school undoubtedly played a big role in supporting my growth as a feminist. I attended an all-women school, so none of us felt any competition during the school day. We were required to wear a uniform and felt no pressure about dressing well or looking attractive; we wore the same uniform every day and no one cared! We were encouraged to pursue all of our interests and to be ourselves. Many of my friends in high school were Indian, Sri-Lankan, Asian- and African-American. To be a feminist there was almost inevitable.

Now, in college, I realize that the issues that my mother was facing (and still faces today) really do exist. I, too, face them now. Never before have I been afraid to speak up in class, or to ask a question, or to participate in a political discussion. Never before have I felt stupid for not knowing a fact. Never have I been interrupted so many times in the middle of a conversation with male friends. And I'd never considered myself unusually lucky to have friends from all different backgrounds. Since my arrival at college I have learned much about feminism that I was not aware of before—issues that my mother never discussed with me until recently. I now realize to what extent feminism requires a woman to fight against all forms of oppression, including racism, anti-Semitism, heterosexism, and classism.

I am slowly beginning to learn what the feminist movement has meant to all women in the past and present. I am also beginning to understand what it meant to my mother eight years ago, and what it meant to me at that time. The picture is becoming clearer. I am ready to call myself a feminist, and to join forces with my mother, who has become a source of pride and support as she travels with me on my own road to self-discovery.

NARRATIVE P

Thinking about Jennifer, 1979

Barbara Hillyer

• • •

Jennifer is fourteen and she is afraid to grow up. Her fear is realistic. It is frightening for a girl to become a woman and even more frightening for a woman to be an adult in our society. But for Jennifer, growing up is more frightening than for most girls because she has to learn that the feminist promise—a girl can be anything she dares try to be—is meaningless. Jennifer is disabled, physically and mentally, and most of the things a man or woman might learn to be are beyond her ability, but not beyond her hope. She is frustrated and angry and afraid.

As her mother, I am frustrated and angry and afraid, too.

• • •

Until she was ten, Jenny fit very well into my understanding of what it means for mothers and daughters to become sisters. She is just a year younger than her sister, and although her development was slower and her body couldn't perform as competently as Megan's, they were plainly on the same track, girls who were learning their capacities, developing individuality, growing through childhood into an expanded, challenging world. We all knew that someday they would be women like me and that my feminist work would make their womanhood better. Supporting their personhood was as rewarding as nurturing them in infancy had been. I was sorry that they had to grow in a sexist society but sure of my ability to give them confidence and pride in being women.

When she was ten, Jenny changed her name to Jennifer, an assertion in which I rejoiced as one who knows the power of naming. She said that since she was growing up, she needed a more grown up name. It was the last gesture she made that fit comfortably into my feminist theory. At the same time, she was beginning to understand and to struggle against accepting the fact that she could not learn the things other children learn, that she was not going, even with difficulty, to become a woman like me or like most other women she knew. My own realization came slower; Jennifer taught me the limits of her life.

At ten, she was angry at the boys in her class who said girls couldn't be football players. Girls, she said, can be anything. Jennifer planned to be a bullfighter. Last year, at thirteen, she planned to be a gymnast. But her body betrays her. She can't

From Feminism and Disability, *by Barbara Hillyer, Norman: University of Oklahoma Press, 1993, 3–8, 245–248.*

walk upstairs with assurance. She is terrified of escalators. The terror is realistic, and the dreams of bullfighting and balance beams are not.

How am I to assimilate these facts into my motherhood without depriving her of dreams? How into my feminism without a biological determinism that will undermine my own belief in womankind?

• • •

One of the strengths of women's culture, I believe, is the high value we have placed on empathy and on meeting the emotional needs of others. That part of my mothering of Jenny has given us both great satisfaction. She has difficulty articulating her feelings, and I have learned to speak them for her. I can sometimes explain to her the meanings of experiences that are very confusing to her. This also is the great strength of her daughtering. I am cerebral and usually repress my emotions. Jenny functions almost entirely on an emotional level; she provides for my deficiency as I do for hers. We love each other deeply, but we don't know how to do the next, hard thing: to enable Jennifer to grow up.

Our interdependency was too much like a traditional marriage, so deeply based on dichotomies: intellectual/emotional, dependent/reliable, weak/strong, passive/aggressive. Of course she must break free, and of course we both broke open as she pulled away.

It is possible for me, with the help of a therapist, a lot of close friends, and a fine library, to regain my emotional self, to become whole. Because some of those friends are sister-daughters I can—or hope I can—achieve some better definition of what it means to mother, to daughter. But here is where my theory stumbles: Jennifer, losing me as her cognitive half, cannot gain that part of her self in any way I can understand. Her mind really does not work very well; its neural connections are as erratic as those that control her muscles.

And I, helplessly watching Jennifer's inability to grow up and her equally frustrating inability to stay a child, realize that my own hope for and patience with other women comes out of the optimistic belief that they are capable of growing up, that they can learn, that each has a consciousness that can be raised.

• • •

It is much too easy to sentimentalize Jennifer's role as my disabled daughter and my own as her mother, to make my nurturing and her childlike nature a permanent, admirable stasis. But she is angry and so am I. Madonna-mothering requires a younger and more passive child. And my rejection of passivity and dependency for myself precludes my wanting it for another woman.

When she was younger, I could present myself as one who copes gracefully with the medical and educational problems of a beautiful "handicapped" little girl. This role-playing had its rewards for both of us; I was admired for my strength and she for her sweetness. But it didn't help either of us to mature. Now we must find ways for her to care for herself and resources to help her do so.

Even the better answers our society offers for disabled people trouble me as a feminist who is also Jennifer's mother. She thinks of herself as homeless, someone who belongs nowhere, and that assessment, like her fear of escalators, is realistic.

Our society has two principal models for homes for dependent people, both based on the traditional nuclear family. The first and most "natural" (i.e., less institutional) of these is marriage, and it is tempting, even to one who mistrusts marriage as an institution, to hope that a woman like Jennifer will marry a nice man who will take care of her. But the wife in such a marriage would be unable either to relate to her partner as a peer or to leave the marriage if it proved unhappy (or even abusive). We have come to understand that a woman's ability to support herself is crucial to the maintenance of options for her, but some disabled people are unable to support themselves.

Indeed, even in sheltered workshops there is an assumption that retarded people will be able to do work involving some physical dexterity (such as cafeteria serving or factory assembly work) and that physically disabled people will be able to rely on mental or verbal competence (as in telephone sales or office work). Where both disabilities occur, a common solution is parental care more appropriate to a younger child. In the best institutions this pattern has recently changed. Efforts are made to acknowledge the emotional and even sometimes the sexual needs of the clients and to treat them less as children. The best case workers avoid the stereotyping inherent in disability "labeling" and try to understand the individuality of the people they help. Some agencies have encouraged marriage between retarded people, for example. Although this is certainly progress over the treatment of dependent adults as if they were children, such marriages are subject to all the deficiencies of marriage as an institution, especially for dependent wives. Where the partners are people whose mental and emotional capacities are, like Jennifer's, especially vulnerable to the influence of television, the traditional sex roles will probably be reinforced by marriage. An agency that avoids labeling by handicap may willingly label by sex role.

• • •

Of course I will be relieved if there are places where Jennifer can be protected and nurtured, perhaps loved and even married. And of course I want her to be accepted as she is, not punished or patronized for her inability to be as intelligent or well coordinated as others. But after the most hopeful and most realistic of planning, I return to those questions whose answers matter most to me and that I cannot answer. Because I believe in the value of an examined life, how can I relate to a woman who cannot examine her life? Since I know the difficulty for women of growing up, how shall I understand a woman who can't grow up entirely? Because I understand mothering to be nurturing independence, how can I mother this dependent woman? As our society's responses to disability range from neglect through sentimentality, how can I object to sex-role stereotyping if it is done with respect? Above all, how can I teach a girl I love that she can't be what she wants to be?

I don't know the answers to any of these questions, but I consider them basic questions for feminism. If conventional femininity is handicapping, an understanding of the double-bind of disabled women is essential to our efforts toward social change. To the extent that feminist theory relies on women's ability to understand their situation, it fails to touch the situation of the woman with mental disabilities. When we argue against female dependency in marriage or elsewhere, we should not ignore the existence of individual women who may be unable to avoid dependency. As our institutions respond to the rights of people with disabilities to live as "normally" as possible, we must remember that "normal" women's lives are often oppressive—inadequate models for the dignity of disabled women.

Thinking about Jennifer and Me, 1992

• • •

Jennifer is probably as happy as she has been since her early, relatively nondisabled childhood. She lives with nine other women who have varying degrees of mental retardation and with a series of house managers and trainers in a large modern house in a small Oklahoma town. She attends classes on such subjects as personal hygiene and laundry sorting in a nearby intermediate care facility and for an hour or two each afternoon she works in a sheltered workshop. She can walk unsupervised a couple of blocks to a convenience store to buy a soft drink, a miraculous new freedom for someone who needed twenty-four-hour-a-day supervision during all of the past eleven years.

My concerns about the reinforcement of traditional sex roles proved well grounded. After twelve years of training (and the invention of a submersible electric razor) Jennifer has learned to shave her legs, but not yet to apply nail polish and makeup; those lessons continue. On a daily basis a more important issue is whether she needs supervision while she showers and washes her hair. Still, the nail polishing lessons go on. Because her appearance now is deviant (she looks and acts "retarded"), the gestures toward conventional feminine appearance may smooth her experience in small town life, but won't make her "blend in."

Jennifer's greatest anxieties during the past ten years have been about boyfriends, marriage, and childbearing, concerns appropriate to her chronological age but invariably provoked by pressures from the workers in her various agencies and from her peers. Her own anxieties of choice have been about why no T-shirts or toys are available in honor of the Beverly Hillbillies and the Dukes of Hazzard. Her present houseparent and trainer are more interested in her getting through the day's routine than in her dating, and so her distress about boys and babies has abated.

• • •

Each year when asked her career goals, she says she wants to be a TV star and resists her trainers' pressures to consider cleaning TV studios instead. Their pressures make her anxious, though, because she wants to please them, or at least not to make them angry. In fact, Jennifer spends a lot of time being upset by what she fears is her inability to meet others' expectations, an anxiety that comes to a crisis when she perceives (rightly) that I don't want her to get married and have children and (perhaps wrongly) that other significant adults (her supervisors and her peers) believe that she should.

I no longer believe that I can persuade all of her teachers and trainers to agree with my view of Jennifer's abilities or to see me as a good mother, nor do I believe I can convince Jennifer that her peers' interpretations of her life are less accurate than those of people without mental disabilities. I no longer expect to persuade women with other disabilities to agree with me or to understand my point of view. I no longer believe that I can be superwoman enough to meet Jennifer's productivity quotas in addition to my own.

What I do know is how to be humanly present with Jennifer as she is, a woman with very serious limitations, intense anxieties, simple pleasures. One by one, and with enormous difficulty, I have given up the roles of interpreter, teacher, trainer, and therapist, until now what I give Jennifer is my physical presence, and access to what she loves best, pizza and "action figures." I still protect her by choosing her placement, attempting to cooperate with her case workers, managing her legal guardianship, and reminding her to wear her glasses. But Jennifer is not the central figure in my life and I am not the focus of hers.

I wanted to know how a girl with such severe limitations could become a woman, a whole person. Jennifer simply grew up. She was always a whole person, one whose disabilities and the behaviors they entail are basic to her personality, are her predominant traits. Now she is a woman with those traits, those behaviors. I believed that my job as her mother was to nurture her independence so that she could be a whole and responsible adult; she became a dependent adult, who needs protection so that she can survive and be responsible for the limited self-care that is within her abilities. She is a survivor, but she is not strong. Both of us know that. What has been harder for both of us to learn is that I too am not strong.

Jennifer's disabilities have handicapped me—socially, of course, because of stigma, but also physically because of stress, and emotionally because of grief. As I have come to terms with these facts, I have learned to live outside the illusion of self-sufficiency and to accept help. I no longer expect reciprocity, nor do I train Jennifer for it. Real acceptance of her particular disabilities includes acceptance of an unequal, uneven relationship. What I have, instead, is the multidirectional reciprocity of a women's community, the reciprocity of sharing the human condition. Like Jennifer, I am one who endures losses, who sometimes refuses to help or be helped, and yet who sometimes helps and sometimes can ask for help.

None of this was true before I began exploring my feminist questions about Jennifer. I did not even know and feel and act as if I were in a bad situation. I did not know that her losses and mine were appropriate occasions for grief, that I could live with such grief and not die of it. I did not yet know that I could not keep her safe.

Exploring the meanings of her womanhood, my motherhood, our lives together as women, enabled me to see that, like her, I am capable of suffering, fragile, human.

I had passed as less limited than I am. I believed women in general to be less limited than we are. Sometimes . . . I have wanted to sound more optimistic, cheerful, and competent than I am, but I have learned that disguising the pain, denying the sorrow, even "managing" too well denies the human connection. What Jennifer has given me is that connection. Jennifer taught me the limits of her life—and mine.

NARRATIVE Q

I Am My Mother's Keeper

Judy Dothard Simmons

After evading marriage and children (the two were linked in my formative years), I am, at age fifty-one, in my fifth year of tending to my mother. She needs help to live with Alzheimer's disease and I am it, although interacting with people whose thoughts and actions proceed slowly makes me grind my teeth.

I've often thought that life makes us go through certain tempering experiences, whether we want them or not. So, I'm not being allowed out of this woman-life without a profound lesson in patience that includes fulfilling the traditional female role of domestic and body servant.

In a *Reader's Digest*–like version of our heartwarming story, I would be the family-values heroine who gives up a high-powered New York media career and discovers the true meaning of life wiping bowel movement off her feisty, seventy-something mother, the spunky, most unforgettable character of the month. My less genteel version of this travail casts Momma as, indeed, a game person playing a poor hand with determination, but I am a conflicted caregiver with one hard-learned tip to offer.

• • •

The death of my grandmother in May 1991 at age one hundred and a half occasioned the unsought-for return of this Yankee to the Bible Belt. When I left Mount Vernon, New York, for Anniston, Alabama, I planned to attend Grandma's funeral, then stay a few weeks to ease Momma through the transition from elderly caretaker of the aged to single, carefree retiree. Right. Momma was a worse-for-wear seventy-five. By July it was clear to my subconscious that I wasn't going anywhere,

From Ms. *7, no. 1 (July/August 1996): 8690. Reprinted by permission of* Ms. *magazine,* so I resolved the dilemma of what I should do by breaking my ankle. I never saw the inside of my New York apartment again.

I had gotten a wake-up call about Momma's mortality in 1987. She had been hospitalized that September, following what was inconclusively diagnosed as a transient ischemic attack—an interruption of blood supply to the brain. I came south then, placed Grandma with a family that did elder care, and took Mom to New York for a vacation.

While she was with me, I kept trying to identify what was wrong with her, because something was. She never wanted to leave the house; when we did, she asked me repeatedly where we were going and why. Suddenly she couldn't abide going into New York City (Mount Vernon is 35 minutes by train from mid-Manhattan). Yet she had lived in the Bronx in the 1950s and later, over several years of summers, had attended Columbia University's Teachers College in Manhattan, earning a master's degree in elementary school administration.

Even in Mount Vernon everything startled her—me, the cat, the wind, a car passing in the street outside. Every morning I would find her standing in the bedroom packing her suitcase. "I've got to go take care of Momma," she would say. I thought she was completely stressed out from doing that already, and I dragged her to a well-recommended internist. Like the physician-friend who referred me, the internist was professionally blasé. Hypertension? Hey, she's a seventy-one-year-old African American woman. Mental confusion? Happens to the best of us eventually. What these people didn't know, what her physicians in Anniston didn't take into account, is that Amanda Catherine Dothard is an extraordinarily intelligent and well-educated woman with an ironic turn of mind and a marvelous capacity for insightful love. All they saw was a little old black lady with a head tremor.

I saw the wide-eyed, cornflake-tan beauty with the hourglass figure who my father fell for. And the zaftig forty-year-old whose mobile lips kept a hint of a smile in a coal-heated classroom with fifty first-graders. And the tough daughter of the soil, who picked cotton to supplement the Negro-teacher salary, even less than the pittance rural systems paid white teachers, so I could continue the piano lessons she started me on before I was four, and have my own typewriter at seven, and receive a private high school education.

I knew the astonishingly courageous woman who, at 45, committed herself to a rude widower with a laborer's lifestyle and seven children. Her comprehending love and stubborn refusal to allow human waste wrought better destinies for the five younger siblings than their birthright promised, and has definitely raised the aspirations and possibilities of their subsequent offspring.

Momma taught little ones for most of her career. She and small human animals seem to complete an electric circuit that mutually lights them up. If there are toddlers in our vicinity at the various eateries we frequent, I seat Momma so she can watch them. Her delight is wholehearted and her reading of their budding characters and desires uncanny. She seems to have infinite wells of patience and compassion.

Momma's basic orientation to the world seems to turn on interest, curiosity, and a willingness to appreciate the workings of things. She graduated from Johnson C. Smith University in 1939 with a bachelor of science in biology and a math minor. She has that wonderful faculty of attention that harvests an abundance of rich impressions from routine events. She combines the scientist's unblinking eye with a nurturer's compassion.

The precipitous loss of such a woman's coping abilities could not be normal decline. It wasn't until 1992, however, that the Alzheimer's diagnosis was made, and then largely because I refused to accept general senility as a verdict. When your relatives regularly live into their nineties, still in the land of the lucid, you don't give up on a spring chicken in her seventies. I was not about to let my mother go gentle into that vegetable night.

The "why" of my choice to stay with her is deeper than the forebrain and larger than words—and that is a wondrous statement coming from a wordsmith, especially a poet. Probing now, as at sore tooth, I loosen a feeling, a concept: connection, and my throat aches, my eyes fill with tears. Our mother-daughter relationship was a case of arrested development. Since we've been living together, I've been surprised at the intensity of feelings that date back to my adolescence, anger and resentment oozing from hidden niches of hurt and betrayal—like, when I was 16 and valedictorian, she didn't come to my high school graduation (she said her principal wouldn't let her off), and then six months later she remarried without my having an inkling that she was even interested in anyone.

I admit I haven't understood the woman, and often I haven't respected her. Loved her, yes, with a strangling ambivalence, but disagreed contemptuously with some choices she made that landed me in situations I detested: boarding school, for instance. And Alabama.

Yet in a lifetime of severing ties and striving for a sometimes arid autonomy, this is the one relationship that commands me to endure things that are for me impossible, unbearable, or potentially obligating. Like doing domestic dirty work myself, or opening my clamshell heart to my stepfamily.

I have at every point underestimated what I've let myself in for in choosing to care for a loved one with Alzheimer's disease (AD). Remaining rational from moment to moment, day to day, takes unusual effort. The unpredictability of Momma's condition undermines my ability to order my life. I can't have expectations about her comprehension and capabilities, and it's surprising how much expectation figures in life: the sun will rise; the ground won't open up and swallow us at our next step; she pulled down her underwear when she went to the toilet this morning, so she'll do the same this afternoon. I wish. I'm called on to live in the moment, as metaphysicians often advise, but that can be anxiety-producing. And, for someone like me who is used to a lot of autonomy, such interdependence and lack of control can generate a fair amount of frustration and resentment.

In the current, downsized version of her existence Momma is still minutely observant. She can spot a piece of lint on the hem of my garment at 50 paces. What drives me nuts is that at the same time she will be completely unaware of her undergarment drooping around her knees. The way AD pairs acuity with vacuity in apparently random ways can feel perfidious to the caregiver.

Fortunately, my agitation is checked and offset by Momma's intelligence, her emotional discipline, her loving disposition, and her grace. Infrequently she says, "I miss Clarissa so" or "I miss Momma." Sometimes I sympathize with her, hug her, and try to help her articulate her loneliness. Other times we talk about the people who are in our lives now and how fortunate we are. And sometimes I play off our shared faculty for unsentimental irony: "Remember her bad qualities and you won't miss her so much," I chivied Momma recently. We laughed and slid past the longing. I wish I could fill in more gaps for Ma, but we've been apart much more than we were together; our store of shared experiences is slender.

She goes to the Carver Seniors Program three days a week. It's a boon to both of us, providing her with stimulation and companionship and making me feel less guilty about not putting everything I have into keeping her going. The other seniors and the staff dote on her and I'm grateful to them for being willing to give her the care that she requires. Some of them know her as the teacher of their children and grandchildren. Others admire the gallantry of her struggle to remain in the world.

They are part of the whole new world I've entered since I started caring for Momma. When I listen to the inexperienced congressional Republicans' plans to reduce or kill these types of services with crippling cuts to social welfare agencies, I know they have no idea about the level of need in this country. At least Momma has a livable income, and she has me; still, we are pressed. She needs physical therapy, for instance, but doesn't qualify under strict Medicare criteria and our budget simply won't stretch any further.

I never felt class jealousy until I was a year or two into caring for Momma and began to see how much what I can do for her is determined by how much money we have. I can't spend all day every day doing things that will enhance Momma's functioning (exercise, handicrafts, speech therapy), in addition to handling her maintenance needs and the domestic load. Why not? Because I'm a person, too, not someone joined to Momma at the hip.

As it is, every time she slips another gear—that's the way I think of it—I'm disturbed on levels I didn't know I had. Here's an example of the latest undevelopment. For a while now, she hasn't been able to tie the name of an article of clothing to the actual garment. Except that she is able to—sometimes. 'Course those times might just be because she's following the direction of my eyes or a hand gesture, so I can't count on her pulling off her shirt on request, if she's in one room and I'm in another.

But, God, why can't she just take her clothes off with some verbal prompting while I put this laundry away and give me a little slack? 'Cause she can't. But since seven o'clock this morning I've been trying to tempt her flagging appetite; and taking her to the bathroom every couple of hours. And going on errands with her in tow so she'll get an outing. And tuning the television to something that she shows signs of enjoying. And giving her medicine one, two, three times, and the fourth still to go. And washing and drying and folding her urine-soaked nightclothes and bed pads. And monitoring her physical state and emotional state because she can't frame the thoughts and then the words to express discomfort or preferences, but she still has them. Stuff registers—like a creepy serial killer on TV who was scaring her—but I have to locate what she's feeling and thinking and name it to her before she can report on her state. And reminding myself that I choose this, I choose this, I choose this, and that her being in this good a condition is due to the miracle drug Tacrine and where would I be without it? And making myself hug her in the midst of my boiling frustration so I can feel how the parkinsonism that goes with Alzheimer's is making the major muscles of her neck, throat, and upper torso turn to stone; so I can feel how frail and frightened she is and how brave she is to still say she wants to go on pushing her loyal turning-80-now body forward in that penguin-like waddle; so I can touch the fact that she is someone, the one, who is love in the world to me, the only love I trust.

My biggest challenge is emotional control. The sustaining rage of my life is my undoing now. It's my response, my defense, my coping mechanism, my motive power; has been for much of my life. Rage against segregation, injustice, amoral capitalism, against petty greed, lyin', cheatin' hearts, and fundamentalists of all kinds. Noble, artistic rage that fueled my ambition to write poems that could change the world. Idealistic, pioneering rage that drove me to hurt myself proving that a woman and a black person could cut it in Fortune 500-land.

But the rage that propelled me toward socially constructive acts of art and freedom struggle is incompatible with the domestic, nurturing enterprise I have undertaken. Yet I still have it. So many frightening realities are bearing down on me that I maintain the little sanity I lay claim to by taking it one day, one hour, one minute at a time—when I can think clearly enough to remember that, when I can hold myself that still.

Here's where the blunder of canceling that [nursing home and custodial care] insurance policy comes back to haunt me. Doing this 24 hours a day, seven days a week, is too much for any thinking body. Being able to pay someone for regular breaks (a day a week, a couple of weekends a month) would make all the difference in my life and probably be refreshing for Momma also.

Failing that, I find myself screaming at Momma, creating a sound barrier that protects me from hitting her. I slam a glass down, hard enough to break it, on the rug. I snatch away the tray bearing the food she won't eat; it's done with ill grace and a punitive attitude, but it defuses the moment, gives me the nanosecond of space and time it takes to demagnify the situation and restore a sane perspective.

And gradually, as Momma continues to live, Alzheimer's disease will continue to disconnect words from concepts and feelings and referents. "Daughter," "Love,"

"Judy" will not add up to anything discernibly meaningful for her. Who will I be without my mother? How will I stand it when she doesn't comprehend that I am her baby—"my one little chick," she called me in 1991 with infinite tenderness when I had broken my ankle. It's like the whole Alabama experience is a black hole and I'll never again reach escape velocity.

'Course it's silly to think that way, because Mother will die.

Then I will have no one and nothing.

Now you see why I'm learning to take one day or less at a time. Now I see why people learn to pray.

• • •

I am being gentled and healed by living in a loving relationship—with my mom. Being around her is instructive. Watching her improvise around the gaps that Alzheimer's gouges into her brain humbles and shames me. She is aware of being changed, impaired, but she doesn't despair and she doesn't complain. Some people would argue that the disease itself, promoting forgetfulness as it does, is its own anesthetic. I say that is wishful thinking on the part of those reluctant to witness a terrible engagement between a human and the impersonal poetics of life, existence, being.

• • •

Momma is driven by the poem of her particular spirit, and committed to it. Every day she rages against the dying of the light. It is amazing to look at the very skeleton of a personality, of a soul . . . no, it is awesome and rather terrifying, for it attests to the loss of the basic tool of human intercourse—the mask. Alzheimer's disease is stripping Momma of the ability to dissemble and disguise that creates our private selves and fosters civility. As a result, her communications and actions reveal the bare bones of her character, not the careful image we are generally at pains to present to others.

Momma is a humble person. I could see all the negatives of that before: lack of self-esteem, a martyr complex, fear of rejection and failure. I thought those were the reasons she buried herself in this hick town with my wicked stepfather and the seven little steps. Maybe so. Maybe more so, her humility stems from her awareness of transcendence, of knowing herself to be a span in the generational bridge that brings human beings over to something above instinctual life. Perhaps she knows intrinsically the worth of her life's work; therefore, no New York ego is required.

The way she is playing the endgame that she must eventually concede is another of her gifts to me. Plagued by incomprehension and deprived of the intellectual activities that were her calling and her pleasure, she continues to synthesize meaning from people and events, and to shape me by her steadfastness into a person more understanding, kinder, than I want to be.

CHAPTER 9

Othermothering

Among the highlights of a trip I took to Illinois several years ago was a giddy game of hide-and-seek with my nephews Noah and Sam, then six years old. One evening, the three of us took a walk. The sidewalk bored Sam and Noah. Flowers, pets, toys, tools, and other attractions in people's yards held much more appeal so they darted and dashed along more interesting pathways. About halfway home they hid behind a wall of dense shrubs bordering someone's large yard. We spent many minutes running and peeking and startling one another around that green fence, often laughing too hard to run. All the rest of the way home—around an old Volkswagon van, a huge storage shed, big bushes—we hid-and-sought until we had no more energy.

During those thirty or forty minutes I felt a closeness to my nephews that is hard to put into words. Maybe "othermothering" is as good a word as any for what I felt. Certainly I, who have never been an official mother in any way, did not feel like a mother. But I did feel the closeness assumed to sustain committed parents. I hoped for a continuing relationship with them that would lead to something like Walter McCloud had with his aunt Sue Rawson. Jane Hamilton describes that bond from Walter's point of view in her novel *The Short History of a Prince*: "Of course his mother had given him life, and yet Sue Rawson, he sometimes grandly thought, had given him his own self, something that may have been even more difficult than birthing a baby. From the very beginning, it seemed, without either the benefit or the obstruction of love, his tall aunt had looked down her beaky nose at him and seen him clearly."[1]

Needless to say, one need not be an aunt or other family member to nurture someone else's daughter or son in a significant, sustaining way. The nurturer might be a neighbor, foster parent, godparent, or teacher.[2] In some racial-ethnic communities such extramaternal nurturance is institutionalized; it is a transgenerational pattern that members take for granted as a feature of life in their community. Generically, this institution might be called *othermothering*. Like all mothering, this type encompasses an array of practices that vary from one to the next community and from one historical period to another.

This chapter was written by Mary F. Rogers.

Othermothering

Mothering cannot be a solo enterprise. A mother has to collaborate to some substantial extent with other people, usually other women. Geraldine Youcha claims "women have always helped other women to be mothers," that women have a "long legacy of shared mothering."[3] Relatively isolated and privatized mothering is the exception, not the norm, in human history and across human societies. Multiple caretaking tends to be the norm, and in those societies "where caretaking by the mother alone prevails, . . . there tends to be more neglect of children."[4]

As we saw in chapter 3, the maternal role comprising a "full-time housewife and child-care provider" is far from universal, even in modern societies.[5] Despite the claims of some "family decline" commentators, the "traditional" or "conventional" nuclear family is in fact neither. That family form emerged with the middle classes during the nineteenth century. While it gained great respectability, it never became the norm among high-income families. Nor did it become normative among working-class and low-income families. By now the so-called traditional nuclear family is no longer normative in the middle sectors of American society either. "Intensely reared" children still show up in such societies, but their rearing is now shared among diverse individuals across various institutional settings.[6]

All societies make such "alternative arrangements for child care when mothers [are] unable or unwilling to care for their own children." These other arrangements typically are "compared to mother care as the standard of optimum child care."[7] Among the ramifications of that pattern is that women seen as "unwilling" to be the primary caregiver for their children are seen as bad in the extreme. For example, the economist, social theorist, and feminist Charlotte Perkins Gilman (1860–1935) "was vilified by the press for divorcing her husband and later sending their daughter to live with him." Margaret Sanger, the preeminent leader of the birth control movement in early twentieth-century American society, "did not fare any better" when her reform efforts took her to Europe without her family.[8] Such harsh censure still occurs today, as was seen when the au pair Louise Woodward became notorious when the child in her care died. The child's mother, a part-time ophthamologist, was widely criticized for working outside the home.

In some communities such judgments are rare, particularly where sizable percentages of mothers are financially forced to work outside the home. Within African American communities, for instance, mothering is seen as a "form of cultural work."[9] Patricia Hill Collins calls that cultural work motherwork, which entails not only struggling so that one's own children survive but also understanding that "individual survival, empowerment, and identity require group survival, empowerment and identity." Motherwork commonly extends, then, to the community's children and beyond.[10] It presupposes substantial othermothering.

As first characterized by Rosalie Riegle Troester, othermothers help bloodmothers "guide and form" their daughters. These othermothers sometimes belong to the bloodmother's kinship network—cousins, for example—but sometimes they do not. In the latter instances othermothers sometimes have "different lives and exemplify values widely divergent from" those of the bloodmother, thus providing girls alternative role models.[11] In narrative R, Elena Featherston describes such a network of othermothers. Drawing on diverse data, Collins enlarged the concept beyond mother-daughter relationships so that othermothering means collaborating with other women in child care and other projects essential to the survival of one's family and community.

Collins emphasizes that in African American communities distinctions among the various women who care for children "are often fluid and changing." Embedded in "organized, resilient, women-centered networks of bloodmothers and othermothers," these mothering women occupy a central place in extended families.[12] Elsa Barkley Brown, for instance, says that on her wedding day one of her "mothers/aunts" told her, "Your mother is my sister, my daughter, my mother, my cousin, and to you I have been and always will be your aunt, your mother, your grandmother, your sister; your children will have an aunt, a grandmother, a greatgrandmother, a mother, a sister, a cousin."[13] Much in line with Brown's memory, Collins points out that when necessity dictated, "temporary child care arrangements turned into long-term care or informal adoption." She also points out that othermothers not only provide support for children but also for bloodmothers.[14]

Some Chicana and Anglo employed mothers in Albuquerque, New Mexico, are illustrative. They

> created women-centered support networks from their own primary kin (usually mothers and sisters) and, if married, their husbands' kin (mothers-in-law and sisters-in-law), plus their friend. . . . [These] working- class women have integrated support networks to include friends, especially friends established in the workplace. It was the sometimes extraordinary support of kin, friends, and even day-care providers that enabled some of them to better handle the contradictions of being working mothers.[15]

These mothers, 70 percent of whom are Chicanas, are extending Mexican and Mexican-American traditions of othermothering that have long sustained heavily burdened mothers. Early in the twentieth century, for example, it was common to find "one or two women who, in addition to working in their own homes, served other families in the community as *curanderas* (healers), *parteras* (midwives), and schoolteachers."[16] The institution of *compadrazgo* (godparenting) also supported mothers and their families. Bonnie Thornton Dill explains that this family system has helped preserve the Mexican community. Besides participating in rites of passage such as baptisms and marriages, godparents act as guardians and also provide financial help, if needed. Traditionally, *compadrazgo* cut across class, racial, and even generational lines.[17]

Ruth Behar, a Cuban American anthropologist, participated in this institution at the behest of Esperanza, a Mexican woman whose experiences she was studying. Behar writes about her husband and herself:

> David and I became *compadres*, spiritual coparents of Esperanza's daughter and her nino Dios. Esperanza and I would from then on address one another as *comadre* and participate in the intimate but respectful friendship and patronage that goes with being *compadres*. A *compadrazgo* relation in rural Mexico is typically forged between persons of high and low economic standing, so that as the better-off person in my relation with Esperanza I would be expected to offer financial or other assistance if she requested it. She would be expected, in turn, to offer me small gifts from time to time.

Behar thus became fictive kin—as-if kin, like kin—to Esperanza and her family.[18]

Puerto Rican American mothers rely on the same institution that Esperanza does to facilitate their motherwork. Ruth Zambrana found that they also created *natural support systems* within their racial-ethnic community that complemented professional caregiving systems in the larger community. Their extended families included not only relatives but also the *compadrazgo* system. Zambrana describes the typical family as including"'blood relatives' and a wide-ranging constellation of 'adoptive relatives' who fulfill either formal or informal functions within the extended family. Informal members consist of close family friends and neighbors who, over a period of years, prove their willingness to be involved in important family matters and events. The term *como familia* (like family) has been used to describe these individuals."[19] Among such individuals are surely many othermothers.

The same broad patterns also hold among Vietnamese Americans. As they resettled in the United States, Vietnamese refugees "actively worked to reconstruct family networksby building kin relationships. In order for this to take place, the criteria for inclusion in the family had become extremely flexible. Thus, close friends were often incorporated into family groups as fictive kin. Also, relationships with relatives who were distant or vaguely known in Vietnam were elevated in importance."[20] Again, comothers or othermothers were probably central to the familial reconstruction the women masterminded.

Often wanting to help their daughters or daughters-in-law and sometimes not involved full-time in the paid labor force, grandmothers are often crucial othermothers. For instance, the Albuquerque mothers' "mothers or mothers-in-law took on a significantly greater amount of child care than sisters or other close kin."[21] That pattern is scarcely exceptional. By 1994, 3.7 million American children lived with a grandparent or other relative, with about one-third of these living in homes where neither their mother nor their father also lived. Fifty to sixty percent of the primary caregivers in these skipped-generation families are grandmothers. This and other versions of "kinship care" are on the rise in American society.[22] Unfortunately, "little is known about relative care," but we do know that grandmother care is its most common form.[23]

Another form of othermothering is stepmothering. In some respects stepmothering may be paradigmatic of othermothering. In "An Open Letter to a Stepmother," a narrative opening her book on stepmothering, Donna Smith delineates the dilemmas and contradictions commonly built into othermothering of all sorts. First, she raises the question of whether anyone "ever aspired to be a stepmother."[24] Girls are widely socialized to aspire to primary motherhood, but othermothering usually emerges as part and parcel of kinship or close friendship with a primary mother. In addition, othermothering may derive from one's occupational commitments, such as teaching.

Second, Smith emphasizes that stepmothers need not be "mother figure[s]" to their stepchild(ren). Instead, they can choose other roles such as friend or "sponsoring adult" (2). Certainly, as their children grow, primary mothers also face significant choices along these lines. Their core connection with their child(ren), however, is usually parental. Primary mothers do not routinely have the wide choice that othermothers enjoy as they carve out their relationships with the children they are co-mothering. If only because the norms of othermothering are more flexible and open-ended than those of mothering, othermothers are less constrained in their practices than primary mothers tend to be.

Third, stepmothering is typically part-time (15). Since more than nine out of ten children in stepfamilies live with their mother but spend selected periods with their father, stepmothers exemplify the part-time character of most othermothering. Theirs is not round-the-clock, year-round mothering but a complementary, support-giving form that usually takes considerably less than a full-time effort.

Fourth, the care associated with stepmothering and other forms of othermothering is usually less than that provided by primary mothers (25). Most othermothers are less involved with child care than primary mothers are, although there is dramatic variation in how much care they provide and for how long a period in a child's life. Some othermothers, such as teachers or counselors, are typically short-term; others, such as foster mothers, are shorter-term than most kin and fictive kin but do provide comprehensive care for some substantial period. Nevertheless, othermothering has a narrower reach than primary mothering. While primary mothers range from virtually no care (that is, routine neglect) to excessive attention (that is, undue preoccupation), those extremes are unlikely among othermothers. If their care tilts toward extremes, it becomes likely that their involvement with the child will be challenged and changed.

Finally, Smith emphasizes that a stepmother is both an insider and an outsider, as are most othermothers (87). Inside and outside the family, inside and outside the child's life, and inside and outside the role of mother, othermothers negotiate a course that leaves them not only with latitude and choice but also with considerable anomaly and little authority compared to primary mothers. Stepmothers' insider/outsider status leaves them open to diverse stereotypes and negative judgments. David Popenoe (see chapter 4) renders such judgments: citing only a single 1988 study, he claims that "the increase of stepfamilies has created serious problems for child welfare" and concludes that "we as a society should be doing much more to halt the growth of stepfamilies." Norval Glenn, also mentioned in chapter 4, says stepparents and stepchildren's relationship with one another "is incidental to the attraction of two adults to one another."[25] His assertion implies that many parents fail to consider carefully how their remarriage will affect their child(ren), a dubious notion at best.

Overall, othermothers face diverse challenges and opportunities, some shared with primary mothers and others peculiar to their social positioning as co-mothers. Their challenges and opportunities intensify when othermothers take money for their maternal work. Commercial othermothering is, to say the least, a prospective minefield where the insider/outsider status assumes its full force. Before turning to commercial othermothering, however, let us look at two other forms of othermothering. Both involve co-mothering outside any tradition such as *compadrazgo* or African American othermothering. The first is lesbian couples becoming parents together. The second, less institutionalized form occurs when a single mother and one of her friends negotiate an othermothering arrangement together.

Lesbian couples have long co-parented, usually because one or both women had already become a mother in a heterosexual marriage. Recently, though, more lesbian couples have been choosing to have a child together. Among lesbian co-parent families Maureen Sullivan found two parenting patterns. Overwhelmingly, the preferred pattern was for the two women to share equal responsibilities for financial support as well as nurture of their child. That type of family involves full-fledged *co-mothering*. By contrast, a few couples favored an arrangement with a primary mother and an othermother—the "Rozzie and Harriet" pattern.[26] This pattern represents a distinctive form of othermothering by the partner who is the breadwinner for the family. She is both like and unlike stepmothers, like and unlike other types of othermothers. Hers is a particularly anomalous position, although it may entail considerably more authority and long-term commitment than most forms of othermothering. The lesbian co-parent partnered with a stay-at-home mom deviates not only from heterosexist norms of family life but also from those norms that apparently prevail in lesbian communities.

Also in a distinctive, nonnormative position is an othermother whose long-term commitment lies outside any tradition such as those found in African American and Latino/a communities. Anndee Hochman tells about one such primary mother and othermother. Cherry, the othermother, is a therapist and writer who has long wanted a child but is infertile. Her partners have been women with grown children or women uninterested in co-mothering. At one juncture Cherry's friend Susan decided to adopt a child. These two friends came up with an arrangement where "Susan would make the decisions and pay the bills for Abra's care. But Cherry's role would be far greater than that of a baby-sitter or friend." The amount of time Cherry has spent with Susan's daughter, Abra, has varied over the years, ranging from a few hours a week during the first months to a day or more each week thereafter.

Hochman calls these two friends the "primary adults in Abra's life." She concludes that together they show not only that primary mothers can depend on othermothers in diverse ways but also that women contemplating motherhood "need not choose between a full-time commitment to children and none at all."[27] Othermothering represents all the choices lying beyond full-time motherhood or no regular involvement with children. Its possibilities reach as far as women's imaginations and children's needs. Elena Featherston's personal narrative, the first accompanying this chapter, beautifully illustrates such possibilities. She describes how mothers can create "godmothering networks" for their children to enrich their cultural as well as interpersonal environments.

Commercial Child Care: Othermothering and Othercare

American day care was first institutionalized during the 1920s and 1930s with nursery schools for middle-income children supposedly at risk of getting too much maternal attention and day nurseries for working-class children whose employed mothers might give them too little attention. Advocates of both institutions presumed that mothers need expert advice and support in order to raise "healthy children."[28] Beginning in 1933 during the Great Depression, the Works Progress Administration established day nurseries for poor children; these nurseries aimed more at providing jobs than assisting mothers. With World War II came the Lanham Act, which established child care centers so that mothers could enter and remain in the labor force. This was the only time in American history when public funds supported child care for other than poor children and their families.[29] Historically, the chief sponsors of extrafamilial child care in American society have been the public welfare system and nonprofit organizations, such as churches and synagogues.[30] The best-known national example is Head Start, which by 1993 "had provided a year of comprehensive early childhood education for more than 13 million poor children in approximately thirteen hundred programs" across the country.[31]

Today about 10 percent of child care involves federal funding but it earmarked only for poor families and usually only covers part of their child care costs.[32] Nonparental child care is something other parents have to pay for entirely out of pocket. Marital status, social class, and number of children make the challenges of finding and funding child care either more or less difficult. As mothers—especially mothers of preschool children—began entering the labor force in substantial numbers during the 1960s, the challenges of finding affordable, high-quality childcare intensified. Now that the majority of these mothers work outside the home, millions of parents face a chronic child care challenge.

Typically, mothers assume the main responsibility of arranging for and overseeing childcare. Yet that responsibility does not evolve "in the same way for all groups of parents."[33] The Albuquerque mothers cannot, for example, readily purchase child care services, so they have to be particularly resourceful about making arrangements with spouses, kin, roommates, or even their other children in order to get the child care they need. For them, "split-shift arrangements" with their spouses are particularly attractive, which is in fact what both Hispano and Anglo couples did whenever possible.[34]

For preschool children of employed parents, parental care by far remains the most common form of child care. Roughly 46 percent of preschool children have that form of primary child care arrangement.[35] While many parents can sustain this arrangement by working different shifts, others manage with one parent working a full-time job and the other working a part-time one. Occasionally, one parent works for wages inside the home, as with family day care providers whose experiences we will soon consider. In any event, much more often than one might expect, employed parents still manage to provide the lion's share of their children's care.

Among the least observed patterns, if only because it is the most expensive on average, is in-home care provided by someone other than a parent or relative. About 3 percent of preschool children get such care. One of its forms is the au pair system that Congress authorized in 1986. This arrangement revolves around a twelve-month "cultural exchange" whereby European, English-speaking workers provide child care at modest fees in American homes. Eight agencies screen participants in the program.[36] Nannies and other in-home child care workers would seem to outnumber au pairs, but the numbers are hard to come by because so many nannies are either undocumented ("illegal") residents or are American citizens who are paid "under the table."

Julia Wrigley interviewed seventy-six in-home child care workers as well as seventy-nine parents using their services. She also interviewed twenty-two heads of agencies that place domestic workers in the Los Angeles and New York areas. Among the workers Wrigley interviewed, forty-one were Latina, mostly from Mexico, El Salvador, and Guatemala; eleven were from the Caribbean. The remainder included fifteen nannies, five each from Ireland and England and the American Midwest, as well as seven European au pairs. Only two African American women were included, in part—according to the heads of the employment agencies—because a lot of parents "refuse to accept black workers." When they do, they expect to pay them less.[37]

Wrigley found that in-home child care varies a lot. Some parents see distinct advantages in hiring foreign-born and other people "different" from themselves. They say it keeps costs down, mitigates against child care workers taking on parental roles, and lets employers assign housecleaning chores (17, 47). On average, the mothers drawn to in-home child care from nonrelatives strongly feel that "group care" is not good enough for their children (144). Sometimes, then, theirs is an elitist as well as racist posture.

With about half of American preschoolers getting their primary child care from their own parents or (occasionally) in-home child care workers, what forms of care do the other half of young children get? As we have seen, relative care is not uncommon. Fourteen to fifteen percent of children under five have that type of child care arrangement. By a ratio of about three to two, the majority get that care in the relative's home rather than their own home.[38] Although only 10 to 11 percent of preschoolers are in it, family day care is the preferred nonfamilial arrangement among parents of preschoolers. In particular, parents of infants and toddlers often seek family day care. Since it typically involves another woman caring for children in her own home, this child care "most closely approximates mother care" and may be a big reason for its popularity with parents. Another appealing circumstance is that the child care provider and the parents tend to be in the same social class, which may make for more comfortable communication as well as similar child care styles.[39]

Family day care is popular in countries besides the United States, but in other countries it is likelier to be regulated. Between 82 and 90 percent of family day care homes in American society are not licensed. Some are operating illegally, but most are smaller in size than the states regulate. William Gormley Jr. generalizes that "regulated family day care providers offer superior care" to that provided in other extrafamilial settings.[40] Regulated or not, one attractive advantage of family day care is its "rich opportunities for play," some of which is specifically "stimulated by the home site."[41] Also, since family day care usually involves one mother providing all the child care, contact between parents and their children's actual caregiver is usually direct as well as frequent. Such contact is widely considered important to all the individuals involved.[42]

From mothers' points of view no feature of their children's child care may be as important as "feeling comfortable" with the caregiver. Susan Kontos and her collaborators found that "[n]either cost nor convenience nor quality of the child's experience in care were the primary reasons that mothers selected care."[43] Their comfort level with the caregiver took precedence over these other factors, which were also important to them. Kontos and her collaborators studied 820 mothers using family day care or relative care for their children under six years old. Living in the areas of Charlotte (North Carolina), Dallas-Fort Worth, and California's San Fernando Valley, these mothers included white (42 percent), African American (23 percent), and Latina (31 percent) women, 80 percent of whom were married and living with their partner. All the groups of mothers put the same five factors at the top of their priorities about their children's care. These factors include attention to safety and cleanliness, the child care provider's attention to and warmth toward the children, and the provider's communication with the parents about their children. Overall, the mothers and their children's caregivers "were in close agreement about what constitutes quality care" (127). Still, more than a quarter of the mothers would choose other care if they could (206). Often, too, family day care providers themselves would choose other employment if they felt they could.

Margaret K. Nelson has studied such providers' experiences in detail. There are roughly 1.8 million family day care providers care in the United States.[44] They scarcely make a good living. Only 18 percent charge $1.50 or more an hour per child, and nearly a third charge $1.00 an hour or less. Overall, their average weekly income for a median workweek of fifty hours was $171, or roughly $3.42 per hour. Once their costs for such things as food and toys are taken into account, these workers' weekly incomes drop to $154, or about $3.08 per hour (41, 42). Even though these figures are somewhat dated, there is no reason to think that these caregivers' incomes have much increased of late, if only because they can charge only what employed parents can afford to pay.

Besides their paltry incomes, these paid othermothers face considerable frustration. For one thing, they often feel socially isolated.[45] A sort of loneliness for adults tends to infiltrate their work lives. Also, Nelson found that they anticipate losing contact with the children they nurture (98). Further, family day care providers often experience problems with parents. A common one is how long some parents want to talk when they pick up their children.[46] At the very time that the child care worker is trying to turn her attention to her own family, some parents seem oblivious to her needs. Such parental behavior bolsters providers' market perspective, Nelson found, enabling them to enforce their fee schedule as well as the rules they set for parents (55). Family day care providers also face the physical and emotional challenge of keeping their wage work and their family life distinct from one another.[47] Finally, these child care workers are "painfully aware that their attachments to the children in their charge [are] rooted in economic relationships."[48] That circumstance perhaps accounts for their inclination toward what Nelson calls their "detached attachment" to the children temporarily in their care (92). Because of these distinct features of their othermothering, family day care providers are hard pressed to find role models in or guidance from other types of othermothers.

Yet family day care providers do share certain experiences with other women in the broad, anomalous role of othermother. Above all, as Nelson emphasizes, theirs is an experience of shared mothering (68–78). For the most part, these child care workers see themselves as mothers and want to take care of their own children in their own homes while earning some income at the same time. Importantly, they value the kind of care they provide (91). Nelson found that while family day care providers readily reject professional models of carework, they cannot "easily dismiss mothering as a model for their involvement with children." What they like about their work is largely all the things that make it motherwork.[49] Miriam Rosenthal concludes that "[t]heir role definition is usually that of a 'substitute mother,' meaning that they are expected to be like mothers," though less important.[50] Her findings about Israeli family day care providers thus resonate with those of Nelson and others about American providers. Among all paid child care workers, family day care providers, working in their own homes, surely come closest to othermothering in their daily practices.

Professional or even business models are supposed to govern the paid work of other child care workers. Their work conditions and their contacts with children and their parents also make their paid work distinct from that of family day care providers. Family day care providers, for instance, sometimes distrust the "emerging professional model of home day care," which they fear will reduce their flexibility, constrain their responsiveness, and make individual attention less a priority.[51] Rosenthal observed that family day care providers act more like mothers than professional preschool teachers do. Nelson made parallel observations when she looked at ten women operating preschools. She found that they "*are* better able than their nonprofessional peers to sustain a market perspective." For the most part, "instead of identifying with their clients, . . . they look outward to a community of professional colleagues."[52]

Over the past few decades, that community has spawned a number of professional and business associations. One is the National Association of Child Care Professionals, whose members own, direct, or administer child care centers. For this organization, a professional perspective includes such insights as this: "Like any business, the child care industry continues to grow, change and challenge its *managers*."[53] There is also the National Child Care Association (NCCA) for owners, administrators, and directors of private, licensed child care centers and preschools. At its Web site, one link is to "Federal Legislative Updates." Another organization for child care providers is USA Child Care, whose Web site notes that "none of the proposed federal initiatives . . . focus on raising child care rates of reimbursement."[54]

The professional/business model of child care also shows up in self-help books for people wanting to start child care businesses, such as Nan Lee Hawkins's *Profitable Child Care: How to Start and Run a Successful Business*. Hawkins surveys the "top ten worries" of prospective center owners, including unjustified lawsuits, hiring a child abuser, fear of competition, dealing with distraught employees, and even using a computer system.[55] Not one of the worries has to do with children, for instance, children getting sick at the center, children unable to get along well with their peers, or children with special needs. Nor do any of the major worries have to do with parents.

By now a lot of for-profit child care centers are not small businesses at all. Some are part of national chains, which in turn are sometimes publicly owned corporations eager for good earnings, high profits, and consistent performance on the financial markets. KinderCare grew from sixty centers in 1974 to 1,100 in 1988. Its growth and that of its corporate counterparts have created a "proprietary lobby," the chief organization of which is the aforementioned NCCA.[56] Neither child psychologists nor other experts on child development steer these organizations or drive this lobby. Like the business of family making examined in chapter 7, the business of child care is growing.

So is the business of entertaining children, whether with toys, videos, television programs, or books. As sociologists and psychologists have long emphasized, the mass media are key agents of socialization for children in modern societies. These corporate media influence children's perceptions, beliefs, and values, as Maureen Reddy illustrates in narrative T. Wanting "to help [their son] Sean resist a racist, sexist system," Reddy and her husband actively seek "alternatives to fill the space resistance creates." Already "supported by friends and by the enlightened day-care center Sean attended," these parents came up short when they sought similar support in toy stores, on television, and at other sites of children's media culture. Reddy's narrative shows their resourceful responses to the biases and erasures they found in the media, while also illustrating the need for some sort of othermothering to take hold there.

Gormley concludes, "The single most unusual feature of the child care industry in the United States is the relatively prominent role played by for-profit day care centers," which account for about 35 percent of all group centers. Gormley adds that for-profit chains are another distinctive feature of American child care, with more than one-sixth of for-profit centers being part of chains. On-site child care at parents' workplaces remains uncommon. Even companies with many female employees usually do not offer it. A notable exception is the "substantial minority" of hospitals with on-site centers that help them recruit and keep nurses and other key personnel.[57]

Amidst this web of childcare providers, credible expressions of concern for children are not easy to find, even among child care "professionals." Nor does it seem easy to find a corporate-sponsored childcare business where one can enthusiastically leave one's child(ren), especially if one is looking for othermothering. At the professional/business end of the paid child care continuum, then, one might better talk about othercare rather than othermothering. Alternatively, one might talk about othermothering in its most constrained, narrow form. In for-profit settings child care workers have few opportunities for full-fledged othermothering—for spontaneity, for sustained attention to a child needing it for a significant period, for familiarity with the child's parent(s) built up over time. In nonprofit centers the picture is unclear, if only because data about them are less accessible.

Yet we do know a good deal about child care workers in general, especially those working outside their own homes. Their work is profoundly demanding and woefully unrewarded. Gormley notes that when compared with those who are compensated at the same level, child care workers are "unusually well-trained and well-educated." That wages/skills gap may why child care workers exhibit two to four times the national average 10 percent rate of annual turnover.[58] The Children's Defense Fund reports that most child care workers earn only somewhat more than the minimum wage, averaging $12,058 per year.[59] Their average weekly incomes range between $190 and $310, and they usually have no benefits and no paid leave. Among center-based child care workers, for instance, only about one out of three receives partial or full medical benefits.[60] Regardless of whether they work in their own homes or at centers, child care workers also face recurrent experiences of powerlessness. Seen as neither competent nor expert, they lack sufficient control over their work and its conditions, face too much bureaucracy and too few resources, and cannot protect their charges as fully as they would like.[61]

These are the common laments of mothers. The work of child care providers is in the end *mothers'* work; it is women's work—the work of caring, nurturing, protecting. Child care has long been feminized and may have become refeminized during the 1980s when news of satanic rituals and other abuse receved lots of media attention. Mary de Young found that among thirty-five "major satanic day care center cases," about half of the sixty-one people facing criminal charges were men. Such circumstances feed the strong tendency in American culture to be suspicious of men who seek contact with young children, which in turn feeds the tendency for men to avoid occupations where their motives are likely to face relentless scrutiny.[62]

Othermothering and Provision of Child Care

Child care provision is a women's issue as a matter of practical course. As consumers and providers of child care, women overwhelmingly predominate. Yet the people making the policies about extrafamilial child care are overwhelmingly men, including legislators as well as executives of for-profit centers. For the most part, their outlook has been stingy and unimaginative, perhaps reflecting prejudice against mothers who dare, even out of necessity, to place their young children in the care of an othermother.

Even in the 1990s, critics of paid othermothering are easy to find. Some have been around a good while—T. Berry Brazelton, Penelope Leach, and Benjamin Spock, for instance. This "Holy Triumvirate" of "baby gurus" basically treats "'othercare' [as] inferior to mothercare."[63] More recently, the father-absence, family-decline authors examined in chapter 4 have adopted the same biased tack. Popenoe says "childrearing by nonrelatives is inherently problematic." Maggie Gallagher, an "affiliate scholar" of Blankenhorn's Institute for American Values, claims that "[a]n emerging body of research suggests that children in full-time day care are less likely to be firmly attached to their parents and are on average more disobedient toward adults and more aggressive toward their peers than children primarily cared for by their parents." She says that sometimes day care even "puts children's cognitive development at risk," as if some children's homes didn't sometimes entail that same risk. Gallagher ultimately leaves day care issues behind and focuses on mothers with full-time jobs outside the home: "Several researchers . . . have found that very young children whose mothers work full-time tend to have poorer relations not only with their mothers but also with their fathers."[64]

The patchwork quilt of child care alternatives available to American parents is only explicable in the context of such biases against employed mothers, plus unrealistic notions about what motherwork entails and how it gets done. As we have seen, mothering is collaborative; maternal practices are profoundly social. Motherwork links mothers not only with their children but also with other women whose help lets primary mothers sustain themselves for the long haul while doing all the other work (paid or not) necessary for their own and their children's survival. If we lived in a society that recognized the collaborative realities of most mothering, comprehensive child care services would be widely available, actually affordable, and of consistently high quality.

In such a society awareness would run deep that mothering has public as well as private dimensions, collective as well as individual facets. In fact, today more and more American "mothers are redefining child rearing from a privatized activity to a social one."[65] As they do so, they rock the boat that the father-absence/family-decline ideologues are trying to redirect. After all, accessible and affordable child care enhances mothers' employment opportunities and enables more of them to achieve a measure of economic self-sufficiency. Accessible, affordable child care is, for example, crucial in programs helping teenage mothers complete high school.[66] In the main, withholding child care services means holding mothers back and, often enough, their children with them.

The priority given to child care services thus reflects the values that predominate in a culture. Focusing on four cross-societal variations in child care services, Michael Lamb and Kathleen Sternberg disclose the dense cultural meanings embedded in such services. First, child care entitlements vary with the emphasis given to gender equality. Second, they vary with how much child care is seen as a private, individual responsibility or as a substantially public, collective responsibility as well. Third, publicly funded child care can be seen as no more than a social welfare provision, or it can be seen as fundamentally an educational provision. Finally, child care services vary with cultural conceptions of childhood and child development.[67] Overall, childcare services in American society imply a relatively low priority put on gender equality; a relatively narrow conception of child rearing as private and individual; little notion of extraparental childcare as an educational opportunity; and notions of children as the property and responsibility of their parents who can adequately oversee their development in their own homes.

Instead of asking "how child care providers contribute to child rearing," some Americans seem more intent on asking how to get mothers of young children back into their homes where they can do the work of properly raising their children.[68] Certainly, that question prevails among father-absence/family-decline critics. That same question, albeit unuttered, may account for the failure of national leaders to support child care provisions capable of promoting American children's development while easing parents' minds about the safety and welfare of their children. Missing from our broader public discourse is any serious concern about the millions of fathers who fail to do their fair share of co-parenting.[69] The intense association of child rearing with mothers perhaps accounts for that silence in everyday discourse, but when policymakers, nonfeminist social scientists, and culture critics sustain that same silence in our public discourse, one begins to suspect that child care in our society reflects stingy attitudes toward mothers' rights and opportunities.

The quality of mothering and othermothering in society is in the end a quality-of-life issue. It has to do with the quality of children's lives and their mothers' lives, to be sure. Yet it has also to do with the quality of civic life, which revolves in large measure around the sense that citizens and their families are respected and esteemed. That sense can only build up when public services reach far enough to make our everyday lives less trying and more dignified.

NARRATIVE R

The Godmother Network

Elena Featherston

I'm African American, Latina, Native American, Irish, Nicaraguan, Scottish, Italian. Did I leave anything out? But, I'm Black, right? I'm creamy tan but I'm Black. Karen is creamy tan, but she is Korean. That means she's Yellow, right? This is silly. We just are what we are.

Alexandria Gomez-Featherston, 1993, age 5

The "godmother network" is an idea playwright Glenda Dickerson shared with me a few years ago. When her teenage daughter began having difficulty during her "coming of age," Glenda found other women to help her ease the child through the hormonal and emotional turbulence of adolescence. This is the way of most indigenous, tribal people. I've modified Glenda's idea just a bit to fit the needs of children of any age.

Group size can vary, but four to nine women friends works well. Ask each woman if she would consider spending one day a month with the child(ren) in your life. It is imperative that the women be different in age, ethnicity, ableness, place of origin, occupation, first language, etc. Mix it up! This is a cross-cultural stew. Godmothers can be homemakers, scientists, single, educators, secretaries, artists, married, lawyers, welfare moms, grandmothers or unmarried childless women. They should be great people who know how to be with a child, and have the time, energy and heart to share with one.

Through one such group, my granddaughter is learning gardening, music, sewing, Spanish, and an understanding of disability. She has developed an empathy with and compassion for the human condition that is rare even among adults. Her godmothers are an African American writer, a Japanese multicultural curriculum developer, a disabled Filipina crisis counselor and film student, a Latina lawyer, a German/Irish housewife, and an African American chemist turned workshop leader. The Japanese curriculum developer speaks Spanish, the writer gardens, the ex-chemist is a world-class quilter, the housewife loves Mexican art and culture, the disabled filmmaking student is teaching her to bake.

From her visits, Alexandria learns more about human diversity than any book can teach, or any misinformation can destroy. She is exposed to households in which all kinds of people and points of view are represented. She hears and often partici-

From Feminist Parenting: Struggles, Triumphs, & Comic Interludes, *edited by Dena Taylor. Crossing Press, 1994. Revised version reprinted by permission of the author.*

pates in conversations about politics, exercise, concerts, broken hearts, current events, science, eco-feminist concerns, human spirituality, and race. She is learning, by example, that individuals can be different and disagree and also respect, honor and even love one another. These experiences teach self-esteem, self-respect, and respect for others, and they impart a sense of empowerment. She knows people of different races, different ethnicities, different spiritual practices, diverse sexualities, and varying degrees of ableness, which is much better than knowing about them. But difference does not diminish her. It is positive. There are many languages to learn, foods to eat, traditions to know, colors to enjoy, and a whole world to explore. Most importantly, she knows, from experience, that we are, in essence, more alike than not.

She is one of those no longer rare little children who treats adults with respect when they deserve it and challenges them when they do not. Recently, I was enraged about some social injustice or another; I can't remember what it was, but at the time I was spitting fire. Alexandria age five, said to me quite gently, "I am a peaceful Black woman, Nana. And you are too, right?" Not taking the hint, I replied, "Peace is always my first option, but I do what seems appropriate to the circumstance." Very thoughtfully, looking me straight in the eye, she replied smiling, "Nana, there really is no other option in the end, is there?" Having made her point, she went off to play. I wondered which of her surrogate moms had taught her that, and allowed her to remind me how easily the connections can be over shadowed by the contradictions.

I knew then that we had made the correct choice, done the right thing. We were helping a small trusting human become fully who and what she was intended to be. The "we" of which I speak is European, African, Native, Latino/a, Hawaiian, college educated, high school dropout, rich, poor and middle class with roots in every corner of this nation and in several countries outside of it.

We were those who loved the innocence in the face of a child enough to cherish it more than we cherished our egos or our ideologies. Truthfully, it is possible that she did more for us than we could ever do for her. She made us a family, a community, and a tribe, not despite but *because* of our differences.

NARRATIVE S

"Why Do White People Have Vaginas?"

Maureen T. Reddy

When Sean was born in November of 1983, Doug and I had been married for four years and living in Minneapolis for almost all of that time, half a continent away from our families. My younger brother, Tom, had recently moved out to live with us, but everyone else awaited from a distance the birth of this first member of the next generation of our families.

The couples in our childbirth class and the women who were in my prenatal exercise class all had their babies before us, and every one had a boy. Both Doug and I assumed we would have a girl, based on some vague, mathematically insupportable idea about odds and just a feeling we both had. We were proved wrong when Sean appeared. When we made our calls an hour or so after Sean was born, everyone was effusively delighted, demanded photos by overnight mail, and announced various plans to fly out to us. The only odd comment came from my mother-in-law, who said, "A boy! That's *wonderful*—Daddy will be so happy! I'm relieved!" Relieved? "Oh, I probably shouldn't tell you this, but it's okay now that Sean's here and he's a boy," Marguerite said, "but Daddy said that if it wasn't a boy, he didn't care what it was." I spluttered a bit, and my mother-in-law said, "Don't take it personally, Maureen; that's what Daddy said to me, too, every time I was pregnant."

Well, *of course*, I took it personally: I am a woman, and a feminist, and objected to this valuing of boys over girls. I also was troubled by this vivid, early reminder that Doug and I would have to struggle with inequitable gender roles for our child, and to help him to resist a racist, sexist system that, on one of its axes, favored him because of his maleness. Or, more accurately, *seemed* to favor him: although maleness carries certain privileges, most of those privileges are in fact reserved for white males. Stereotypes of black masculinity—rapacious sexuality, violence, danger, threat—shorten black men's lives and mock the very notion of male privilege.

I also knew that simply resisting stifling race/gender definitions would not be enough: we would have to provide alternatives to fill the space resistance creates. In a world that offers few positive public images of black maleness, we would have to seek them out while also countering the vast number of soul-destroying stereotypes. . . . We did not want Sean to see black men in general or himself in particular through that racist lens, but I was not at all certain how Doug and I could help

From Crossing the Color Line: Race, Parenting and Culture, *by Maureen T. Reddy. New Brunswick, N.J.: Rutgers University Press, 1994, 43–58. Reprinted by permission of Rutgers University Press.*

him to see himself through his own eyes, unclouded by racism or sexism. In addition to the obvious counter to racism unconditional love and real self-esteem provide, we both wanted to foster in Sean a sense of wide possibility through carefully choosing books and toys for him, and through encouraging lots of fantasy play.

One of the simpler pleasures of parenting, we thought, would be giving Sean toys and playing with him—wrong, wrong, wrong, as we learned on our first excursion to a toy store when Sean was just a few weeks old. Because Doug and I were among the first of our friends to have children, we had not been toy shopping since we were little more than children ourselves, and we therefore had no clear idea about what toys were available. Before our baby's birth, we had decided to buy toys on a gender-neutral basis—blocks, trucks, stuffed animals, and dolls, regardless of our child's sex—and to ban war toys and Barbie, for obvious reasons. We had guessed that black dolls would be hard to find, but otherwise we had given little thought to race as a factor in toy shopping. After all, what could race have to do with blocks? Plenty, we discovered.

That first trip to a big toy store was enlightening: we found aisle upon aisle of toys of all varieties in packages that depicted only white children playing with them. At most, one-fifth of the toys we saw incorporated no exclusionary race or gender codes on their packages. Even fancy yuppie toys, carefully aimed at both sexes—European crib mobiles and the like—came in packages adorned with pictures of white babies. In the doll aisle, blond, blue-eyed dolls outnumbered black dolls fifty to one, and the only black male dolls were Cabbage Patch Kids, which were new to the market the year Sean was born and almost impossible to get. In an effort to support progressive manufacturers, we tried to buy toys that showed some sensitivity to racial diversity in their packaging, but we also ended up buying a lot of things that had to be removed from their boxes before we gave them to Sean. Obviously, though, we could not control everything in Sean's life as easily as we discarded troubling toy wrappings, and we knew that he would be bombarded by images and messages quite contrary to the vision of self we hoped to foster. What effect would these images have on him? And how powerful would our parental influence be? We waited, and hoped.

At about two and a half or three, Sean began to say things that suggested he understood both race and sex as categories—as interrelated categories, in fact—and that he was trying to figure out the principles that govern those categories. Like most preschoolers, Sean had a passion for categorization and a sometimes overwhelming desire to organize the elements of his world into a system that made sense to him. He was single-mindedly dedicated to grasping the abstract principles to be extrapolated from specific observations. Sean was a tiny scientist, Doug and I were his reference library, and the world was his laboratory.

One evening, Sean asked me if he would get a vagina when he grew up. After explaining that he would always have a penis but no vagina, I remarked that I had been born with a vagina and still have one, and that his father was born with a penis and still has that. "Your sex doesn't change when you grow up," I concluded. A series of questions from Sean followed, focusing on people we know and whether they have vaginas or penises. That was the end of that, I thought. Months later, Sean once again brought up the penis/vagina issue, but phrased it this way: "Why do white people have vaginas, Mom?" He evidently thought genitalia determined race, not sex: generalizing from me and his father, Sean assumed all black people have penises, and all white people have vaginas. I had to return to our list of friends, reiterate who had penises and who vaginas, and remind him of each person's race before Sean would believe that a penis meant you were male, whether black or white, and a vagina meant you were female, independent of race.

Racial differences were apparently more noticeable to Sean than were sex differences, and I suppose this could have been predicted. After all, we were making major efforts to raise Sean in a gender-free way, emphasizing that the only real differences between boys and girls were biological. We were supported by friends and by the enlightened day-care center Sean attended, where both staff and parents identified themselves as feminists. Perhaps most important, when he was a toddler Sean never saw commercial television. At three, he did not choose playmates or toys on a gender-appropriate basis, nor did he seem to think much about differences between boys and girls, especially in comparison to several other children we knew, who made a big deal about gender roles from an early age. Sean could see skin-color differences between Doug and me, and knew that I have a vagina and Doug has a penis. He never saw other people naked, so he had no opportunity to notice black females with vaginas and white males with penises. It makes perfect sense, then, that he would jumble everything up and figure that skin color and genitalia were linked.

• • •

From about age three, Sean began to realize that racial differences were meaningful in some way beyond mere skin color, but he wasn't clear on what these meanings might be. For instance, he announced to me that people get darker as they get older and that dark people are older than light people. This makes sense as a general statement about the origins of humankind, but that wasn't his point. "No," I explained, "skin color isn't age-related. People come in all different colors and pretty much stay that way. Daddy was dark brown when he was little, and he's still dark brown. I was sort of pink when I was a baby and I'm still pink. You were light brown as a baby and you're still light brown." This seemed to make sense to Sean, and he moved on to another question ("Why is Big Bird yellow?").

• • •

Sometimes Sean's mistakes about race and/or gender amused us, as when he first saw a program on commercial television and I had to explain advertisements to him. The short version of this long explanation was that you can't believe everything you see in ads, because the advertisers are trying hard to sell their products, not to let you know all sides of any issue. Sean snorted knowingly and said, "I *know,* Mom. Commercials are stupid. Like that ad for washing soap. Everyone knows that Moms don't do the laundry!"

Occasionally, Sean's mistakes alerted Doug and me to real problems. For instance, from his early infancy, we sought out books for Sean that showed both girls and boys engaged in various activities, rejecting books that encoded gender stereotypes. We also found books for him that featured black children in a variety of roles, not just as the background figures they too often are in children's literature. When we couldn't find books that incorporated racial diversity, we purchased stories about humanoid animals, figuring these were better than all-white texts. Then, at three, Sean started critiquing the pictures in his books. "*That's* not the mom," he'd say, pointing to the black mother in *Jamaica's Find,* or "Where's the dad?" as we looked at a page in a book about a white boy who was shown sitting on his father's lap. We realized that there was not a single children's book available that reflected Sean's family situation. Although many books showed black and white children playing together, no book that we found showed black and white people as members of the same family: in the world of children's literature we were invisible, nonexistent.

Actually, that's not quite true: searching through bibliographies of children's literature, I did find books about interracial families, but none I wanted to share with Sean. Rather like the literary and sociological treatments of interracial couples as pathological . . . most children's books about interracial families fall into the problem/solution genre, treating interracial families as posing special problems. Most of these books are about adoption . . . and therefore did not reflect Sean's life. Others . . . treat the initial rejection of the interracial family by white relatives—the problem—and the eventual growth of love between white grandparents and black children—the solution. Although well-meant and perhaps valuable, such books were of no use to us. At that stage in his life, Sean's interracial family was simply a *fact,* not a problem, and we wanted to find materials that acknowledged or reflected that fact. Most children's books depicting relationships between blacks and whites—even nonfamilial ones—posit such relationships as problem-ridden. Generally, the white characters are at the center of the story, which focuses on their learning about blacks and simultaneously discovering the evils of racism.

In this highly theoretical age, talking about the impact of popular culture or the uses of literature in simple terms is faintly embarrassing. However, whenever I ask students in my introduction to theory course why they are English majors, they inevitably respond with some version of "I like to read. Literature teaches me about myself and about other people." Although these students realize that literature does a lot of other things as well, this sort of comment is always their *first* response to the question. Numerous autobiographies by black writers remark on the poisonous lesson they learned as children from books that completely ignored their existence. Indeed, a recognition of literature's reflective or reinforcing function underlay early efforts to integrate African-American and women's literature into the curricula of colleges and universities. Sean's remarks to us indicated that he was certainly looking for images of himself and his world when he looked at books. At that young age, however, he doubted the books and thought they were wrong, as opposed to seeing our family as unusual, unlike others, "wrong."

Looking now for Ailis [their daughter] who is fascinated by books, as well as for Sean, we have found exactly one "nonproblem" book about interracial families—Sarah Garland's *Billy and Belle,* which a black librarian at our local library put aside for me because she thought Belle resembled Ailis—and few about blacks and whites together in any kind of relationship that do not centralize the white child's consciousness. This may be one reason that Sean now most often reads fantasy books featuring characters that are other than human, such as Brian Jacques's Redwall series and J. R. R. Tolkien's Hobbit books. Toni Morrison has described her writing of *The Bluest Eye* as partly motivated by her need to write the book she wanted to read; I am convinced that this same desire, this hunger, for self-affirming, truth-telling tales fuels the current boom in black women's literature. Adult children of interracial couples will have to write their own books, as their experience is not only marginalized but totally erased in currently available children's literature.

My unsuccessful quest for children's literature that reflected Sean's daily environment paralleled my own search for child-care books that seriously addressed issues of race and gender, and that did more than merely acknowledge the existence of interracial families—sadly, few books did even that much. The books that addressed race progressively (such as James P. Comer and Alvin R. Poussaint's *Black Baby and Child Care*) said little about gender, while the books that addressed parents like us who wanted to avoid reinscribing traditional gender definitions (such as Letty Cottin Pogrebin's *Growing Up Free*) said little about race. At the same time, I continued to hunt for fiction for myself that depicted interracial relationships, and found very little other than tragic tales of sorrow, loss, and death. Even fewer of the few exceptions I found included children, and I was hungry for information about this crucial part of my life. I needed something to rub up against, to give me some sense of history, of shared experience. Jane Lazarre's *The Mother Knot* was the only book I found that gave me what I needed, and the sheer *relief,* the amazing exhilaration I felt while reading Lazarre's book taught me how deep my need was. In looking for literature that reflected my family's circumstances, I was looking for visibility, for verification of our existence, in some sense. Of course, that was exactly what Sean wanted, too, and our absence from literature—and from movies, television programs, catalogues, and even toy boxes—obviously worried him.

Television presents problems akin to those of literature, but its pervasiveness and its consequent power in shaping consciousness are more troubling. We have always closely supervised Sean's television watching, restricting him to a maximum of four hours weekly of "approved" (by us) shows, with few of these on commercial television until very recently. Nonetheless, Sean absorbed a lot of information about television from other children. At three, for instance, he often played "He-Man," a game he learned at day care from children who watched the cartoon. The superhero's cry—"I am the Master of the Universe!"—lost something between television and day care, as Sean would run around the campus of the college where I then taught, shouting, "I am the Master of the University!" He learned about violent characters, about gender divisions (She-Ra certainly had a subordinate role to He-Man in the games), and about consumer culture. Once, when we capitulated to Sean's insistent wish that we go to McDonald's, we discovered that he wasn't interested in the food, but in the toys that came with Happy Meals. As we drove home from that lunch, Sean playing happily in the back seat with his toy, he cried out, "Collect them all, Mom! Collect them all!" Television's effect even on a nonwatcher clearly was profound.

Television's erasure of race's importance, even in the current crop of shows featuring black characters, blatantly serves conservative ideology, as of course the common depiction of women as objects also does. As a medium, television sends out two conflicting messages, both comforting to whites: (1) race does not matter because blacks are just like whites and have the same life chances as whites (never, of course, that whites are just like blacks); and (2) blacks are naturally completely different from whites, and are therefore dangerous enemies of civilization. In either case, black liberation efforts are irrelevant, just as feminism is portrayed as irrelevant. Television is really *for* white viewers, I think, with most programs teaching all of us how to be white and to desire whiteness. Even some supposedly progressive children's programs on PBS incorporate prevailing race/gender hierarchies. *Sesame Street,* for instance, portrays a variety of racial possibilities, but sharply limits gender roles: all of the really lovable, active muppets are male. *Mister Rogers' Neighborhood is* notably pale, and reproduces familiar gender codes as well. To give PBS its due, *Reading Rainbow,* which Sean loved, gave him a wonderful black male image in LeVar Burton, who consistently came across as an intelligent, thoughtful man who loved to read and who could learn to do *anything,* from hot-air ballooning to scuba diving. I wish there were even one program aimed at small children with an equally positive black female image. *Where in the World Is Carmen Sandiego?* has Lynn Thigpen as the Chief, but the program is aimed at an older audience. Nevertheless, Ailis and I sometimes watch it with Sean just so that she can see a strong black woman (and a multiracial group of children whose intelligence and knowledge are applauded) on television. Movies made for children, including critically acclaimed Disney animated features like *The Little Mermaid* and *Beauty and the Beast,* tell the same old story: boys *do* while girls *are;* if you're white, you're right, and if you're black, get back.

Although our first impulse was to ban all television watching and to allow few movies, Doug and I realized that such a radical approach might easily backfire and make television seem even more desirable due to its forbiddenness. Instead, we tried to help Sean to develop a critical consciousness about television, watching television programs with him so that we could talk about what we saw instead of allowing him to consume these images passively. . . . Children do not have the critical repertoire and psychological sophistication that enable some adults to resist seductive screen images, but I believe even small children can be taught the rudiments of resistance.

Once, during a commercial for the construction toys he has always loved, Sean turned to me and said, "Isn't it funny that they only show white kids in this ad? They should come to our house and take pictures of *me* playing!" Sometimes Sean completely resisted the message ads sent, appearing oblivious to the implications of certain commercials. For instance, at age four he had a big collection of "My Little Pony" figures, yet never commented on the fact—apparently did not even notice—that all of the commercials we saw for these toys showed only girls playing with them. Arriving at day care one day with several of these ponies grasped in his hands, Sean was met at the door by a boy who said scornfully, "Those are *girl* toys! Are you a girl?" Sean, seeming surprised, replied, "No, I'm a boy—I have a penis," which effectively silenced his critic. As the other child walked away, Sean cast me a look that said, "Is that kid weird or what?" and ran off to play with his friends.

The fundamental miscommunication in this incident—Sean was talking about sex, while the other child was talking about gender—worked to Sean's advantage, as Sean's ignorance of gender requirements continued to do for several years. Sean did not fully recognize gender codes *as* gender codes until he was six or so, and even then dismissed them as "stupid." But then, beginning in second grade, Sean occasionally came home from school with stories about playground disputes that were rooted in gender. Several boys insisted on sex segregation, and persistently tried to limit soccer games to boys. This posed a major problem for Sean, because one of his closest friends was a girl. . . .

• • •

Two years later, the gender boundaries seemed even stronger and enclosed a much smaller territory, but Sean was then the veteran of numerous gender-based conflicts and seemed to take them in stride. Last spring he told me that some of the boys at school were making fun of him for playing with trolls. Apparently there was a new commercial on television that said something like "Girls like nice, cute, little trolls, but boys like Battle Trolls!" A few boys were using this commercial to tease Sean and other boys who liked all kinds of trolls. Our dialogue:

Sean: I *hate* those stupid commercials, because now some kids are saying only girls play with trolls.

Me: Which kids say that?

Sean: Well, not the girls and not most of the boys, either. Just Bill and some of the other guys who think they're real macho—which is pretty funny, because they're not macho at all!

Me: Sean, what do you think "macho" means?

Sean: Oh, you know: tough and able to beat people up and that kind of stuff, but they're not macho, they're *dumb* and just need to think there's something special about them, so they get into saying who can do what and trying to find something they can make fun of. I'm smarter than they are, and I'm bigger so they can't beat me up, plus the teacher would go crazy if they ever even tried to fight someone . . .

Me: What do you do when they tease you?

Sean: Ignore them, mostly, or else turn it into a joke.

Me: How do you feel when they tease, honey? Are your feelings hurt?

Sean: No, but they can be aggravating, I guess.

Me: Well, it's hard to be different and to make your own choices about what you like. If you wanted to stop the teasing, what would you do?

Sean: I guess I'd pretend I didn't really like trolls, which is what George did—he told Bill his mother *makes him* bring trolls to school! But I'm not going to do that, Mom—they can tease me if they want, but I'm not going to let them run my life like that. I think they should think about why they worry so much about everyone else's business! Maybe they'd have more friends and better stuff to do if they didn't spend all their time trying to get people to be like them.

I look across the table at my nine-year-old son and am so proud of him that I'm speechless. I don't think I had Sean's courage at nine, or his total lack of interest in peer approval, although I do have both of those traits as an adult. After a minute of companionable silence, I say, "Sean, I think you are pretty terrific!" He looks puzzled—why the drama?—and then says, "You are, too, Mom. We're a lot alike." Sitting there with Sean, I realize that he is right about our similarities, even in ways he probably is not considering. Socially, we are both in the "insider without" position: people who do not want unearned, false privileges and who prefer the difficult but rewarding task of making up our own lives as we go along to the comparative ease of accepting long-standing rules.

• • •

CHAPTER 10

Mothering as Political Action

Modern Western cultures typically portray motherhood as a private, domestic activity requiring little skill. As Jessica Benjamin, among others, emphasizes, the mothers portrayed this way have no consciousness beyond the maternal subjectivity that defines them.[1] Such cultural depictions infiltrate the identities of many mothers while shaping others' perceptions of them. This chapter debunks these depictions by looking at mothers as public agents whose projects sometimes become political as well as collective.

Let's begin with a taken-for-granted circumstance: "Since time immemorial, women have . . . stitch[ed] the threads of everyday life together," especially as mothers.[2] The support systems that women create through informal visiting, gossiping, and mutual aid, the meals and quilts and gardens we make, the letters and cards we send all sustain community. All this activity usually goes unnoticed, "except when it is not done or is the subject of complaint."[3]

This chapter focuses on less taken-for-granted maternal projects, specifically, women's advocacy and politicking as mothers. These less institutionalized, more public forms of maternal activism enlarge our understanding of motherwork while underscoring women's contributions to civic life. One well-known example is Mothers Against Drunk Drivers (MADD). Begun in 1980 by Candy Lightner, whose thirteen-year-old daughter had been killed by a repeat-offender drunk driver, this maternalist organization illustrates how mostly middle-income, white mothers organized effectively for reformist purposes.[4] This chapter centers, however, on less publicized instances of maternal politics among working-class and poor women and middle-class women of color. These instances show how motherhood can engage women as political actors, even when they are financially strapped or bear the burdens of racism as well as sexism. That activist motherhood emerges under such constraints reveals a lot about motherwork as extra-domestic and public as well as home-based and private.

Publicly activist motherwork challenges the private/public dichotomy that continues to sustain separate-spheres thinking throughout much of American society. At the same time such motherwork, like other forms of women's ac-

This chapter was written by Mary F. Rogers.

tivism, raises the broad question of what distinguishes feminist from nonfeminist activism. That question is important because, on the one hand, women activists are often belittled as "women's libbers" or "man-hating feminists" and, on the other hand, some women activists are decidedly nonfeminist or even antifeminist. Mapping the intersections between maternalism and feminism thus makes practical as well as theoretical sense.

First-Wave Feminism and Social Motherhood

North American and Western European women laid the foundations of modern welfare states. Their movement for suffrage intertwined with their efforts, often as mothers, to achieve social reforms that would improve the lot of children and mothers. We have long known, however superficially, that nonmarried, educated othermothers such as Jane Addams and other activists in the settlement house movement helped shift the political landscape during the early twentieth century.[5] By now we are learning more about their (usually) married counterparts who entered the political arena as mothers. Sociologist Theda Skocpol's voice has been prominent among the tellers of these more obscure stories.

In *Protecting Soldiers and Mothers: The Political Origins of Social Policy in the United States*, Skocpol traces the emergence of maternalist politics during the Progressive Era. She indicates that between the 1870s and the early twentieth century American women widely participated in women's clubs. Albion Fellows Bacon may have been fairly typical of "progressive" white mothers. A wife and the mother of four children, she started her "reform career as a volunteer member of the sanitation committee of Evansville's Civic Improvement Society." She went on to serve as a "friendly visitor" for that Indiana community's "associated charities." Bacon was in effect a community social worker.[6]

Bacon's membership in a civic improvement society paralleled many married women's memberships in clubs formed for their own edification and development. In Greenwich Village, Atlanta, Knoxville, and Chicago as well as in the Pacific Northwest, middle-class women's associations gave them roles beyond home and church.[7] Eventually, some of their clubs sponsored reformist as well as cultural activities. Other associations were established specifically for reformist ends, such as the Southern Council for Women and Children in Industry, founded in Atlanta in 1930.[8]

Particularly likely to eventuate in reformist efforts were the "maternal associations" that had begun cropping up in New England and several other places during the 1820s and 1830s. The first was perhaps the Portland, Maine, association established in 1815. As early as 1832, Utica's maternal association launched *Mother's Magazine*, which remained an influential publication until 1888.[9] These mothers' associations and other women's organizations catapulted women into public life using notions such as "municipal housekeeping" and "social motherhood." Eventually some became national organizations.

Alongside the General Federation of Women's Clubs (GFWC), founded in 1890, was another key women's organization of that era, the National Congress of Mothers (NCM), established seven years later. The NCM sought to increase maternal influence in society and "empower mothers through education and organization." The NCM had a distinctly feminist dimension, even though its focus was empowering mothers rather than securing women's equal rights. Its leaders used terms such as "mother-work" that now have renewed currency among feminists. By 1920 the NCM had 190,000 members in thirty-seven states.[10]

The National Congress of Mothers lobbied for juvenile courts and child labor laws as well as mothers' pensions, which were legislated by forty states between 1911 and 1920. The latter "authorized local government authorities to make regular payments directly to impoverished mothers (and occasionally other caretakers) of dependent children," thus reducing the number of juvenile candidates for foster homes or orphanages.[11] Both the NCM and the GFWC played key roles in getting state legislatures to approve such measures. Even the most influential of their members could not, however, prevent the adoption of eligibility criteria favoring "blameless" or "good" mothers. The Pensions Movement went beyond merely criticizing "unfit mothers." It "set in place a system which . . . surveilled their homes, established them as tax burdens and referred those deemed unfit to sterilization programs."[12] Not surprisingly, "Pensions were nowhere near enough to support full-time motherhood, even in frugal homes. And aid recipients were usually prohibited from doing better-paid, full-time labor."[13]

Maternalist reformers were more successful in expanding the federal machinery promoting child welfare. Paramount among their achievements was the federal Children's Bureau; established in 1912, it functioned as "something close to the central directorate of [a] possible maternalist welfare state." Skocpol infers that that maternalist welfare state "would have done much more than earlier or later U.S. systems of social provision to help children rather than the elderly, to benefit women directly rather than through the wage-earning capacities of husbands, and to buffer families from the full impact of participation in capitalist labor markets."[14]

It is tempting to speculate about what sort of welfare state might have emerged had its maternalist originators worked closely across the social lines dividing women of color from white women, lower- and working-class from higher-class women, homosexual from heterosexual women, and foreign- from native-born women. As historian Leila J. Rupp points out, first-wave feminists organizing across national boundaries thought motherhood could "unite all women." They treated it as a "universal power."[15] Had such insights taken sustained hold, modern welfare states might be less biased against women, especially those facing multiple oppressions. Put differently, had early maternalist efforts been more thoroughly feminist, their long-term impact might have been greater.

Skocpol implies such promise when she notes how "single" women and married mothers forged alliances during the Progressive Era. Specifically, the "cooperation between [single] social settlement leaders and organized married women" rested on "shared beliefs about women's roles in society and about the morally justifiable need for reform." Even though the social settlement leaders often had no children of their own, they saw themselves as "public mothers."[16] These two groupings of women also overlapped in other ways. For one thing, high maternal and infant mortality rates made not only mothers[17] but also mothers' sisters, cousins, aunts, and friends fearful of death. Mobilized by loss and the prospect of further losses through death, nonmothers joined mothers in espousing reforms capable of alleviating their fears.

For another thing, some nonmarried leaders in maternalist politics were in fact mothers (and often had women as their life partners). As Estelle Freedman points out, the first woman physician in American society, Elizabeth Blackwell, was an adoptive single mother. One of her Progressive Era counterparts was Miriam Van Waters, who worked for reforms primarily in the juvenile justice system. Also "single," Van Waters adopted a daughter, which was unusual but scarcely unheard of among professional women of her day.[18] She and her counterparts constituted a little-known bridge between the single nonmothers and married mothers involved in maternalist politics early in the twentieth century.

For maternalist politics to succeed, bridges also had to be built across various classes and races of women. In the former respect Skocpol credits Progressive Era reformist women with promoting "solidarity between privileged and less privileged women." Higher-class women, for example, did "try to embrace as sisters, as fellow mothers" those who might benefit from mothers' pensions.[19] Skocpol says virtually nothing about bridges among women of different races, but others have pointed out their characteristic weakness.

The African American women's club movement was separate from the white women's, both structurally and ideologically. In their own local and national organizations African American women during the Progressive Era were more accepting of employed mothers and single mothers than their white counterparts were.[20] African American club women's activism was part of their community othermothering. As such, it was characteristically interclass and intraracial.[21] Also distinguishing African American women's maternalist politics early in the century were their greater efforts at building private institutions. Seeing the state "less as a potential friend and more as a roadblock," African American women facing race-segregated institutions created social services organizations within their own communities.[22]

African American women's maternalist politics were often rooted in or connected with their churches, which had come to "signify public space" or a "public sphere" supporting diverse activities.[23] African American women often held their Mothers' Conferences there.[24] In a sense their maternalist politics revolved around "social movement communities" that "buil[t] on prior commitments to local communities and traditions."[25] Unlike their white counterparts, who were carving out niches for themselves in the white- and male-monopolized public sphere, African American maternalists were expanding their responsibilities in a black-monopolized public space where they had already been contributing a great deal as members. Ironically enough, church activities were where white and black maternalists (and other women) sometimes met. As Evelyn Brooks Higginbotham observes, the last twenty years of the nineteenth century saw "black and white women . . . linked in evangelical work."[26]

Whatever the specific contexts and purposes of their activism, Progressive Era maternalists—both African American and European American—spoke an influential language. Theirs were mothers' voices. Theirs were voices articulating "a 'personalized' culture of commitment" and a macro-level "strategic personalism" emphasizing personal bonds.[27] Perhaps such personalistic rhetoric was necessary among people who could not vote.[28] Lacking suffrage, women mobilized other women less as anonymous citizens and more as personal agents, especially mothers. Today's continuing use of personalistic rhetoric—among toxic waste activists, for instance—reflects the same pattern insofar as grassroots politics rests on nonelectoral processes such as community organizing. In addition, nonprofessional women may "keep the issues 'emotional' and 'personal' since this provides a solid basis from which [they] can speak" credibly and persuasively.[29]

In any event, maternalist politics early in the twentieth century deployed a richly nuanced rhetoric of motherwork. As Patricia Hill Collins uses it, "motherwork" serves to "soften the existing dichotomies between private and public, family and work, the individual and the collectivity, identity as individual autonomy and identity growing from the collective self-determination of one's group."[30] As Molly Ladd-Taylor similarly conceptualizes it, motherwork comprises not only "childrearing in the home" but also maternalist reform activities that express "social motherhood."[31] Even though Ladd-Taylor's definition has to do with the Progressive Era, its ramifications are generic. Motherwork refers to all those undertakings culturally associated with motherhood and mothering that advance the development of one's own child(ren), other children, and one's community. "Motherwork" is a concept worthy of further exploring among contemporary feminists. It might promote the progressive ends Skocpol envisions: "Feminists must . . . articulate values and political goals that speak to the well-being of all American families. If feminists can find better ways to do these things, organized women will again be at the forefront of social provision in the United States."[32]

Maternal Mobilization: Child Care and Breastfeeding

Before turning to contemporary maternalism, a brief disucssion of maternalist politics following World War II might prove helpful. The post–World War II campaign for publicly funded child care in California is instructive, as is the establishment of La Leche League on the eve of second-wave feminism. Each shows how maternalist politics can both affirm and challenge traditional conceptions of motherwork and thus be both nonfeminist and feminist.

Given the demand for female labor force participation during World War II, the federal government spent about $52 million financing nonmaternal child care. Ellen Reese points out that more than one hundred thousand children in forty-seven states had enrolled in more than three thousand nursery school and "extended school" programs by 1945.[33] At the end of the war, the federal government withdrew its support. Four states—California, Massachusetts, New York, Washington—responded with allocations for child care, but only in California were these substantial enough to maintain a sizable percentage of the existing centers. California's 1946 allocation launched "the oldest, continuous state child care program in the country," which is only available to poor families (567).

Reese argues that even though California's child care movement was an employed-mothers' movement, women from all classes participated (571). These cross-class alliances promoted success, as did the participation of key organizations and officials. Women's organizations "made up 40 percent of all organizations" that appealed to the governor for state-funded childcare centers. These included businesswomen's, professional women's, and working-class women's organizations. The common ground these organizations carved out was, says Reese, "unusual at this time" (577).

Maternalism fueled this effort. Reese notes the maternalist rhetoric in many mothers' letters to the governor in support of state-funded centers. They emphasized their financial need to work rather than their "desire to work" (575). They also underscored their maternal commitment by emphasizing the difficulty of finding other sources of care as well as their desire for high-quality care (576). As with the mothers' letters, the organizations commonly emphasized children's needs rather than women's desire to work outside the home.

Under the relatively opportune circumstances at hand, including a state surplus and a sympathetic governor, the coalition succeeded (581). Yet Reese concludes that one must recognize the limitations of maternalist rhetoric. In order to build diverse coalitions such rhetoric cannot be taken to the point where men are, at least implicitly, excluded and child care comes to be seen as a "women's issue" (584). As we will see in the last section of the chapter, political efficacy often requires such a limited or implicit feminism.

Much less public and less overtly political was the postwar effort of some mothers to promote breastfeeding. Theirs was more a cultural than a reformist politics. In 1956 seven mothers first met in the home of Mary White, one of the seven. In 1958 they incorporated their organization—La Leche League—and published its *Womanly Art of Breastfeeding*, which has sold more than two million copies.[34] The League publishes a bimonthly magazine called *New Beginnings*, which includes articles on such topics as breastfeeding adopted babies, breastfeeding with implants, and "extended breastfeeding" (breastfeeding for more than a year). It emphasizes mother-to-mother support and advice as well as a "natural" rather than "scientific" approach to breastfeeding.

The seven founders of La Leche League were Roman Catholic, middle-income mothers interested in religious ecumenism as well as natural childbirth and breastfeeding. In 1964, La Leche League held its first national meeting in Chicago with more than four hundred mothers and one hundred or so babies in attendance. This maternalist organization now ranks second only to Alcoholics Anonymous among American self-help groups, which is how La Leche League "has always cast itself."[35] Yet its invitation to mothers was not historically an open-ended one. During the late 1960s the League openly criticized employed mothers. Twenty years later, however, it published a book for "working mothers," and *New Beginnings* now features many articles on breastfeeding for mothers who work outside the home.[36]

Given the emergence of second-wave feminism on the heels of the League's establishment, feminism was part of the cultural landscape La Leche League aimed to influence with its self-help, mother-to-mother approach. Overall, its relationship with feminism is complex. Lynn Weiner says the League's founders saw themselves as "early feminists" and "often appropriate[d] the language of feminism," even though most "rejected feminist philosophy." Linda Blum and Elizabeth Vandewater join Weiner in emphasizing that La Leche League anticipated the women's health care movement. Blum and Vandewater go on to indicate that League members' thinking resonated with that of cultural feminists promoting "motherly" values and practices. They conclude that the League's stance is "less than coherent," if only because "maternalist ideologies like La Leche League's both mesh and compete with feminist discourses."[37] Or, as Weiner puts it, the League's maternalism "implies an empowered motherhood defined by 'female' qualities that would improve society," yet its ideology also affirms a narrow set of roles for women.[38] The activism at hand is thus like other varieties of maternalism examined thus far—a mix of decidedly nonfeminist as well as significantly feminist elements.

Perhaps symptomatic of La Leche League's paradoxical stance is the makeup of its 1998 board of directors. All seventeen directors, including the executive director, are women; all are mothers. Such a composition suggests that othermothers have no central role to play in the organization. In addition, all but three of the directors have more than two children; the remaining three have two children each, which sends a pronatalist as well as maternalist message.[39] One wonders at the absence of mothers with "only" one child, just as one wonders at the absence of any mention of adoptive mothers. Such absences illustrate how maternalism typically stresses women's agency and influence but mostly in their private-sphere roles. Moreover, maternalism makes it hard to overcome the cultural binaries that breastfeeding challenges, such as the one between stay-at-home ("full-time") mothers and employed mothers.

Global Maternalism

Around the world, maternal activism is often peace activism. Harriet Hyman Alonso says that such activism typically presupposes "women's maternal qualities."[40] Narrative T, Martha Boesing's "Statement to the Court," is a plea from a maternalist peace activist demanding a peaceful world for her own and other children.

Globally, maternalist politics have also taken shape around issues of land-use reform, women's access to natural resources, workers' rights, public housing reform, political terrorism and torture, and dictatorial regimes.[41] A great deal of maternal activism also revolves around children's health, welfare, and education. From black middle-class mothers' efforts to raise the birth weight of lower-class mothers' babies to Latina and Anglo mothers' efforts to enhance their children's educational outcomes, mothers' collective efforts on behalf of their children have been enormous and consequential.[42] One powerful stimulus for such actions is having a disabled daughter or son. Studying one group of such mothers, Parnel Wickham-Searl found that their efforts often arose from their disagreements with professionals involved with their children and their marginalization from their children's programs.[43] On behalf of their children as well as themselves mothers have also been active in welfare rights and welfare reform, with their activism often seen as feminist as well as maternalist. As Eileen Boris points out, for example, "[a]fter 1972, when recipients gained control, the National Welfare Rights Organization [NWRO] became identified with black feminism."[44]

One group meriting detailed attention is the welfare mothers on Las Vegas's Westside whose activism began with efforts to secure clothing for their children returning to school one autumn in the late 1960s. These African American mothers living in a public housing project soon became aware of the NWRO begun in 1967. That organization gave them a sense that "welfare mothers were citizens, with the same rights and responsibilities as other citizens." Armed with that consciousness, the Westside mothers went on to organize marches, lobby state legislators, and do every other political thing capable of transforming their community. Eventually, with help from "Legal Services and the League of Women Voters, the women of West Las Vegas created a nonprofit corporation through which they could apply for funds to help revitalize their devastated community." Called Operation Life, the welfare mothers' nonprofit organization opened the Westside's first medical facility in 1973. There they did children's health screening and administered the first Women and Infant Care (WIC) nutrition program in Nevada. Annelise Orleck reports, "It was the first and only WIC program in the country to be administered by poor women themselves."

Orleck goes on to report even more impressive results: "Four years later, the federal Office of Economic Opportunity approved Operation Life's application to become a Community Development Corporation. By 1981 it had brought millions of dollars in federal grant monies and investments into the Westside. Operation Life . . . was now the largest property owner in the community. It had constructed a senior citizen housing project, several units of low-income housing, and would soon begin building a modern, fully equipped community medical center." Operation Life's leader, Ruby Duncan, was by then nationally known. President Jimmy Carter appointed her to the National Advisory Council on Economic Opportunity, and she twice led a delegation of Operation Life members to Democratic national conventions.

Sadly, these mothers' achievements were eventually undermined. By the late 1980s the federal Department of Health and Human Services (HHS) dictated that Operation Life must operate its clinic with a conservative group that was seeking federal funds for a health center or lose its HHS funding. Operation Life lost its momentum. Nevertheless, it showed that "no one is more expert on the problems of women and children living in poverty than poor mothers themselves." The events that eventuated in its undoing also show that "when poor women do what their critics demand of them, when they struggle to get an education, to organize, to develop programs that enhance services to their communities—as the Las Vegas women and as women's groups across the United States did in the 1970s—they are faced with fierce resistance from the same state workers, ministers and politicians who speak so fervently about welfare mothers' responsibility to become independent."[45]

Let us look at one last arena where mothers around the globe organize on behalf of their families and communities—environmentalism. A paramount example is Love Canal, a toxic chemical dump in Niagara Falls, New York.

The toxic substances in the canal, located three blocks from Lois Gibbs's home, made her two children seriously ill. She and others fought back for the sake of their children. Gibbs says, "Mostly all of the activities were done by women." Gibbs also reports several circumstances familiar to environmental maternalists. For one thing, "politicians are moved by public images." Just as significantly, maternalist activism does not presuppose an assertive personality. Gibbs recalls: "Prior to all of this I was a very shy, introverted person. I was afraid to talk. I wouldn't even teach church classes to adults. I would do it for children but not for adults. At school I had few friends. I wasn't into sports or clubs of any sort. So it was really difficult for me to move . . . into a more aggressive, confrontational and articulate person who could speak to other people."[46]

But Gibbs learned to do just that. Working primarily with other mothers, she saw to it that "all 900 families in the community were relocated." Gibbs herself went on to establish the Center for Health, Environment and Justice (CHEJ) in 1981. The CHEJ remains "the only national environmental organization in the United States started and run by grassroots organizers."[47]

Lois Gibbs's counterparts include mothers active in the environmental justice movement. That movement aims at countering the exploitation of minority and low-income neighborhoods as sites for dumping hazardous wastes and otherwise degrading the community's environment (see narrative U). Gibbs's counterparts also include hundreds of thousands of mothers around the world who have learned lessons and pursued activism like hers. Her counterparts include mothers and other women protesting industrial waste dumps in three Spanish towns. In Gibraleon, one of the communities, these mothers established an "unprecedented, constant presence on the street," where they often sewed, knitted, or cleaned vegetables as they protested environmental degradation. Their other strategies included banging pots and pans from their windows and rooftops during the night, visiting imprisoned activists, attending trials, and even "form[ing] a musical group to motivate and educate the community with their music."[48] In Upper Silesia, a region of Poland, the women who started the "Tested Food for Silesia" program to minimize the chances of contaminated food reaching the market were all professional engineers as well as mothers.[49]

Joni Seager generalizes: "Women are the backbone of virtually every environmental group around the world. With few exceptions, women constitute approximately 60 to 80 percent of the membership of most environmental organizations—averaging 60 percent of the membership of general-interest environmental groups, 80 percent or more of small grassroots groups and animal-rights groups."[50] Like other analysts, Seager is quick to point out that "as sustainers of families, it is often women who first notice environmental degradation" (271). She concludes, "For reasons both banal and deep, it 'matters' what mothers say and do, and women can often bring attention to their cause if they speak as mothers. But a maternalism-based analysis can paint women into a corner—or, rather, keep women in the corner that society has cordoned off for them" (278). To the paradoxes of activist mothering as both enabling (or empowering) and constraining (or disempowering), we now turn.

Maternalism as a Political Action Paradigm

Among white working-class women involved in toxic waste activism Celene Krauss found that "the private world of family ultimately became a source of personal strength, empirical knowledge, and political strategy in the public sphere."[51] As we saw, activist mothering makes personalism a strategic political resource. It also demonstrates the efficacy of caring in a world turned dispassionate and bureaucratic in its social provisioning. Maternalist activists thus vindicate and affirm motherwork. Maternalists' empowerment is multipronged.

So are the limitations of maternalist standpoints and strategies. On the other side of empowerment stands the prospect of reinforcing the gendered, unfair division of carework, centrally including motherwork. This prospect, which troubles many feminists, is less obvious than the empowering side of maternalism. Thus, I explore it here without meaning to discount the personal empowerment and community transformation that often derive from activist mothering.

Maternalism is most disempowering when it mobilizes women in support of social hierarchies based on race, social class, nationality, age, sexual orientation, or even gender itself. Historically, maternalism has sometimes portrayed women as little more than "guardians of their racial, social class, or national identities and futures."[52] Typically, such maternalism narrows womanhood to the work of perpetuating a group by birthing and raising its members along tradition-bound lines. Often this right-wing maternalism rests on a belief in women's moral superiority and purity, not unlike what some cultural feminists propound, as we saw in chapter 1. Here, though, that belief makes some mothers agents of traditionalism and group hate supporting fascism or armed struggle.[53]

Most activist motherhood involves no such extremes. As we have seen, maternalism commonly revolves around various social-justice aims. Even then, it is sometimes problematic. Molly Ladd-Taylor cites three generic problems with the maternalist perspective.[54] First, it presupposes differences between women and men, mothers and fathers, which it tends neither to question nor challenge. Instead, maternalism stresses the "distinctively feminine or maternal quality of certain values, qualities, or ways of thinking."[55] Yet maternal characteristics are historically and culturally variable. As Kathleen Uno indicates, for instance, maternalism failed to emerge as a perspective in early modern Japan (1600–1867), mostly because mothers were often not the primary caretakers of their children and so maternalist logic could not readily take hold.[56]

Second, Ladd-Taylor charges maternalism with erasing or ignoring the diversity among mothers. Alison Bailey illustrates that erasure by juxtaposing two maternalist concepts—Sara Ruddick's "maternal thinking" and Patricia Hill Collins's "motherwork." The latter, she says, reflects a "clearly identifiable location" distinct from Ruddick's " 'nearly universal' version."[57] Collins focuses on activities that reflect the historically specific experiences of racial-ethnic mothers trying to ensure their children's and communities' survival. That mothers are active in race-hate and other right-wing movements also shows how diverse they are. That diversity gets little attention in most maternalist perspectives, however.

Third, according to Ladd-Taylor, maternalism largely idealizes home-centered identities for women. Sabina Lovibond observes that "there is considerable difficulty in saying anything celebratory about motherhood without seeming to accept reimmersion in the world of 'normal' femininity."[58] Affirming mothers' contributions as caregivers runs the risk of also affirming the cultural conflation of femininity with caregiving. Even though influential theorists such as Ruddick emphasize that "mothering" is not reserved for women, for most people "mothering" has enormous feminine resonance. Put differently, maternalism often offers a "limited vision of women's rights and responsibilities."[59] For example, it typically lodges no strong protest against "the identity of 'woman' or 'mother,' as currently constituted."[60]

Yet maternalism sometimes challenges the very notions it sometimes reinforces. While it may at times bolster the institution of motherhood or cultural dichotomies about "good" versus "bad" mothers, at other times it challenges the institutional boundaries around motherhood and cultural dichotomies such as "full-time" versus employed mother. Thus, in principle, maternalism would seem consistently to have feminist potential. How much that potential gets actualized depends on the sociopolitical context of any specific maternalist project or movement. At its best, maternalism might be said to affirm motherwork while "also seek[ing] to transform [its] practice."[61] At its best, then, maternalism is soundly feminist.

In its other versions maternalism is often implicitly and ambiguously feminist. Typically, politics demands substantial pragmatism. Explicitly calling themselves feminists would be a setback for most maternalists in action. As Dollie Burwell points out in Narrative U, women activists already face derisive, stigmatizing labels, including "activist," "troublemaker," or "agitator." Providing one's opponents yet another "negative" label for their rhetorical arsenal would usually be foolhardy, especially when the issues at hand are not narrowly about women's rights. Typically, as Burwell indicates, they are about civil- or human-rights violations.

Yet Burwell does see herself and her maternalist collaborators as carrying on a tradition of their foremothers who "had the commitment and found the time to fight for justice and freedom." Especially when those same women also see themselves as waging a "struggle for empowerment," their work surely entails feminism regardless of whether they characterize it that way among themselves or in public. Political and other constraints may make such characterizations problematic and thus render maternalist feminism implicit or even ambiguous more often than not.

All the while, whatever limitations maternalism exhibits also apply to feminism in many practical instances. Take Ladd-Taylor's second two criticisms of maternalism, for instance. On the one hand, like some maternalists, some nonmaternalist feminists have ignored or downplayed the dramatic diversity among mothers. On the other hand, feminists sometimes valorize wage-based work and occupational identities for women, whether intentionally or not, just as maternalists sometimes valorize home-based and maternal identities for them. For a swift illustration let us look at Gwendoyn Mink's feminist analysis of the Personal Responsibility Act (PRA), which mistakenly passes for "welfare reform." Support for the PRA's harsh measures designed to reduce "welfare rolls" was strong, even among feminists and their supposed supporters. It was strong enough that the National Organization for Women's "Legal Defense and Education Fund appeal for funds to support an economic justice litigator aroused so much hate mail that the organization stopped doing direct mail on the welfare issue."[62] Analyzing the coalitions that built up around "welfare reform," Mink concluded that "feminists do not always act in the interest of other women," especially those seen as "different from them." She notes, for example, the "failure to make reliable allies of five white Democratic women in the Senate," including self-identified feminists like Pat Schroeder (D-CO), and "most white Democratic women in the House" (x, 3). (See chapters 2 and 3 on the PRA.) As Mink implies and NOW's participation indicates, many feminists fought the PRA, particularly its severe limits on lifetime eligibility for welfare assistance.[63] Yet feminist resistance to the PRA was far from dramatic. Like maternalism, whether explicitly feminist or not, feminism has limitations rooted in its specific real-world circumstances.

Among the circumstances limiting maternalists are most mothers' real-life situations. Typically, maternalism starts from their motherwork and extends it into the realms of society, culture, and politics. Its focus on mothers and motherwork can mobilize mothers around their maternal experiences and resources as readily as it can reinforce the maternal institution and its constraints (see chapter 3). Whichever way it tilts, maternalism reaches women more comprehensively and diffusely than any other perspective could. The vast majority of women are mothers or strongly support mothers and motherwork.

Yet mothers' commonplace constraints are considerable. Even high-status mothers with diverse options for entering public life face institutional and cultural hurdles. In electoral politics (as distinct from social-justice politics), for example, wives and mothers continue to be disadvantaged. Among members of state legislatures women are much likelier than men to be nonmarried. While they are just as likely to be parents, they are much less likely to have children under the age of twelve.[64] Thus, even relatively high-status mothers are to some extent held back in electoral politics where business as usual largely presupposes that one is either not a parent or has the advantage of a coparent who provides most of the child care.

By contrast with such high-status women, most women's resources are woefully narrow, but far from insignificant. Social-justice politics is capable of making great use of mothers' resources while empowering them in the process, as Burwell illustrates alongside the examples offered in this chapter. Perhaps in the end "maternalism" can be thought of as "home building," a less gender-skewed term. Indeed, it may be gender-open to the extent that the first of its terms is commonly associated with women, the second with men. In any event, this generic activity represents a "tradition that has no name," namely, the tradition of constructing "public homeplaces."[65] Women's organizations commonly carry on this tradition, but nothing implies that only women can do this nurturing work in communities and beyond.

Alongside homebuilding, we might think in terms of an *ecological ethic* based on the notions of connection or interdependence, social justice, and environmental responsibility. Such an ethic entails an abiding awareness of relationship—human relationships, interspecies relationships, human-plant relationships, and so forth. We cannot survive, let alone thrive, without connections. Like the caring labor Ruddick emphasizes, an ecological ethic ordains "relational work in which others' responses serve as an intrinsic and primary measure of achievement."[66]

Whatever rhetoric we decide upon as citizens, activists, and family makers, we do well to combat the woeful fact that "motherwork finds few adherents today."[67] This book is just one of many feminist attempts to change that cultural and political fact. It is as much a maternalist as a feminist project. It has aimed to affirm mothers, to counteract narrow and biased notions about them, to convey their perspectives and voices, and to demonstrate both the profundity and the diversity of their work. In the end our own maternalism revolves around the conviction that whatever we call our commitment to social justice—maternalism, home building, an ecological ethic, or something else—its enactment must entail the diverse labor that mothers commonly do amidst their various circumstances and prospects.

NARRATIVE T

Statement to the Court

Martha Boesing

Martha Boesing delivered this statement to the court at her trial for criminal trespass, on February 21, 1983. As a member of the Honeywell Project, Boesing had blocked access to Honeywell Corporation headquarters in November 1982; at this trial, she and thirty-three codefendants were found guilty and sentenced to twenty hours of community service. In April 1983, Boesing was again arrested in a civil-disobedience action at Honeywell headquarters. In June, a jury found her and thirty-five others not guilty.

My name is Martha Boesing. I am a playwright and the artistic director of At the Foot of the Mountain, a Minneapolis-based women's theater. My most recent play, *Ashes, Ashes, We All Fall Down,* a ritual drama about nuclear war and the denial of death, was the result of years of research on the economics and politics of militarism and the weapons industry. I have spent most of my adult life trying to effect change through democratic channels and through my work as a theater artist. I am forty-seven years old. I speak here today as a woman and a mother of three children.

As a mother I am often confused about how to help my children make wise decisions for themselves. One day I extol the virtues of a free and open education and the next I tell them they can't watch TV until they finish their homework. One day I tell them to eat what they like, their bodies know intuitively what they need; and the next I say, "Okay, that's it—no more junk food in this house!" I flounder like this because I have no training and very little support for this work and there are days when I'm the one who needs the parenting, even more than they do.

But I do try not to lie to them. I try to tell them the truth as I see it at any given moment. I cannot tell them that they are growing up into a benign world where they will be given an equal opportunity to succeed at whatever they wish to do with their lives, when the television, the newspapers, and their own nightmares belie this reality. They want to know whether there is even going to be a world for them. They want to know why they should prepare themselves for a life that cannot be lived, a life that is doomed from the start.

I have asked my children since they were very little not to use violence. No punching each other out, no toy guns inside the house, no hitting. You work things out by talking them over, or you go to your room until everyone cools out a little. That's the

From Hurricane Alice: A Feminist Review *1, no. 2 (fall/winter 1983/84): 1. Reprinted by permission of the author.*

rule. I cannot therefore turn around and support the rights of one nation to murder another, with my votes and my tax money. And I cannot tacitly agree that it's all right for Honeywell, a major industry in my neighborhood, to build cluster bombs which are right now killing hundreds of people in Lebanon and Southeast Asia. Which standard are they supposed to believe? And I cannot say, "What those other guys do is none of our business," because it is the business of all of us. It is our own lives we are talking about and the lives of our own children.

I believe that Honeywell and the thousands of other corporations who make profits from wars, such as Control Data, Sperry Univac, and FMC Corporation, are run by men who have lost touch with reality. They have clogged up their imaginations, so that they no longer see the faces of the people whom these bombs are killing today, so that they no longer see the faces of their own children whom these bombs will kill tomorrow.

And I believe it is the women, because we are the ones who give birth and because for the most part we are the ones who are asked to raise and nurture the children, who understand the connections and the bonding each one of us has with all living creatures. It is up to us, and to our brothers who are willing to share in this terrifying task of nurturing a new generation of life on the planet, to educate those whose creative intelligence has been stifled.

We live on a precipice. It is not a tolerable place to live, to breathe, to work, to die, to raise children. We must say no to those who are pushing us nearer and nearer to the edge.

And so I sit on Honeywell's doorstep—and since they are determining the fate of all of us, it is no longer a private doorstep—hoping to wake them up and bring them to their senses. Raising children gives one a certain kind of patience. I am willing to sit on this doorstep over and over again, for as long as it takes for them to hear our passionate plea for life.

I have three very beautiful, intelligent children. I have been deeply blessed. They bring enormous joy into my life. I do this for them, and for your children, and for all their friends both known and unknown to them and to us. I pray for a world that is sane and safe for them all to grow up in.

NARRATIVE U

Sometimes the Road Gets Lonely

Dollie Burwell

It is not easy being a mother and an activist. It is even more difficult for a mother to be an activist in a small rural community in North Carolina, especially a small rural county like Warren County, where 65 percent of the 18,000 population are African Americans. Many times being an activist can cause you to be called names that are not pleasant to be called. You are often labeled a "troublemaker." Mothers are often asked why aren't they home taking care of the children instead of out causing trouble. Sometimes when you are labeled a troublemaker in a small rural community, it can really cause problems for you.

When you are a mother and an activist in a small community, sometimes the road gets lonely and it gets difficult. Sometimes you can feel like you are not making a difference. Sometimes you can really feel like giving up the struggle. . . .

As an environmental activist in my community, I am constantly struggling to educate people about the danger of hazardous and toxic waste landfills and incinerators. Many times I am disliked by government officials and by waste management companies officials because I tell people the truth. I tell them that jobs and prosperity and economic growth do not come with hazardous and toxic waste landfills and incinerators. That people living in areas where these facilities are located do not get high-paying jobs; what they get are strange diseases and health problems. I tell them that these waste management companies prey on poor and minority communities when they locate these facilities because they know that they are vulnerable and sometimes lack education and knowledge. I tell them that the government officials in these communities are just looking for a way to increase the tax base and provide jobs.

Of course, this does not make me popular with the powers that be. Especially when these waste management companies promise so much—shopping centers, jobs, economic and industrial growth. To a small county with double-digit unemployment, these promises sound like the best thing since sliced bread!

This happened a few years ago in Northampton County, North Carolina, a county adjacent to where I live. A waste management company promised county government officials a shopping center, lots of jobs and a few other goodies. Since

Northampton County is one of the state's poorest counties, these promises sounded to county government officials like they were Godsent. They believed that the county could really benefit from having a hazardous and toxic waste incinerator. They were convinced that this facility would provide hundreds of jobs for people, and people would look upon them as real leaders for having made this move for the county. Northampton County is also about 70 percent African American.

One night at a hearing, one of the officials called me a troublemaker. He told the people that I didn't know what I was talking about. The incinerator was going to be safe, he said, and all I did was go around the state talking to people and discouraging economic development by instilling fear in the people of the community. I was just an outside agitator. When I got up to speak I thanked him for the compliment. Of course he looked at me like, "What is this fool talking about? I know I'm not crazy. I did not compliment her."

So I said, "Mr. Clark, I know you are wondering what kind of compliment you gave me. But you called me an agitator. If you don't believe that that's a compliment, the next time you wash your clothes you just take the agitator out of your washer and see if you don't have just a bunch of wet dirty clothes. I want to thank you for calling me an agitator because you are right, what I'm going to do for Northampton County is get all the dirt out and leave this county clean." I don't think Mr. Clark called any other activist an agitator.

For a very long time a myth existed that environmental problems were only the concern of white, middle-class males. But from native lands to urban ghettos, from welfare rolls to university rolls, mothers and minorities are fighting back against toxic siege and impacting the environmental justice movement. I feel that I can best explain how mothers have played a role in environmental activism and how mothers are fighting back against toxic siege by telling the 1982 story of how mothers of predominantly black, rural, mostly poor Warren County, North Carolina, struggled against the state's siting of a polychlorinated biphenyl (PCB) landfill resulting in more than five hundred arrests of mostly women and children.

Before the Warren County demonstrations, racial and ethnic communities had been only marginally involved with issues of hazardous and toxic wastes. In the fall of 1982, mothers and daughters, fathers and sons of Warren County launched one of the largest civil rights demonstrations since the 1960s. But let me back up a bit. During the summer of 1978, a transformer company illegally and deliberately sprayed 31 gallons of PCB fluid along 240 miles of roadside in fourteen counties of North Carolina. In some areas concentrations were as high as 10,000 parts per million, two hundred times above the level the Environmental Protection Agency designates as safe.

After examining ninety potential sites, the state of North Carolina officially announced its intention to bury 40 cubic yards of this PCB-laced soil in the town of Afton. Citizens of the community felt deeply that the state's decision to bury the PCBs in Warren County was based solely on the fact that the Afton was 85 percent

African American. Citizens felt this way because in choosing this site, the Environmental Protection Agency had to waive two of its very important requirements. One of their requirements was that the bottom of the landfill had to be at least 50 feet above the groundwater table. At the Warren County site, the landfill would be only 7 feet above the groundwater. The second important requirement that they waived was that a site had to have a thick and permeable soil formation such as large clay pans. Warren County's soil samples showed only small amounts or no clay presence. But in spite of that, on June 4, 1979, the Environmental Protection Agency waived these requirements and gave the state of North Carolina final approval to construct the landfill on the Afton site. The citizens of Warren County felt that their civil rights had been violated.

Many people in the community believed that EPA and the government would, in fact, protect them. They firmly believed that if there had to be a landfill, it would have to meet all the requirements. When the EPA waived these requirements, people were infuriated. Some people were ready to resort to violence. Once the landfill was constructed, someone cut up the plastic liner that the state had put in. Many people were ready to actually shoot anyone who drove a truck bringing PCB-laced soil into the county. This is where I believe the church was extremely helpful in our struggle. The church played a major role by encouraging people to pray and put their faith into action. This prevented people from becoming violent. Though our community is poor, its people are very proud. We have a lot of working-class people whose lands were inherited from generations past. People did not want to see their land destroyed.

My affiliation with the Southern Christian Leadership Conference (SCLC) and the United Church of Christ Commission for Racial Justice had taught me what nonviolent civil disobedience could accomplish. So I immediately gathered people together and told them that there were other ways to prevent the state and EPA from destroying our community. I told them that I believed that we could save our community though nonviolent struggle. So we began to meet at church and pray and march and protest. We invited other civil rights organizations and churches to join us in our struggle. Spirituality was a major part of the movement.

Mothers argued vigorously that the state's decision to put the landfill in Warren County was based on racial and political grounds. The fact that Warren County had the highest percentage of African-Americans of any county in the state, the fact that the county was rural, mostly poor, had very little voting power and almost no economic power were the reasons why the state was putting the landfill in Warren County. Scientific data indicated that the Warren County site was not the best site. Mothers in Warren County joined other citizens in filing a lawsuit to prevent the state from hauling toxic and hazardous waste to the Warren County landfill. This suit was dismissed by the state court. Mothers then joined other citizens in persuading the Warren County Board of Commissioners to file a second lawsuit. But the Commissioners got a lot of pressure from the state, and they later withdrew the lawsuit. But that didn't stop the mothers of Warren County.

Mothers came out to public hearings, bringing their children and letting the state know that they would not stand by and let them dump poison on their children. Many mothers knew that they were fighting more than just a one-time PCB dump. Because by that time, Governor James B. Hunt was saying that the state needed a permanent hazardous and toxic waste facility. The state had purchased a 100-acre tract of land and had an option to purchase an additional 240-acre tract in the Afton community.

By 1982, when the trucks began to roll into Warren County, headed for the landfill, we knew we had to act. From September 15 to October 27, 1982, over five hundred people were arrested. Hundreds of mothers in Warren County literally laid their bodies in front of trucks filled with PCB-contaminated soil to stop the unjust dumping of toxic waste in their community. We knew that laying our bodies in front of those trucks was risky, but we were willing to put our lives on the line for justice.

For six weeks, more than two hundred mothers marched from three to four miles every day, many engaging in civil disobedience, and many were arrested. We prayed, we sang, we met every day at the church. We asked God to bless us and protect us, but we knew we had to continue the struggle. During that six-week period, I was arrested and jailed five times. On one occasion I spent three days in jail with four other mothers including Mrs. Evelyn Lowery, convener of the SCLC women and the wife of Joseph Lowery, who was then president of the Southern Christian Leadership Conference. We spent our time in jail writing a statement on behalf of the children. But many of our children wanted to speak for themselves. They participated in the demonstrations and marches and many were also arrested.

I remember, on the very first day of the demonstrations, I was getting my ten-year-old daughter all ready to go to school—or so I thought. I had made breakfast and laid out her clothes so that she could get dressed and catch the bus for school when she informed me that she was not going to school but was going to the march. I told her that in all probability I would be arrested and that it would really be better if she went on to school. She said, "Well, Mom, I have my aunt's telephone numbers. I am probably going to get arrested too, so if you get arrested I will call my aunt. They will give me one phone call, won't they?"

Now, I was willing to put my life on the line. But when it came right down to it, as a mother, I just didn't know whether I wanted my ten-year-old daughter to put her life on the line. Though it was a difficult decision for me to say "yes" to her, I had to do it. I could not in good conscience be hypocritical. I couldn't let her believe that justice was important enough for me to fight for but that it was not important enough for her to fight for.

So as expected, both of us were arrested that day. Just as I was being taken to jail I saw her being taken to another paddy wagon. Then I saw her being stopped by all these reporters. I saw tears running down her face as she talked to the reporters. I panicked—I tried to get out of the paddy wagon but they wouldn't let me. I could see her talking but I couldn't hear what she was saying. I was by this time crying myself. I had to stay in jail for the rest of the day wondering why she was crying. I thought perhaps she had become frightened.

But, as it turned out, she did get her telephone call from juvenile hall and called my sister to pick her up. And later that day when I got out, I saw her on television. I heard her say to the anchor person that she was not afraid of going to jail. She said, "I'm afraid of what this waste is going to do to my family and to the people." She had actually believed that we were going to keep the trucks from dumping the soil. And when she saw the trucks going in after they had started taking us away she became hurt because she believed that the people were really going to die from this waste and she was devastated. People who saw her on the national news all over the country called; they sent funds and some of them came to participate. The children played a major role in helping to get the attention of the media and other support. I think people could have seen me or some other adult crying and not been so moved to action, but seeing a ten-year-old crying, they came to our aid.

I believe that without the mothers of Warren County there would not have been an environmental justice movement. The environmental justice movement is just emerging and the old environmental movement is being redefined. While I was talking to Patsy Ruth Oliver, I indicated to her that I was featured in the Audubon Society magazine as activist of the month and I also expressed how overwhelmed I was at being featured. She said, "Well if you think that's something, I was featured in *Sierra*." So the environmental justice movement is emerging and we really have mothers to thank for that because out of that struggle in Warren County, North Carolina, came a whole new environmental justice movement.

"We haven't told you why the Commission for Racial Justice got involved in environmental justice," Dr. Benjamin F. Chavis Jr. told the audience at the 1991 First National People of Color Environmental Leadership Summit held in Washington, D.C. Dr. Chavis, the former Executive Director of the United Church of Christ Commission for Racial Justice and the NAACP [National Association for the Advancement of Colored People], is also the publisher of one of the nation's leading environmental studies, "Toxic Waste and Race in the United States." "God did not whisper," he told the crowd. "God spoke to us through an African American woman, a woman who led her children and her community to jail. This woman started this leadership summit. If it had not been for her, the Commission for Racial Justice would not have gotten involved. A lot of accolades have gone toward our organization, but I want to give credit where credit is due. It was Dollie Burwell and other African American sisters like her that caused us to take seriously the life and the consequence of the environmental struggle."[1]

The mothers who struggled for environmental justice in Warren County, North Carolina, struggled in the same tradition and in the same spirit as their foremothers who cooked, fed their children, washed and ironed their clothes, cleaned their house, went to work on their jobs, and still had the commitment and found the time to fight for justice and freedom. As the mothers laid their bodies in front of trucks, as they were hauled off to jail by more than two hundred state troopers, they knew that they were neither politically nor economically powerfully enough to stop the trucks. But they knew that they had to take a stand for their children's sake. They knew that the media would not do them justice in telling the story of the struggle, but it did not matter because they knew in their hearts that they were doing the right thing.

We may not have stopped that one dump, but we stopped others. Mothers in Warren County forced the state of North Carolina to give back to the county 95 of the 100 acres of land that it had purchased. The state did not exercise its option to purchase the 240 additional acres. The governor called a moratorium on landfills in North Carolina. Mothers also lobbied to get legislation passed that prevented any other hazardous or toxic waste facility from being located within a 100-mile radius of the county.[2]

Mothers in Warren County continue to struggle for empowerment, both politically and economically. In 1982, following the demonstrations, Eva M. Clayton, an African American woman and mother, was elected to the Warren County Board of Commissioners and then elected by her colleagues to chair the board, becoming the first African American woman in the state to chair a Board of Commissioners. In 1992, this same woman and mother became the first African American woman to be elected to the U.S. House of Representatives from North Carolina. She was also the first African American to be elected president of the Democratic freshman class. In 1988 another mother, Patsy Hargrove, became the second African American woman and mother to be elected to the Warren County Board of Commissioners. That same year, a Native American mother and an African American mother were also elected to the Warren County Board of Education.

Wanting to be sure that if any other large tracts of land were sold to anybody I would be in a position to find out who they were and why were they buying the land, I ran for Register of Deeds, and as a result of winning the election I became the first African American woman to manage all of the county's real property and vital records. All of these mothers ran very vigorous and well-managed campaigns and were reelected for second terms in 1992.

There are many mothers of all races in our communities who are struggling for environmental justice and fighting back against the toxic siege. Many of you have heard of Lois Gibbs, the white mother who led the struggle of Love Canal, New York. . . . You may also have heard of Joanna Guthierez, a Hispanic mother, and her four-hundred-member "Mothers of East Los Angeles." This woman gave lectures and circulated petitions to churchgoers after Sunday Mass and organized weekly marches and successfully stopped a toxic waste incinerator that was slated for the mostly poor and Hispanic community of Vernon, California, where she lived.

But you probably have not heard of Janice Dickerson, an African American mother and organizer working every day with families along an 80-mile strip between New Orleans and Baton Rouge, Louisiana, known as Cancer Alley, to stop the toxic siege and environmental racism. You probably have not heard of Jesse Dearwater, a Native American mother and founder of Native Americans for a Clean Environment, who lost her job as a hairdresser because she dared to spread the word in her community of Iron, Oklahoma, about the town's largest industry that was also the town's largest hazardous waste producing industry, and who organized and struggled daily against toxic aggression and environmental racism.

Within our communities the voices of women really must be acknowledged. Environmental racism deals a double blow to women because women are the ones who usually wind up caring for the sick babies and families. Mothers are playing very important roles in social and political change in the country. As this new movement for environmental justice emerges, it will be even more important that the role of mothers be lifted up and their voices heard.

Notes

1. [Original] [e]ditor's note: Other environmental leaders credit the Warren County demonstrations with pressuring the EPA to issue the 1992 landmark report, *Environmental Equity: Reducing Risk for All Communities*, which correlated race and income level with hazardous waste dump sites nationwide. Says Robert Bullard, former University of California Riverside sociologist and editor of *Confronting Environmental Racism*, "This study was only initiated after massive civil disobedience protests in predominantly African American Warren County." See Bullard, ed., *Confronting Environmental Racism: Voices from the Grassroots* (Boston: South End Press, 1993).

2. In 1992, the state of North Carolina announced that it was going to transfer contaminated water from the Warren County dump to Emille, Alabama. Burwell led her community in protest, saying that "environmental justice is not taking contamination from one poor black community to another poor black community." The protesters forced the state to set up a commission, chaired by Burwell, to find a suitable technology to detoxify the Warren County landfill. They are still searching for answers.

Epilogue

When we began working on the project that turned into this book, we were surprised by the enormity of the feminist literature on motherhood, mothering, and mothers. Although we had both taught courses on family issues for years, this was the first time we had "narrowed" our focus to motherhood. Far from it being a narrow topic, however, we found a literature so immense we had trouble keeping up with it. Not only did we find that feminist theorists, researchers, and activists had made motherhood a central concern for decades, we also found ourselves in the midst of a contemporary explosion of such work. Even as we bring our work on this book to a close, every new issue of *The Women's Review of Books*, *Ms.* magazine, *Gender & Society*, and *Contemporary Sociology*, among others, introduces us to more feminist articles and books on motherhood. There are now websites devoted to motherhood, as well as a professional organization, the Association for Research on Mothering, which publishes a journal and organizes several conferences a year.[1] Our selected bibliography represents less than a third of the books and articles we cite in our chapters, and those citations represent a small portion of the materials we came across in the course of our work. A feminist bibliography on motherhood could constitute a book in itself. Indeed, such a book was published in the early 1990s, Penelope Dixon's *Mothers and Mothering: An Annotated Feminist Bibliography*, although we've seen very few references to it.[2]

Our surprise at the enormity of the feminist literature on motherhood suggested to us that a synthesis of that literature was due. Focusing on the three major themes we found within it, we pulled together between the two covers of this book feminist analyses of social constructions of motherhood, maternal bodies, and mothering in everyday life. We also made room for personal stories written by mothers and others who care for children.

In the preceding pages we have traveled most of the challenging pathways that we set out to explore and analyze. Our work has enlarged our insights into the lived realities of mothering and mothers' relationships with their children, as well as the social, political, and historical dimensions of motherhood. We have renewed our appreciation of the utter singularity of every mother-child relationship, the unique challenges each mother faces in her very own biographical situation, the pressures on mothers to do extraordinary things with ordinary—often even paltry—resources, and the divide between the public rhetoric valorizing mothers and the treatment they actually face in the home, the workplace, the birthplace, the court, the welfare office, the halls of Congress, and elsewhere.

Although we have come a long way, our work has made us vividly aware of gaps in the literature on motherhood as well as in our own analyses. In this closing statement, we focus on the gaps we felt most poignantly as we researched and wrote our book.

Despite our pairing of mothers and children in the title of our book, we found a split between the literature on mothers and the literature on children. There is a massive literature exploring motherhood, much of it qualitative research that includes mothers' perspectives on their maternal identities, their mothering, and their children. Likewise, there is a massive literature exploring childhood, some of which looks at whether and how children's needs are met through interactions with their parents. There is a dearth of research, however, that simultaneously takes into account both mothers' and children's needs, desires, and perspectives concerning their relationships. Jessica Benjamin's theoretical work is a major exception to this pattern (see chapter 5), and our chapter 8 includes some research that focuses on mothers and children together. Nonetheless, we need to know more about mothers' and children's lived experiences of one another, how they support and frustrate each others' needs, desires, and development, how they grow in connection with and apart from each other, and how they deal with stresses and strains that impinge on their relationships. We need long-term, qualitative studies on mother-child relationships as they develop over the life course, relationships that are likely to be among the longest lasting in many people's lives.

Another gap has to do with motherwork in relation to specific institutions and cultural arenas, especially schooling, moral (or religious) education, and popular culture. Mothers often spend enormous time and energy seeking and then monitoring child care arrangements for their preschool children, yet they spend an even greater number of years monitoring and participating in their children's K–12 schooling. What is involved in this aspect of parenting? What kinds of relationships do mothers develop with their children's teachers and schools? When are parents and teachers most successful (and least successful) in working together to support children's education? What happens when mothers and teachers share or don't share social characteristics such as race, class, gender, and sexual orientation? How do children experience their mothers' involvement (or lack of involvement) in their education?[3]

Similarly, research on mothers' own schooling remains atypical and underdeveloped. We need to know how maternal aspirations and responsibilities sometimes stimulate a return to school and how educational institutions sometimes impede mothers' schooling, particularly when they are set up for students without substantial child care responsibilities. We need to know as well how mothers' roles as students affect their motherwork, both in the short and the long run. Wendy Luttrell has begun this work by showing in vivid detail what a return to school entails for working-class mothers as well as what it means to them as mothers.[4]

Also falling short is research on how mothers attend to children's moral education, whether or not that includes formal or informal religious training. Even though mothers have borne the brunt of this sweeping responsibility since the middle of the nineteenth century, little is documented about their satisfactions and frustrations as moral educators of their daughters and sons. What kinds of stories do different mothers tell their children about truth telling, social justice, kindness, and environmental awareness? How do mothers of various social backgrounds talk to children about their ethnic, racial, religious, and national identities? How do they introduce them to inequalities that structure not only our society but also global relations? How do mothers instruct children about community, fellowship, and teamwork? About family, neighborhood, and civic life? What do mothers in various situations do about "manners" and politeness? Where do they see their greatest successes and their biggest challenges? And how do children respond to their mothers' efforts at moral education? Sara Ruddick and Patricia Hill Collins have set the theoretical stage for these questions (see chapter 1), but qualitative work on these issues is still needed.

Popular culture's influence on children and on mother-child relationships is another area meriting fuller attention. The corporate media spew out video games, cartoons, books, videos, movies, compact discs, television programs, computer games, and comic books, spinning a web of enormous influence. By shaping children's consciousness along lines that often diverge from mothers' preferences and priorities, these media impinge on mothers' relationships with their children in ways we need to articulate precisely and rigorously.

While schooling, moral education, and popular culture figure prominently in nearly every mother's motherwork, there are other institutional and cultural arenas that mothers contend with. How do mothers negotiate relationships with pediatricians and other medical experts, particularly mothers whose children have special medical needs? How do mothers deal with other professionals who have an impact on their children's lives, such as social workers, school counselors, foster care staff, and psychologists?

We also found gaps in the personal narrative genre. Not surprisingly, socially privileged mothers—especially those privileged in terms of social class—are more likely to have time to write and more likely to have access to outlets for publishing their reflections. Poor and working-class mothers are less likely to get their stories written and published. For example, there are many strong qualitative studies about poor teen mothers, but their stories are noticeably absent from the personal narrative genre. Likewise, the late 1990s saw the publication of several good qualitative studies about drug-dependent mothers (see the notes to chapter 2), but we found only one narrative written by a mother recovering from drug abuse.[5] Qualitative research typically includes the voices and perspectives of those who are studied (a major strength of this research method), but we also need to hear women's stories in the extended form that personal narratives make possible. Moreover, we have yet to hear the full, diverse stories of many other mothers: adoptive mothers, birth mothers, mothers in prison, and mothers with disabilities, to name a few.

What about fathers? Except for chapter 4 our focus has been on mothers, and that focus may trouble or frustrate some readers. Rather than a gap in the literature or our analyses, however, we think of our focus on mothers in a different light. The institution of fatherhood has a distinctly different history from the institution of motherhood. Consequently, for most people, fathering has different meanings from mothering, and fathers' parenting experiences typically differ from those of mothers. To give just one example illustrating this divergence: the index of Michael Kimmel's *Manhood in America: A Cultural History* lists only 22 pages (in a 335-page text) under the entry "fatherhood."[6] We mention this not to criticize Kimmel, a profeminist sociologist whose work we respect, but to point out the more tenuous relationship between manhood and fatherhood than between womanhood and motherhood. If there were a book titled, *Womanhood in America: A Cultural History*, we can be sure that motherhood would figure prominently within it, whether it was written from a feminist perspective or not. By focusing on mothers, mothering, and motherhood in our book, then, we are not suggesting that fathers are unimportant or that they need to remain secondary as child nurturers. Indeed, for most mothers most of the time, fathers are of paramount importance. A feminist literature on fatherhood, fathers, and fathering is beginning to blossom, a development we heartily welcome. Boundaries between the literatures on mothers and fathers will begin to blur when the everyday care of and responsibility for children become as central to most fathers' lives and identities as they have been and continue to be for most mothers' lives and identities.

Finally, we want to address a topic that we barely skimmed in chapters 1 and 9 and that remains underrepresented in the feminist literature: similarities and differences among women across the mother/nonmother divide. Perhaps we are acutely aware of this gap because one of us is a mother and one of us is not. The everyday experiences of mothers and nonmothers, even among women who share class, race, and other social characteristics, usually differ radically. As a mother and a nonmother, we have felt how much our everyday lives take shape around our parental statuses. Our daily round of activities and responsibilities, the things that most tug at our consciousness, and our fears, dreams and fantasies, all reflect our parental statuses to some extent. In addition, mothers and nonmothers face different cultural treatment. Even though motherwork is not highly valued in our society, a certain status accompanies motherhood in many communities. Thus, women who are not mothers are likely to be seen, at least by some people, as socially deviant. "Why don't you have children?" is a culturally intelligible question; "why *do* you have children?" is not.

Our work together has renewed our appreciation of the differences between women who are mothers and women who are not, but it has also renewed our appreciation of their similarities. What most women have in common is a commitment both within and beyond their families to caregiving. Across the mother/nonmother divide, many women devote a lot of their time and energy to nurturing others, whether in jobs such as teacher, child care worker, nurse, secretary, or babysitter, or in their personal lives as sister, daughter, aunt, wife, partner, neighbor, and friend. We believe that the boundary that sometimes makes it seem that mothers and nonmothers live in two different worlds can and should be transcended. Transcending that boundary means understanding and respecting commonalities as well as differences.

In closing, then, we acknowledge that many questions remain unanswered about motherwork, mothers' (and others') relationships with children, and the role of caregiving in many women's lives. At the same time, we hope our work has provoked our readers to think in new ways about the diverse realities of mothers' and children's lives, and the emotional, political debates about motherhood that rage around us.

Notes

Notes to Introduction

1. Jane Smiley, "Mothers Should," *New York Times Magazine,* April 5, 1998, 37, 39.

2. Sara Ruddick, "Rethinking 'Maternal' Politics," in *The Politics of Motherhood: Activist Voices from Left to Right*, ed. A. Jetter, A. Orleck, and D. Taylor (Hanover, N.H.: University Press of New England, 1997), 370.

3. These questions are grounded in the sociological traditions of social constructionism, the sociology of knowledge, phenomenology, and symbolic interaction.

4. Ellen Ross, "New Thoughts on 'The Oldest Vocation': Mothers and Motherhood in Recent Feminist Scholarship," *Signs: Journal of Women in Culture and Society* 20, no. 2 (winter 1995): 397–413; Molly Ladd-Taylor, "Love, Work, and the Meanings of Motherhood," *Journal of Women's History* 8, no. 3 (fall 1996): 219–227; Donna Bassin, Margaret Honey, and Meryle Mahrer Kaplan, "Introduction," in *Representations of Motherhood*, ed. D. Bassin, M. Honey, and M. M. Kaplan (New Haven. Conn.: Yale University Press, 1994), 9; Maureen T. Reddy, Martha Roth, and Amy Sheldon, "Prologue: What Is 'Feminist Mothering'?" in *Mother Journeys: Feminists Write about Mothering*, ed. M. T. Reddy, M. Roth, and A. Sheldon (Minneapolis: Spinsters Ink, 1994), 1.

5. We planned to reprint excerpts from Cherríe Moraga's "Waiting in the Wings: Reflections on a Radical Motherhood," in *The Politics of Motherhood*, 288–310. Although we held out hope of reaching her before our book went into production in order to get permission to reprint her essay, we did not succeed in doing so. We regret that our book is missing the eloquent voice of this Chicana lesbian poet.

Notes to Chapter 1

1. Seven of the twenty-two students in this class were mothers; two were stepmothers; one was visibly pregnant. One student had suffered a second-trimester miscarriage shortly before the course began; another had a miscarriage during the semester. All but one of the students were women, and five (including two of the mothers) were African American, Asian American, or Latina. One woman proudly called herself a "grand-dyke," referring to her lesbian partnership with a new grandmother. Many of the students had nieces and nephews, and several had responsibility for children as babysitters or nannies.

2. The relationship between motherhood and feminism is a huge topic. Although the three issues I address in this chapter are central to a strong understanding of that relationship, my examples, of necessity, are selective. Other chapters in the book cover the ideas of prominent theorists, researchers, and activists who do not show up here.

3. See for example, Gerda Lerner, *The Grimké Sisters from South Carolina: Pioneers for Woman's Rights and Abolition* (New York: Schocken Books, 1967); Angela Davis, *Women, Race, and Class* (New York, Vintage, 1983); Miriam Schneir, ed., *Feminism: The Essential Historical Writings* (New York: Random House, 1972).

4. Ann Oakley, "Feminism, Motherhood and Medicine—Who Cares?" in *What Is Feminism?* ed. J. Mitchell and A. Oakley (New York: Pantheon Books, 1986), 129.

5. "Declaration of Sentiments and Resolutions, Seneca Falls," in *Feminism: The Essential Historical Writings*, 76–82.

6. Sojourner Truth, "Ain't I a Woman," in *Feminism: The Essential Historical Writings*, 94–95.

7. Stephanie J. Shaw, "Mothering under Slavery in the Antebellum South," in *Mothering: Ideology, Experience, and Agency*, ed. E. N. Glenn, G. Chang, and L. R. Forcey (New York: Routledge, 1994), 237–258.

8. Linda Gordon, "Why Nineteenth-Century Feminists Did Not Support 'Birth Control' and Twentieth-Century Feminists Do: Feminism, Reproduction, and the Family," in *Rethinking the Family: Some Feminist Questions*, ed. B. Thorne with M. Yalom (New York: Longman, 1982), 42.

9. Linda Gordon, *Pitied But Not Entitled: Single Mothers and the History of Welfare, 1890–1935* (New York: Free Press, 1994); Molly Ladd-Taylor, *Mother-Work: Women, Child Welfare, and the State, 1890–1930* (Urbana: University of Illinois Press, 1994).

10. Two points of clarification. First, feminists were active in the middle decades of the twentieth century, though not as publicly as feminists were before 1920 and after 1960. Leila J. Rupp and Verta Taylor, *Survival in the Doldrums: The American Women's Rights Movement, 1945 to the 1960s* (New York: Oxford University Press, 1987). Second, liberal feminists, such as those who founded the National Organization for Women in 1966, were not tied as directly to the social movements of this time period as were radical feminists; the latter are my focus in this section of the chapter. Leila J. Rupp and Verta Taylor, "The Women's Movement Since 1960: Structure, Strategies, and New Directions," in *American Choices: Social Dilemmas and Public Policy Since 1960*, ed. R. H. Bremner, G. W. Reichard, and R. J. Hopkins (Columbus: Ohio University Press, 1986), 75–104.

11. Lauri Umansky, *Motherhood Reconceived: Feminism and the Legacies of the Sixties* (New York: New York University Press, 1996). Throughout this chapter I rely heavily on Umansky's book, the only detailed history of second-wave feminism's relationship to motherhood.

12. M. Rivka Polatnick, "Diversity in Women's Liberation Ideology: How a Black and a White Group of the 1960s Viewed Motherhood," *Signs: Journal of Women in Culture and Society* 21, no. 3 (spring 1996): 685–688.

13. Umansky, *Motherhood Reconceived*, 13. Radical feminists are often distinguished from socialist feminists, who prioritize capitalism in their analyses of gender oppression, and from liberal feminists, who seek reform within existing systems.

14. Polatnick, "Diversity in Women's Liberation Ideology," 690, 702, 682–683. Page numbers that follow in the text refer to this article. We use this method throughout the book; page numbers in the text always refer to the previously cited article or book.

15. Umansky, *Motherhood Reconceived*, 79.

16. Ibid., 80–81; Polatnick, "Diversity in Women's Liberation Ideology," 686.

17. Mount Vernon group, cited in Polatnick, "Diversity in Women's Liberation Ideology," 686.

18. Umansky, *Motherhood Reconceived*, 21–25.

19. Polatnick, "Diversity in Women's Liberation Ideology," 690, 691.

20. African American feminists have argued this point cogently. See Patricia Hill Collins, *Black Feminist Thought: Knowledge, Consciousness, and the Politics of Empowerment* (Boston: Unwin Hyman, 1990), 133–137; and Barbara Christian, "An Angle of Seeing: Motherhood in Buchi Emecheta's *Joys of Motherhood* and Alice Walker's *Meridian*," in *Mothering*, 95–120.

21. Polatnick, "Diversity in Women's Liberation Ideology," 701.

22. Umansky, *Motherhood Reconceived*, 46–50.

23. Shulamith Firestone, *The Dialectic of Sex: The Case for Feminist Revolution* (New York: William Morrow, 1970), 8–9.

24. Ann Snitow, "Feminism and Motherhood: An American Reading," *Feminist Review*, no. 40 (spring 1992), 35–36.

25. Umansky, *Motherhood Reconceived*, 32, 53–55.

26. Ibid., chapter 2.

27. Adrienne Rich's ideas have been pivotal in this regard. We address her work in chapters 3 and 5.

28. Mary O'Brien, *Reproducing the World: Essays in Feminist Theory* (Boulder, Colo.: Westview Press, 1989), 22.

29. Gerda Lerner, *The Creation of Patriarchy* (New York: Oxford University Press, 1986), 9.

30. Mary O' Brien, *The Politics of Reproduction* (Boston: Routledge & Kegan Paul, 1981), 54, 52–64.

31. Lerner, *The Creation of Patriarchy*, 46. Lerner defines patriarchy in a more general way than O'Brien does. "Patriarchy . . . means the manifestation and institutionalization of male dominance over women and children in the family and the extension of male dominance over women in society in general. It implies that men hold power in all the important institutions of society and that women are deprived of access to such power. It does *not* imply that women are either totally powerless or totally deprived of rights, influence, and resources" (239); emphasis in original.

32. Robbie Pfeufer Kahn, *Bearing Meaning: The Language of Birth* (Urbana, Ill: University of Illinois Press, 1995), 102.

33. Evelyn Fox Keller, "From Secrets of Life to Secrets of Death," in *Body/Politics: Women and the Discourses of Science*, ed. M. Jacobus, E. F. Keller, and S. Shuttleworth (New York: Routledge, 1990), 186, 187, 181.

34. Lise Vogel, *Mothers on the Job: Maternity Policy in the U.S. Workplace* (New Brunswick, N.J.: Rutgers University Press, 1993), 14, 28.

35. Ibid, 54–56; Rupp and Taylor, "The Women's Movement Since 1960," 80–82, 86.

36. Vogel, *Mothers on the Job*, 38.

37. Nancy R. Hooyman and Judith Gonyea, *Feminist Perspectives on Family Care: Policies for Gender Justice* (Thousand Oaks, Calif.: Sage, 1995), 224.

38. Vogel, *Mothers on the Job*, 150–156, quote on 156. Vogel points out that in all European countries, Canada, and many developing nations, "working mothers and their children enjoy broad health care coverage, including hospital and physician ex-

penses during pregnancy, for childbirth, and for postnatal care; the coverage is generally provided through a national health care system. A new mother has the right to a paid leave of absence no shorter than fourteen weeks, and often considerably longer. While on paid leave, she receives cash benefits amounting to as much as 90 percent to 100 percent of her pay. . . . Not only are women workers able to return from their leaves to the same or a comparable job, but seniority, pensions, and other benefits are preserved. Once a mother is back at work, child care is often available" (35–36).

39. Kahn, *Bearing Meaning*, 103.

40. Vogel and Kahn recognize that "equality" is a complex concept with a particular history in Western societies. For a brief discussion of its complexities, see Mary F. Rogers, *Contemporary Feminist Thought* (New York: McGraw Hill, 1998), 43–47.

41. Umansky, *Motherhood Reconceived*, chapter 4; Heather Jon Maroney, "Embracing Motherhood: New Feminist Theory," *Canadian Journal of Political and Social Theory* 9, no. 1–2 (winter/spring 1985): 40–64; Roberta Hamilton, "Feminism and Motherhood, 1970–1990: Reinventing the Wheel?" *Resources for Feminist Research* 19, no. 3/4 (September/December 1990): 23–32.

42. Robin Morgan, *Going Too Far: The Personal Chronicle of a Feminist* (New York: Vintage Books, 1978), 8.

43. Umansky, *Motherhood Reconceived*, 13.

44. Jane Alpert, cited in Umansky, *Motherhood Reconceived*, 110.

45. Umansky, *Motherhood Reconceived*, 106–108, 127.

46. Sara Ruddick, "Maternal Thinking," *Feminist Studies* 6, no. 2 (summer 1980): 347–349; emphasis in original.

47. Sara Ruddick, *Maternal Thinking: Toward a Politics of Peace* (Boston: Beacon Press, 1989).

48. Alison Bailey, "Mothering, Diversity, and Peace Politics," *Hypatia* 9, no. 2 (spring 1994): 188–198.

49. Patricia Hill Collins, "Shifting the Center: Race, Class, and Feminist Theorizing about Motherhood," in *Mothering*, 45–65.

50. Ellen Ross, "New Thoughts on 'The Oldest Vocation': Mothers and Motherhood in Recent Feminist Scholarship," *Signs: Journal of Women in Culture and Society* 20, no. 2 (winter 1995): 398. Similarly, Margaret A. Simons suggests that Ruddick's analysis does not allow for the rage of a mother or child who has been abused. Simons, "Motherhood, Feminism and Identity," *Women's Studies International Forum* 7, no. 5 (1984): 353.

51. Umansky, *Motherhood Reconceived*, 101.

52. Snitow, "Feminism and Motherhood," 33. See also Judith Stacey, "Are Feminists Afraid to Leave Home? The Challenge of Conservative Pro-Family Feminism," in *What Is Feminism?*, 208–237.

53. See Susan Faludi, *Backlash: The Undeclared War Against American Women* (New York: Anchor Books, 1991).

54. Snitow, "Feminism and Motherhood," 41.

55. See, for example, Carolyn M. Morell, *Unwomanly Conduct: The Challenges of Intentional Childlessness* (New York: Routledge, 1994); Mardy S. Ireland, *Reconceiving Women: Separating Motherhood from Female Identity* (New York: Guilford Press, 1993).

56. Gayle Letherby, "Mother or Not, Mother or What? Problems of Definition and Identity," *Women's Studies International Forum* 17, no. 5 (1994): 525–532.

57. Morell, *Unwomanly Conduct*, 21.

58. The complex relationship between feminism and motherhood is discussed in several review essays: Ross, "New Thoughts on 'The Oldest Vocation;' " Alice Adams, "Maternal Bonds: Recent Literature on Mothering," *Signs: Journal of Women in Culture and Society* 20, no. 2 (1995): 414–427; Lisa D. Brush, "Love, Toil, and Trouble: Motherhood and Feminist Politics," *Signs: Journal of Women in Culture and Society* 21, no. 2 (1996): 429–454; Molly Ladd-Taylor, "Love, Work, and the Meanings of Motherhood," *Journal of Women's History* 8, no. 3 (Fall 1996): 219–227; Carol Sternhell, "Motherhood is Powerful," *The Women's Review of Books* 14, no. 7 (April 1997): 5–7.

59. Sylvia Ann Hewlett, *A Lesser Life: The Myth of Women's Liberation in America* (New York: William Morrow, 1986), 184. For critiques of Hewlett's ideas, see Umansky, *Motherhood Reconceived*, 1–2; and Noreen Connell, "Feminists and Families: 'A Lesser Life' and Other Lies," *The Nation* 243, no. 4 (August 16/23, 1986): 106–108.

60. Michele M. Moody-Adams, "Feminism by Any Other Name," in *Feminism and Families*, ed. H. L. Nelson (New York: Routledge, 1997), 77, 78.

61. Dale Spender, *Women of Ideas (And What Men Have Done to Them)* (London: ARK Paperbacks, 1982), 13.

Notes to Chapter 2

1. Mothers with disabilities receive little attention in the feminist social science literature on motherhood. See Susan Shaul, Pamela J. Dowling, and Bernice F. Laden, "Like Other Women: Perspectives of Mothers with Physical Disabilities," in *Women and Disability: The Double Handicap*, ed. M. J. Deegan and N. A. Brooks (New Brunswick, N.J.: Transaction Books, 1985), 133–142.

2. Molly Ladd-Taylor and Lauri Umansky, "Introduction," in *"Bad" Mothers: The Politics of Blame in Twentieth-Century America*, ed. M. Ladd-Taylor and L. Umansky (New York: New York University Press, 1998), 3.

3. See the special issue on lesbian mothering of the *Journal of the Association for Research on Mothering* 1, no. 2 (fall/winter 1999). See also Gillian A. Dunne, "Opting into Motherhood: Lesbians Blurring the Boundaries and Transforming the Meaning of Parenthood and Kinship," *Gender & Society* 14, no. 1 (February 2000): 11–35; and Susan E. Dalton and Denise D. Bielby, " 'That's Our Kind of Constellation': Lesbian Mothers Negotiate Institutionalized Understandings of Gender within the Family," *Gender & Society* 14, no. 1 (February 2000): 36–61.

4. Sandra Pollack, "Lesbian Parents: Claiming Our Visibility," in *Feminist Frontiers III*, ed. L. Richardson and V. Taylor (New York: McGraw-Hill, 1993), 264; William B. Rubenstein, *Sexual Orientation and the Law: Cases and Materials* (St. Paul, Minn.: West, 1997), 801.

5. Ellen Lewin, *Lesbian Mothers: Accounts of Gender in American Culture* (Ithaca, N.Y.: Cornell University Press, 1993), 1.

6. Ibid., 19.

7. Lauri Umansky, *Motherhood Reconceived: Feminism and the Legacies of the Sixties* (New York: New York University Press, 1996), 42.

8. Kath Weston, *Families We Choose: Lesbians, Gays, Kinship* (New York: Columbia University Press, 1991), 168–169. On the emergence of the gay liberation movement in 1969, see John D'Emilio and Estelle B. Freedman, *Intimate Matters: A History of Sexuality in America* (New York: Harper & Row, 1988), 318–325.

9. Weston, *Families We Choose*, 168. Arlene Stein, *Sex and Sensibility: Stories of a Lesbian Generation* (Berkeley: University of California Press, 1997), 133.

10. Lewin, *Lesbian Mothers*, 199, note 1.

11. William B. Rubenstein, *Lesbians, Gay Men, and the Law*, (New York: New Press, 1993), 492.

12. Pollack, "Lesbian Parents," 264.

13. Lewin, *Lesbian Mothers*, 3.

14. Christine J. Allison, "The Making of a 'Bad' Mother: A Lesbian Mother and Her Daughters," in *"Bad" Mothers*, 254.

15. Rubenstein, *Lesbians, Gay Men, and the Law*, 492, 500–502. See Rubenstein, *Sexual Orientation and the Law*, 813–823, for the Sharon Bottoms case, in which the per se and nexus tests were used at different times. In 1995, the Virginia Supreme Court upheld Bottoms's loss of custody of her child to Bottoms's mother, in part because of social condemnation the child would experience due to his mother's lesbianism.

16. Charlotte J. Patterson, "Children of Lesbian and Gay Parents," in *Advances in Clinical Child Psychology*, ed. T. H. Ollendick and R. J. Prinz (New York: Plenum Press, 1997), 19: 246.

17. Ibid., 243–245; 264. A major limitation of the research to date is that differences of race, ethnicity, and social class have not been studied (247–248).

18. Ibid., 245.

19. *M.P. v. S.P.*, Superior Court of New Jersey, Appellate Division, 1979, reprinted in Rubenstein, *Sexual Orientation and the Law*, 832.

20. Pollack, "Lesbian Parents," 267.

21. Laura Benkov, "Yes, I Am a Swan: Reflections on Families Headed by Lesbians and Gay Men," in *Mothering against the Odds: Diverse Voices of Contemporary Mothers*, ed. C. G. Coll, J. L. Surrey, and K. Weingarten (New York: Guilford Press, 1998), 117.

22. Sarah Bruckner, "Two Moms, Two Kids, and a Dog" in *Mother Journeys: Feminists Write about Mothering*, ed. M. T. Reddy, M. Roth, and A. Sheldon (Minneapolis: Spinsters Ink., 1994), 35–46; Cheryl Muzio, "Lesbians Choosing Children: Creating Families, Creating Narratives," *Journal of Feminist Family Therapy* 7, no. 3/4 (1995), 33–45.

23. Ronald Smothers, "Gay Couples Cleared to Adopt Jointly," *New York Times*, December 18, 1997, A25.

24. Benkov, "Yes, I Am a Swan," 125.

25. See, for example, Rubenstein, *Sexual Orientation and the Law*, 881, on the 1989 antidiscrimination statute in Massachusetts, which does not cover foster placements.

26. Phyllis Burke, *Family Values: A Lesbian Mother's Fight for Her Son* (New York: Vintage Books, 1993), xi–xii. See also Linda Mulley, "Lesbian Motherhood and Other Small Acts of Resistance," in *Politics of Motherhood: Activist Voices from Left to Right*, ed. A. Jetter, A. Orleck, and D. Taylor (Hanover, N.H.: University Press of New England, 1997), 311–321; Julie Ainslie and Kathryn M. Feltey, "Definitions and Dynamics of Motherhood and Family in Lesbian Communities," *Marriage and Family Review* 17, no. 1–2 (fall 1991): 63–86; and Virginia Casper, Steven Schultz, and Elaine Wickens, "Breaking the Silences: Lesbian and Gay Parents and the Schools," *Teachers College Record* 94, no. 1 (fall 1992): 109–137.

27. Marc Lacey, "Teen-age Birth Rate in U.S. Falls Again," *New York Times*, October 27, 1999, A14.

28. Kristin Luker, *Dubious Conceptions: The Politics of Teenage Pregnancy* (Cambridge: Harvard University Press, 1996), 142–143.

29. Note, however, that some teen mothers who might otherwise be deemed exemplary have experienced discrimination. Two seventeen-year-old mothers, for example, sued their local school board, claiming they were denied membership in the National Honor Society because they were pregnant (Ethan Bronner, "Lawsuit on Sex Bias by Two Mothers, 17," *New York Times*, August 6, 1998, A12).

30. Sue Books, "Fear and Loathing: The Moral Dimensions of the Politicization of Teen Pregnancy," *Journal of Thought* 31, no. 1 (spring 1996): 9. See also Susan Douglas and Meredith Michaels, "The Mommy Wars: How the Media Turned Motherhood into a Cat Fight," *Ms.* 10, no. 2 (February/March 2000): 62–68. This article compares the media's idealization of celebrity moms to its demonization of welfare moms.

31. Luker, *Dubious Conceptions*, 11, 81–82; Harrell R. Rodgers, Jr., *Poor Women, Poor Children: American Poverty in the 1990s*, 3rd ed. (Armonk, N.Y.: M. E. Sharpe, 1996) 158.

32. Lacey, "Teen-age Birth Rate in U.S. Falls Again," A14; Tamar Lewin, "Birth Rates for Teen-agers Declined Sharply in the 90's," *New York Times*, May 1, 1998, A17. Lewin notes, "While black teen-agers still have babies at almost twice the rate of whites, their birth rate declined 21 percent from 1991 to 1996, and is now at the lowest level ever reported. There were 91.7 births for every 1,000 black teen-age women ages 15 to 19 in 1996, while whites had 48.4 per 1,000, and Hispanic teen-agers had 101.6" (A17). While teen birth rates have declined, teen mothers in the 1950s were much more likely to be married, at least by the time they gave birth, than teen mothers today (Luker, *Dubious Conceptions*, 8). "Rates of birth to unmarried mothers have indeed climbed dramatically over the past 20 years. This rise, though, has been most dramatic among those in the 20- to 24-year and 24- to 29-year age ranges, not among those in their teenage years" (Patricia Flanagan, "Teen Mothers: Countering the Myths of Dysfunction and Developmental Disruption," in *Mothering Against the Odds*, 240).

33. Luker *Dubious Conceptions*, 7.

34. Ibid., 124, 110, 111.

35. Rickie Solinger, Review essay on *Dubious Conceptions* in *Contemporary Sociology* 26, no. 1 (January 1997): 3; emphasis in original.

36. Ruth Sidel, *Keeping Women and Children Last* (New York: Penguin, 1996), 87–88.

37. Demie Kurz, *For Richer, For Poorer: Mothers Confront Divorce* (New York: Routledge, 1995), 30.

38. Luker, *Dubious Conceptions*, 124, 126–127. See also Sidel, *Keeping Women and Children Last*, 90–92, for statistical breakdowns on women who are employed and simultaneously receive welfare; women who alternate between employment and welfare; and those who are more "welfare-reliant."

39. Linda Gordon, *Pitied But Not Entitled: Single Mothers and the History of Welfare 1890–1935* (New York: Free Press, 1994), 11–12.

40. Valerie Polakow, *Lives on the Edge: Single Mothers and Their Children in the Other America* (Chicago: University of Chicago Press, 1993), 79–80.

41. Luker, *Dubious Conceptions*, 41.

42. Flanagan, "Teen Mothers," 239.

43. Luker, *Dubious Conceptions*, 135.

44. See also Randall Stokes and Albert Chevan, "Female-Headed Families: Social and Economic Context of Racial Differences," *Journal of Urban Affairs* 18, no. 3 (1996): 245–268.

45. Luker, *Dubious Conceptions*, 141–142.

46. Giving a child up for adoption has become less and less common for all women since the 1960s. By the late 1980s, only 3 percent of white women and 1 percent of black women were giving up their children for adoption. Young women who surrender their children are probably more like those who abort and less like those who keep their babies. They usually come from well-off families, do well in school, and have high aspirations (Luker, *Dubious Conceptions*, 162). See also Rickie Solinger, "Race and 'Value': Black and White Illegitimate Babies in the U.S.A., 1945–1965," *Gender & History* 4, no. 3 (autumn 1992): 343–363.

47. Luker, *Dubious Conceptions*, 170–171.

48. Rickie Solinger, "Poisonous Choice," in *"Bad" Mothers*," 394; emphasis in original.

49. Gwendolyn Mink, *Welfare's End* (Ithaca, N.Y.: Cornell University Press, 1998), 65.

50. Katha Pollitt, "Let Them Sell Lemonade," *The Nation* 268, no. 6 (February 15, 1999): 11.

51. Lauren M. Rich and Sun-bin Kim, "Patterns of Later Life Education among Teenage Mothers," *Gender & Society* 13, no. 6 (December 1999): 814–815.

52. Dorothy Roberts, *Killing the Black Body: Race, Reproduction, and the Meaning of Liberty* (New York: Pantheon Books, 1997), 153.

53. Laura E. Gomez, *Misconceiving Mothers: Legislators, Prosecutors, and the Politics of Prenatal Drug Exposure* (Philadelphia: Temple University Press, 1997), 11–12, 14, 29; Roberts, *Killing the Black Body*, 155, 153.

54. Gomez, *Misconceiving Mothers*, 76–78. Prosecutions tapered off during the early and mid-1990s. Drew Humphries, *Crack Mothers: Pregnancy, Drugs, and the Media* (Columbus: Ohio State University Press, 1999), chapter 3.

55. Gomez, *Misconceiving Mothers*, 17; Roberts, *Killing the Black Body*, 158. See Drew Humphries, *Crack Mothers: Pregnancy, Drugs, and the Media* (Columbus: Ohio State University Press, 1999), chapter 5, for a summary of research on drug-affected children.

56. Roberts, *Killing the Black Body*, 156.

57. Gomez, *Misconceiving Mothers*, 17. For a close look at such mothers' perspectives, see Phyllis L. Baker and Amy Carson, " 'I Take Care of My Kids': Mothering Practices of Substance-Abusing Women," *Gender & Society* 13, no. 3 (June 1999): 347–363; Claire E. Sterk, *Fast Lives: Women Who Use Crack Cocaine* (Philadelphia: Temple University Press, 1999), chapter 4; and Sheigla Murphy and Marsha Rosenbaum, *Pregnant Women on Drugs: Combating Stereotypes and Stigma* (New Brunswick, N.J.: Rutgers University Press, 1999).

58. Gomez, *Misconceiving Mothers*, 25, 18.

59. Roberts, *Killing the Black Body*, 173. See also, Gomez, *Misconceiving Mothers*, 77.

60. Roberts, *Killing the Black Body*, 173–174, 164–165.

61. Ibid., 175, 172; emphasis in original.

62. Gomez, *Misconceiving Mothers*, 101. The general failure of legislators and prosecutors to criminalize prenatal drug exposure has hinged in large part on the courts' refusal to treat the fetus as a child. South Carolina is the exception in this regard (110). Indeed, in May 1998, the U.S. Supreme Court declined to hear a case, leaving intact

the South Carolina law that allows a pregnant woman to be prosecuted for endangering her fetus. *Ms.* 9, no. 2 (September/October 1998): 14.

63. Roberts, *Killing the Black Body*, 159–160. See also Gomez, *Misconceiving Mothers*, 75; and Humphries, *Crack Mothers*, 129–139.

64. Roberts, *Killing the Black Body*, 187–190; Humphries, *Crack Mothers*, 118–126; Sterk, *Fast Lives*, 133–143. Nonetheless, when women do have access to high-quality programs, such programs can be very effective. Mary R. Haack, *Drug-Dependent Mothers and Their Children: Issues in Public Policy and Public Health* (New York: Springer, 1997), xviii.

65. Gomez, *Misconceiving Mothers*, 2.

66. Susan Bordo, *Unbearable Weight: Feminism, Western Culture, and the Body* (Berkeley: University of California Press, 1993), 72–79. See also Katha Pollitt, " 'Fetal Rights': A New Assault on Feminism," in *"Bad" Mothers*, 285–298; and Barbara Katz Rothman, *Recreating Motherhood: Ideology and Technology in a Patriarchal Society* (New York: W. W. Norton, 1989), 159–168.

67. Roberts, *Killing the Black Body*, 10–19 and chapter 4; Humphries, *Crack Mothers*, 11–12.

68. Roberts, *Killing the Black Body*, 183, 184. The 1996 infant mortality rates are from U.S. Department of Health and Human Services, "Facts on Infant Mortality," (www.healthystart.net.factualcharts/imchart4_b.htm [11–16–98]). Infant mortality rates include deaths up to one year; they do not include stillbirths.

69. In 1993, 22.7 percent of children under eighteen were poor in the United States. Among black children, 46.1 percent were poor; among white children, 17.8 percent; and among Hispanic children, 40.9 percent (Rodgers, *Poor Women, Poor Children*, 10–13; 112, 122–125).

70. For a good discussion of the limits of foster care see Annette R. Appell, "On Fixing 'Bad' Mothers and Saving Their Children," in *"Bad" Mothers*, 356–380.

71. Books, "Fear and Loathing," 15; Polakow, *Lives on the Edge*, 43–44; Ladd-Taylor and Umansky, "Introduction," in *"Bad" Mothers*, 2.

Notes to Chapter 3

1. Jessie Bernard, *The Future of Motherhood* (New York: Dial Press, 1974), vii.

2. Thomas S. Weisner and Ronald Gallimore, "My Brother's Keeper: Child and Sibling Caretaking," *Current Anthropology* 18, no. 2 (June 1977): 170.

3. Bernard, *The Future of Motherhood*, 9, 14.

4. Adrienne Rich, *Of Woman Born: Motherhood as Experience and Institution*, 10th anniversary ed. (New York: W. W. Norton, 1986 [1976]), 34, 13. Writing in the tradition of radical feminism, Rich defines patriarchy as an "identifiable sexual hierarchy" that has persisted through much of human history and within diverse social and political systems (xxiv). Other feminists, particularly those writing in the socialist feminist tradition, view patriarchy as a particular social form in which men ruled households as fathers, and by extension ruled churches, cities, and nations. In this view, patriarchy (but not male-dominance) came to an end with the Industrial Revolution when production moved out of the home. See, for example, Barbara Ehrenreich and Deirdre English, *For Her Own Good: 150 Years of the Experts' Advice to Women* (New York: An-

chor Books, 1979), 7–12. See my chapter 1 of this book for further discussion of the concept of patriarchy.

5. Glenda Riley, *Inventing the American Woman: An Inclusive History*, vol. 2, *Since 1877*, 2nd ed. (Wheeling, Ill.: Harlan Davidson, 1995), 365.

6. Rich, *Of Woman Born*, 276–277.

7. Evelyn Nakano Glenn, Grace Chang, and Linda Rennie Forcey, eds., *Mothering: Ideology, Experience, and Agency* (New York: Routledge, 1994); Rima D. Apple and Janet Golden, eds., *Mothers & Motherhood: Readings in American History* (Columbus: Ohio University Press, 1997).

8. Elizabeth Badinter, *The Myth of Motherhood: An Historical View of the Maternal Instinct* (London: Souvenir Press, 1981), 40–43, 58–72.

9. Edward Shorter, *The Making of the Modern Family* (New York: Basic Books, 1975), 26–28; Badinter, *The Myth of Motherhood*, 29–39; Sharon Hays, *The Cultural Contradictions of Motherhood* (New Haven, Conn.: Yale University Press, 1996), 23–25; Philippe Ariès, *Centuries of Childhood: A Social History of Family Life*, trans. R. Baldick (New York: Vintage, 1962), 356–357.

10. Robert H. Bremmer, ed., *Children and Youth in America: A Documentary History*. Vol. I: 1600–1865 (Cambridge: Harvard University Press, 1970), 149.

11. Ariès, *Centuries of Childhood*, 47, 127.

12. Badinter, *The Myth of Motherhood*, chapter 5; Shorter, *The Making of the Modern Family*, 181–204; Hays, *The Cultural Contradictions of Motherhood*, 25; Ariès, *Centuries of Childhood*.

13. Molly Ladd-Taylor and Lauri Umansky, "Introduction," in *"Bad" Mothers: The Politics of Blame in Twentieth-Century America,* ed. M. Ladd-Taylor and L. Umansky (New York: New York University Press, 1998), 6–7; Sara M. Evans, *Born for Liberty: A History of Women in America* (New York: The Free Press, 1989), 68–70; Nancy F. Cott, *The Bonds of Womanhood: "Woman's Sphere" in New England, 1780–1835* (New Haven, Conn.: Yale University Press, 1977), 64–74.

14. Ladd-Taylor and Umanski, "Introduction," 7; Linda K. Kerber, *Women of the Republic: Intellect and Ideology in Revolutionary America* (Chapel Hill: University of North Carolina Press, 1980), 227–231, 283–287; Bernard Wishy, *The Child and the Republic: The Dawn of Modern American Child Nurture* (Philadelphia: University of Pennsylvania Press, 1968), vii, 26–32.

15. Ladd-Taylor and Umanski, "Introduction," 7; Cott, *The Bonds of Womanhood*, 74–75, 90–91, 104–105, 118–120.

16. Michael Grossberg, "Who Gets the Child? Custody, Guardianship, and the Rise of a Judicial Patriarchy in the Nineteenth Century," *Feminist Studies* 9, no. 2 (summer 1983): 235–260.

17. Evelyn Nakano Glenn, "Social Constructions of Mothering: A Thematic Overview," in *Mothering*, 14–15.

18. Rickie Solinger, "Poisonous Choice," in *"Bad" Mothers*, 382.

19. Glenn, "Social Constructions of Mothering," 5–6. "In 1880, 73.3 percent of black single women and 35.4 percent of black married women in seven southern cities reported paid jobs. Among white women only 23.8 percent of the single and 7.3 percent of the married reported paid employment. Even where family income, husband's employment, and demographic factors are held constant, black women were still far more

likely to work than white women" (Alice Kessler-Harris, *Out to Work: A History of Wage-Earning Women in the United States* [New York: Oxford University Press, 1982], 123).

20. Hays, *The Cultural Contradictions of Motherhood*, 36; Christine Stansell, *City of Women: Sex and Class in New York, 1789–1860* (New York: Alfred A. Knopf, 1986), 11–18, 52–53.

21. Ladd-Taylor and Umansky, "Introduction," 8.

22. Molly Ladd-Taylor, *Mother-Work: Women, Child Welfare and the State, 1890–1930* (Urbana: University of Illinois Press, 1994), 4.

23. Hays, *The Cultural Contradictions of Motherhood*, 39.

24. Ladd-Taylor and Umansky, "Introduction," 9, 10.

25. Ruby Takanishi, "Childhood as a Social Issue: Historical Roots of Contemporary Child Advocacy Movements," *Journal of Social Issues* 34, no. 2 (1978): 8–28; Valerie Polakow, *Lives on the Edge: Single Mothers and their Children in the Other America* (Chicago: University of Chicago Press, 1993), 32; Hays, *The Cultural Contradictions of Motherhood*, 41; Ladd-Taylor, *Mother-Work*, chapters 2 and 3; Molly Ladd-Taylor, *Raising a Baby the Government Way: Mothers' Letters to the Children's Bureau 1915–1932* (New Brunswick N.J.: Rutgers University Press, 1986), 1–2.

26. Polakow, *Lives on the Edge*, 31–32. See also Linda Gordon, *Heroes of Their Own Lives: The Politics and History of Family Violence, Boston 1880–1960* (New York: Viking, 1988).

27. Hays, *The Cultural Contradictions of Motherhood*, 42.

28. Lynn Y. Weiner, *From Working Girl to Working Mother: The Female Labor Force in the United States, 1820–1980* (Chapel Hill: University of North Carolina Press, 1985), 83.

29. Alice Kessler-Harris, "The Debate over Equality for Women in the Workplace: Recognizing Differences," in *Families and Work*, ed. N. Gerstel and H. E. Gross (Philadelphia: Temple University Press, 1987), 520–539.

30. Hays, *The Cultural Contradictions of Motherhood*, 43; Weiner, *From Working Girl to Working Mother*, 103.

31. Ladd-Taylor and Umansky, "Introduction," 11.

32. Linda Gordon, *Pitied But Not Entitled: Single Mothers and the History of Welfare*, 1980–1935 (New York: Free Press, 1994), 142, 114, 136, 142.

33. Ladd–Taylor and Umansky, "Introduction," 10; Ehrenreich and English, *For Her Own Good*, chapters 6 and 7.

34. Hays, *The Cultural Contradictions of Motherhood*, 45.

35. Ibid., 47–48; Ladd-Taylor and Umansky, "Introduction," 11; Ehrenreich and English, *For Her Own Good*, 225–235.

36. Jacquelyn Litt, "Pediatrics and the Development of Middle-Class Motherhood," *Research in the Sociology of Health Care* 10 (1993), 161, 162, 164, 165, 168.

37. Barbara Miller Solomon, *In the Company of Educated Women: A History of Women and Higher Education in America* (New Haven, Conn.: Yale University Press, 1985), 63.

38. Nancy F. Cott, *The Grounding of Modern Feminism* (New Haven, Conn.: Yale University Press, 1987), 165. Carolyn M. Morell, *Unwomanly Conduct: The Challenges of Intentional Childlessness* (New York: Routledge, 1994), 19–20. Morell cites a June 1988 U.S. Census Bureau document reporting that "fifteen percent of women forty to forty-four years old were childless" at that time (11). See also Kathleen Gerson, *Hard Choices:*

How Women Decide about Work, Career, and Motherhood (Berkeley: University of California Press, 1985), table A.5, 236.

39. Litt, "Pediatrics and the Development of Middle-Class Motherhood," 167.

40. Barbara Reskin and Irene Padavic, *Women and Men at Work* (Thousand Oaks, Calif.: Pine Forge Press, 1994), 24; and "Facts on Working Women," in *Perspectives: Women's Studies*, ed. Renae Bredin (Boulder, Colo.: Coursewise, 1998), 3.

41. Alice Abel Kemp, *Women's Work: Degraded and Devalued* (Englewood Cliffs, N.J.: Prentice-Hall, 1994), 173.

42. In 1964, 48.5 percent of black women were in the labor force compared to 38.7 percent of all women (the majority of whom were white). By 1991 that gap had closed; 57 percent of black women were employed compared to 57.3 percent of all women. In that same year, 52.3 percent of Hispanic women worked for wages (Kemp, *Women's Work*, 177).

43. Ladd-Taylor and Umansky, "Introduction," 14.

44. Mimi Abramovitz, *Regulating the Lives of Women: Social Welfare Policy from Colonial Times to the Present*, rev. ed. (Boston: South End Press, 1996), 318–319; Frances Fox Piven and Richard A. Cloward, *Regulating the Poor: The Functions of Public Welfare* (New York: Pantheon Books, 1971), 134, 138, 308–309; Gwendolyn Mink, *Welfare's End* (Ithaca, N.Y.: Cornell University Press, 1998), 47–48; Joanne L. Goodwin, " 'Employable Mothers' and 'Suitable Work': A Reevaluation of Welfare and Wage Earning for Women in the Twentieth-Century United States," in *Mothers & Motherhood*, 539–564.

45. Ladd-Taylor and Umansky, "Introduction," 13.

46. Susan Bordo, *Unbearable Weight: Feminism, Western Culture, and the Body* (Berkeley: University of California Press, 1993), 121–122.

47. Hays, *The Cultural Contradictions of Motherhood*, 50, 51, 54.

48. John D'Emilio and Estelle B. Freedman, *Intimate Matters: A History of Sexuality in America* (New York: Harper & Row, 1988), 250.

49. Dorothy Roberts, *Killing the Black Body: Race, Reproduction, and the Meaning of Liberty* (New York: Pantheon Books, 1997), 97, 231–232.

50. Philip R. Reilly, *The Surgical Solution: A History of Involuntary Sterilization in the United States* (Baltimore. Md.: Johns Hopkins University Press, 1991), 94–95.

51. Roberts, *Killing the Black Body*, 93, 96, 97.

52. Rich, *Of Woman Born*, xx.

53. For example, Christina Baker Kline, ed., *Child of Mine: Writers Talk about the First Year of Motherhood* (New York: Delta [Dell Publishing], 1997); Camille Peri and Kate Moses, eds., *Mothers Who Think: Tales of Real-Life Parenthood* (New York: Villard, 1999); Traci Dyer, ed., *Mother Voices: Real Women Write about Growing into Motherhood* (Naperville, Ill.: Sourcebooks, 1999); Amy Benson Brown and Kathryn Read McPherson, eds., *The Reality of Breastfeeding: Reflections by Contemporary Women* (Westport, Conn.: Bergin & Garvey, 1998). Many mothers have published personal narratives in the past, but there has been an explosion of such writing in recent years.

54. See also Harriet Edwards, *How Could You? Mothers Without Custody of Their Children* (Freedom, Calif: The Crossing Press, 1989); and Rosie Jackson, *Mothers Who Leave: Behind the Myth of Women Without Their Children* (London: HarperCollins, Pandora, 1994).

55. Martha McMahon, *Engendering Motherhood: Identity and Self-Transformation in Women's Lives* (New York: Guilford Press, 1995), 176, 175, 176; emphasis in original.

56. Verta Taylor, *Rock-a-by Baby: Feminism, Self-Help, and Postpartum Depression* (New York: Routledge, 1996), 39.

57. See Wendy Hollway and Bird Featherstone, eds., *Mothering and Ambivalence* (London: Routledge, 1997).

58. Shari L. Thurer, *The Myths of Motherhood: How Culture Reinvents the Good Mother* (New York: Houghton Mifflin, 1994), xxiv.

59. Hays, *The Cultural Contradictions of Motherhood*, 134–148.

60. Denise A. Segura, "Working at Motherhood: Chicana and Mexican Immigrant Mothers and Employment," in *Mothering*, 212.

61. Alison I. Griffith and Dorothy E. Smith, "Constructing Cultural Knowledge: Mothering as Discourse," in *Women and Education: A Canadian Perspective*, ed. J. S. Gaskell and A. T. McLaren (Calgary, Alberta: Detselig Enterprises Limited, 1987), 99–100. Stephanie Coontz points out that the way teachers assign homework (for example, during the week versus on weekends) can end up advantaging one family form or another (*The Way We Really Are: Coming to Terms with America's Changing Families* [New York: Basic Books, 1997]), 170–171).

62. See, for example, Signithia Fordham, *Blacked Out: Dilemmas of Race, Identity, and Success at Capital High* (Chicago: University of Chicago Press, 1996); Maureen T. Reddy, *Crossing the Color Line: Race, Parenting, and Culture* (New Brunswick, N.J.: Rutgers University Press, 1994), chapter 5.

63. Sharon R. Liff, *No Place Else to Go: Homeless Mothers and Their Children Living in Urban Shelters* (New York: Garland, 1996), 126.

64. Arlie Hochschild, *The Second Shift: Working Parents and the Revolution at Home* (New York: Viking, 1989); Scott Coltrane, *Family Man: Fatherhood, Housework, and Gender Equity* (New York: Oxford University Press, 1996).

65. Lynet Uttal, "Custodial Care, Surrogate Care, and Coordinated Care: Employed Mothers and the Meaning of Child Care," *Gender & Society* 10, no. 3 (June 1996): 291–311.

66. Gwendolyn Mink, *Welfare's End* (Ithaca, N.Y.: Cornell University Press, 1998).

67. Ronnie J. Steinberg, " 'A Want of Harmony': Perspectives on Wage Discrimination and Comparable Worth," in *Comparable Worth and Wage Discrimination: Technical Possibilities and Political Realities*, ed. H. Remick (Philadelphia: Temple University Press, 1984), 23.

68. Mink, *Welfare's End*, 28, 25, 26.

69. Rich, *Of Woman Born*, 280.

Notes to Chapter 4

1. Several authors emphasize the unreliable gender-neutrality of "parenting"; see Susan Rae Paterson, "Against 'Parenting,' " in *Mothering: Essays in Feminist Theory*, ed. J. Trebilcot (New York: Rowman & Allanheld, 1984), 62–69; Anne Woollett and Ann Phoenix, "Motherhood As Pedagogy: Developmental Psychology and the Accounts of Mothers of Young Children" in *Feminisms and Pedagogies of Everyday Life*, ed. C. Luke (Albany: State University of New York Press, 1996), 82.

2. Arlie Russell Hochschild with A. Machung, *The Second Shift* (New York: Viking Press, 1989); Janet Saltzman Chafetz, " 'I Need a (Traditional) Wife!': Employment Family Conflicts," in *Workplace/Women's Place: An Anthology*, ed. D. Dunn (Los Angeles: Roxbury, 1997), 118.

3. Arlene Skolnick and Stacey Rosencrantz, "The New Crusade for the Old Family," *The American Prospect* 18 (summer, 1994): 59–65; Dana Mack, *The Assault on Parenthood: How Our Culture Undermines the Family* (New York: Simon and Schuster, 1997).

4. Sylvia Ann Hewlett and Cornel West, *The War Against Parents: What We Can Do for America's Beleaguered Moms and Dads* (Boston: Houghton Mifflin, 1998), 39.

5. See, for instance, Phyllis L. Baker and Amy Carson, " 'I Take Care of My Kids': Mothering Practices of Substance-Abusing Women," *Gender & Society* 13, no. 3 (June, 1999): 347–363.

6. Sara McLanahan and Gary Sandefur, *Growing Up with a Single Parent: What Hurts, What Helps* (Cambridge: Harvard University Press,1994); David Blankenhorn, *Fatherless America* (New York: Basic Books, 1995); David Popenoe, *Life without Father: Compelling New Evidence That Fatherhood and Marriage Are Indispensable for the Good of Children* (New York: Free Press, 1996).

7. See, for example, John D'Emilio and Estelle B. Freedman, *Intimate Matters: A History of Sexuality in America* (New York: Harper & Row, 1988), 216–217; also, Stephanie J. Shaw, "Mothering under Slavery in the Antebellum South," in *Mothering: Ideology, Experience, and Agency*, ed., E. N. Glenn, G. Chang, and L. R. Forcey (New York: Routledge, 1994).

8. I mean neither to demonize these groups nor to imply they are wholly problematic. Instead, I mean to leave room for the "slippery area between ideals and resources" where "we find gender negotiated, managed, and lived." Sally K. Gallagher and Christian Smith found that evangelical Protestants, for example, "negotiate gender in much the same way others of different or no religious worldviews do—borrowing from, resisting, and participating in the larger structures of which they are part"; see "Symbolic Traditionalism and Pragmatic Egalitarianism: Contemporary Evangelicals, Families, and Gender," *Gender & Society* 13, no. 2 (April 1999): 230.

9. Sylvia Ann Hewlett and Cornel West, "A Parenting Movement," *Tikkun* 13, no. 3 (May/June, 1998): 29–30; this publication identifies Hewlett as the founder and president of the National Parenting Association and West as a member of its board. Also see Wade F. Horn, David Blankenhorn, and Mitchell B. Pearlstein, eds., *The Fatherhood Movement: A Call to Action* (Lanham, Md.: Lexington Books, 1999).

10. Judith Stacey, *In the Name of the Family: Rethinking Family Values in the Postmodern Age* (Boston: Beacon Press, 1996), 54.

11. Http://www.americanvalues.org; 05-28-99; Stacey notes that Popenoe once cochaired the Council on Families with Elshtain; *In the Name of the Family*, 54.

12. Sylvia Ann Hewlett, *When the Bough Breaks: The Cost of Neglecting Our Children* (New York: Basic Books, 1991), ix.

13. David Popenoe, *Disturbing the Nest: Family Change and Decline in Modern Societies* (New York: Aldine de Gruyter, 1988), viii.

14. See note 6.

15. Blankenhorn also likes to cite Popenoe. Among the thirty-seven footnotes for "American Family Dilemmas" are a dozen citations of Popenoe's work; see David Blankenhorn, "American Family Dilemmas," in *Rebuilding the Nest: A New Commitment to the American Family*, ed. D. Blankenhorn, S. Bayme, and J. B. Elshtain (Milwaukee: Family Service America, 1990), 3–25. Popenoe has a chapter ("Family Decline in

America," 39–51) in the same volume, as does Hewlett ("Good News? The Private Sector and Win-Win Scenarios," 207–226).

16. Scott Coltrane, "Family Policy Wonderland" (a review of Margrit Eichler's *Family Shifts*), *Contemporary Sociology* 27, no. 3 (May 1998): 231; Norval Glenn, *Closed Hearts, Closed Minds: The Textbook Story of Marriage* (New York: Institute for American Values, 1997). Coltrane points out that Glenn is director of research for the Council on Families.

17. Barbara Dafoe Whitehead, *The Divorce Culture* (New York: Alfred A. Knopf, 1997), 4.

18. Mack, *The Assault on Parenthood*, 15.

19. Amitai Etzioni, *The Spirit of Community: The Reinvention of American Society* (New York: Touchstone Books, 1994), 2.

20. Mary Midgley and Judith Hughes observe that communitarianism "provide[s] a new impetus for this panic [about familial breakdown] and a new hope for resolution"; see their "Are Families Out of Date?" in *Feminism and Families*, ed. H. L. Nelson (New York: Routledge, 1997), 55. One example of the overlap is the publication of a paper by Glenn from his study of textbooks on the family; see Norval Glenn, "A Textbook Assault on Marriage," *The Responsive Community* 7, no. 4 (fall 1997): 56–66. Another example is that Blankenhorn and Etzioni are among the thirty people on the Senior Advisory Council of the National Commission on Civic Renewal.

21. Francine Deutsch has shown how working-class couples pursue shared childcare by working different shifts, and Anita Ilta Garey has shown how night-shift nurses sometimes pass themselves off as "stay-at-home," as opposed to "working," mothers; see Deutsch, "Traditional Ideologies, Nontraditional Lives," *Sex Roles* 38, no. 5/6 (March 1998): 331–62; Garey, "Constructing Motherhood on the Night Shift: 'Working Mothers' as 'Stay-at-Home Moms,'" *Qualitative Sociology* 18, no. 4 (winter 1995): 415–437.

22. Http://www.slip.net/~ccf/; 05-28-99. For another pointed response to Blankenhorn's and other restorationists' thinking, see Sara Ruddick, "The Idea of Fatherhood," in *Feminism and Families*, 205–220.

23. Kenneth Clatterbaugh, *Contemporary Perspectives on Masculinity: Men, Women, and Politics in Modern Society* (Boulder, Colo.: Westview Press, 1997), 38.

24. Simon Duncan and Rosalind Edwards, "Introduction: A Contextual Approach to Single Mothers and Paid Work," in *Single Mothers in an International Context: Mothers or Workers*, ed. S. Duncan and R. Edwards (London: UCL Press, 1997), 6.

25. See Martha de Acosta, "Single Mothers in the USA: Unsupported Workers and Mothers," in *Single Mothers in an International Context*, 81–113.

26. Paul R. Amato, "Single-Parent Households As Settings for Children's Development, Well-Being, and Attainment: A Social Network/Resources Perspective," *Sociological Studies of Children* 7 (1995): 37.

27. Alisa Burns and Cath Scott, *Mother-Headed Families and Why They Have Increased* (Hillsdale, N.J.: Lawrence Erlbaum Associates, 1994), 193. Amato makes the point this way: "The important consideration . . . is not the number of parents in the household but the number of available adults and the quantity and quality of resources that these adults provide"; (Amato, "Single-Parent Households," 30).

28. Christopher Jencks and Kathryn Edin, "Do Poor Women Have a Right to Bear Children?" *The American Prospect* 20 (winter 1995): 43.

29. Richard Weissbourd, "Divided Families, Whole Children," *The American Prospect* 18 (summer 1994): 68, 70.

30. Arlene Skolnick, "Family Values: The Sequel," *The American Prospect* 32 (May-June 1997): 94.

31. Michael R. Stevenson and Kathryn N. Black, *How Divorce Affects Offspring: A Research Approach* (Dubuque, Iowa: WCB Brown and Benchmark, 1995), 130.

32. Ibid., 127.

33. Sara S. McLanahan, "The Consequences of Single Motherhood," *The American Prospect* 18 (summer 1994): 49.

34. Nancy Folbre, *Who Pays for the Kids? Gender and the Structures of Constraint* (New York: Routledge, 1994), 257.

35. As Judith Stacey puts it, "Dada-ism functions as proxy rhetoric for antifeminist, antigay, xenophobic, and antiwelfare sentiments"; "Dada-ism in the 1990s: Getting Past Baby Talk about Fatherlessness," in *Lost Fathers: The Politics of Fatherlessness in America*, ed. C. R. Daniels (New York: St. Martin's Press, 1998), 73. Dorothy Roberts also discusses the antiwelfare thrust of the New Familism: "The Absent Black Father," in *Lost Fathers*, 157.

36. Robert L. Griswold, *Fatherhood in America: A History* (New York: Basic Books, 1993), 262.

37. Terry Arendell, *Fathers & Divorce* (Thousand Oaks, Calif.: Sage, 1995), 45, 78, 88, 89.

38. Carl E. Bertoia and Janice Drakich, "The Fathers' Rights Movement," in *Fatherhood: Contemporary Theory, Research, and Social Policy*, ed. W. Marsiglio (Thousand Oaks, Calif.: Sage, 1995), 236, 242, 250.

39. Michael A. Messner, *Politics of Masculinities: Men in Movements* (Thousand Oaks, Calif.: Sage, 1997), 27; Ken Abraham, *Who Are the Promise Keepers? Understanding the Christian Men's Movement* (New York: Doubleday, 1997), 57.

40. Donna Minkowitz, "In the Name of the Father," *Ms.* 6, no. 3 (November/December 1995): 69.

41. See Kathleen Gerson, "An Institutional Perspective on Generative Fathering: Creating Social Supports for Parenting Equality," in *Generative Fathering: Beyond Deficit Perspectives*, ed. Alan J. Hawkins and David C. Dollahite (Thousand Oaks, Calif.: Sage, 1997), 42; David C. Dollahite, Alan J. Hawkins, and Sean E. Brotherson, "Fatherwork: A Conceptual Ethic of Fathering as Generative Work," in *Generative Fathering*, 21; Francine M. Deutsch, Julianne B. Lussier, and Laura J. Servis, "Husbands at Home: Predictors of Paternal Participation in Childcare and Housework," *Journal of Personality and Social Psychology* 65, no. 6 (1993): 1154–1166.

42. Irwin Garfinkel, Jennifer L. Hochschild, and Sara S. McLanahan, "Introduction," in *Social Policies, for Children*, ed. Irwin Garfinkel, Jennifer L. Hochschild, and Sara S. McLanahan (Washington, D.C.: The Brookings Institution, 1996), 27.

43. See Stacey, *In the Name of the Family*; see also Richard Collier, *Masculinity, Law and the Family* (London: Routledge, 1995), especially 180–190, 215–251.

44. Wini Breines, Margaret Cerullo, and Judith Stacey, "Social Biology, Family Studies, and Antifeminist Backlash," *Feminist Studies* 4, no. 1 (February 1978): 62.

45. Robert L. Griswold, "The History and Politics of Fatherlessness," in *Lost Fathers*, 29.

Notes to Chapter 5

1. Simone de Beauvoir, *The Second Sex,* trans. H. M. Parshley (1949; New York: Bantam Books, 1961), 159, 164, 165.

2. Nancy F. Cott, *The Grounding of Modern Feminism* (New Haven, Conn.: Yale University Press, 1987), 20.

3. John D'Emilio and Estelle B. Freedman, *Intimate Matters: A History of Sexuality in America* (New York: Harper & Row, 1989), xvi.

4. Lauri Umansky, *Motherhood Reconceived: Feminism and the Legacies of the Sixties* (New York: New York University Press, 1996), 27–29.

5. Michelle Fine, *Disruptive Voices: The Possibilities of Feminist Research* (Ann Arbor: University of Michigan Press, 1992), 34–37.

6. D'Emilio and Freedman, *Intimate Matters*, 358.

7. Norma Coates, "Moms Don't Rock: The Popular Demonization of Courtney Love," in *"Bad" Mothers: The Politics of Blame in Twentieth-Century America*, ed. M. Ladd-Taylor and L. Umansky (New York: New York University Press, 1998), 326, 328, 329, 330, 331.

8. Ellen Lewin, *Lesbian Mothers: Accounts of Gender in American Culture* (Ithaca, N.Y.: Cornell University Press, 1993), 166, 169–170.

9. Renee A. Monson, "State-ing Sex and Gender: Collecting Information from Mothers and Fathers in Paternity Cases," *Gender & Society* 11, no. 3 (June 1997): 284, 285.

10. Gwendolyn Mink, *Welfare's End* (Ithaca, N.Y.: Cornell University Press, 1998), 90–93, 43.

11. Sharon Thompson, " 'Drastic Entertainments': Teenage Mothers' Signifying Narratives," in *Uncertain Terms: Negotiating Gender in American Culture*, ed. F. Ginsburg and A. L. Tsing (Boston: Beacon Press, 1990), 278.

12. Jane Flax, "Mothers and Daughters Revisited," in *Daughtering and Mothering: Female Subjectivity Reanalysed*, ed. J. van Mens-Verhulet, K. Schreurs, and L. Woertman (London: Routledge, 1993), 149. On Ruddick's theorizing, see chapter 1 of this book.

13. Starhawk, "The Sacredness of Pleasure," in *Bisexual Politics: Theories, Queries, and Visions*, ed. N. Tucker (New York: Haworth Press, 1995), 327. Also see Susan Griffin, *The Eros of Everyday Life: Essays on Ecology, Gender, and Society* (New York: Anchor Books, 1996), 52. Griffin says eros is "at the heart of existence."

14. Audre Lorde, "Uses of the Erotic: The Erotic as Power," in *Sister Outsider: Essays and Speeches* (Freedom, Calif.: The Crossing Press, 1984), 55, 53.

15. For a discussion of Barthes' notion of *jouissance* in connection with *plaisir*, see John Fiske, *Understanding Popular Culture* (1989; London: Routledge, 1996), 51, 54–56.

16. Judith Butler, *Gender Trouble: Feminism and the Subversion of Identity* (New York: Routledge, 1990).

17. Flax, "Mothers and daughters revisited," 148.

18. Alison Hawthorne Deming, *Temporary Homelands: Essays on Nature, Spirit and Place* (1994; New York: Picador, 1996), 37.

19. Sigmund Freud perhaps best theorizes the extent and ramifications of such siphoning; see *Civilization and Its Discontents*, trans. J. Strachey (1930; New York: W. W. Norton, 1962).

20. Sally Hacker, *Pleasure, Power, and Technology: Some Tales of Gender, Engineering, and the Cooperative Workplace* (Boston: Unwin Hyman, 1989), xvi, 45; also see Claudia Springer, *Electronic Eros: Bodies and Desire in the Postindustrial Age* (Austin: University of Texas Press, 1996).

21. Adrienne Rich, *Of Woman Born: Motherhood as Experience and Institution* (New York: Bantam Books, 1977), 289.

22. Greta Gaard, "Towards a Queer Ecofeminism," *Hypatia* 12, no. 1 (winter 1997): 133.

23. Arundhati Roy, *The God of Small Things* (New York: HarperPerennial, 1998), 210.

24. See also Kate Moses, "A Mother's Body," in *Mothers Who Think: Tales of Real-life Parenthood,* ed. C. Peri and K. Moses (New York: Villard, 1999), 176–181.

25. Iris Marion Young, "Breasted Experience: The Look and the Feeling," in *The Politics of Women's Bodies: Sexuality, Appearance, and Behavior*, ed. R. Weitz (1992; New York: Oxford University Press, 1998), 133.

26. Barbara Katz Rothman, *Recreating Motherhood: Ideology and Technology in a Patriarchal Society* (New York: W. W. Norton, 1989), 100.

27. Pam Carter, "Breast Feeding and the Social Construction of Heterosexuality, or 'What Breasts Are Really For,' " in *Sex, Sensibility and the Gendered Body*, ed. J. Holland and L. Adkins (New York: St. Martin's Press, 1996), 103.

28. Young, "Breasted Experience," 129.

29. Susan Bordo, *Unbearable Weight: Feminism, Western Culture, and the Body* (Berkeley: University of California Press, 1993), 20.

30. Young, "Breasted Experience," 129.

31. Carter, "Breast Feeding," 100.

32. Young, "Breasted Experience," 132.

33. Http://www3.islandnet.com/~bedford/br-fem.html; 11/06/98; emphasis added.

34. Naomi Baumslag and Dia L. Michels, *Milk, Money, and Madness: The Culture and Politics of Breastfeeding* (Westport, Conn.: Bergin & Garvey, 1995), xxxi.

35. Young, "Breasted Experience," 128; also see Carter, "Breast Feeding," 116.

36. Young, "Breasted Experience," 133.

37. Carter, "Breast Feeding," 104; Pam Carter, *Feminism, Breasts and Breast-Feeding* (New York: St. Martin's Press, 1996), 232.

38. Carter, "Breast Feeding," 150.

39. Carter, *Feminism, Breasts, and Breastfeeding*, 141, 142. See also Amy Benson Brown and Kathryn Read McPherson, eds., *The Reality of Breastfeeding: Reflections by Contemporary Women* (Westport, Conn.: Bergin and Garvey, 1998). In this collection of personal narratives, many women mention the sensual aspects of breastfeeding. They also discuss the difficulties of breastfeeding, such as not having enough milk, getting infections (mastitis), and becoming exhausted from sleepless nights.

40. For example, Janet Shibley Hyde, John D. DeLamater, E. Ashby Plant, and Janis M. Byrd, "Sexuality during pregnancy and the year postpartum," *The Journal of Sex Research* 33, no. 2 (1996): 143–151.

41. Cindy A. Stearns, "Breastfeeding and the Good Maternal Body," *Gender & Society* 13, no. 3 (June 1999): 312, 313.

42. Ibid., 312; Baumslag and Michels, *Milk, Money, and Madness*, 235–236.

43. Robbie Pfeufer Kahn, *Bearing Meaning: The Language of Birth* (Urbana: University of Illinois Press, 1995), 361.

44. Stearns, "Breastfeeding and the Good Maternal Body," 319.

45. Young, "Breasted Experience," 134.

46. Kahn, *Bearing Meaning*, 367, 368.

47. Linda M. Blum, *At the Breast: Ideologies of Breastfeeding and Motherhood in the Contemporary United States* (Boston: Beacon Press, 1999), 167–171.

48. Young, "Breasted Experience," 134.

49. Carter, *Feminism, Breasts, and Breastfeeding*, 134, 158.

50. Carter, "Breast Feeding," 105.

51. Lauri Umansky, "Breastfeeding in the 1990s: The Karen Carter Case and the Politics of Maternal Sexuality," in *"Bad" Mothers*, 299–309.

52. Mira Crouch and Lenore Manderson find that new mothers sometimes have "the experience of 'falling in love' with their infant." *New Motherhood: Cultural and Personal Transitions in the 1980s* (Langhorne, Pa.: Gordon and Breach Science Publishers, 1993), 117. These researchers studied Australian mothers.

53. George Ritzer, *Enchanting a Disenchanted World: Revolutionizing the Means of Consumption* (Thousand Oaks, Calif.: Pine Forge Press, 1999).

54. Barbara Stern and Morris B. Holbrook, "Gender and Genre in the Interpretation of Advertising Text," in *Gender Issues and Consumer Behavior*, ed. J. A. Costa (Thousand Oaks, Calif.: Sage, 1994), 11–41.

55. Ellen Seiter, *Sold Separately: Children and Parents in Consumer Culture* (New Brunswick, N.J.: Rutgers University Press, 1995), 3.

56. Georg Simmel, "On Flirtation," in *Georg Simmel: On Women, Sexuality, and Love*, tr. Guy Oakes (New Haven, Conn: Yale University Press, 1984), 143, 151.

57. Barbara Ehrenreich and Deirdre English, *For Her Own Good: 150 Years of the Experts' Advice to Women* (New York: Anchor Books, 1979), 221–222.

58. Betty Friedan, *The Feminine Mystique* (New York: Dell, 1963).

59. Nancy Chodorow, *The Reproduction of Mothering: Psychoanalysis and the Sociology of Gender* (Berkeley: University of California Press, 1978).

60. Jessica Benjamin, "The First Bond," in *The Women and Language Debate*, ed. C. Roman, S. Juhasz, and C. Miller (1988; New Brunswick, N.J.: Rutgers University Press, 1994), 171.

61. Kahn, *Bearing Meaning*, 376–377.

Notes to Chapter 6

1. In 1995, there were 311 abortions for every 1,000 live births in the United States. Tamar Lewin, "Abortion Rate Declined Again in '95, U.S. Says, But Began Rising Last Year," *New York Times*, December 6, 1997, A10.

2. See, for example, Rose Wiles, " 'I'm Not Fat, I'm Pregnant': The Impact of Pregnancy on Fat Women's Body Image," in *Women and Health: Feminist Perspectives*, ed. S. Wilkinson and C. Kitzinger (London: Taylor & Francis, 1994), 33–48.

3. Thirty-one percent of pregnancies may end in miscarriage. Anthony R. Scialli, "Miscarriage: executive summary," (Arlington, Va.: Chlorine Chemistry Council, 1998) www.c3.org/library/miscarriage/html, 5-27-99. See also Frances M. Boyle, *Mothers Bereaved by Stillbirth, Neonatal Death or Sudden Infant Death Syndrome: Patterns of Distress and Recovery* (Aldershot, England: Ashgate, 1997); Rosanne Cecil, ed., *The Anthropology of Pregnancy Loss: Comparative Studies in Miscarriage, Stillbirth and Neonatal Death*

(Oxford: Berg, 1996); Wendy Simonds and Barbara Katz Rothman, *Centuries of Solace: Expressions of Maternal Grief in Popular Literature* (Philadelphia: Temple University Press, 1992); Shulamit Reinharz, "What's Missing in Miscarriage?" *Journal of Community Psychology* 16, no. 1 (1988): 84–103.

4. Barbara Katz Rothman, "The Give and Take of Adoption," in *Recreating Motherhood: Ideology and Technology in a Patriarchal Society* (New York: W. W. Norton, 1989), 125–132; Judith Modell, " 'How Do You Introduce Yourself as a Childless Mother?': Birthparent Interpretations of Parenthood," in *Storied Lives: The Cultural Politics of Self-Understanding*, ed. G. C. Rosenwald and R. L. Ochberg (New Haven, Conn.: Yale University Press, 1992), 76–94; and Christine E. Edwards and Christine L. Williams, "Adopting Change: Birth Mothers in Maternity Homes Today, *Gender & Society* 14, no. 1 (February 2000): 160–183.

5. This is a powerful theme in Cherríe Moraga's personal narrative about her pregnancy: "Waiting in the Wings: Reflections on a Radical Motherhood, in *The Politics of Motherhood: Activist Voices from Left to Right*, ed. A Jetter, A. Orleck, and D. Taylor (Hanover, N.H.: University Press of New England, 1997), 288–310. We wanted to include Moraga's narrative in our book but were unable to reach her to get permission to reprint it before our book went into production.

6. Verta Taylor, *Rock-a-by Baby: Feminism, Self-Help, and Post-Partum Depression* (New York: Routledge, 1996).

7. For example, Barbara Katz Rothman, *In Labor: Women and Power in the Birthplace*, rev. ed. (1982; New York: W. W. Norton, 1991); Richard W. Wertz and Dorothy C. Wertz, *Lying-In: A History of Childbirth in America* (New York: The Free Press, 1977); Judith Walzer Leavitt, *Brought to Bed: Childbearing in America, 1750–1950* (New York: Oxford University Press, 1986); Judith Pence Rooks, *Midwifery and Childbirth in America* (Philadelphia: Temple University Press, 1997); Janet Carlisle Bogdan, "Losing Birth: The Erosion of Women's Control Over and Knowledge About Birth, 1650–1900," in *Changing Education: Women as Radicals and Conservators*, ed. J. Antler and S. K. Biklen (Albany: State University of New York, 1990), 83–101; Barbara Ehrenreich and Deirdre English, *For Her Own Good: 150 Years of the Experts' Advice to Women* (Garden City, N.Y.: Anchor Books, 1979); Lauri Umansky, *Motherhood Reconceived: Feminism and the Legacies of the Sixties* (New York: New York University Press, 1996), chapter 2.

8. Leavitt, *Brought to Bed*, 14–19; Jacqueline Jones, *Labor of Love, Labor of Sorrow: Black Women, Work, and the Family, From Slavery to the Present* (New York: Vintage, 1985), 61.

9. Leavitt, *Brought to Bed*, 20–22

10. Wertz and Wertz, *Lying-In*, 128.

11. Brigitte Jordan, *Birth in Four Cultures: A Crosscultural Investigation of Childbirth in Yucatan, Holland, Sweden, and the United States*, 4th ed., revised and expanded by Robbie Davis-Floyd (Prospect Heights, Ill.: Waveland Press, 1993).

12. Leavitt, *Brought to Bed*, 37–38.

13. Laurel Thatcher Ulrich, " 'The Living Mother of a Living Child': Midwifery and Mortality in Post-Revolutionary New England," in *Mothers & Motherhood: Readings in American History*, ed. R. D. Apple and J. Golden (Columbus: Ohio State University Press, 1997), 176, 178, 180, 184–186.

14. Rothman, *In Labor*, 52, 54. The American Medical Association was formed in 1847. Leavitt, *Brought to Bed*, 265.

15. Leavitt, *Brought to Bed*, 171, 267.

16. Kahn, *Bearing Meaning*, 119; Rooks, *Midwifery and Childbirth in America*, 450.

17. Rothman, *In Labor*, 75–76; Beth Rushing, "Ideology in the Reemergence of North American Midwifery," *Work and Occupations* 20, no. 2 (February 1993): 55.

18. Leavitt, *Brought to Bed*, 39, 19, 27.

19. Ibid., 203; Ulrich, " 'The Living Mother of a Living Child,' " 192.

20. Leavitt, *Brought to Bed*, 172, 203, 43, 50.

21. Ibid., 176–177; Joan J. Mathews and Kathleen Zadak, "The Alternative Birth Movement in the United States: History and Current Status," in *Mothers & Motherhood*, 279.

22. Leavitt, *Brought to Bed*, 182–184.

23. Gertrude Jacinta Fraser, *Afro-American Midwives, Biomedicine and the State: An Ethnohistorical Account of Birth and Its Transformation in Rural Virginia* (Ph.D. diss., Johns Hopkins University, 1988), 23. In the Deep South, birthing women used the services of midwives well into the 1970s (23–24).

24. Leavitt, *Brought to Bed*, 267, 268. For the sake of comparison, I have translated mortality rates if they appeared in a form other than "1 out of ___."

25. F. Gary Cunningham, Paul C. MacDonald, Norman F. Gant, Kenneth J. Leveno, Larry C. Gilstrap III, Gary D.V. Hankins, and Steven L. Clark, *Williams Obstetrics*, 20th ed. (Stamford, Conn.: Appleton & Lange, 1997), 6; Ulrich, " 'The Living Mother of a Living Child,' " 178, 180. Fraser discusses early twentieth-century studies in Richmond, Virginia, and in New Jersey that reported lower maternal mortality rates for midwives (1 in 149) than doctors (1 in 128). *Afro-American Midwives*, 35, 39.

26. Leavitt, *Brought to Bed*, 188, 183, 194.

27. Cunningham et al., *Williams Obstetrics*, 3, 6. This major medical text acknowledges that maternal mortality is underreported. Also, throughout the twentieth century, the maternal mortality rates of black women have been two to four times greater than those of white women (3–5).

28. U.S. Department of Health and Human Services, "Facts about Infant Mortality," (www.healthystart.net/factsheet.html; 10-29-98). When we place these mortality rates in cross-national context, we get a less heartening picture. In 1993, the U.S. had the twenty-fifth lowest infant mortality rate among industrialized countries. U.S. Department of Health and Human Services, "Facts about Infant Mortality".

29. Henci Goer, *Obstetric Myths Versus Research Realities: A Guide to the Medical Literature* (Westport, Conn.: Bergin & Garvey, 1995), 334.

30. Rothman, *In Labor*, 43–44. The study was conducted by Lewis E. Mehl, "Research on Childbirth Alternatives: What Can It Tell Us about Hospital Practice?" in *21st Century Obstetrics Now!* ed. L. Stewart and D. Stewart (Chapel Hill. N.C.: National Association of Parents & Professionals for Safe Alternatives in Childbirth [NAPSAC], 1977).

31. Robbie E. Davis-Floyd, *Birth as an American Rite of Passage* (Berkeley: University of California Press, 1992), 182.

32. Paula A. Treichler, "Feminism, Medicine, and the Meaning of Childbirth," in *Body/Politics: Women and the Discourses of Science*, ed. M. Jacobus, E .F. Keller, and S. Shuttleworth (New York: Routledge, 1990), 116.

33. Brigitte Jordan, "Authoritative Knowledge and Its Construction," in *Childbirth and Authoritative Knowledge: Cross-Cultural Perspectives*, ed. R. E. Davis-Floyd and C. F. Sargent (Berkeley: University of California Press, 1997), 57, 58; emphasis in original.

34. Rothman, *In Labor*, 29–49; Davis-Floyd, *Birth as an American Rite of Passage*, 160–161; Emily Martin, *The Woman in the Body: A Cultural Analysis of Reproduction* (Boston: Beacon Press, 1987), 54–67.

35. Kahn, *Bearing Meaning*, 8; 24 n. 10; 238.

36. Rooks, *Midwifery and Childbirth in America*, 450. In 1985, the World Health Organization stated that "there is no justification in any specific geographic region to have more than 10 to 15% cesarean section births" (cited in Marsden Wagner, "Confessions of a Dissident," in *Childbirth and Authoritative Knowledge*, 374). The cesarean rates are much lower in other developed countries than in the United States (Cunningham et al., *Williams Obstetrics*, 511).

37. Rothman, *In Labor*, chapter 9; Rushing, "Ideology in the Reemergence of North American Midwifery;" Mathews and Zadak, "The Alternative Birth Movement in the United States;" Robbie Davis-Floyd and Elizabeth Davis, "Intuition as Authoritative Knowledge in Midwifery and Home Birth," in *Childbirth and Authoritative Knowledge*, 315–349. Rooks, *Midwifery and Childbirth in America*, chapters 7, 8, and 9; Umansky, *Motherhood Reconceived*, chapter 2; Julie K. Childers, *The Boston Birth Center: An Ethnographic Case Study of Institutional Capture in the Women's Health Movement* (Ph.D. diss., Boston College, 2000).

38. Rooks, *Midwifery and Childbirth in America*, 450.

39. Davis-Floyd, *Birth as an American Rite of Passage*, 160–161; Rothman, *In Labor*, chapters 1 and 3; Martin, *The Woman in the Body*, chapter 9; Bonnie Fox and Diana Worts, "Revisiting the Critique of Medicalized Childbirth: A Contribution to the Sociology of Birth," *Gender & Society* 13, no. 3 (June 1999): 338.

40. Kahn, *Bearing Meaning*, chapters 7 and 11; Louis M. Hellman and Jack A. Pritchard, eds., *Williams Obstetrics*, 14th ed., New York: Appleton-Century-Crofts, 1971); Boston Women's Health Collective, *Women and Their Bodies: A Course* (Somerville, Mass.: New England Free Press, 1970). Beginning with the 1973 edition, the book's name was changed to *Our Bodies, Ourselves: A Book by and for Women* (New York: Simon and Schuster, 1973). Kahn was a member of the Boston Women's Health Collective.

41. Cited in Kahn, *Bearing Meaning*, 211.

42. Susan Bordo, "Are Mothers Persons? Reproductive Rights and the Politics of Subject-ivity," in *Unbearable Weight: Feminism, Western Culture, and the Body* (Berkeley: University of California Press, 1993), 78–88. Since the Angela Carder case in the late 1980s, court-ordered cesareans may have been laid to rest, but Bordo, along with others, maintains that the subjectification of the fetus and desubjectification of pregnant women continues unabated. See also Ruth Hubbard, "The Politics of Fetal/Maternal Conflict," in *Power and Decision*, 318–319; Rothman, *Recreating Motherhood*, 159–168; Susan Squier, "Fetal Subjects and Maternal Objects: Reproductive Technology and the New Fetal/Maternal Relation," *The Journal of Medicine and Philosophy* 21, no. 5 (October 1996): 515–535.

43. Cindy Martin, "Maternal Consequences," December 18, 1997 (unpublished essay used with the author's permission; emphasis in original), citing Bordo, "Are Mothers Persons?" 76.

44. Kahn, *Bearing Meaning*, 331.

45. Cunningham et al., *Williams Obstetrics*, 660.

46. In 1996, a substantial proportion of women nationwide received no prenatal

care in the first trimester of their pregnancies: 29 percent of black women; 28 percent of Latinas; and 16 percent of white women. U.S. Department of Health and Human Services, "Facts about infant mortality" (www.healthystart.net/factsheet.html; 10-29-98).

47. Judy Wajcman, "Delivered into Men's Hands? The Social Construction of Reproductive Technology," in *Power and Decision: The Social Control of Reproduction*, ed. G. Sen and R. C. Snow (Boston: Harvard School of Public Health, Harvard University Press, 1994), 166.

48. Rayna Rapp, "Constructing Amniocentesis: Maternal and Medical Discourses," in *Uncertain Terms: Negotiating Gender in American Culture*, ed. F. Ginsburg and A. L. Tsing (Boston: Beacon Press, 1990), 31–32.

49. Rayna Rapp, "The Power of 'Positive' Diagnosis: Medical and Maternal Discourses on Amniocentesis," in *Representations of Motherhood*, ed. D. Bassin, M. Honey, and M. M. Kaplan (New Haven, Conn.: Yale University Press, 1994), 207.

50. Barbara Katz Rothman, *The Tentative Pregnancy: How Amniocentesis Changes the Experience of Motherhood*, rev. ed. (1986; New York: W. W. Norton, 1993), 6.

51. Carole H. Browner and Nancy Press, "The Production of Authoritative Knowledge in American Prenatal Care," in *Childbirth and Authoritative Knowledge*, 125–126.

52. Emily Martin, "The Ideology of Reproduction: The Reproduction of Ideology," in *Uncertain Terms*, 304, 305. Robbie Davis-Floyd and Carolyn F. Sargent discuss the lack of research on middle-class women of color's birth experiences in "Introduction," *Childbirth and Authoritative Knowledge*, 9, 25 n. 7.

53. See also Margarita A. Kay, "Mexican, Mexican American, and Chicana Childbirth," in *Twice a Minority: Mexican American Women*, ed. M. B. Melville (St.Louis: C.V. Mosby, 1980), 57.

54. Martin, "The Ideology of Reproduction," 309; emphasis in original.

55. Martin, "Maternal Consequences," citing Bordo, "Are Mothers Persons?" 79. Similarly, Fraser heard accounts from African American women in Virginia about physicians and nurses ignoring their pain during childbirth. *Afro-American Midwives*, 75–76.

56. Davis-Floyd, *Birth as an American Rite of Passage*, 2–4, 190, 199–202.

57. Fox and Worts, "Revisiting the Critique of Medicalized Childbirth, 326–346.

58. Lisa Rose Gates, "The Mystery and Mystique of Natural Childbirth," in *Courage of Conviction: Women's Words, Women's Wisdom*, ed. L. A. M. Perry and P. Geist (Mountain View, Calif.: Mayfield, 1997), 185–200.

59. Iris Marion Young, "Pregnant Embodiment: Subjectivity and Alienation," in *Throwing Like a Girl and Other Essays in Feminist Philosophy and Social Theory* (Bloomington: Indiana University Press, 1990), 165–166.

60. Sara Ruddick, "Thinking Mothers/Conceiving Birth," in *Representations of Motherhood*, 39.

61. Rothman, *Recreating Motherhood*, 97–98.

62. Martin, *The Woman in the Body*, 164.

63. Davis–Floyd, *Birth as an American Rite of Passage*, 102.

Notes to Chapter 7

1. Linda J. Lacey, " 'O Wind, Remind Him That I Have No Child': Infertility and Feminist Jurisprudence," *Michigan Journal of Gender & Law* 5, no. 1 (1998): 165, 203.

Rayna Rapp makes the same observation about discussions of prenatal diagnoses; see "The Power of 'Positive' Diagnosis: Medical and Maternal Discourses on Amniocentesis," in *Representations of Motherhood*, ed. D. Bassin, M. Honey, and M. M. Kaplan (New Haven, Conn.: Yale University Press, 1994), 217.

2. Paul Lauritzen, *Pursuing Parenthood: Ethical Issues in Assisted Reproduction* (Bloomington: Indiana University Press, 1993), ix, 3.

3. Margarete Sandelowski, *With Child in Mind: Studies of the Personal Encounter with Infertility* (Philadelphia: University of Pennsylvania Press, 1993), 10; 11.

4. Marta Kirejczyk, "Cassandra's Warnings: Feminist Discourse, Gender and Social Entrenchment of In Vitro Fertilization in the Netherlands," *European Journal of Women's Studies* 1, no. 2 (autumn, 1994): 161.

5. Sarah Franklin, "Making Miracles: Scientific Progress and the Facts of Life," in *Reproducing Reproduction: Kinship, Power, and Technological Innovation*, ed. S. Franklin and H. Ragone (Philadelphia: University of Pennsylvania Press, 1998), 113.

6. Elizabeth Bartholet, "Adoption Rights and Reproductive Wrongs," in *Power and Decision: The Social Control of Reproduction*, ed. G. Sen and R. C. Snow (Cambridge: Harvard University Press, 1994), 186.

7. Anne Woollett, "Having Children: Accounts of Childless Women and Women with Reproductive Problems," in *Motherhood: Meanings, Practices and Ideologies*, ed. A. Phoenix, A. Woollett, and E. Lloyd (London: Sage Publications, 1991), 50.

8. Caroline Whitbeck, "Ethical Issues Raised by the New Medical Technologies," in *Women and New Reproductive Technologies: Medical, Psychosocial, Legal, and Ethical Dilemmas*, ed. J. Rodin and A. Collins (Hillsdale, N.J.: Lawrence Erlbaum Associates, 1991), 58.

9. Lauritzen, *Pursuing Parenthood*, 32, 33, 34, 35.

10. Franklin, "Making Miracles," 107, 108.

11. Sandelowski, *With Child in Mind*, 50; Judith N. Lasker and Susan Borg, *In Search of Parenthood: Coping with Infertility and High-Tech Conception* (Boston: Beacon Press, 1987), 17. For some women, infertility treatments become "like an addiction"; see Phyllis O. Ziman Tobin with Barbara Aria, *Motherhood Optional: A Psychological Journey* (Northvale, N.J.: Jason Aronson Inc., 1998), 109.

12. Lasker and Borg, *In Search of Parenthood*, 29.

13. For first-person narratives, see Jill Bialosky and Helen Schulman, eds., *Wanting a Child: Twenty-Two Writers on Their Difficult But Mostly Successful Quests for Parenthood in a High-Tech Age* (New York: Farrar, Straus and Giroux, 1998).

14. Deborah Lynn Steinberg, "The Depersonalisation of Women through the Administration of *In Vitro* Fertilization," in *The New Reproductive Technologies*, ed. M. McNeil, I. Varcoe, and S. Yearley (New York: St. Martin's Press, 1990), 113. Like Sandelowski, Steinberg emphasizes the ambiguity of infertility.

15. Helena Michie and Naomi R. Cahn, *Confinements: Fertility and Infertility in Contemporary Culture* (New Brunswick, N.J.: Rutgers University Press, 1997), 8. Like Lauritzen, these authors have experienced infertility firsthand.

16. Sandelowski, *With Child in Mind*, 245; Whitbeck, "Ethical Issues," 58.

17. Lasker and Borg, *In Search of Parenthood*, 16, 145.

18. Judith Lorber, "Choice, Gift, or Patriarchal Bargain? Women's Consent to *In Vitro* Fertilization in Male Infertility," *Hypatia* 4, no. 3 (fall 1989): 25, 33.

19. See, for example, Leslie King and Madonna Harrington Meyer, "The Politics of

Reproductive Benefits: U.S. Insurance Coverage of Contraceptives and Infertility Treatments," *Gender & Society* 11, no. 1 (February, 1997): 8–30.

20. Elizabeth Heitman and Mary Schlachtenhaufen, "The Differential Effects of Race, Ethnicity, and Socioeconomic Status on Infertility and Its Treatment," in *New Ways of Making Babies: The Case of Egg Donation*, ed. C. B. Cohen (Bloomington: Indiana University Press, 1996), 195, 197; Elaine Tyler May, *Barren in the Promised Land: Childless Americans and the Pursuit of Happiness* (New York: Basic Books, 1995), 12.

21. May, *Barren in the Promised Land*, 12.

22. Lacey, " 'O Wind,' " 191.

23. Diane Houghton and Peter Houghton, *Coping with Childlessness* (London: George Allen & Unwin, 1984), 91.

24. Lasker and Borg, *In Search of Parenthood*, 20, 21; Houghton and Houghton, *Coping with Childlessness*, 47.

25. Ruth L. Ozeki, *My Year of Meats* (New York: Penguin Books, 1998), 159.

26. Sarah Franklin, "Deconstructing 'Desperateness': The Social Construction of Infertility in Popular Representations of New Reproductive Technologies," in *The New Reproductive Technologies*, 204; Lasker and Borg, *In Search of Parenthood*, 11.

27. Sandelowski, *With Child in Mind*, 79.

28. Lasker and Borg, *In Search of Parenthood*, 25.

29. Barbara Menning founded Resolve in 1973 when she was diagnosed as infertile and came up short when seeking medical expertise and social support; see Ruth Macklin, *Surrogates & Other Mothers: The Debates over Assisted Reproduction* (Philadelphia: Temple University Press, 1994), 25.

30. Sandelowski, *With Child in Mind*, 226ff.

31. Lisa Sowle Cahill, "Moral Concerns about Institutionalized Gamete Donation" in *New Ways of Making Babies*, 80.

32. Robyn Rowland, *Living Laboratories: Women and Reproductive Technologies* (Bloomington: Indiana University Press, 1992), 19, 22, 25, 30.

33. Lauritzen, *Pursuing Parenthood*, 31.

34. Charis Cussins, "Producing Reproduction: Techniques of Normalization and Naturalization in Infertility Clinics" in Franklin and Ragone, *Reproducing Reproduction*, 75.

35. Houghton and Houghton, *Coping with Childlessness*, 44; Sandelowski, *With Child in Mind*, 23.

36. Lauritzen, *Pursuing Parenthood*, 135.

37. Predictably, postmenopausal women are the most common targets of such judgments; see Jennifer A. Parks, "On the Use of IVF by Post-menopausal Women," *Hypatia* 14, no. 1 (winter 1999): 77–96. Women in their late thirties and early forties sometimes face that same judgment.

38. Lasker and Borg, *In Search of Parenthood*, 15.

39. Bartholet, "Adoption Rights," 187. Bartholet reports that others are less fortunate. By the time they "exhaust their treatment options" they no longer have "the will, the energy, or the resources to pursue their adoptive options" (187). Betsy Smith, Janet L. Surrey, and Mary Watkins, all adoptive mothers, indicate that some do "come to adoption through the disappointment of infertility" but that others adopt "for personal, political, or moral reasons"; see their " 'Real' Mothers: Adoptive Mothers Resisting Marginalization and Re-Creating Motherhood," in *Mothering Against the Odds: Diverse Voices*

of Contemporary Mothers, ed. C. G. Coll, J. L. Surrey, and K. Weingarten (New York: Guilford Press, 1998), 194.

40. Sandelowski, *With Child in Mind*, 74; Lasker and Borg, *In Search of Parenthood*, 26.

41. Margaret Marsh and Wanda Ronner, *The Empty Cradle: Infertility in America from Colonial Times to the Present* (Baltimore: Johns Hopkins University Press, 1996), 255.

42. Ibid., 172–174, 236, 241, 248.

43. Lasker and Borg, *In Search of Parenthood*, 27, 52, 53.

44. Susan Merrill Squier, *Babies in Bottles: Twentieth-Century Visions of Reproductive Technologies* (New Brunswick, N.J.: Rutgers University Press, 1994), 2.

45. Julien S. Murphy, "Is Pregnancy Necessary? Feminist Concerns about Ectogenesis," *Hypatia* 4, no. 3 (fall 1989): 67, 78, 79.

46. Marsh and Ronner, *The Empty Cradle*, 66, 163, 297, 203; also see Naomi Pfeffer, *The Stork and the Syringe: A Political History of Reproductive Medicine* (Cambridge, England: Polity Press, 1993). Nancy Lublin indicates that because AID is similar to the acronym AIDS, TDI—therapeutic donor insemination—is often used instead; see Lublin, *Pandora's Box: Feminism Confronts Reproductive Technology* (Lanham, Md.: Rowman & Littlefield, 1998), 18.

47. Lasker and Borg, *In Search of Parenthood*, 33, 34, 42.

48. Ibid., 35, 36, 43.

49. Ibid., 38; Gina Maranto, *Quest for Perfection: The Drive to Breed Better Human Beings* (New York: Scribner's, 1996), 180, 11.

50. Lori B. Andrews, "The Sperminator," *New York Times* magazine, March 28, 1999, 62.

51. See, for instance, Cherrie Moraga, "Waiting in the Wings: Reflections on a Radical Motherhood," in *The Politics of Motherhood: Activist Voices from Left to Right*, ed. A. Jetter, A. Orleck, and D. Taylor (Hanover, N.H.: University Press of New England, 1997), 228–310; Francie Hornstein, "Children by Donor Insemination: A New Choice for Lesbians" in *Test-Tube Women: What Future for Motherhood?* ed. R. Arditti, R. D. Klein, and S. Minden (London: Pandora Press, 1984), 373–381. In that same volume is the story of the six British women who formed the Feminist Self Insemination Group; see Renate Duelli Klein, "Doing It Ourselves: Self Insemination," 382–390.

52. Lasker and Borg, *In Search of Parenthood*, 45, 46.

53. Http://www.surrogacyagency.com/surrogacy/index.html; 06-30-98.

54. Delores S. Williams, "Black Women's Surrogacy Experiences and the Christian Notion of Redemption," in *After Patriarchy: Feminist Transformations of the World Religions*, ed. P. M. Cooey, W. R. Eakin, and J. B. McDaniel (Maryknoll, N.Y.: Orbis Books, 1991), 1.

55. See Michelle Stanworth, "Reproductive Technologies and the Destruction of Motherhood" in *Reproductive Technologies: Gender, Motherhood, and Medicine*, ed. Michelle Stanworth (Minneapolis: University of Minnesota Press, 1987). *Reproductive Technologies*, 26; Steinberg, "The Depersonalisation of Women," 78.

56. Lasker and Borg, *In Search of Parenthood*, 77.

57. Barbara Katz Rothman, *Recreating Motherhood: Ideology and Technology in a Patriarchal Society* (New York: W. W. Norton, 1989), 90, 91. Rothman discusses "Pregnancy as a Relationship" on pages 90–105.

58. Christine Overall, *Ethics and Human Reproduction: A Feminist Analysis* (Boston: Allen & Unwin, 1987), 190.

59. Rowland, *Living Laboratories*, 238.

60. Helena Ragone, "Incontestable Motivations," in *Reproducing Reproduction*, 119.

61. Katha Pollitt, "Checkbook Maternity: When Is a Mother Not a Mother?" in Katha Pollitt, *Reasonable Creatures: Essays on Women and Feminism* (New York: Vintage Books, 1995), 100, 101.

62. Katha Pollitt, "Contracts and Apple Pie: The Strange Case of Baby M," in *Reasonable Creatures*, 63–80.

63. Thomas A. Shannon, *Surrogate Motherhood: The Ethics of Using Human Beings* (New York: Crossroad Publishing, 1988), 79; emphasis in original.

64. Natalie Angier, "Baby in a Box," *New York Times* magazine, May 16, 1999, 88.

65. Stanworth, "Reproductive Technologies," 22, 26.

66. Rothman, *Recreating Motherhood*, 237; emphasis in original.

67. Ann Oakley, "From Walking Wombs to Test-Tube Babies" in *Reproductive Technologies*, 52.

68. See, for instance, Shannon, *Surrogate Motherhood*, x.

69. Sara Ann Ketchum, "Selling Babies and Selling Bodies," *Hypatia* 4, no. 3 (fall 1989): 117; also see Overall, *Ethics and Human Reproduction*, 181–185.

70. See also Gena Corea, "The Reproductive Brothel," in *Man-Made Women: How New Reproductive Technologies Affect Women*, ed. G. Corea, R. D. Klein, J. Hanmer, H. B. Holmes, B. Hoskins, M. Kishwar, J. Raymond, R. Rowland, and P. Sternbacher (London: Hutchinson and Company, 1985), 43, 44, 47.

71. Susan Ince, "Inside the Surrogate Industry" in *Test-Tube Women*, 111; Ketchum, "Selling Babies," 119; Overall, *Ethics and Human Reproduction*, 130. Similarly, current U.S. divorce laws presuppose that "the law cannot permit people to be bound to a promise when they and their relationship have fundamentally changed." If pregnancy is a dynamic relationship, the same logic applies to surrogacy contracts; see Mary Lyndon Shanley, " 'Surrogate Mothering' and Women's Freedom: A Critique of Contracts for Human Reproduction," *Signs* 18, no. 3 (1993): 630.

72. Rosemarie Tong, "Toward a Feminist Perspective on Gamete Donation and Reception Policies," in *New Ways of Making Babies*, 148.

73. Susan E. Chase, personal communication, 09-25-98.

74. Andrews, "The Sperminator," 65. Also see Sarah Franklin, "Making Representations: The Parliamentary Debate on the Human Fertilisation and Embryology Act," in *Technologies of Procreation: Kinship in the Age of Assisted Conception*, ed. J. Edwards, S. Franklin, E. Hirsch, F. Price, and M. Strathern, (Manchester, England: Manchester University Press, 1993), 96–131; Brenda M. Baker, "A Case for Permitting Altruistic Surrogacy," *Hypatia* 11, no. 2 (spring 1996): 34–48. Baker notes that "Canada's Royal Commission on New Reproductive Technologies rejects all forms of surrogacy arrangement under the rubric of objecting to commercial surrogacy" (34).

75. See Lacey, " 'O Wind,' " for a survey of these stances.

76. Lublin, *Pandora's Box*, 23, 63.

77. Ketchum, "Selling Babies," 120; Lauritzen, *Pursuing Parenthood*, 112, 113; Overall, *Ethics and Human Reproduction*, 134; Laura M. Purdy, *Reproducing Persons: Issues in Feminist Bioethics* (Ithaca, N.Y.: Cornell University Press, 1996), 214–215.

78. The first quote comes from Shannon, *Surrogate Motherhood*, 164; the second is from Overall, *Ethics and Human Reproduction*, 126.

79. Maranto, *Quest for Perfection*, 24.

80. Http://www.surrogacyagency.com/surrogacy/index.html; 06-30-98; emphasis added.

81. Stanworth, "Reproductive Technologies," 28–32.

82. Michelle McCaffery, "Foetal Subjectivity and the Rise of Paternal Rights," *Irish Journal of Feminist Studies* 1, no. 1 (March 1996): 23; Sarah Franklin, "Postmodern Procreation: A Cultural Account of Assisted Reproduction," in *Conceiving the New World Order: The Global Politics of Reproduction*, ed. F. D. Ginsburg and R. Rapp (Berkeley: University of California Press, 1995), 325.

Notes to Chapter 8

1. Kathy Weingarten, "Sidelined No More: Promoting Mothers of Adolescents as a Resource for Their Growth And Development," in *Mothering Against the Odds: Diverse Voices of Contemporary Mothers*, ed. C. G. Coll, J. L. Surrey, and K. Weingarten (New York: Guilford Press, 1998), 34, 23.

2. Jill McLean Taylor, Carol Gilligan, and Amy M. Sullivan, *Between Voice and Silence: Women and Girls, Race and Relationship* (Cambridge: Harvard University Press, 1995), 3, 74, 4. The earlier studies are Lyn Mikel Brown and Carol Gilligan, *Meeting at the Crossroads: Women's Psychology and Girls' Development* (New York: Ballantine Books, 1993); and Carol Gilligan, Nona P. Lyons, and Trudi J. Hanmer, eds., *Making Connections: the Relational Worlds of Adolescent Girls at Emma Willard School* (Cambridge: Harvard University Press, 1990).

3. Donna Eder, with Catherine Colleen Evans and Stephen Parker, *School Talk: Gender and Adolescent Culture* (New Brunswick, N.J.: Rutgers University Press, 1995), especially chapter 8.

4. Taylor et al., *Between Voice and Silence*, 95.

5. For examples of straightforward sex education classes, see Carolyn Mackler, "Sex Ed: How Do We Score?" *Ms.* 9, no. 5 (August/September 1999): 66–73.

6. Taylor et al., *Between Voice and Silence*, 114–115.

7. Elaine Bell Kaplan, "Black Teenage Mothers and Their Mothers: The Impact of Adolescent Childbearing on Daughters' Relations with Mothers," *Social Problems* 43, no. 4 (November 1996): 427. See also Elaine Bell Kaplan, *Not Our Kind of Girl: Unraveling the Myths of Black Teenage Motherhood* (Berkeley: University of California Press, 1997).

8. Patricia Flanagan, "Teen Mothers: Countering the Myths of Dysfunction and Developmental Disruption," in *Mothering Against the Odds*, 238–254.

9. Kaplan, "Black Teenage Mothers and Their Mothers," 433.

10. The classic feminist text is Judith Lewis Herman, with Lisa Hirschman, *Father-Daughter Incest* (Cambridge: Harvard University Press, 1981).

11. Ibid., vii, 9–11, 39–40.

12. Judith Green, "Mothers in 'Incest Families': A Critique of Blame and Its Destructive Sequels," *Violence Against Women* 2, no. 3 (September 1996): 324, 325.

13. Herman, *Father-Daughter Incest*, 71, 72, 73.

14. Green, "Mothers in 'Incest Families,' " 329.

15. See also Janis Tyler Johnson, *Mothers of Incest Survivors: Another Side of the Story* (Bloomington: Indiana University Press, 1992), 110–111.

16. Green, "Mothers in 'Incest Families,' " 337–338.

17. See also Johnson, *Mothers of Incest Survivors*, 116.

18. Nancy Chodorow and Susan Contratto, "The Fantasy of the Perfect Mother," in *Rethinking the Family: Some Feminist Questions*, ed. B. Thorne with M. Yalom (New York: Longman, 1982), 54–75.

19. Green, "Mothers in 'Incest Families,' " 334–335.

20. Elizabeth Diem, "Unravelling the Myth of the Perfect Mother with Mothers of Early Adolescent Girls," in *Redefining Motherhood: Changing Identities and Patterns*, ed. S. Abbey and A. O'Reilly (Toronto: Second Story Press, 1998), 175, 183.

21. Chodorow and Contratto, "The Fantasy of the Perfect Mother," 68–69.

22. bell hooks, *Talking Back: Thinking Feminist, Thinking Black* (Boston: South End Press, 1989), 85. Other feminist scholars argue that contemporary feminism has not paid sufficient attention to mothers' violence against children. See Dorothy E. Roberts, Motherhood and Crime," *Social Text* 42 (spring 1995): 99–123; Linda Gordon, "Feminism And Social Control: The Case of Child Abuse and Neglect," in *What Is Feminism?* ed. J. Mitchell and A. Oakley (New York: Pantheon, 1986), 63–84; Nancy Scheper-Hughes, *Death Without Weeping: The Violence of Everyday Life in Brazil* (Berkeley: University of California Press, 1992).

23. Jennifer Crew Solomon, "Child Sexual Abuse by Family Members: A Radical Feminist Perspective," *Sex Roles* 27, nos. 9/10 (November 1992): 474, 473.

24. Rose Stone, "Night Song for the Journey: A Self-Critical Prelude to Feminist Mothering," in *Mother Journeys: Feminists Write about Mothering*, ed. M. T. Reddy, M. Roth, and A. Sheldon (Minneapolis, Minn.: Spinsters Ink, 1994), 237.

25. Rose L. Glickman, *Daughters of Feminists* (New York: St. Martin's Press, 1993), xiv, xv, xvi, 22, 24, 27, 29. See also Barbara J. Risman and Kristen Myers, "As the Twig Is Bent: Children Reared in Feminist Households," *Qualitative Sociology* 20, no. 2 (summer 1997): 229–252.

26. Harriet Lerner, *The Mother Dance: How Children Change Your Life* (New York: HarperCollins, 1998), 170.

27. Glickman, *Daughters of Feminists*, 30.

28. Christina Looper Baker and Chirsina Baker Kline, *The Conversation Begins: Mothers and Daughters Talk about Living Feminism* (New York: Bantam Books, 1996).

29. Baker and Kline, *The Conversation Begins*, chapters 5 and 23.

30. Penelope Sky, "How You Change the World," in *Feminist Parenting: Struggles, Triumphs & Comic Interludes*, ed. D. Taylor (Freedom, Calif.: The Crossing Press, 1994), 243.

31. Carole Klein, *Mothers and Sons* (Boston: Houghton Mifflin, 1984), 149.

32. Olga Silverstein and Beth Rashbaum, *The Courage to Raise Good Men* (New York, Viking, 1994), 232.

33. Olga Silverstein in an untitled sidebar, *Ms.* 4, no. 3 (November/December, 1993): 46; emphasis in original.

34. Robyn Rowland and Alison Thomas, "Mothering Sons: A Crucial Feminist Challenge," *Feminism and Psychology* 6, no. 1 (1996): 96.

35. Patricia J. Williams, "Whose Hoop Dream Is It, Anyway?" *New York Times* magazine, April 5, 1998, 53.

36. Robin Morgan, "Raising Sons," *Ms.* 4, no. 3 (November/December 1993): 36. Morgan's is just one part of this multiauthored essay.

37. Audre Lorde, "Man Child: A Black Lesbian Feminist's Response" in *Sister Outsider: Essays and Speeches* (Freedom, Calif.: The Crossing Press, 1984), 78, 73.

38. Taylor, *Feminist Parenting.*

39. Carolina Mancuso, " 'But Will He Be a Normal Boy?' Raising a Feminist Son," in *Feminist Parenting*, 175–180; emphasis in original.

40. Janneke van Mens-Verhulst, "Introduction," in *Daughtering and Mothering: Female Subjectivity Reanalysed*, ed. J. van Mens-Verhulst, K. Schreurs, and L. Woertman (London: Routledge, 1993), xiii–xv.

41. Liesbeth Woertman, "Mothering in Context: Female Subjectivities and Intervening Practices," in *Daughtering and Mothering*, 61.

42. Bertram J. Cohler and Henry U. Grunebaum, *Mothers, Grandmothers, and Daughters: Personality and Childcare in Three-Generation Families* (New York: John Wiley, 1981), 40, 1. These researchers focus on four Italian-American families.

43. Pat O'Connor, "The Adult Mother/Daughter Relationship: A Uniquely and Universally Close Relationship?" *Sociological Review* 38, no. 2 (May 1990): 316, 317.

44. Karen L. Fingerman, "Being More Than a Daughter: Middle-Aged Women's Conceptions of Their Mothers," *Journal of Women & Aging* 9, no. 4 (1997): 67.

45. See Rosemary Blieszner, Paula M. Usita, and Jay A. Mancini, "Diversity and Dynamics in Late-Life Mother-Daughter Relationships," *Journal of Women & Aging* 8, nos. 3/4 (1996): 5–24.

46. Janneke van Mens-Verhulst, "Introduction," in *Daughtering and Mothering*, xiii.

47. See, for instance, Rosa Ainley, ed., *Death of a Mother: Daughters' Stories* (New York: Pandora, 1994); and Karin Cook, "What Did You Wish for Me?" in *Letters of Intent: Women Cross the Generations to Talk About Family, Work, Sex, Love and the Future of Feminism*, ed. A. Bondoc and M. Daly (New York: The Free Press, 1999), 184–186. For a parallel volume of sons' stories, see Bob Blauner, ed., *Our Mothers' Spirits: On the Death of Mothers and the Grief of Men* (New York: HarperCollins, 1997).

48. Catherine Foote, Mary Valentich, and Leslie Gavel, "When Mothers of Adult Daughters Die: A New Area of Feminist Practice," *Affilia* 11, no. 2 (summer 1996): 148, 157.

Notes to Chapter 9

1. Jane Hamilton, *The Short History of a Prince* (New York: Random House, 1998), 17.

2. See, for instance, Karen Case, "African American Othermothering in the Urban Elementary School," *The Urban Review* 29, no. 1 (1997): 25–39.

3. Geraldine Youcha, *Minding the Children: Child Care in America from Colonial Times to the Present* (New York: Scribner's, 1995), 13.

4. Diane Eyer, *Motherguilt: How Our Culture Blames Mothers for What's Wrong with Society* (New York: Times Books, 1996), 202.

5. Duane F. Alexander, "Foreword," in *Child Care in Context: Cross-Cultural Perspectives*, ed. M. E. Lamb, K. J. Sternberg, C. Hwang, and A. G. Broberg, (Hillsdale, N.J.: Lawrence Erlbaum Associates, 1992), xviii.

6. Sandra Scarr, *Mother Care/Other Care* (New York: Basic Books, 1984).

7. Judith D. Auerbach and Gary A. Woodill, "Historical Perspectives on Familial and Extrafamilial Child Care: Toward a History of Family Day Care," in *Family Day Care: Current Research for Informed Public Policy*, ed. D. L. Peters and A. R. Pence (New York: Teachers College Press, 1992), 9.

8. Lois Banner, *Women in Modern America: A Brief History*, 3rd ed. (New York: Harcourt Brace College Publishers, 1995), 107.

9. Stanlie M. James, "Mothering: A Possible Black Feminist Link to Social Transformation?" in *Theorizing Black Feminisms: The Visionary Pragmatism of Black Women*, ed. S. M. James and A. P. A. Busia (London: Routledge, 1993), 44.

10. Patricia Hill Collins, "Shifting the Center: Race, Class, and Feminist Theorizing about Motherhood," in *Mothering: Ideology, Experience, and Agency*, ed. E. N. Glenn, G. Chang, and L. R. Forcey (New York: Routledge, 1994), 47, 48.

11. Rosalie Riegle Troester, "Turbulence and Tenderness: Mothers, Daughters, and 'Othermothers' in Paule Marshall's *Brown Girl, Brownstones*," *SAGE: A Scholarly Journal on Black Women* 1, no. 2 (fall 1984): 13.

12. Patricia Hill Collins, "The Meaning of Motherhood in Black Culture and Black Mother/Daughter Relationships," *SAGE* 4, no. 2 (fall 1987): 4–5. Sometimes siblings are among a child's othermothers, as is common in Africa today; see Michael E. Lamb and Kathleen J. Sternberg, "Sociocultural Perspectives on Nonparental Child Care," in *Child Care in Context*, 22.

13. Elsa Barkley Brown, "Mothers of Mine," *SAGE* 6, no. 1 (summer 1989): 8.

14. Collins, "The Meaning of Motherhood," 5.

15. Louise Lamphere, Patricia Zavella, and Felipe Gonzales, with Peter B. Evans, *Sunbelt Working Mothers: Reconciling Family and Factory* (Ithaca, N.Y.: Cornell University Press, 1993), 273.

16. Nan Elasser, Kyle MacKenzie, and Yvonne Tixier Y. Vigil, *Las Mujeres* (New York: The Feminist Press, 1980), 10; cited by Bonnie Thornton Dill, "Fictive Kin, Paper Sons, and *Compadrazgo*: Women of Color and the Struggle for Family Survival," in *Women of Color in U.S. Society*, ed. M. Baca Zinn and B. T. Dill (Philadelphia: Temple University Press, 1993), 159.

17. Dill, "Fictive Kin," 163, 164.

18. Ruth Behar, *Translated Woman: Crossing the Border with Esperanza's Story* (Boston: Beacon Press, 1993), 5, 7.

19. Ruth E. Zambrana, "Puerto Rican Families and Social Well-Being" in *Women of Color in U.S. Society*, 140.

20. Nazli Kibria, "Migration and Vietnamese American Women: Remaking Ethnicity," in *Women of Color in U.S. Society*, 254.

21. Lamphere, Zavella, and Gonzales, *Sunbelt Working Mothers*, 242.

22. Denise Burnette, "Grandparents Raising Grandchildren in the Inner City," *Families in Society* 78, no. 5 (September/October 1997): 489, 490; Beverly Davidson, "Service Needs of Relative Caregivers: A Qualitative Analysis," *Families in Society* 78, no. 5 (September/October 1997): 502.

23. Susan Kontos, Carollee Howes, Marybeth Shinn, and Ellen Galinsky, *Quality in Family Child Care and Relative Care* (New York: Teachers College Press, 1995), 2, 8.

24. Donna Smith, *Stepmothering* (New York: St. Martin's Press, 1990), 53.

25. David Popenoe, "The Evolution of Marriage and the Problem of Stepfamilies: A Biosocial Perspective," in *Stepfamilies: Who Benefits? Who Does Not?*, ed. A. Booth and

J. Dunn (Hillsdale, N.J.: Lawrence Erlbaum Associates, 1994), 5, 21; Norval D. Glenn, "Biology, Evolutionary Theory, and Family Social Science," in *Stepfamilies*, 49.

26. Maureen Sullivan, "Rozzie and Harriet: Gender and Family Patterns of Lesbian Coparents," *Gender & Society* 10, no. 6 (December 1996): 747–767.

27. Anndee Hochman, *Everyday Acts & Small Subversions: Women Reinventing Family, Community, and Home* (Portland, Oreg.: Eighth Mountain Press, 1994), 111, 112.

28. Elizabeth Rose, "Taking on a Mother's Job: Day Care in the 1920s and 1930s," in *"Bad" Mothers: The Politics of Blame in Twentieth-Century America*, ed. M. Ladd-Taylor and L. Umansky (New York: New York University Press, 1998), 67, 68.

29. Youcha, *Minding the Children*, 307, 309.

30. Abbie Gordon Klein, *The Debate over Child Care 1969–1990: A Sociohistorical Analysis* (Albany: State University of New York Press, 1992), 63.

31. Youcha, *Minding the Children*, 347.

32. Alison Clarke-Stewart, *Daycare*, rev. ed. (Cambridge: Harvard University Press, 1993), 57.

33. Julia Wrigley, "Children's Caregivers and Ideologies of Parental Inadequacy," in *Circles of Care: Work and Identity in Women's Lives*, ed. E. K. Abel and M. K. Nelson (Albany: State University of New York Press, 1990), 305.

34. Lamphere, Zavella, and Gonzales, *Sunbelt Working Mothers*, 217, 242.

35. William T. Gormley, Jr., *Everybody's Children: Child Care As a Public Problem* (Washington, D.C.: The Brookings Institution, 1995), 16.

36. Youcha, *Minding the Children*, 351.

37. Julia Wrigley, *Other People's Children* (New York: Basic Books, 1995), xiii, 10.

38. Gormley, *Everybody's Children*, 16.

39. Auerbach and Woodill, "Historical Perspectives," 9–10.

40. Gormley, *Everybody's Children*, 80, 81.

41. Betsy Squibb and Joel King, "Play in Home Spaces in Family Child Care," *Child & Youth Care Forum* 25, no. 3 (June 1996): 202.

42. Margaret Henry, *Young Children, Parents and Professionals: Enhancing the Links in Early Childhood* (London: Routledge, 1996), 176.

43. Kontos et al., *Quality in Family Child Care and Relative Care*, 143. Mothers differ in how they define the role of their children's paid caregivers. Some see them as offering only custodial care; others, as offering mother-substitute care; still others, as offering complementary care; see Lynet Uttal, "Custodial Care, Surrogate Care, and Coordinated Care: Employed Mothers and the Meaning of Child Care," *Gender & Society* 10, no. 3 (June 1996): 291–311.

44. Margaret K. Nelson, *Negotiated Care: The Experience of Family Day Care Providers* (Philadelphia: Temple University Press, 1990), 4.

45. Ibid., 199; also see Deborah Rutman, "Child Care as Women's Work," *Gender & Society* 10, no. 5 (October 1996): 640.

46. Virginia K. Molgaard, "Caregivers' Perceptions of the Relationship between the Family Day Care Business and Their Own Families," *Child & Youth Care Forum* 22, no. 1 (February 1993): 65. About half of the 185 family day care providers Molgaard studies mentioned this problem, one among a host of frustrations that led to mixed or negative feelings about their work among a quarter of these providers in Iowa. Another sign of frustration is the high turnover among child care workers. Nelson found that their median time in this work is only three years; Nelson, *Negotiated Care*, 195.

47. Nelson, *Negotiated Care*, 639–640.

48. Elaine Enarson, "Experts and Caregivers: Perspectives on Underground Day Care," in *Circles of Care*, 239.

49. Margaret K. Nelson, "Mothering Others' Children: The Experiences of Family Day Care Providers," in *Circles of Care*, 213, 215.

50. Miriam K. Rosenthal, *An Ecological Approach to the Study of Child Care: Family Day Care in Israel* (Hillsdale, N.J.: Lawrence Erlbaum Associates, 1994), 69, 91.

51. Enarson, "Experts and Caregivers," 239, 240.

52. Rosenthal, *An Ecological Approach to the Study of Child Care*, 69; Nelson, *Negotiated Care*, 194.

53. Http://www.naccp.org; 07-08-98.

54. Http://nccanet.org, 07-08-98; http://www.usachildcare.org, 07-08-98.

55. Nan Lee Hawkins with Heldi Kane Rosenholtz, *Profitable Child Care: How to Start and Run a Successful Business* (New York: Facts on File, 1993), 236–243.

56. Clarke-Stewart, *Daycare*, 54–55; Abbie Gordon Klein, *The Debate over Child Care 1969–1990: A Sociohistorical Analysis* (Albany: State University of New York Press, 1992), 158. Klein observes that during the 1980s, for-profit child care grew at an annual rate of 10 to 12 percent, while the nonprofit sector grew at less than half that rate (143). She also reports that for-profit providers began lobbying in 1973 and organized the present lobby, the NCCA, in 1988 (158).

57. Gormley, *Everybody's Children*, 68, 147.

58. Ibid., 27, 29.

59. Http://www.children'sdefense.org; 07-08-98.

60. Tia R. Keenan, "Child Care Worker," *Ms.* 9, no. 4 (June/July 1999): 45.

61. Rutman, "Child Care," 635.

62. Mary de Young, "The Devil Goes to Day Care: McMartin and the Making of a Moral Panic," *Journal of American Culture* 20, no. 1 (Spring 1997): 24; also see Susan B. Murray, " 'We All Love Charles': Men in Child Care and the Social Construction of Gender," *Gender & Society* 10, no. 4 (August 1996): 368–385.

63. Eyer, *Motherguilt*, 4.

64. Popenoe, "The Evolution of Marriage," 19, 20; Maggie Gallagher, "Day Careless," *National Review* 50, no. 1 (January 26, 1998): 37, 42.

65. Uttal, "Custodial Care," 309.

66. Lamb and Sternberg, "Sociocultural Perspectives," 4; Jay Fagan, Martha M. Dore, and Nessa Math, "Pregnant and Mothering Adolescents' Attitudes about Day Care," *Child & Youth Care Forum* 20, no. 5 (October 1991): 354.

67. Lamb and Sternberg, "Sociocultural Perspectives," 8–9.

68. Uttal, "Custodial Care," 309.

69. See also Karen Swift, "Contradictions in Child Welfare: Neglect and Responsibility," in *Women's Caring: Feminist Perspectives on Social Welfare*, ed. C. T. Baines, P. M. Evans, and S. M. Neysmith (Toronto: McClelland and Stewart, 1991), 265.

Notes to Chapter 10

1. Jessica Benjamin, *The Bonds of Love: Psychoanalysis, Feminism, and the Problem of Domination* (New York: Pantheon Books, 1988), 78, 81–82. We discuss Benjamin's ideas in chapter 5.

2. Lena Dominelli, "Women in the Community: Feminist Principles and Organising in Community Work," *Community Development Journal* 30, no. 2 (April 1995): 133.

3. Ibid. For diverse illustrations, see Penny Weiss and Marilyn Friedman, eds., *Feminism and Community* (Philadelphia: Temple University Press, 1995).

4. Http://www.madd.org; 07-02-98. In 1994 Lightner began working "as a lobbyist for a consortium of the nation's brewers. Her assignment was to convince members of Congress to ease restrictions on the sale of alcohol"; see Annelise Orleck, "Tradition Unbound: Radical Mothers in International Perspective," in *The Politics of Motherhood: Activist Voices from Left to Right*, ed. Alexis Jetter, Annelise Orleck, and Diana Taylor (Hanover, N.H.: University Press of New England, 1997), 12.

5. Addams's place in American history is multifaceted. She (1931) and Emily Greene Balch (1946) are the only two American women who have won the Nobel Peace Prize, both for their work with the Women's International League of Peace and Freedom. Harriet Hyman Alonso, "Nobel Peace Laureates, Jane Addams and Emily Greene Balch: Two Women of the Women's International League for Peace and Freedom," *Journal of Women's History* 7, no. 2 (summer 1995): 6–26.

6. Lois Banner, *Women in Modern America: A Brief History*, 3rd ed. (New York: Harcourt Brace, 1995), 95.

7. See Judith Schwarz, *Radical Feminists of Heterodoxy, Greenwich Village 1912–1940* (Lebanon, N.H.: New Victoria, 1982); Darlene Rebecca Roth, *Matronage: Patterns in Women's Organizations, Atlanta, Georgia, 1890–1940* (Brooklyn, N.Y.: Carlson, 1994); Marsha Wedell, *Elite Women and the Reform Impulse in Memphis, 1875–1915* (Knoxville: University of Tennessee Press, 1991); Muriel Beadle and the Centennial History Committee, *The Fortnightly of Chicago: The City and its Women, 1873–1973* (Chicago: Henry Regnery, 1973); Sandra Haarsager, *Organized Womanhood: Cultural Politics in the Pacific Northwest, 1840–1920* (Norman: University of Oklahoma Press, 1997).

8. See Landon R. Y. Storrs, "Gender and the Development of the Regulatory State: The Controversy over Restricting Women's Night Work in the Depression-Era South," *Journal of Policy History* 10, no. 2 (1998): 179–206. Storrs indicates that to a significant extent the Southern Council had racially inclusive ends and used maternalist arguments.

9. Ibid., 35, 40, 41.

10. Theda Skocpol, *Protecting Soldiers and Mothers: The Political Origins of Social Policy in the United States* (Cambridge: Harvard University Press, 1992), 334, 336.

11. Ibid., 424; also see Joanne L. Goodwin, "An American Experiment with Paid Motherhood: The Implementation of Mothers' Pensions in Early Twentieth-Century Chicago," *Gender & History* 4, no. 3 (autumn 1992): 323–342.

12. Allison C. Carey, "Gender and Contemporary Sterilization Programs in America: 1907–1950," *Journal of Historical Sociology* 11, no. 1 (March,1998): 94; also see Lisa D. Brush, "Worthy Widows, Welfare Cheats: Proper Womanhood in Expert Needs Talk about Single Mothers in the United States, 1900 to 1988," *Gender & Society* 11, no. 6 (December,1997): 740.

13. Skocpol, *Protecting Soldiers and Mothers*, 476.

14. Ibid., 523, 524.

15. Leila J. Rupp, *Worlds of Women: The Making of an International Women's Movement* (Princeton, N.J.: Princeton University Press, 1997), 85–86; see also Molly Ladd-Taylor, *Mother-Work: Women, Child Welfare, and the State, 1890–1930* (Urbana: University of Illinois Press, 1994), 34.

16. Skocpol, *Protecting Soldiers and Mothers*, 18.

17. Ladd-Taylor, *Mother-Work*, 18.

18. Estelle B. Freedman, *Maternal Justice: Miriam Van Waters and the Female Reform Tradition* (Chicago: University of Chicago Press, 1996), 153; also see Lillian Faderman, *To Believe in Women: What Lesbians Have Done for America—A History*. (Boston: Houghton Mifflin, 1999).

19. Skocpol, *Protecting Soldiers and Mothers*, 538, 479.

20. Eileen Boris, "The Power of Motherhood: Black and White Activist Women Redefine the 'Political,' " in *Mothers of a New World: Maternalist Politics and the Origins of Welfare States*, ed. Seth Koven and Sonya Michel (New York: Routledge, 1993), 227; Linda Gordon, "Black and White Visions of Welfare: Women's Welfare Activism, 1890–1945," in *"We Specialize in the Wholly Impossible": A Reader in Black Women's History*, ed. Darlene Clark Hine, Wilma King, and Linda Reed (Brooklyn, N.Y.: Carlson, 1995), 468.

21. Katrina Bell McDonald, "Black Activist Mothering: A Historical Intersection of Race, Gender, and Class," *Gender & Society* 11, no. 6 (December 1997): 774, 776.

22. Among these were schools and day nurseries as well as birth control clinics and birth control education in their local communities. African American organizations such as the Mothers' Health Association of the District of Columbia and the National Negro Housewives League sponsored such initiatives.

23. Evelyn Brooks Higginbotham, *Righteous Discontent: The Women's Movement in the Black Baptist Church 1880–1920* (Cambridge: Harvard University Press, 1993), 7.

24. Boris, "The Power of Motherhood," 224.

25. Suzanne Staggenborg, "Social Movement Communities and Cycles of Protest: The Emergence and Maintenance of a Local Women's Movement," *Social Problems* 45, no. 2 (May 1998): 183.

26. Higginbotham, *Righteous Discontent*, 90.

27. Staggenborg, "Social Movement Communities," 183; Jennifer Bickham Mendez, "Of Mops and Maids: Contradictions and Continuities in Bureaucratized Domestic Work," *Social Problems* 45, no. 1 (February 1998): 129. Mendez analyzes micro-level uses of strategic personalism among domestic workers seeking "personalistic relations with employers/clients."

28. Skocpol, *Protecting Soldiers and Mothers*, 319.

29. J. Timmons Roberts, "Negotiating Both Sides of the Gate: Gender, Hazardous Facility Workers and Community Responses to Technological Hazards," *Current Sociology* 45, no. 3 (July 1997): 159.

30. Patricia Hill Collins, "Shifting the Center: Race, Class, and Feminist Theorizing about Motherhood," in *Mothering: Ideology, Experience, and Agency*, ed. Evelyn Nakano Glenn, Grace Chang, and Linda Rennie Forcey (New York: Routledge, 1994), 47–48.

31. Ladd-Taylor, *Mother-Work*, 2.

32. Skocpol, *Protecting Soldiers and Mothers*, 539.

33. Ellen Reese, "Maternalism and Political Mobilization: How California's Postwar Child Care Campaign Was Won," *Gender & Society* 10, no. 5 (October 1996): 567.

34. Http://www.lalecheleague.org, 07-02-98; Lynn Y. Weiner, "Reconstructing Motherhood: The La Leche League in Postwar America," *Journal of American History* 80, no. 4 (March 1994): 1357.

35. Weiner, "Reconstructing Motherhood," 1360, 1369; Linda M. Blum and Eliza-

beth A. Vandewater, " 'Mother to Mother': A Maternalist Organization in Late Capitalist America," *Social Problems* 40, no. 3 (August 1993): 286, 296.

36. Weiner, "Reconstructing Motherhood," 1374; Blum and Vandewater, " 'Mother to Mother,'" 288; http://www.lalecheleague.org.

37. Weiner, "Reconstructing Motherhood," 1376, 1379; Blum and Vandewater, " 'Mother to Mother,' " 289, 297.

38. Weiner, "Reconstructing Motherhood," 1358, 1359.

39. Http://www.lalecheleague.org.

40. Alonso cited in Anne Marie Pois, "Foreshadowings: Jane Addams, Emily Greene Balch, and the Ecofeminism/Pacifist Feminism of the 1980s," *Peace & Change* 20, no. 4 (October 1995): 449–450; also see Noel Sturgeon, *Ecofeminist Natures: Race, Gender, Feminst Theory, and Political Action* (New York: Routledge, 1997), 69–72; Yael Azmon, "War, Mothers, and a Girl with Braids: Involvement of Mothers' Peace Movements in the National Discourse of Israel," *Israel Social Science Research* 12, no. 1 (1997): 109–128.

41. Bina Agarwal, "Gender, Resistance and Land: Interlinked Struggles over Resources and Meanings in South Asia," *Journal of Peasant Studies* 22, no. 1 (October 1994): 81–125; Esther Wangari, Barbara Thomas-Slayter, and Dianne Rocheleau, "Gendered Visions for Survival: Semi-Arid Regions in Kenya," in *Feminist Political Ecology: Global Issues and Local Experiences*, ed. Dianne Rocheleua, Barbara Thomas-Slayter, and Esther Wangari (London: Routledge, 1996), 127–154; Virginia Rinaldo Seitz, "Class, Gender, and Resistance in the Appalachian Coalfields," in *Community Activism and Feminist Politics: Organizing across Race, Class, and Gender*, ed. Nancy A. Naples (New York: Routledge, 1998), 213–236; Roberta M. Feldman, Susan Stall, and Patricia A. Wright, " 'The Community Needs to Be Built by Us': Women Organizing in Chicago Public Housing," in *Community Activism and Feminist Politics*, 257–274; Margorie Agosin, "Amidst the Smoke We Remember: Mothers of the Plaza de Mayo," in *Radically Speaking: Feminism Reclaimed*, ed. Diane Bell and Renate Klein (North Melbourne, Australia: Spinifex Press, 1996), 470–478; Jean Bethke Elshtain, "The Mothers of the Disappeared: Passion and Protest in Maternal Action," in *Representations of Motherhood*, ed. Donna Bassin, Margaret Honey, and Meryle Mahrer Kaplan (New Haven, Conn.: Yale University Press, 1994), 75–91.

42. See McDonald, "Black Activist Mothering"; Naomi Abrahams, "Negotiating Power, Identity, Family, and Community: Women's Community Participation," *Gender & Society* 10, no. 6 (December, 1996): 768–796; Mary Prado, "Creating Community: Mexican American Women in Eastside Los Angeles," in *Community Activism and Feminist Politics*, 275–300.

43. Parnel Wickham-Searl, "Politics and Personal Pursuits: The Experience of Mothers of Children with Severe Disabilities," *Journal of Health and Human Services Administration* 12, no. 4 (spring 1995): 423–424.

44. Eileen Boris, "When Work Is Slavery," *Social Justice* 25, no. 1 (spring 1998): 35.

45. Annelise Orleck, " 'If It Wasn't for You I'd Have Shoes for My Children': The Political Education of Las Vegas Welfare Mothers," in *The Politics of Motherhood*, 103, 107, 111, 112, 114, 115.

46. Alexis Jetter, " 'What Is Your Wife Trying to Do—Shut Down the Chemical Industry?' An Interview with Lois Gibbs," in *The Politics of Motherhood*, 31, 38, 41.

47. Ann Marie Dobosz, "Polluters Beware," *Ms.* 9, no. 4 (June/July 1999): 38.

48. Josepa Bru-Bistuer, "Spanish Women Against Industrial Waste: A Gender Perspective on Environmental Grassroots Movements," trans. Moya Hallstein and Annette Ramos, in *Feminist Political Ecology*, 107–108.

49. Anne C. Bellows, "Where Kitchen and Laboratory Meet: The 'Tested Food for Silesia' Program," in *Feminist Political Ecology*, 251–270.

50. Joni Seager, *Earth Follies: Coming to Feminist Terms with the Global Environmental Crisis* (New York: Routledge, 1993), 263–264.

51. Celene Krauss, "Challenging Power: Toxic Waste Protests and the Politicization of White, Working-Class Women," in *Community Activism and Feminist Politics*, 143; also see Abrahams, "Negotiating Power," 781–782; Bru-Bistuer, "Spanish Women," 115; Orleck, "Tradition Unbound," 115.

52. Kathleen Blee, "Mothers in Race-Hate Movements" in *The Politics of Motherhood*, 249.

53. See, for instance, Glen Jeansonne, *Women of the Far Right: The Mothers' Movement and World War II* (Chicago: University of Chicago Press, 1996); Julie Peteet, "Icons and Militants: Mothering in the Danger Zone," *Signs: Journal of Women in Culture and Society* 23, no. 1 (autumn 1997): 103–129; Gilda Zwerman, "Mothering on the Lam: Politics, Gender Fantasies and Maternal Thinking in Women Associated with Armed, Clandestine Organizations in the United States," *Feminist Review* 47 (summer 1994): 33–56.

54. Ladd-Taylor, *Mother-Work*, 201, 45.

55. Patricia Boling, "The Democratic Potential of Mothering," *Political Theory* 19, no. 4 (November 1991): 608.

56. Kathleen S. Uno, "Maternalism in Modern Japan," *Journal of Women's History* 5, no. 2 (fall 1993): 126.

57. Alison Bailey, "Mothering, Diversity, and Peace Politics," *Hypatia* 9, no. 2 (spring 1994): 188, 193. Sabina Lovibond the most influential versions of maternalism valorize "the life lived by the twentieth-century Western, bourgeois married woman"; see "Maternalist Ethics: A Feminist Assessment," *South Atlantic Quarterly* 93, no. 4 (fall 1994): 789.

58. Lovibond, "Maternalist Ethics," 788.

59. Sonya Michel, "The Limits of Maternalism: Policies Toward American Wage-Earning Mothers during the Progressive Era," in *Mothers of a New World*, 308.

60. Lovibond, "Maternalist Ethics," 789–790.

61. John Power and Deane Curtin, "Mothering: Moral Cultivation in Buddhist and Feminist Ethics," *Philosophy East & West* 44, no. 1 (January 1994): 8.

62. Gwendolyn Mink, *Welfare's End* (Ithaca, N.Y.: Cornell University Press, 1998), 7.

63. See, for example, Rhonda M. Williams and Carla L. Peterson, "The Color of Memory: Interpreting Twentieth-Century U.S. Social Policy from a Nineteenth-Century Perspective," *Feminist Studies* 24, no. 1 (spring 1998): 7–25. Williams and Peterson characterize "welfare reform" as "a racialized and gendered class war." In that same issue of *Feminist Studies* also see, among other pertinent articles, Eva Feder Kittay, "Dependency, Equality, and Welfare" (32–43), and Felicia Kornbluh, "The Goals of the National Welfare Rights Movement: Why We Need Them Thirty Years Later" (65–78).

64. Debra L. Dodson, "Change and Continuity in the Relationship between Private Responsibilities and Public Officeholding: The More Things Change, the More They Stay the Same," *Policy Studies Journal* 25, no. 4 (winter 1997): 572, 573.

65. Mary Field Belenky, Lynne A. Bond, and Jacqueline S. Weinstock, *A Tradition That Has No Name: Nurturing the Development of People, Families, and Communities* (New York: Basic Books, 1997), 156.

66. Sara Ruddick, "Thinking Mothers/Conceiving Birth," in *Representations of Motherhood*, 34.

67. Boris, "When Work Is Slavery," 41.

Notes to Epilogue

1. Association for Research on Mothering, Room 726, Atkinson College, York University, 4700 Keele St. Toronto, Canada, M3J 1P3. See also the "Mothers Who Think" section of www.salon.com.

2. Penelope Dixon, *Mothers and Mothering: An Annotated Feminist Bibliography* (New York: Garland, 1991).

3. See Sharon Abbey, Joyce Castle, and Cecilia Reynolds, "Comparing How Mothers Influence the Education of Daughters and Sons," in *Redefining Motherhood: Changing Identities and Patterns*, ed. S. Abbey and A. O'Reilly (Toronto: Second Story Press, 1998), 29–58; Maureen T. Reddy, *Crossing the Color Line: Race, Parenting, and Culture* (New Brunswick, N.J.: Rutgers University Press, 1994), chapter 5; and Signithia Fordham, *Blacked Out: Dilemmas of Race, Identity, and Success at Capital High* (Chicago: University of Chicago Press, 1996). In chapter 6 of *School Work: Gender and the Cultural Construction of Teaching* (New York: Teachers College Press, 1995), Sari Knopp Biklen looks at mother-teacher relations from teachers' points of view.

4. Wendy Luttrell, *Schoolsmart and Motherwise: Working-class Women's Identity and Schooling* (New York: Routledge, 1997). See also Lauren M. Rich and Sun-Bin Kim, "Patterns of Later Life Education among Teenage Mothers," *Gender & Society* 13, no. 6 (December 1999): 798–817.

5. Sheila Fay Braithwaite, "Motherhood: The First Step on the Road to Recovery," in *Mother Journeys: Feminists Write about Mothering*, ed. M. T. Reddy, M. Roth, and A. Sheldon (Minneapolis, Minn.: Spinsters Ink, 1994),133–141.

6. Michael Kimmel, *Manhood in America: A Cultural History* (New York: Free Press, 1996).

Selected Bibliography

Abbey, Sharon M., and Andrea O'Reilly, eds. *Redefining Motherhood: Changing Identities and Patterns*. Toronto: Second Story Press, 1998.

Abel, Emily K., and Margaret K. Nelson, eds. *Circles of Care: Work and Identity in Women's Lives*. Albany: State University of New York Press, 1990.

Abrahams, Naomi. "Negotiating Power, Identity, Family, and Community: Women's Community Participation." *Gender & Society* 10, no. 6 (December 1996): 768–796.

Abramovitz, Mimi. *Regulating the Lives of Women: Social Welfare Policy from Colonial Times to the Present*. Rev. ed. Boston: South End Press, 1996.

Adams, Alice. "Maternal Bonds: Recent Literature on Mothering." *Signs: Journal of Women in Culture and Society* 20, no. 2 (1995): 414–427.

Apple, Rima D., and Janet Golden, eds. *Mothers & Motherhood: Readings in American History*. Columbus: Ohio University Press, 1997.

Badinter, Elizabeth. *The Myth of Motherhood: An Historical View of the Maternal Instinct*. London: Souvenir Press, 1981.

Baines, Carol T., Patricia M. Evans, and Sheila M. Neysmith, eds. *Women's Caring: Feminist Perspectives on Social Welfare*. Toronto: McClelland and Stewart, 1991.

Baker, Christina Looper, and Christina Baker Kline. *The Conversation Begins: Mothers and Daughters Talk about Living Feminism*. New York: Bantam Books, 1996.

Bassin, Donna, Margaret Honey, and Meryle Mahrer Kaplan, eds. *Representations of Motherhood*. New Haven, Conn.: Yale University Press, 1994.

Baumslag, Naomi, and Dia L. Michels. *Milk, Money, and Madness: The Culture and Politics of Breastfeeding*. Westport, Conn.: Bergin & Garvey, 1995.

Benjamin, Jessica. *The Bonds of Love: Psychoanalysis, Feminism, and the Problem of Domination*. New York: Pantheon Books, 1998.

Benkov, Laura. "Yes, I am a Swan: Reflections on Families Headed by Lesbians and Gay Men." In *Mothering Against the Odds: Diverse Voices of Contemporary Mothers*, edited by Cynthia Garcia Coll, Janet L. Surrey, and Kathy Weingarten, 113–133. New York: Guilford Press, 1998.

Bernard, Jessie. *The Future of Motherhood*. New York: The Dial Press, 1974.

Blum, Linda M. *At the Breast: Ideologies of Breastfeeding and Motherhood in the Contemporary United States*. Boston: Beacon Press, 1999.

Books, Sue. "Fear and Loathing: The Moral Dimensions of the Politicization of Teen Pregnancy." *Journal of Thought* 31, no. 1 (spring 1996): 9–24.

Boyle, Frances M. *Mothers Bereaved by Stillbirth, Neonatal Death or Sudden Infant Death Syndrome: Patterns of Distress and Recovery*. Aldershot, England: Ashgate, 1997.

Brown, Amy Benson, and Kathryn McPherson, eds. *The Reality of Breastfeeding: Reflections by Contemporary Women*. Westport, Conn.: Bergin & Garvey, 1998.

Brush, Lisa D. "Love, Toil, and Trouble: Motherhood and Feminist Politics." *Signs: Journal of Women in Culture and Society* 21, no. 2 (1996): 429–454.

———. "Worthy Widows, Welfare Cheats: Proper Womanhood in Expert Needs Talk about Single Mothers in the United States, 1900 to 1988." *Gender & Society* 11, no. 6 (December 1997): 720–746.

Carter, Pam. *Feminism, Breasts and Breastfeeding*. New York: St. Martin's Press, 1996.

Cecil, Roseanne, ed. *The Anthropology of Pregnancy Loss: Comparative Studies in Miscarriage, Stillbirth and Neonatal Death*. Oxford: Berg, 1996.

Childers, Julie K. "The Boston Birth Center: An Ethnographic Case Study of Institutional Capture in the Women's Health Movement." Ph.D. diss., Boston College, 2000.

Chodorow, Nancy. *The Reproduction of Mothering: Psychoanalysis and the Sociology of Gender*. Berkeley: University of California Press, 1978.

Chodorow, Nancy, and Susan Contratto. "The Fantasy of the Perfect Mother." In *Rethinking the Family: Some Feminist Questions*, edited by Barrie Thorne with Marilyn Yalom, 54–75. New York: Longman, 1982.

Coll, Cynthia Garcia, Janet L. Surrey, and Kathy Weingarten, eds. *Mothering Against the Odds: Diverse Voices of Contemporary Mothers*. New York: Guilford Press, 1998.

Dalton, Susan E., and Denise D. Bielby. " 'That's Our Kind of Constellation': Lesbian Mothers Negotiate Institutionalized Understandings of Gender within the Family." *Gender & Society* 14, no. 1 (February 2000): 36–61.

Davis-Floyd, Robbie E. *Birth as an American Rite of Passage*. Berkeley: University of California Press, 1992.

Davis-Floyd, Robbie, and Carolyn F. Sargent, eds. *Childbirth and Authoritative Knowledge: Cross-Cultural Perspectives*. Berkeley: University of California Press, 1997.

Dill, Bonnie Thorton. "Fictive Kin, Paper Sons, and *Compadrazgo*: Women of Color and the Struggle for Family Survival." In *Women of Color in U.S. Society*, edited by Maxine Baca Zinn and Bonnie Thornton Dill, 149–169. Philadelphia: Temple University Press, 1993.

Dixon, Penelope. *Mothers and Mothering: An Annotated Feminist Bibliography*. New York: Garland, 1991.

Dowd, Nancy E. *In Defense of Single-Parent Families*. New York: New York University Press, 1997.

Dunne, Gillian A. "Opting into Motherhood: Lesbians Blurring the Boundaries and Transforming the Meaning of Parenthood and Kinship." *Gender & Society* 14, no. 1 (February 2000): 11–35.

Edwards, Christine E., and Christine L. Williams. "Adopting Change: Birth Mothers in Maternity Homes Today." *Gender & Society* 14, no. 1 (February 2000): 160–183.

Edwards, Harriet. *How Could You? Mothers Without Custody of Their Children*. Freedom, Calif.: The Crossing Press, 1989.

Ehrenreich, Barbara, and Deirdre English. *For Her Own Good: 150 Years of the Experts' Advice to Women*. New York: Anchor Books, 1979.

Flanagan, Patricia. "Teen Mothers: Countering the Myths of Dysfunction and Developmental Disruption." In *Mothering Against the Odds: Diverse Voices of Contemporary Mothers* edited by Cynthia Garcia Coll, Janet L. Surrey, and Kathy Weingarten, 238–254. New York: Guilford Press, 1998.

Folbre, Nancy. *Who Pays for the Kids? Gender and the Structures of Constraint.* New York: Routledge, 1994.

Fox, Bonnie, and Diana Worts. "Revisiting the Critique of Medicalized Childbirth: A Contribution to the Sociology of Birth." *Gender & Society* 13, no. 3 (June 1999): 326–346.

Franklin, Sarah, and Helena Ragone, eds. *Reproducing Reproduction: Kinship, Power, and Technological Innovation.* Philadelphia: University of Pennsylvania Press, 1998.

Fraser, Gertrude Jacinta. "Afro-American Midwives, Biomedicine and the State: An Ethnohistorical Account of Birth and Its Transformation in Rural Virginia." Ph.D. diss., Johns Hopkins University, 1988.

Gallagher, Sally K., and Christian Smith. "Symbolic Traditionalism and Pragmatic Egalitarianism: Contemporary Evangelicals, Families, and Gender." *Gender & Society* 13, no. 2 (April 1999): 211–233.

Glenn, Evelyn Nakano, Grace Chang, and Linda Rennie Forcey, eds., *Mothering: Ideology, Experience, and Agency.* New York: Routledge, 1994.

Glickman, Rose L. *Daughters of Feminists.* New York: St. Martin's Press, 1993.

Goer, Henci. *Obstetric Myths Versus Research Realities: A Guide to the Medical Literature.* Westport, Conn.: Bergin & Garvey, 1995.

Gomez, Laura E. *Misconceiving Mothers: Legislators, Prosecutors, and the Politics of Prenatal Drug Exposure.* Philadelphia: Temple University Press, 1997.

Goodwin, Joanne L. " 'Employable Mothers' and 'Suitable Work': A Reevaluation of Welfare and Wage Earning for Women in the Twentieth-Century United States." In *Mothers and Motherhood: Readings in American History*, edited by Rima D. Apple and Janet Golden, 539–564. Columbus: Ohio University Press, 1997.

Goodwin, Joanne L. "An American Experiment with Paid Motherhood: The Implementation of Mothers' Pensions in Early Twentieth-Century Chicago." *Gender & History* 4, no. 3 (autumn 1992): 323–342.

Gordon, Linda. *Heroes of Their Own Lives: The Politics and History of Family Violence, Boston 1880–1960.* New York: Viking, 1998.

———. *Pitied But Not Entitled: Single Mothers and the History of Welfare, 1890–1935.* New York: Free Press, 1994.

Green, Judith. "Mothers in 'Incest Families': A Critique of Blame and Its Destructive Sequels." *Violence Against Women* 2, no. 3 (September 1996): 322–348.

Griffith, Alison I., and Dorothy E. Smith. "Constructing Cultural Knowledge: Mothering as Discourse." In *Women and Education: A Canadian Perspective*, edited by Jane S. Gaskell and Arlene Tigar McLaren, 87–103. Calgary, Alberta: Detselig Enterprises Limited, 1987.

Grossberg, Michael. "Who Gets the Child? Custody, Guardianship, and the Rise of Judicial Patriarchy in the Nineteenth Century." *Feminist Studies* 9, no. 2 (summer 1983): 235–260.

Hamilton, Roberta. "Feminism and Motherhood, 1970–1990: Reinventing the Wheel?" *Resources for Feminist Research* 19, no. 3/4 (September–December 1990): 23–32.

Hays, Sharon. *The Cultural Contradictions of Motherhood.* New Haven, Conn.: Yale University Press, 1996.

Herman, Judith Lewis, with Lisa Hirschman. *Father-Daughter Incest.* Cambridge: Harvard University Press, 1981.

Hochman, Anndee. *Everyday Acts & Small Subversions: Women Reinventing Family, Community, and Home*. Portland, Oreg.: Eighth Mountain Press, 1994.

Hochschild, Arlie, with Anne Machung. *The Second Shift: Working Parents and the Revolution at Home*. New York: Viking, 1989.

Hollway, Wendy, and Bird Featherstone, eds. *Mothering and Ambivalence*. London: Routledge, 1997.

Humphries, Drew. *Crack Mothers: Pregnancy, Drugs, and the Media*.Columbus: Ohio State University Press, 1999.

Ireland, Mardy S. *Reconceiving Women: Separating Motherhood from Female Identity*. New York: Guilford Press, 1993.

Jackson, Rosie. *Mothers Who Leave: Behind the Myth of Women without Their Children*. London: HarperCollins, Pandora 1994.

Johnson, Janis Tyler. *Mothers of Incest Survivors: Another Side of the Story*. Bloomington: Indiana University Press, 1992.

Kahn, Robbie Pfeufer. *Bearing Meaning: The Language of Birth*. Urbana Ill.: University of Illinois Press, 1995.

Kaplan, Elaine Bell. "Black Teenage Mothers and Their Mothers: The Impact of Adolescent Childbearing on Daughters' Relations with Mothers." *Social Problems* 43, no. 4 (November 1996): 427–433.

King, Leslie, and Madonna Harrington Meyer. "The Politics of Reproductive Benefits: U.S. Insurance Coverage of Contraceptives and Infertility Treatments." *Gender & Society* 11, no. 1 (February 1997): 8–30.

Klein, Carole. *Mothers and Sons*. Boston: Houghton Mifflin, 1984.

Ladd-Taylor, Molly. "Love, Work, and the Meanings of Motherhood." *Journal of Women's History* 8, no. 3 (fall 1996): 219–227.

———. *Mother-Work: Women, Child Welfare, and the State, 1890–1930*. Urbana, Ill.: University of Illinois Press, 1994.

Ladd-Taylor, Molly, and Lauri Umansky, eds. *"Bad" Mothers: The Politics of Blame in Twentieth-Century America* New York: New York University Press, 1998.

Lamphere, Louise, Patricia Zavella, and Felipe Gonzales, with Peter B. Evans. *Sunbelt Working Mothers: Reconciling Family and Factory*. Ithaca, N.Y.: Cornell University Press, 1993.

Lasker, Judith N., and Susan Borg. *In Search of Parenthood: Coping with Infertility and High-Tech Conception*. Boston: Beacon Press, 1987.

Leavitt, Judith Walzer. *Brought to Bed: Childbearing in America, 1750–1950*. New York: Oxford University Press, 1986.

Letherby, Gayle. "Mother or Not, Mother or What Problems of Definition and Identity." *Women's Studies International Forum* 17, no. 5 (1994): 525–532.

Lewin, Ellen. *Lesbian Mothers: Accounts of Gender in American Culture*. Ithaca, N.Y.: Cornell University Press, 1993.

Liff, Sharon R. *No Place Else to Go: Homeless Mothers and Their Children Living in Urban Shelters*. New York: Garland, 1996.

Litt, Jacquelyn. "Pediatrics and the Development of Middle-Class Motherhood." *Research in the Sociology of Health Care* 10 (1993): 161–173.

Lorber, Judith. "Choice, Gift, or Patriarchal Bargain? Women's Consent to *In Vitro* Fertilization in Male Infertility." *Hypatia* 4, no. 3 (Fall 1989): 23–36.

Lorde, Audre. "Man Child: A Black Lesbian Feminist's Response." In *Sister Outsider: Essays and Speeches*. Freedom, Calif.: The Crossing Press, 1984.

Lublin, Nancy. *Pandora's Box: Feminism Confronts Reproductive Technology*. Lanham, Md.: Rowman & Littlefield, 1998.

Luker, Kristin. *Dubious Conceptions: The Politics of Teenage Pregnancy*. Cambridge: Harvard University Press, 1996.

Maroney, Heather Jon. "Embracing Motherhood: New Feminist Theory." *Canadian Journal of Political and Social Theory* 9, no. 1–2 (winter/spring 1985) :40–64.

Martin. Emily. "The Ideology of Reproduction: The Reproduction of Ideology." In *Uncertain Terms: Negotiating Gender in American Culture*, edited by Faye Ginsburg and Anna Lowenhaupt Tsing, 300–314. Boston: Beacon Press, 1990.

———. *The Woman in the Body: A Cultural Analysis of Reproduction*. Boston: Beacon Press, 1987.

Mathews, Joan J. and Kathleen Zadak. "The Alternative Birth Movement in the United States: History and Current Status." In *Mothers & Motherhood: Readings in American History*, edited by Rima D. Apple and Janet Golden, 278–292. Columbus: Ohio State University Press, 1997.

McDonald, Katrina Bell. "Black Activist Mothering: A Historical Intersection of Race, Gender, and Class." *Gender & Society* 11, no. 6 (December 1997): 773–795.

McMahon, Martha. *Engendering Motherhood: Identity and Self-Transformation in Women's Lives*. New York: Guilford Press, 1995.

Michie, Helena, and Naomi R. Cahn. *Confinements: Fertility and Infertility in Contemporary Culture*. New Brunswick, N.J.: Rutgers University Press, 1997.

Mink, Gwendolyn. *Welfare's End*. Ithaca, N.Y.: Cornell University Press, 1998.

Moody-Adams, Michele M., "Feminism by Any Other Name." In *Feminism and Families*, edited by H. L. Nelson, 76–89. New York: Routledge, 1997.

Moraga, Cherríe. *Waiting in the Wings: Portrait of a Queer Motherhood*. Ithaca, N.Y.: Firebrand Books, 1997.

Morell, Carolyn M. *Unwomanly Conduct: The Challenges of Intentional Childlessness*. New York: Routledge, 1994.

Morgan, Robin. "Raising Sons." *Ms*. 4, no. 3 (November/December 1993): 36–41.

Murphy, Sheigla, and Marsha Rosenbaum. *Pregnant Women on Drugs: Combating Stereotypes and Stigma*. New Brunswick, N.J.: Rutgers University Press, 1999.

Murray, Susan B. " 'We All Love Charles': Men in Child Care and the Social Construction of Gender." *Gender & Society* 10, no. 4 (August 1996): 368–385.

Naples, Nancy A., ed. *Community Activism and Feminist Politics: Organizing across Race, Class, Gender*. New York: Routledge, 1998.

Nelson, Margaret K. *Negotiated Care: The Experience of Family Day Care Providers*. Philadelphia: Temple University Press, 1990.

Patterson, Charlotte J. "Children of Lesbian and Gay Parents." In *Advances in Clinical Child Psychology,* edited by Thomas H. Ollendick and Ronald J. Prinz, 19:235–282. New York: Plenum Press, 1997.

Peteet, Julie. "Icons and Militants: Mothering in the Danger Zone." *Signs: Journal of Women in Culture and Society* 23, no. 1 (autumn 1997): 103–129.

Phoenix, Ann, Anne Woollett, and Eva Lloyd, eds. *Motherhood: Meanings, Practices and Ideologies*. London: Sage, 1991.

Polakow, Valerie. *Lives on the Edge: Single Mothers and Their Children in the Other Amer-*

ica. Chicago: University of Chicago Press, 1993.

Polatnick, M. Rivka. "Diversity in Women's Liberation Ideology: How a Black and a White Group of the 1960s Viewed Motherhood." *Signs: Journal of Women in Culture and Society* 21, no. 3 (spring 1996): 679–706.

Pollack, Sandra. "Lesbian Parents: Claiming Our Visibility." In *Feminist Frontiers III*, edited by Laurel Richardson and Verta Taylor, 263–270. New York: McGraw Hill, 1993.

Rapp, Rayna. "Constructing Amniocentesis: Maternal and Medical Discourses." In *Uncertain Terms: Negotiating Gender in American Culture*, edited by Faye Ginsburg and Anna Lowenhaupt Tsing, 28–42. Boston: Beacon Press, 1990.

———. "The Power of 'Positive' Diagnosis: Medical and Maternal Discourses on Amniocentesis." In *Representations of Motherhood*, edited by Donna Bassin, Margaret Honey, and Meryle Mahrer Kaplan, 204–219. New Haven, Conn.: Yale University Press, 1994.

Reddy, Maureen T. *Crossing the Color Line: Race, Parenting, and Culture*. New Brunswick, N.J.: Rutgers University Press, 1994.

Reddy, Maureen T., Martha Roth, and Amy Sheldon, eds. *Mother Journeys: Feminists Write about Mothering*. Minneapolis: Spinsters Ink, 1994.

Reilly, Philip R. *The Surgical Solution: A History of Involuntary Sterilization in the United States*. Baltimore: Johns Hopkins University Press, 1991.

Rich, Adrienne. *Of Woman Born: Motherhood as Experience and Institution*. New York: Bantam Books, 1977.

Roberts, Dorothy. *Killing the Black Body: Race, Reproduction, and the Meaning of Liberty*. New York: Pantheon Books, 1997.

Rocheleau, Dianne, Barbara Thomas-Slayter, and Esther Wangari, eds. *Feminist Political Ecology: Global Issues and Local Experiences*. London: Routledge, 1996.

Rooks, Judith Pence. *Midwifery and Childbirth in America*. Philadelphia: Temple University Press, 1997.

Ross, Ellen. "New Thoughts on 'The Oldest Vocation': Mothers and Motherhood in Recent Feminist Scholarship." *Signs: Journal of Women in Culture and Society* 20, no. 2 (winter 1995): 397–413.

Rothman, Barbara Katz. *In Labor: Women and Power in the Birthplace*. New York: W.W. Norton, 1991 [1982].

———. *Recreating Motherhood: Ideology and Technology in a Patriarchal Society*. New York: W. W. Norton, 1989.

———. *The Tentative Pregnancy: How Amniocentesis Changes the Experience of Motherhood*. New York: W. W. Norton, 1993 [1986].

Rowland, Robyn. *Living Laboratories: Women and Reproductive Technologies*. Bloomington: Indiana University Press, 1992.

Rowland, Robyn, and Alison Thomas. "Mothering Sons: A Crucial Feminist Challenge." *Feminism and Psychology* 6, no. 1 (1996): 93–99.

Ruddick, Sara. "Maternal Thinking," *Feminist Studies* 6, no. 2 (summer 1980): 342–367.

———. *Maternal Thinking: Toward a Politics of Peace*. Boston: Beacon Press, 1989.

———. "Thinking Mothers/Conceiving Birth." In *Representations of Motherhood*, edited by Donna Bassin, Margaret Honey, and Meryle Mahrer Kaplan, 29–45. New Haven, Conn.: Yale University Press, 1994.

Rushing, Beth. "Ideology in the Reemergence of North American Midwifery." *Work and Occupations* 20, no. 2 (February 1993): 46–67.

Rutman, Deborah. "Child Care as Women's Work." *Gender & Society* 10, no. 5 (October 1996): 629–49.

Sandelowski, Margarete. *With Child in Mind: Studies of the Personal Encounter with Infertility*. Philadelphia: University of Pennsylvania Press, 1993.

Segura, Denise A. "Working at Motherhood: Chicana and Mexican Immigrant Mothers and Employment." In *Mothering: Ideology, Experience, and Agency*, edited by Evelyn Nakano Glenn, Grace Chang, and Linda Rennie Forcey, 211–233. New York: Routledge, 1994.

Seiter, Ellen. *Sold Separately: Children and Parents in Consumer Culture*. New Brunswick, N.J.: Rutgers University Press, 1995.

Shaw, Stephanie J. "Mothering Under Slavery in the Antebellum South." In *Mothering: Ideology, Experience, and Agency*, edited by Evelyn Nakano Glenn, Grace Chang, and Linda Rennie Forcey, 237–258. New York: Routledge, 1994.

Sidel, Ruth. *Keeping Women and Children Last*. New York: Penguin, 1996.

Silverstein, Olga and Beth Rashbaum. *The Courage to Raise Good Men*. New York: Viking, 1994.

Simonds, Wendy, and Barbara Katz Rothman. *Centuries of Solace: Expressions of Maternal Grief in Popular Literature*. Philedelphia: Temple University Press, 1992.

Skocpol, Theda. *Protecting Soldiers and Mothers: The Political Origins of Social Policy in the United States*. Cambridge: Harvard University Press, 1992.

Smith, Donna. *Stepmothering*. New York: St. Martin's Press, 1990.

Snitow, Ann. "Feminism and Motherhood: An American Reading." *Feminist Review* no. 40 (spring 1992): 32–51.

Solinger, Rickie. "Poisonous Choice." In *"Bad Mothers": The Politics of Blame in Twentieth-Century America*, edited by Molly Ladd-Taylor and Lauri Umansky, 381–402. New York: New York University Press, 1998.

Squier, Susan Merrill. *Babies in Bottles: Twentieth Century Visions of Reproductive Technologies*. New Brunswick, N.J.: Rutgers University Press, 1994.

Stacey, Judith. *In the Name of the Family: Rethinking Family Values in the Postmodern Age*. Boston: Beacon Press, 1996.

Stearns, Cindy A. "Breastfeeding and the Good Maternal Body." *Gender & Society* 13, no. 3 (June 1999): 308–325.

Sterk, Claire E. *Fast Lives: Women Who Use Crack Cocaine*. Philadelphia: Temple University Press, 1999.

Sullivan, Maureen. "Rozzie and Harriet: Gender and Family Patterns of Lesbian Coparents." *Gender & Society* 10, no. 6 (December 1996): 747–767.

Takanishi, Ruby. "Childhood as a Social Issue: Historical Roots of Contemporary Child Advocacy Movements." *Journal of Social Issues* 34, no. 2 (1978): 8–28.

Taylor, Dena, ed. *Feminist Parenting: Struggles, Triumphs & Comic Interludes*. Freedom, Calif.: The Crossing Press, 1994.

Taylor, Jill McLean, Carol Gilligan, and Amy M. Sullivan. *Between Voice and Silence: Women and Girls, Race and Relationship*. Cambridge: Harvard University Press, 1995.

Taylor, Verta. *Rock-a-by Baby: Feminism, Self-Help, and Postpartum Depression*. New York: Routledge, 1996.

Thorne, Barrie with Marilyn Yalom, eds. *Rethinking the Family: Some Feminist Questions*. New York: Longman, 1982.

Thurer, Shari L. *The Myths of Motherhood: How Culture Reinvents The Good Mother*. New York: Houghton Mifflin, 1994.

Troester, Rosalie Riegle. "Turbulence and Tenderness: Mothers, Daughters, and 'Othermothers' in Paule Marshall's *Brown Girl, Brownstones*." *SAGE: A Scholarly Journal on Black Women* 1, no. 2 (fall 1984): 13–16.

Ulrich, Laurel Thatcher. " 'The Living Mother of a Living Child': Midwifery and Mortality in Post-Revolutionary New England." In *Mothers & Motherhood: Readings in American History*, edited by Rima D. Apple and Janet Golden, 175–197. Columbus: Ohio State University Press, 1997.

Umansky, Lauri. *Motherhood Reconceived: Feminism and the Legacies of the Sixties*. New York: New York University Press, 1996.

Uttal, Lynet. "Custodial Care, Surrogate Care, and Coordinated Care: Employed Mothers and the Meaning of Child Care." *Gender & Society* 10, no. 3 (June 1996): 291–311.

van Mens-Verhulet, Janneke, Karlein Schreurs, and Liesbeth Woertman, eds. *Daughtering and Mothering: Female Subjectivity Reanalysed*. London: Routledge, 1993.

Vogel, Lise. *Mothers on the Job: Maternity Policy in the U.S. Workplace*. New Brunswick, N.J.: Rutgers University Press, 1993.

Weiner, Lynn Y. *From Working Girl to Working Mother: The Female Labor Force in the United States, 1820–1980*. Chapel Hill: University of North Carolina Press, 1985.

Wertz, Richard W. and Dorothy C. Wertz. *Lying In: A History of Childbirth in America*. New York: The Free Press, 1977.

Young, Iris Marion. "Breasted Experience: The Look and the Feeling." In *The Politics of Women's Bodies: Sexuality, Appearance, and Behavior*, edited by Rose Weitz, 125–136. New York: Oxford University Press, 1998.

Zwerman, Gilda. "Mothering on the Lam: Politics, Gender Fantasies and Maternal Thinking in Women Associated with Armed, Clandestine Organizations in the United States." *Feminist Review* 47 (summer 1994): 33–56.

Index

About the Authors

Susan E. Chase teaches sociology and women's studies at the University of Tulsa. She is the author of *Ambiguous Empowerment: The Work Narratives of Women School Superintendents*. Mary F. Rogers teaches sociology and women's studies at the University of West Florida. She is the author of *Barbie Culture* and several other books.